CONTENTS

Foreword

No one is more knowledgeable about judicial clerkships than Professor Todd Peppers. Just when you think he has exhausted the subject, he comes up with a new wrinkle, as in this absorbing collection of recollections by former clerks on the federal courts of appeals, federal district courts, and state supreme courts.

The clerkships on these courts are much different from clerkships on the Supreme Court. The cachet may not be as great, and the law firm bonuses upon completion of service may not be as high. But the jobs are every bit as important and in many ways every bit as difficult as clerkships on the Supreme Court.

The state and federal appellate courts are where law first shifts from relative informality to a more formal posture, from a greater emphasis on finding facts to a de novo review of questions of law. And on those legal issues, the clerks and judges whom they serve struggle with far less assistance than clerks on the Supreme Court.

The briefing and argument in state and federal appellate courts is strikingly uneven, and judge and clerk alike are sometimes forced to make the best of presentations whose quality leaves much to be desired. The number of amicus briefs in those courts is increasing but remains far below that of the Supreme Court. I tell my clerks that we need to make the best call under law that we can, but prepare to watch thirty or so different amici complain to the Supreme Court how appallingly wrong we were.

All this is to say that the clerks on the lower federal and highest state courts will be dealing with law in a more primitive state. But this is not all bad—the lower courts have the chance to shape a case before the issues are frozen, which they often are by the time they reach the highest court.

Some lower court clerks arrive with the thought that their clerkship is a stepping stone to a clerkship at the Supreme Court. That is altogether understandable, but at the same time a big mistake. Experiences should not be instrumental but valued for their own intrinsic worth.

From the perspective of the bench, clerks are family. If not sons and daughters, then certainly nieces and nephews. The marvelous recollections in this volume show the deep bonding between clerk and judge, the intergenerational communication that is equaled nowhere else in government, the education into the workings of an entirely co-equal branch, the opportunity to vitally contribute to the functioning of our indispensable judicial system, and the chance to become ambassadors for the values of that system long after the clerkship ends.

All these are open to every clerk on every court, no matter what the perceived prestige of the judge or tribunal might appear to be.

It is difficult to point to one or two essays as especially illustrative of the inimitable clerkship experience. All the essays make a special contribution because every judge and every clerk is unique. And even the briefest sampling conveys the unparalleled education and mentorship a clerkship yields. Justice Ruth Bader Ginsburg, for instance, credits Judge Edmund L. Palmieri with teaching her not only about the art of good judging, but also about "the art of good living." David M. Dorsen notes how Judge Henry Friendly "would light up with joy" when a clerk challenged him with a cogent counterargument. Anna R. Hayes describes the inner workings of the North Carolina Supreme Court from her vantage point as a clerk for Justice Susie Marshall Sharp. Ronald Krotoszynski recounts the role Judge Frank M. Johnson Jr.'s clerks played—including writing bench memoranda, opinion drafts, and speeches—in shaping the civil rights movement of the mid-twentieth century. And Barry Sullivan writes how Judge John Minor Wisdom showed his clerks "by his example that one could be a great lawyer and judge without being crotchety or cynical or sour."

These recollections also show judges and clerks operating in many different ways. It's all a question of what works for the judge. Some judges, such as Judge Burnita Shelton Matthews, keep their doors open so that clerks may pop in at will. Others, such as Judge Henry Friendly, maintain a more remote and intimidating presence. Some judges are more openly critical when a clerk makes a mistake. Others, like Judge Frank M. Johnson Jr., respond with measured advice. In terms of work flow, some judges recruit their clerks' help as they prepare for oral argument, whether through memoranda or verbal sparring matches. Others, like Judge John Minor Wisdom, prefer to prepare on their own.

Don't let these differences mislead you. Certain clerking principles are universal. Since a judge must be conversant with many more cases than a clerk, the clerk must know his or her cases cold. Particularly impressive is the clerk who answers accurately on the spot a judge's factual inquiry about a case, without having to say "I'll get back to you on that." A good clerk must also be a

OF COURTIERS & PRINCES

CONSTITUTIONALISM AND DEMOCRACY

Gregg Ivers and Kevin T. McGuire, Editors

OF

Stories of Lower Court
Clerks and Their Judges

COURTIERS
& PRINCES

Edited by Todd C. Peppers

University of Virginia Press | Charlottesville and London

University of Virginia Press
© 2020 by the Rector and Visitors of the University of Virginia
All rights reserved
Printed in the United States of America on acid-free paper

First published 2020

9 8 7 6 5 4 3 2 1

Library of Congress Cataloging-in-Publication Data

Names: Peppers, Todd C., editor.
Title: Of courtiers and princes : stories of lower court clerks and their judges /
    edited by Todd C. Peppers, University of Virginia Press.
Description: Charlottesville : University of Virginia Press, 2020. | Series:
    Constitutionalism and democracy | Includes bibliographical references
    and index.
Identifiers: LCCN 2020039797 (print) | LCCN 2020039798 (ebook) |
    ISBN 9780813944593 (cloth) | ISBN 9780813944609 (ebook)
Subjects: LCSH: Clerks of court—United States. | Law clerks—United States. |
    Judicial process—United States.
Classification: LCC KF8807 .O3 2020 (print) | LCC KF8807 (ebook) |
    DDC 347.73/16—dc23
LC record available at https://lccn.loc.gov/2020039797
LC ebook record available at https://lccn.loc.gov/2020039798

Cover photographs: Judge Damon Keith in chambers with law clerks Claude Bailey
(far left), Renee Chenault, and Gerry Hargrove (*top;* Detroit Free Press via ZUMA
Press); Judge Jerome Frank (far left) with Judge Augustus Hand (second from right)
at the wedding of their law clerks, Carmel "Kim" Prashker Ebb and Larry Ebb (*bottom;* photograph courtesy of the Ebb family)

CONTENTS

Foreword

No one is more knowledgeable about judicial clerkships than Professor Todd Peppers. Just when you think he has exhausted the subject, he comes up with a new wrinkle, as in this absorbing collection of recollections by former clerks on the federal courts of appeals, federal district courts, and state supreme courts.

The clerkships on these courts are much different from clerkships on the Supreme Court. The cachet may not be as great, and the law firm bonuses upon completion of service may not be as high. But the jobs are every bit as important and in many ways every bit as difficult as clerkships on the Supreme Court.

The state and federal appellate courts are where law first shifts from relative informality to a more formal posture, from a greater emphasis on finding facts to a de novo review of questions of law. And on those legal issues, the clerks and judges whom they serve struggle with far less assistance than clerks on the Supreme Court.

The briefing and argument in state and federal appellate courts is strikingly uneven, and judge and clerk alike are sometimes forced to make the best of presentations whose quality leaves much to be desired. The number of amicus briefs in those courts is increasing but remains far below that of the Supreme Court. I tell my clerks that we need to make the best call under law that we can, but prepare to watch thirty or so different amici complain to the Supreme Court how appallingly wrong we were.

All this is to say that the clerks on the lower federal and highest state courts will be dealing with law in a more primitive state. But this is not all bad—the lower courts have the chance to shape a case before the issues are frozen, which they often are by the time they reach the highest court.

Some lower court clerks arrive with the thought that their clerkship is a stepping stone to a clerkship at the Supreme Court. That is altogether understandable, but at the same time a big mistake. Experiences should not be instrumental but valued for their own intrinsic worth.

From the perspective of the bench, clerks are family. If not sons and daughters, then certainly nieces and nephews. The marvelous recollections in this volume show the deep bonding between clerk and judge, the intergenerational communication that is equaled nowhere else in government, the education into the workings of an entirely co-equal branch, the opportunity to vitally contribute to the functioning of our indispensable judicial system, and the chance to become ambassadors for the values of that system long after the clerkship ends.

All these are open to every clerk on every court, no matter what the perceived prestige of the judge or tribunal might appear to be.

It is difficult to point to one or two essays as especially illustrative of the inimitable clerkship experience. All the essays make a special contribution because every judge and every clerk is unique. And even the briefest sampling conveys the unparalleled education and mentorship a clerkship yields. Justice Ruth Bader Ginsburg, for instance, credits Judge Edmund L. Palmieri with teaching her not only about the art of good judging, but also about "the art of good living." David M. Dorsen notes how Judge Henry Friendly "would light up with joy" when a clerk challenged him with a cogent counterargument. Anna R. Hayes describes the inner workings of the North Carolina Supreme Court from her vantage point as a clerk for Justice Susie Marshall Sharp. Ronald Krotoszynski recounts the role Judge Frank M. Johnson Jr.'s clerks played—including writing bench memoranda, opinion drafts, and speeches—in shaping the civil rights movement of the mid-twentieth century. And Barry Sullivan writes how Judge John Minor Wisdom showed his clerks "by his example that one could be a great lawyer and judge without being crotchety or cynical or sour."

These recollections also show judges and clerks operating in many different ways. It's all a question of what works for the judge. Some judges, such as Judge Burnita Shelton Matthews, keep their doors open so that clerks may pop in at will. Others, such as Judge Henry Friendly, maintain a more remote and intimidating presence. Some judges are more openly critical when a clerk makes a mistake. Others, like Judge Frank M. Johnson Jr., respond with measured advice. In terms of work flow, some judges recruit their clerks' help as they prepare for oral argument, whether through memoranda or verbal sparring matches. Others, like Judge John Minor Wisdom, prefer to prepare on their own.

Don't let these differences mislead you. Certain clerking principles are universal. Since a judge must be conversant with many more cases than a clerk, the clerk must know his or her cases cold. Particularly impressive is the clerk who answers accurately on the spot a judge's factual inquiry about a case, without having to say "I'll get back to you on that." A good clerk must also be a two platoon player, alert to the best defenses against opposing views and to the most effective offensive thrusts. All this within the framework of seeking justice under law, which after all is the ultimate aim of the entire enterprise.

I could go on, but that would spoil all the fun. Readers who have never clerked will come to understand the influential and often mysterious institution that the judicial clerkship has become. Former clerks will find here touchstones of their own experiences and say to themselves: "I'm glad I did this."

As indeed you should be.

J. Harvie Wilkinson III

Preface

This book is the third and final volume in a trilogy of collected essays published by the University of Virginia Press. The first, *In Chambers: Stories of Supreme Court Law Clerks and Their Justices* (2012), was coedited with Dr. Artemus Ward of Northern Illinois University. The volume features essays by former clerks and historians about working for some of the giants in United States Supreme Court history. Oliver Wendell Holmes Jr. Louis D. Brandeis. Felix Frankfurter. Hugo Black. Earl Warren. Thurgood Marshall. And Ruth Bader Ginsburg.

The second volume of essays, *Of Courtiers & Kings: More Stories of Supreme Court Law Clerks and Their Justices* (2015), was coedited with Clare Cushman, director of publications at the Supreme Court Society. It also offers stories about Supreme Court justices and their clerks, with the wrinkle that many of the essays examine the law clerk hiring and utilization practices of those justices who have not received the same historical scrutiny as a Holmes or Brandeis—justices such as William Howard Taft, James Clark McReynolds, Stanley Reed, Potter Stewart, Warren Burger, and David Souter. Although the justices may not be as prominent, Clare and I found that the stories of their relationships with their clerks were fascinating and, in many instances, more interesting because they had not been told before.

This current volume of essays changes the focus from U.S. Supreme Court justices to lower federal and state court judges. The majority of cases filed in state and federal courts never make it to the U.S. Supreme Court, and over the last one hundred years every type of lower court judge has learned to depend on law clerks. Federal appeals court judges. State supreme court justices. Federal district court judges. Federal magistrate judges and bankruptcy judges. State appeals court judges. State trial court judges. Even state court judges in "specialty" courts, such as family and probate courts. In short, the young men and women who clerk in lower courts are relevant judicial actors with important stories to tell about the judges, the legal issues, and the cases that directly impact the thousands and thousands of plaintiffs and defendants who pass through their courtrooms. And if we want to understand the judiciary in a comprehensive sense, including the role that law clerks play in federal and state courts, then we have to take these other courts and clerks seriously—especially because these lower courts do not receive the same level of public or scholarly scrutiny as the Supreme Court.

Although lower court clerkships are not as prestigious as U.S. Supreme Court positions, the essays that follow reveal similarities across the federal and state courts. Judges and justices typically seek out candidates who attended good law schools, earned strong grades, and held positions on law review or other student publications. Interviews are often offered to the top candidates as a means of determining whether the applicants are personally compatible with the judge and staff.

In making hiring decisions, judges often favor candidates from elite law schools as well as their own alma maters. While systematic studies on the academic and socioeconomic backgrounds of lower court clerks have not been conducted, we should still ask whether the patterns of racial discrimination and academic elitism in the hiring of U.S. Supreme Court law clerks are also found in the selection of lower court clerks. Moreover, law clerks in the lower federal and state courts are given a host of job duties—from reviewing appeals and writing bench memoranda to drafting judicial opinions. As with U.S. Supreme Court law clerks, the substantive responsibilities assigned to clerks raise questions as to whether the clerks have the training and experience to competently carry out their duties as well as whether the clerks wield inappropriate levels of influence over the judicial process. This collected volume of essays does not answer these questions, however, but instead provides some case studies through which readers might arrive at their own tentative conclusions.

When I started this project, I initially approached authors who could provide essays from a cross-section of lower federal and state courts and thereby highlight the different tasks assigned to clerks in federal trial courts versus state and federal appeals courts. Moreover, I sought out contributors who clerked for well-known jurists, such as former California Supreme Court justice Roger Traynor or Fifth Circuit Court of Appeals judges Frank M. Johnson Jr., Elbert Tuttle, and John Minor Wisdom. One might think of these judges as "the greats" of the lower courts.

As my list of essayists grew, however, I noticed that a unique pattern was emerging—a number of the essays featured stories about clerking for judges who are not widely known by judicial scholars. Instead, they were lesser-known jurists who had battled discrimination and shattered glass ceilings. In reading the essay drafts, I found that their stories were as compelling as tales of clerking for judicial superstars. These groundbreaking jurists include North Carolina Supreme Court justice Susie Marshall Sharp and California Supreme Court justice Rose Bird, the second and third women to hold positions on state supreme courts. Juanita Kidd Stout, the first African American woman to sit on a state's highest court. Burnita Shelton Matthews, the first woman to be nominated for a seat on the federal district court bench. Damon Keith and Leon Higginbotham Jr., two of the first African American men who overcame systemic discrimination to rise to the federal appeals court bench. And Ruth Bader Ginsburg, the first woman to be selected as a law clerk by the legendary federal district court judge Edmund L. Palmieri and one of the first women to serve as a law clerk in the federal court system.

In reading the stories of more obscure judges, one cannot help but reflect on the fickle nature of judicial fame and glory. While some of these judges are not household names, they are all well-educated, thoughtful, and skilled jurists as well as admirable human beings. The fact that they did not serve on the United States Supreme Court reminds us that being a judicial "superstar" is due as much to the mysterious workings of the cosmos (to paraphrase Oliver Wendell Holmes Jr.) than anything else. Or put another way, sometimes it's better to be lucky than smart.

Finally, the essays contained in this book offer a rare peek at the rich personalities of the men and women who have sat on our nation's courts. They include vignettes about jurists who love drag races, barbeques, hunting, fresh blueberries, woodworking, and good whiskey. We meet judges who motivate their clerks to achieve the superlative, sometimes through mentoring and sometimes through intimidation and fear. We learn how these judges approach their work and decide legal issues. And see that their black robes do not protect these judges from professional and personal struggles, be they heated retention elections, terminal illnesses, or the devastating loss of a spouse.

A word of caution. While these essays do not swerve into hagiography, only a handful of the essays contain even a whiff of candid observation about the foibles and frailties of the profiled judges (the exception being David Dorsen's essay on Judge Henry Friendly). When I started approaching former law clerks about this project, I did contact individuals who clerked for judges whose difficult personalities were an open secret. Despite off-the-record conversations about awful clerkship experiences, the former clerks declined to submit essays for this book. Some cited a duty of confidentiality, although I pushed back and argued unsuccessfully that the duty does not extend to the issue of toxic personalities. Others—whose judges were still active—were clearly concerned about retaliation. And a few seemed to be protective of their former employers, despite the grueling nature of the clerkship.

I regret that my powers of persuasion were not stronger. The goal of this book is to present an accurate picture of the clerkship experience, and not all law clerks are fortunate enough to work for judges who treated them with kindness and respect. Or took an interest in being a mentor. By not speaking out, former law clerks help create a distorted picture of the clerkship institution. Moreover, the failure to publicly discuss bad clerkships denies current law students the information necessary to make an informed decision about where to submit clerkship applications. Finally, remaining silent about an abusive judge has the effect, in my opinion, of allowing the abuse to continue in the future.

As I end this introduction, I want to briefly thank three people who made this project possible. The first is Dick Holway, my acquisitions editor at the University of Virginia Press. Without Dick's support and confidence, none of the three volumes of essays on law clerks would have been published. The second is Professor Chad Oldfather of the Marquette University Law School, with whom I have shared a friendship since our first year of law school. Not only did Chad contribute an essay to this volume, but he unselfishly offered advice and feedback through this entire process—including reading all the submitted essays. He is a prominent legal scholar in his own right, and I consider myself lucky to have such a talented, unofficial editor looking over my shoulder. The third is Judi Pinckney, my administrative assistant for the last sixteen years. Judi has proofread and edited every book that I have written. Her assistance has been invaluable.

Finally, I want to thank my wife, Michele. During the span of this project, our family weathered a terrible series of deaths and illnesses. Without her love, I would never have completed this book.

Todd C. Peppers
January 2020

OF COURTIERS & PRINCES

I Clerking for State Court Judges

ROLAND E. BRANDEL AND JAMES E. KRIER

Clerking for Roger J. Traynor

J ustice Roger J. Traynor was born in Utah in 1900, the son of a miner and
drayman. He left after high school to undertake undergraduate and graduate studies at the University of California, Berkeley, eventually earn-
ing (simultaneously) a Ph.D. in political science and a law degree from Boalt
Hall, the university's law school. He practiced law for just a few months, then
returned to the university to teach in its political science department. A year
later, in 1930, he joined the law faculty, where he worked until his appointment
to the California Supreme Court in 1940. He became chief justice in 1964,
retired in 1970, and died in 1983.[1]

Justice Traynor's obituary in the *New York Times* said he "was often called one
of the greatest judicial talents never to sit on the United States Supreme Court
and was voted one of the nation's outstanding judges whenever his professional
colleagues were polled."[2] Other tributes spoke of him as "the ablest judge of
his generation," and "an acknowledged leader in every field that he touched."[3]
These memorial statements merely confirmed a long-standing reputation. Walter Schaefer, another great state supreme court justice, said in 1961 that Justice
Traynor was, and had been for many years, "the nation's number one state court
judge." Five years later, Schaefer "removed the state court qualification."[4]

Schaefer called Justice Traynor "a judge's judge," but he was also a law professor's judge, not least, perhaps, because he had been a law professor himself
and went about his judicial work in a famously scholarly way. He published
law review articles regularly throughout his years as a judge and wrote judicial opinions that still figure prominently in law school casebooks—especially
those focused on contracts, torts, and choice of law. He built personal and professional relationships with law professors, and—of particular interest here—
relied on them to recommend law clerks for his chambers.

The selection process was more informal than the practice of many prominent judges then and still is, in two important respects. First, there was no

formal Traynor clerk selection committee, but rather a wide and shifting network of law professors from across the country, whose individual judgment he trusted. This virtually guaranteed a geographically diverse pool of candidates. Second, although he used personal interviews with candidates, he did not insist upon them.

Traynor clerks came from law schools located throughout the United States, with those from California included but not treated preferentially. All of our group of five who worked in his chambers from mid-1966 to mid-1967 came from out of state: the University of Chicago, Columbia University, the University of Illinois, New York University, and the University of Wisconsin. As is typical of law clerks, we were fresh out of school, but the authors of this essay were several years older than our colleagues, thanks to time in the military between college and law school.

There were career employees on Justice Traynor's legal staff as well, most prominently Don Barrett. He was hired by the justice right out of law school in 1948. A year later, Barrett became the senior staff attorney and continued in that position until the justice's retirement in 1970 (he also served, from 1964 until his own retirement in 1981, as principal attorney for the California Supreme Court). We are not sure of the total number of Traynor staffers during our year of clerking, but do know that Donald Wright, who succeeded Justice Traynor as chief justice, had a total of twelve, eight of them career employees. Judges, lawyers, and legal scholars across the country have long held the California Supreme Court in high esteem, and clerkships with any of its justices were coveted positions (a Traynor clerkship especially so). It opened doors to future opportunities, including clerkships with justices of the United States Supreme Court. It forged important personal and professional relationships. It put one in regular company with a stimulating group of excellent attorneys—fellow clerks, the clerks in other chambers, and attorneys from the attorney general's primary office housed in the court's complex. (The building's cafeteria was shared by all, as was an abiding interest in the legal and political issues of the tumultuous 1960s.) And all of this in marvelous San Francisco!

A common benefit of judicial clerkships is some degree of regular face-to-face meetings with the boss, but sitting daily at the feet of the master was not a feature of our year of clerking. That was a marked shift from his practice in the quarter century before his appointment as chief justice, when he regularly worked through, in one-on-one sessions with his clerks, every detail of an opinion, from an insistence on precise, critical thinking to close scrutiny of word choice. Once he became chief justice, the extraordinary and time-consuming duties of managing California's vast judicial system made such close ongoing supervision impossible.

Happily, however, we enjoyed a very close alternative to the real thing, which gets us back to Don Barrett, the senior staff attorney. Don, a big, gangly man with a ready smile and a subtle sense of humor, was our shepherd. Merely being in his presence eased any anxieties we might be suffering about our clerking duties. He took over the supervisory tasks that Justice Traynor had previously performed personally, and it is hard to imagine a better surrogate. We quickly learned that with Don supervising every step of our work, it would turn out fine in the end. It is not hyperbole to say that he had a complete mastery of California law (including the pages on which it appeared) and any other body of law, state or federal, that might have a bearing on whatever issues we had at hand. If what we submitted for his approval had problems, they would be fixed—by us! Never did he tell us what to do. He would simply ask questions, usually with a Cheshire grin that we knew to be a tease. Had we considered a certain judicial opinion unmentioned in our draft? Noticed that a federal statute was involved in our case? Read a certain law review article by Justice Traynor? This was Don's version of the Socratic method.

And we *did* have some time with our judge. The decision process at the court during our tenure had several stages. Litigants would submit petitions for hearing, bunches of which were submitted to the chambers of each justice, who would in turn assign them to the law clerks, who would in turn write conference memoranda recommending a grant or denial. When a petition was granted, the case would be assigned to a justice, who would have a clerk prepare a calendar memorandum, in essence a full, carefully researched draft opinion circulated among all the justices (sometimes we were asked by Justice Traynor to review calendar memos prepared by other chambers). After discussion, the justices tentatively voted on the calendar memorandum prior to the time at which oral arguments were heard.

California attorneys were familiar with this process, but oftentimes unaware of Justice Traynor's particular approach to oral arguments. His practice at arguments was to interject leading questions designed to assist counsel in making their case by helping them clarify points made in their briefs or at the oral argument itself. His intentions were entirely beneficent, but based on our observations at arguments, we came to suspect that nervous counsel, wary that they were being led into a highly public and fatal trap, feared otherwise. So an exchange might all too often proceed as: "Traynor: Counsel, with respect to your characterization of case A, didn't you mean to say X?" (Interpretation X was supportive of counsel's goal and completely consistent with the already written tentative opinion.) Wary counsel might say: "Oh no, your honor. I must have been misunderstood," and proceed to take several rhetorical steps backward on the otherwise road to victory.

Justice Traynor's clerks were assigned other projects in addition to drafting memoranda, such as researching and drafting speeches or law review articles for him. But far and away the most intimidating task was drafting calendar memos and final opinions. We knew that the justice took very seriously not only the task of resolving every dispute before the court, but also determining how the resolution of the particular dispute would impact the future development of the bodies of substantive and procedural law that were involved in the particular case; that he welcomed academic critiques of his decisions and drew from them to develop and refine his ideas; and that his opinions received careful attention and had enormous impact on state and federal judicial and legislative developments, on academic scholarship, and on future generations of law students.

This made drafting a heady, and weighty, experience, to say the least. Yet the Traynor approach was to figuratively drop a case file on our desks with an instruction to write the calendar memo that would ultimately become the draft opinion. That instruction and nothing more. There was not so much as a hint (from Justice Traynor or Don Barrett) at the desired result nor the reasoning to get there. But once the inevitable "there must be some mistake, I haven't even passed the bar exam yet, what do I do?" emotional crisis subsided, all of the Traynor clerks launched into the challenge with vigor. That method put a premium on independent thinking, research, and cogitation on what the justice's views most likely would be, as well as a largely unavailing effort to think like and write like one of the nation's most respected doctrinal jurists.

That aspect of the clerkship was a challenging but wonderfully rewarding experience, in part because it always concluded by meeting with the justice to go over our work in the court's capacious high-ceilinged conference room. Given the setting and the occasion, one might think that these meetings would be intimidating, but they were not. It helped knowing that Don Barrett had approved our work product, but what made all the difference was Justice Traynor's manner. His peers knew him to be a man without arrogance or condescension. In his relationships with us, he was that and more. He made clear that he respected us, and that he had, accordingly, high expectations. He cheered the best of our work with pronounced enthusiasm and noted our shortcomings (including our many embarrassing solecisms) with mild but instructive chiding. All the while, he engaged in his habits of chewing gum, parking it on an ashtray while he smoked an unfiltered Camel cigarette, finishing the cigarette, and retrieving the gum.

If we didn't sit at the feet of the master, at least a fortunate few of us got to ride with him in a limousine provided by the state. Justice Traynor and Don Barrett drove in to work from Berkeley, where both of them lived. Any Traynor clerks residing in the East Bay were invited to ride along, provided they appeared at the specified pickup points. This was a nice perk for the lowly likes of us. Krier's pickup spot was at a corner next to a gas station. One day as he stood waiting, an employee from the station wandered over to have a cigarette. He asked Krier if he was waiting for a ride to work, and when Krier said he was, the guy said words to the effect, "I hope your ride gets here soon. The boss will be mad if you're late." Then the limo pulled up. The guy looked at Krier and said, "Wow! I guess you're the boss."

Every trip was, in several respects, always the same: Don at the wheel of the limo, the justice in the front passenger seat, the clerk or clerks and sometimes an honored guest in the back. And every trip was devoted to conversation, with no distractions like the car radio. But every trip's conversation was different. We remember discussions of pending cases, a recall drive aimed at the justices, the tension between an independent judiciary and a representative political system, and a wide range of jurisprudential topics. Candor was welcome and practiced. Sometimes the justice would comment on the views expressed by a distinguished guest who rode with us the day before, telling us with amusement the points he thought we scored.

How rare and appreciated was the privilege of those hours of intimate discussion with a jurist of such extraordinary talents, experience, and humanity, not just willing but eager to engage the views of the likes of us—lacking in experience and knowledge, but possessed of the certainty and righteousness of the young.

Justice Traynor was always interested in, and happy to visit with, individual former clerks and to assist them in pursuing their careers with a well-placed phone call or letter of recommendation. He was a warm, considerate, quiet, scholarly, somewhat private man. Time we spent with him was always a pleasure. However, neither he nor his former clerks organized large social events in the nature of reunions.

The clerkship system at the California Supreme Court has changed since our day. Now each justice is supported by a judicial assistant and five career staff attorneys (the chief justice has a larger staff), though several justices have opted to employ annual law clerks in lieu of some of their allotted career attorney positions. And San Francisco has changed, too. Our annual salary of $8,500 was enough to make residing in the city affordable, even if we had children and an unemployed spouse. But the cost of housing in San Francisco has far outpaced inflation in general from then to now. Today's clerk would have to devote about 75 percent of their income to rent housing there. We doubt that many of them reside in the City by the Bay.

Notes

1. Our background sketch is drawn from fuller accounts in Leonard G. Ratner, "Reflections of a Traynor Law Clerk—with Some Emphasis on Conflict of Laws," *Southern California Law Review* 44 (1970); G. Edward White, "Tribute to Roger Traynor." *Virginia Law Review* 69, no. 8 (1983): 1381–86; and Geoffrey C. Hazard Jr., *The Jurisprudence of Justice Roger Traynor: Twenty-Third Chief Justice of California* (San Francisco: University of California, Hastings College of the Law, 2015), 11–17.

2. Les Ledbetter, "Roger J. Traynor, California Justice," *New York Times*, May 17, 1983, 6.

3. The quoted remarks are taken from "In Memoriam—Roger J. Traynor," *California Law Review* 71 (1983):1037–71, collecting essays by, among others, Warren Burger, Henry Friendly, and Walter Schaefer.

4. Walter V. Schaefer, "A Judge's Judge," *California Law Review* 71 (1983): 1050–52.

MARGARET CONNORS

Juanita Kidd Stout

Personal Reflections on a Woman of Firsts

The Beginning

Justice Juanita Kidd Stout and I first crossed paths when she spoke at my high school, an all-female Catholic academy. I have scant recollection of what she said[1] and probably recollect her visit only because her juvenile sentencing record had made headlines.[2] Some twenty-one years later, our paths would once again intersect in a way I could never have imagined.

On Martin Luther King Day of 1988, I happened to catch a news spot covering Governor Robert Casey's appointment of Judge Stout[3] as a justice of the Supreme Court of Pennsylvania.[4] An interim appointee, Justice Stout would serve until the vacancy she assumed could be filled by election, at that point presumed to be January 1989. Shortly after learning of the appointment, I received a telephone call from Judge Stout. She had gotten my information from Judge William D. Hutchinson,[5] who knew I had taken a hiatus from practicing law due to the birth of my second child. A practical woman to her core, Justice Stout sought a clerk with experience and turned to a former justice for a reference. We arranged to meet in her Philadelphia Chambers where she sat as a trial judge in the Philadelphia Court of Common Pleas.

On the appointed day, I entered the antechamber to Justice Stout's office. Greeted by a woman, seated at a typewriter, I announced my name and purpose. The woman swiveled her chair back toward another woman, also seated at a typewriter, and announced, "Margaret Connors is here to see you." I attempted to hide my amazement. As was her habit, Justice Stout was working at her own typewriter. I later learned that Justice Stout, an organ player and terrific musician, invariably did her own typing. She used a mechanical typewriter as she did not favor the electric models. Those old enough can remember the pinky finger strength needed to push the "shift" key on such typewriters. Justice Stout was a champ when it came to the mechanical keyboard. In fact, unable to find a legal position when she finished her law studies, Justice Stout worked as a legal secretary. She was proficient at typing and shorthand; she was proud of both.

We proceeded to her inner office, where she asked if I would agree to serve as her administrative law clerk. At that time, administrative law clerks "led" the clerking team and, as the name implies, also assumed some administrative duties. After a brief discussion of the schedule flexibility I would need with a newborn, I eagerly accepted her offer.

The Prequel

The granddaughter of a slave who had toiled in Alabama, Juanita Kidd Stout's family immigrated to Oklahoma. As she recounted to me, opportunities provided by the Homestead Act proved the impetus for the move. Her parents, both school teachers, had settled in Wewoka, Oklahoma, where the Justice learned to read before first grade. She graduated early both from grade school and high school. Her unflagging academic pursuit and indefatigable work ethic no doubt arose in large measure from the influence of her mother. Justice Stout spoke of her often as a strict, though loving, mentor who instilled the value of education.

In order to attend high school, Justice Stout related how she had been compelled to leave her parents and make a somewhat lengthy, arduous trip to the home of an aunt who lived near a segregated high school, the only high school open to her. She sorely missed life with her parents, whom she could visit only on weekends. But she wanted a high school education and more. Throughout her life Justice Stout preached the inestimable value of education. Known to require written essays from juveniles convicted in her courtroom, she often bemoaned the lack of education as a reason for society's ills.

Upon attaining her college degree at the University of Iowa, Justice Stout returned to a teaching position in Oklahoma where she ultimately met her future husband and fellow teacher, Otis Stout. The Second World War interrupted their relationship, and Justice Stout moved to Washington, D.C.

William Hamilton Houston, an African American lawyer in the firm of Houston, Houston and Hastie, hired Justice Stout as a secretary.[6] Thus was born her love of the law. When Otis Stout returned from war, they married, and she was able to use the G.I. Bill to study law at Indiana University while her husband pursued a graduate degree. The couple thereafter moved to Philadelphia. Unable to find a law firm that would hire her,[7] Justice Stout then became a secretary to Judge William H. Hastie of the Third Circuit Court of Appeals.[8]

Ultimately Justice Stout opened her own law practice with a fellow female lawyer. Eventually, she secured a position in the Philadelphia District Attorney's Office, where she attained recognition for her prodigious work ethic. She relished relating how she regularly rose at 4:00 a.m. and was almost always first at the office. Her work ethic and work product caught the attention of her superiors. It also led to her becoming the first African American woman to be elected to the Philadelphia Court of Common Pleas, hence the chambers where we first met in 1988.

In Medias Res

Following her Supreme Court swearing-in, Justice Stout moved to new chambers in Philadelphia's City Hall. Its entryway sat between her private office and a large room for her four full-time clerks. Justice Stout also had a part-time "allocatur" clerk who assisted in reviewing the Pennsylvania equivalent of certiorari petitions. Three secretaries/assistants worked in the middle room, which also housed a seating area for visitors. Unlike the justices of the United States Supreme Court, justices of the Pennsylvania Supreme Court maintained separate chambers in diverse areas of the Commonwealth and heard cases in three venues: Philadelphia, Harrisburg, and Pittsburgh. At the time only one other justice maintained an office in City Hall, and only one other had chambers in the city itself. Others on the seven-member court had chambers in Pittsburgh.

Justice Stout had initially chosen a diverse staff with two women and two men serving as full-time clerks. The clerks were also diverse as to race. Only one of her clerks attended an Ivy League law school. As was the case with me, Justice Stout was flexible with all her clerks when it came to their schedules. As long as the work got done, she did not care when it was done. She trusted us implicitly to put in the required hours. Harkening back to her 4:00 a.m. wake-up while at the district attorney's office, she was often the second person to arrive at chambers. With a four-month-old and a two-year-old, I was usually first to arrive but also usually the first to leave.

As administrative law clerk, my duties included organizing the office from scratch. The paperwork could be overwhelming, so establishing a system to organize and track it constituted a somewhat herculean task. Cheerful as always, Justice Stout encouraged our combined staff efforts to unpack and organize chambers for the influx of allocaturs, appeals, miscellaneous docket filings, proposed rule changes, and other matters that awaited and thereafter arrived continuously. We managed.

The full-time clerks worked in one room that also housed a small bathroom. Despite this open-air forum, we were able to focus on the work at hand. Justice Stout's needs and wishes were clear. Clerks worked on the preparation of allocatur memoranda, which entailed outlining the parties, issues, lower-court finding, and a recommendation as to whether to grant or deny an appeal. Clerks reviewed matters filed in the miscellaneous docket, outlined them, and made a recommendation to grant or deny.[9] Rule changes also underwent preliminary review by a clerk, who would prepare a memo and recommendation.

Insofar as cases that the court actually heard, the vast majority had undergone preliminary review, per allocatur petitions, and were before the court as a matter of its discretion.[10] Clerks prepared bench memos. More detailed than allocatur reviews, bench memos nonetheless outlined the parties, facts, legal issues, outcome, and reasoning of the lower courts accompanied by the clerk's recommendation as to disposition. Justice Stout permitted her clerks to attend oral argument of any matter argued in Philadelphia. The appellate courtroom was a short walk from our chambers. Since the court also sat in Harrisburg and Pittsburgh, a clerk of her choosing would accompany her to these respective cities when the court was in session.

Following oral argument the court would preliminarily discuss, vote on, and assign cases to a justice in the majority for an opinion. Justice Stout, in turn, would write her own opinions or assign a case to a clerk for a preliminary, yet intensively researched and written, draft. Extremely approachable, Justice Stout welcomed, and often initiated, discourse with her clerks. She was wont to pronounce, "The law should make sense. If it doesn't we should make it make sense!" We spent many hours discussing cases, questioning factual assumptions, checking the original record, and researching precedent. Justice Stout carefully listened to, and read, her clerks' work.[11] Hers was unvaryingly and perforce the ultimate decision.

Not to be overlooked in any description of the clerks' duties was citing and sourcing each other's work as well as the work of other chambers.[12] In an age of instant, computer access to cases, regulations, and court rules, together with their annotations, cross-references, and histories, it is difficult to imagine the time consumed in this task. One had to literally "hit the books," often manually copying cited cases in order to read and annotate them for use in a contemporary opinion. *Shepherds,* a publication of which many attorneys may now be unaware, comprised the de rigueur, cumbersome method of checking case history.

In addition to the painstaking task of citing and sourcing, clerks largely handwrote their work. At some point our clerk's office obtained a single, very large word processor that no one knew how to use.[13] It was a hit-or-miss learning process, as a result of which the machine was largely neglected. As a rule, the secretaries typed the clerks' work. Of course the Justice did her own typing. No one had email. I do not even recollect a fax machine, and the sheer volume of paperwork would have overwhelmed those early machines with their glossy, smelly paper. We had rotary telephones.

Not once did Justice Stout ask me, or as far as I know any other clerk, to perform personal work outside our judicial duties. An extremely affable woman, with a quick wit, she did dine with me and my family at least twice.[14] Fond of quoting her mother, Justice Stout would say, "There are no big I's and little u's in this world." In other words, no title or distinction made one person better than another.

Also fond of recounting cases she had heard, late in the day Justice Stout would sometimes regale her clerks with astounding facts gleaned in her courtroom. Particularly memorable was the case of a woman who murdered another by performing a somewhat surgically precise C-section in the course of stealing the victim's baby. There was also the case of paternal puzzlement and fecundation ab extra. Justice Stout could have scripted a television series, had she so chosen.

Years later on a cross-country trip my family of four stopped in Tulsa to visit her. I remember a large organ in her living room that she played at the request of my children. We had lunch together whereupon she most predictably took us on a tour of her local public library. We lingered in the children's section, where, after reading my children a story, she impressed the importance, and the joy, of reading upon my three-year-old and six-year-old. Learning certainly constituted a guiding light in her view of the life well led.

The End

I last saw Justice Stout in a hospital room. A member of her Common Pleas Court staff telephoned me to say she wanted me to know she was ill and hospitalized. On our last visit she related that she had been experiencing chest pain during a homicide trial, took a lunch break, and walked to the hospital, which I do not believe she ever left. She was diagnosed with leukemia. Nonetheless her spirits were invariably high, and she joked about a mutual friend, about to have his fourth child in just a few years. Her wry sense of humor intact, she quipped, "Does he know where they are coming from?" Justice Stout succumbed to leukemia in 1998.

During my clerkship with Justice Stout, I remained keenly aware of what a remarkable, yet also ordinary, woman she was: remarkable in her ethics, intelligence, and accomplishments, despite the many hurdles she had faced, yet ordinary in her self-effacement, practicality, and disdain of pomp and circumstance. I reminded myself regularly that working with[15] her would probably prove a highlight in my legal career. Thirty years later, I can aver I was correct.

Notes

This essay is a personal recollection of time spent, both inside and outside chambers. It is written some thirty years after the fact and represents a purely personal attempt to paint an accurate portrait of Justice Juanita Kidd Stout, as I came to know her.

1. Contrastingly Justice Stout's oratory helped inspire my best friend to become a lawyer years before I did.

2. Justice Stout herself confirmed sewing a skirt comprised a routine sentence she imposed on female juvenile offenders. This unorthodox imposition had a male counterpart that I do not recollect. I do know she at times required an essay and often lamented the grammar and spelling thus evoked.

3. "Judge" Stout at that time sat on the bench of the Court of Common Pleas of Philadelphia.

4. Justice Stout would joke that Governor Casey felt sorry for her because they had once shared a losing ticket.

5. I had clerked for Judge Hutchinson when he sat on the Supreme Court of Pennsylvania. By January 1988, he had assumed a seat on the Third Circuit Court of Appeals.

6. William Houston, also a person of many firsts, practiced law and taught at Howard University. According to Justice Stout, he was an architect of the successful strategy that led to the landmark decision of the United States Supreme Court in *Brown v. Board of Education*. Justice Stout held him in great esteem.

7. One ought not forget that Justice Stout faced discrimination both because of her gender and her race. Her pragmatic and optimistic diligence indubitably forged her pioneer path where many might have faltered.

8. Judge Hastie had practiced law with William Houston when Justice Stout served as a secretary to the latter. Like William Houston, Judge Hastie enjoyed Justice Stout's deep admiration.

9. I found this a challenging task as filings to the miscellaneous docket, often pro se, posed unique and difficult legal issues, that is, issues outside the norm in many instances.

10. Certain matters, such as death penalty cases, were automatically appealable by statute. Very few cases enjoyed this mandatory appeal status.

11. The only tense moment I ever experienced with Justice Stout occurred when I submitted a writing that used "elude" when it should have used "allude," much to my embarrassment.

12. Opinions circulated by other chambers underwent vigorous review with a written report to Justice Stout.

13. My recollection is that it was a word processor, but it could have been an early-model computer. It was half the size of my desk, and I taught myself to use it as a word processor albeit sparingly.

14. Sometime in the early 1990s, "Judge" Stout, who was then serving as a senior judge to the Homicide Division of the Philadelphia Court of Common Pleas, joined several clerks and some members of her Common Pleas staff for brunch.

15. She would surely correct me if I used the preposition "for." A quintessential egalitarian, she saw our work as collaborative.

ANNA R. HAYES

Clerking for North Carolina's First Lady of the Law

North Carolina Supreme Court Justice Susie Marshall Sharp

W hen Governor Terry Sanford appointed Susie Marshall Sharp to be the first woman on the North Carolina Supreme Court in 1962, she had already been known for decades as "the first" and usually "the only" woman in her professional endeavors. She addressed her first—all male—jury in 1929, at a time when women lawyers were all but nonexistent and women trial lawyers practically unknown. It would be another seventeen years before women in North Carolina were allowed to serve on a jury.[1] When Governor Kerr Scott named her as the first woman on the state's Superior Court in 1949, the idea of a female trial court judge was unimaginable. Crowds turned up just to see her, and one newspaperman expressed his expectation of seeing a man named Susie occupying the bench. But by the time she ascended to the North Carolina Supreme Court, a dozen years before she became the first woman in the United States to be elected chief justice of a state supreme court, Susie Sharp had long since tired of the "woman angle." She often said, "Work has no sex." Her unwavering focus was on the pursuit of excellence, and this is what her law clerks would always remember.

Justice Sharp was a short, carefully dressed and coiffed woman with what could be perceived as a forbidding manner. She carried a parasol to protect her creamy complexion from the sun, and a pistol in her handbag to protect the rest of her. She was fondly known as "Her Majesty" to her father's old law partner and perhaps to others, but in fact she possessed a considerable sense of humor. Once her clerks got to know her, they found her to be a warm and charming person, albeit without compromise when it came to work.

The Court

In 1962 the North Carolina Supreme Court was a bastion of tradition. The seven justices hewed to precedent in the law and to unreconstructed views on the role of women. Justice Hunt Parker, for example, was so bound to precedent that he boasted he had never written an original word in his supreme court opinions, and was widely believed to think women should be invisible except at dinner. Terry Sanford, however, who had been elected governor in no small part due to the enthusiasm of women voters, was ready to break the mold when Chief Justice Wallace Winborne was forced by ill health to retire. Meeting with the chief justice to accept his letter of resignation, Sanford suggested that he might appoint Susie Sharp to fill the new vacancy on the court. Visibly distressed, Winborne said, "Governor, the supreme court is a man's court."[2]

Undaunted, Sanford named Susie Sharp to the court, and it proved one of his most popular, well-regarded appointments. The governor's office had to hire two secretaries to handle the congratulatory mail. Meanwhile, at the court the justices' ingrained chivalry assured the new justice a cordial welcome, and her stellar performance soon earned their deep respect. It helped that Justice Sharp, born in 1907 and herself imbued with southern ladylike tradition, was not overtly threatening, and moreover she had studied the ways of men for a lifetime. She displayed the usefulness of her researches when, during her first months on the court, Justice Parker seemed unable to refrain from a dissenting vote on her opinions. She found, however, that if she included one of his opinions among the supporting authorities in her draft opinion, his objections dwindled noticeably. "It's just unbelievable," she remarked to her law clerk, Andy Vanore,[3] "how we now have no trouble with Justice Parker."[4]

Clerk Selection

Justice Sharp inherited her first law clerk, Dick Jones,[5] from Chief Justice Winborne upon his retirement. It was an abrupt descent for the young man, from clerking for the chief to clerking for the newest member of the court. Justice Sharp teased him about it, but Jones was in fact hugely relieved. At the time, although the degree to which the justices relied on their clerks varied somewhat, the tradition that "every Judge does his homework" was very strong.[6] In the matter of opinion writing, it was not the norm for a justice to allocate this responsibility to a law clerk, who no matter how brilliant was merely a brand-new graduate of law school. Chief Justice Winborne, however, had begun to suffer from some of the deficits of age, with the result that his clerks had perforce begun writing his opinions. Jones to his terror had found himself functioning in part as the de facto chief justice.[7] The safe harbor of clerk to "Number 7" had its appeal.

Jones soon found, however, that he still had an important role to play. Justice Sharp, whose intellect was never in doubt, had been a notoriously bad speller her entire life and had an insecure relationship with the rules of grammar. She was unaccustomed to expressing herself in writing, and during her thirteen years as a trial court judge she had never needed to do so. When she handed Jones a draft of her first opinion, he was appalled. Granted, he had been an English major, but he found the draft disjointed, much too long, and overall so dreadful that he felt it would be a disservice to let her circulate it to the other justices. But, as he later recalled, "I didn't know her well enough, to be honest with you, to know whether I could level with her or not." In preparation for discussing the draft with her, he made a second copy. On the original, he indicated a few token remarks and corrections, but on the other he "red-lined the hell out of it. I just tore it all to pieces."[8]

At their conference, Jones apparently betrayed some of his reservations, and Justice Sharp pressed him, asking, "Now what do you really think of it?" When she saw the heavily corrected copy, she said, "Oh, my. Is it that bad?" She then made him sit down and tell her why.[9] She was a fast learner. Jones never had to edit her again, although she continued to rely on him for careful proofreading. In the future she would always recruit clerks who could be counted on "to know the difference between a restrictive and a nonrestrictive clause."[10] She would become known as a perfectionist in every aspect of her writing, working tirelessly to shape facts, legal scholarship, and logic into a bulletproof conclusion. Her opinions, written over a span of seventeen years, still stand out as models of lucidity.

Those first months on the court with their steep learning curve revealed Justice Sharp's sense of humor as well as her fortitude. In her journal she wrote, "My law clerk alternates between uncertainty, despair, disgust and compassion in his attitude toward me. I turn out to be right just often enough to keep him unsettled."[11] Although she appreciated constructive criticism, she made up her own mind. As she would later tell another clerk, Henry Manning,[12] "Remember that whenever two people agree about anything all the time, one of them is unnecessary."[13] And she occasionally revealed a certain wicked glee when she bested one of her bright young assistants. Dick Jones was the subject of one chortling report, in which she said, "I put the Jones boy in his place this morning." He had spent two days on a will case and produced a lengthy memo saying that no error could be found. "It didn't seem to me that he hit the point," Justice Sharp wrote. "I began trying to search myself. In less than ten minutes I had found a one-page opinion which disposed of the matter summarily . . . I suppose that was just one of those things and that I had a happy accident, but 'I wouldn't have taken a pretty [penny] for it.'"[14]

When Jones's clerk year ended, Justice Sharp joined the other members of the court in the annual law clerk search. As it happened, that year the standard operating procedure nearly resulted in a serious shortage of clerks. Andy Vanore, recalling his interview with Justice Sharp, said, "She told me that if I were selected, absolutely, positively, I had to pass the bar, because that was a requirement of the court. . . . Two or three weeks thereafter, she called me and said, 'Mr. Vanore, I'd like to offer you the position. I want to reiterate that you have to pass the bar.' I said, 'No problem, Justice Sharp, I think I will ease through that with no difficulty,' or something to that effect. And of course, it turned out that in '62, more than 50 percent of the applicants failed the bar." This included four of the seven law clerks selected for the coming year. According to Vanore, it was the highest percentage of failure before or since. When he got the letter from the State Bar telling him that he had failed, he called Justice Sharp to give her the news. She said, "Well, Mr. Vanore, I'm very sorry. You do recall that I made it clear that you had to pass the bar."

Understandably despondent, Vanore did not go out of his house for three or four days. But then he got a call from Justice Sharp, who said that in light of the fact that more than half the clerks had failed the bar exam, they were suspending the rule, and she would like him to report for work. "Justice Sharp and I laughed many, many times about that conversation," Vanore said.[15]

The justices tended to draw their clerks from their own law school, predominantly the University of North Carolina or Wake Forest University. By far the majority of Justice Sharp's clerks were graduates of the UNC law school. Although some UNC clerks got interviews through other channels, most during these years piled into a couple of cars, popularly known as the "cattle cars," and drove from Chapel Hill to Raleigh for a day of interviewing. Each justice had a (not so) secret feeder system. Over the years Justice Sharp relied heavily on Dickson Phillips, then dean of the law school at UNC and, later, on Professor Bill Aycock to recommend potential applicants. Bill Kennerly[16] recalled, "I took, you know, a sample of my legal writing with me . . . but I remember her saying, 'If Dickson Phillips says you can do it, then I don't need to read a brief you wrote for Constitutional Law.'"[17] She tended to like her clerks to have had law review experience and to be at the top of their class, although not necessarily number one or two.

Once Justice Sharp had the recommendation from her law school spy, she generally considered the clerk to be hired even if the individual was still considering other options. Bob Sumner[18] had actually accepted a clerkship at the United States District Court for the Middle District in North Carolina, with Chief Judge Eugene A. Gordon, the day before his appointment for an interview with Justice Sharp. Somewhat unusually, she had asked him to meet her on a Saturday at her office in her hometown of Reidsville. He recalled that it was a dreary, rainy day, and when he arrived at the door of her old-fashioned office, it appeared to be completely dark. Eventually she answered his knock, and led him to a small room at the back, where there was a single light on. "That's the way she was. I mean, she was so frugal. She wasn't going to run up the electric bill there at the law office when she would come home on the weekends."

Sumner never got the opportunity to tell her that he had accepted a position at the federal court. Justice Sharp launched right in with what good things she had heard about him and how much she was looking forward to working with him. Sumner, flummoxed, heard himself saying, "Yeah, well, I'm looking forward to coming too." They talked for about an hour and a half. The entire time, Sumner said, "I was sitting there thinking . . . I'm not even out of law school and I'm going to get disbarred. They won't even let me take the bar exam. . . . I'm either going to make a judge on the Supreme Court mad at me, which means I'll lose every case ever down there, or I'm going to be barred from federal court." Sumner recalled, "I really felt like I was in a bad fix. . . . But I knew I couldn't tell her I wasn't coming." Fortunately, Judge Gordon took the news in stride and with a laugh, offering Sumner the option to postpone for a year.[19]

One clerk who had the temerity to ask for time to think about Justice Sharp's clerkship offer was Billy Sturges.[20] Sharp was then chief justice and in her last year on the court. Sturges had submitted his application to clerk at the United States Supreme Court but in the meantime had been summoned to interview at the North Carolina court. Justice Sharp offered him the job during the interview, whereupon, as Sturges recalled with a laugh, "You know, I had these applications pending at the U.S. Supreme Court, and . . . I said, 'Gosh, could I get back with you shortly about it?' And I walked out of the office, I walked down the hallway and got to the elevator, and I realized—I think I've made a mistake." He walked back to her office, knocked on the door, and said, "I want to accept that offer right now."[21]

It was not until 1974 that the court had a female law clerk. Fittingly, it was Justice Sharp who selected her. Recommended by Dean Phillips at the UNC law school, Betsy Cochrane (later Bunting)[22] had the further advantage of having grown up in Charlotte next door to one of North Carolina's few women lawyers, Lelia Alexander, an old friend of Justice Sharp's, who also recommended her. Justice Sharp, however, had reservations. After interviewing the tall young lady, who was given to wearing short skirts and green eyeshadow, she sought counsel from her longtime secretary, Virginia Lyon, and her close companion, Chief Justice William H. Bobbitt. Miss Lyon was against a female clerk, but conceded that she should not be deprived of the job on the basis of gender if she was otherwise qualified.[23] Undecided, Justice Sharp pondered the example of Judge Naomi Morris on the North Carolina Court of Appeals, the only other woman judge in the state's appellate system, who always insisted on a male clerk who could "chaperone her at night."[24] But in her journal she recorded Chief Justice Bobbitt's reminder, "It was not held against me because I was a girl."[25]

In the end, she offered Cochrane the job on the condition that she would "leave off green eyeshadow, put her skirt to her knees and put up her hair."[26] In truth, Cochrane's traditional upbringing as a Southern debutante and sorority girl had provided her with a style in conspicuous contrast to that of the five or six other women in her law school class, aggressive bra burners all.[27] Justice Sharp not only was repelled by that kind of militant unattractiveness, but she deemed it counterproductive. There was no reason why being attractive and being competent should be mutually exclusive. Why make matters more difficult by alarming your male colleagues?

Cochrane herself had not given much thought to how she might be received at the court. If you do your job, she thought, why should anyone care?[28] "It wasn't really until I saw the reaction of some of the other judges and more particularly some of the other clerks that I realized that it was something," she would recall. They were "stunned. Absolutely stunned."[29] Among other things, she was discouraged from working at the court after hours, both on the grounds of safety and the (unspoken) fear that wives would disapprove. After a few months, however, the shock wore off a bit, and Cochrane settled in, boosted by occasional remarks from Justice Sharp, who would say, "You know sometimes we run into male egos and male attitudes. We just have to find another way around. There's always another way around."[30]

In the fall of 1974, Susie Sharp won the statewide election for chief justice, and in the final two years of her tenure, 1977–79, she had two law clerks.

Although she never hired another female clerk, the ice had been broken, and other justices soon had women clerking for them.

General Court Routine

The North Carolina Supreme Court held two terms each year, in the spring and the fall. During hearing weeks, the court heard arguments in the morning. In the afternoon, the justices met in conference to discuss that day's cases. These discussions were conducted formally according to written rules and in strict confidentiality. A preliminary vote was taken on each case, with votes to affirm recorded above a line drawn on the page, votes to reverse recorded below. Justices were said to have voted "above the line" or "below the line." These votes were not written in stone, however. Henry Manning recalled that following a conference vote in which her erstwhile nemesis Justice Parker had voted on the opposite side of the line, Justice Sharp told him, "Go find me a North Carolina case on point, find a Virginia case on point. And if you can't find a Virginia case on point, go to the Queen's Bench. That's because they're the only jurisdictions that he will listen to."[31]

At the last conference each week, justices chose which opinions each would write, following a rotation initially established according to seniority, limited only in that the opinion-writing justice must have voted in the majority. The last case left on the table was known as "Hobson's Choice," invariably the most difficult or undesirable of the lot. Every third week of the term was devoted solely to drafting opinions, with no oral arguments. Once a month during each term the court voted whether to approve the written opinions. Those ready for release were carried by a messenger to the clerk's office, where interested parties and the press could instantly know which justice had written each opinion because their jackets were color-coded. A lavender jacket announced one of Justice Sharp's opinions.

Differing views on cases before the court notwithstanding, collegiality among the justices was another long-held tradition, perhaps most apparent in the court's regular custom of proceeding down the main street of the state capital to have lunch at a popular cafeteria. In this the court differed from those of other states, where members of the highest court, if they dined together, were more likely to do so in a private dining room. But in North Carolina, known as a "valley of humility" between the two "mountains of conceit" on its northern and southern borders, citizens of Raleigh were accustomed to the sight of the court walking to lunch and standing in the cafeteria line. They lined up in order of seniority, except that Southern gallantry decreed that Justice Sharp, even when she was the most junior justice, precede her male colleagues. Sometimes the clerks would eat at the same cafeteria, but never at the justices' table.[32]

Justice Sharp's Interactions with Clerks

Justice Sharp's clerks, particularly in her first years on the court, had a heavy work load. When she went on the court in 1962, there was no intermediate court of appeals, and the right of appeal from the trial court was virtually unlimited. Unlike the United States Supreme Court or many other appellate courts, the North Carolina Supreme Court could not refuse to hear any properly presented appeal—even if the court had previously ruled on the issue involved or the law was well settled. The first year Justice Sharp was on the court, it issued 379 written opinions.[33] Two years later, the total had soared to 473.[34] Rulings in the 1960s from the United States Supreme Court, such as those guaranteeing criminal defendants' right to remain silent and indigent criminal defendants' right to counsel, resulted in a huge increase in cases in the appellate system.[35] By the mid-1960s, the North Carolina Supreme Court was thought to have the heaviest volume of appeals in the country.[36] Moreover, the junior justice was responsible for the swollen volume of prisoner petitions until 1964, when they were divided among all the justices.

Facing this massive mountain of work, the clerks soon discovered that Justice Sharp was a workaholic, and that as an unmarried woman living alone, without the need to go home to a family at night, she was more often than not at the office until late. Some relief came with the establishment of the North Carolina Court of Appeals in 1967, but Justice Sharp's work habits did not change.[37] The clerks' (very spartan) offices were on a separate floor of the Justice Building, and every justice had a buzzer with which to summon his or her clerk. A buzz from Justice Sharp meant a flying exit out the door, sometimes without time to put on one's jacket.[38] More than most other clerks, Justice Sharp's were often found at the office on weekends and even holidays. Gary Chamblee,[39] one of her last clerks, remembered working late nights on a case during Christmas that year. Justice Sharp told him with some exasperation, "You know, I just can't work as hard as I used to. I used to be able to work until 9:00 or 10:00 and wouldn't be tired at all. And now, by 8:30 or 9:00 I'm tired!" Chamblee himself, having been hard at work since 7:30 or 8:00 that morning, said, "*I* was whupped."[40]

Some insight into Justice Sharp's stamina may be gained by another of Chamblee's recollections. "She would take a walk, I guess every day . . . around the Capitol, around 5:00. And I went with her on those walks sometimes." By this time in her life, Justice Sharp was beginning to show some symptoms of what is called Dowager's Syndrome, her shoulders starting to bow a bit. She told Chamblee, "You know, the doctors say that there's nothing that can really be done about it. But I still think exercise might help, walking. I've found in my life that there are very few things in life where trying harder doesn't help."[41]

In preparation for oral argument, Justice Sharp would ask her clerk to do a memo for each case, summarizing the evidence, the appellant and appellee contentions, the issues, and perhaps some argument analysis. Justice Sharp herself would have read every word of the briefs and the record prior to the oral argument.

Once the cases were assigned, she would ask for legal research. Cases generally were well briefed by the time they arrived at the North Carolina Supreme Court, but there was always review and further research to be done, some of which Justice Sharp might do herself. As a fresh graduate of law school, at least one clerk had to learn that there was more to legal research than case law, which had been the primary focus of his legal education. C. H. Pope[42] remembered that he had very little knowledge of the General Statutes, and that sometimes Justice Sharp would say, "Well, I believe there's a statute that does so-and-so." Speaking of the General Statutes, she often said, "There's a lot of law in those books."[43] Joe Eason[44] similarly recalled being ignorant of the supplement containing the latest legislation and thus learned that all his labor on a case was almost worthless because it took no account of a recent statutory amendment by the legislature.[45]

If the facts in the case were murky, Justice Sharp might even bring in outside experts for illumination. Jim Billings[46] recollected a very complicated real estate case in which he simply could not understand the survey that was part of the evidence. Finally, Justice Sharp called in a surveyor with whom they spent the better part of one day, maps taped up all over the walls.[47]

When it came to drafting an opinion, Justice Sharp sometimes would ask her clerk for a draft or an outline. She herself, however, wrote her opinions, in longhand, in her stocking feet or wearing Dr. Scholl's sandals, at a stand-up desk. All her clerks would remember hours spent standing side by side with her at that desk, revising opinions.

All her clerks also remembered what a perfectionist she was as she wrote and revised. Invariably, she was behind all the other members of the court in finishing her opinions. A good deal of this had to do with her desire to provide clarity for the trial judge, whose need for guidance in deciding cases was something with which she had years of personal experience. Joe Eason, who clerked toward the end of her tenure, said that she would make him read the opinions aloud to her, to be sure that they were clear and understandable.[48] Revisions entailed physical cutting and pasting because it was not until the end of her time on the court that word processors replaced typewriters. Final copies of opinions were typed by the incomparable Virginia Lyon as an original and six sets of copies done with carbon paper.

Clerk's Role in a Major Case

As a member of a court profoundly committed to stare decisis, Justice Sharp shared this prevailing philosophy. Unlike some of her colleagues, however, she was willing to examine a case in the light of changed circumstances and common sense.[49] It was her clerk Henry Manning who was responsible for what would perhaps become her most famous case, *Rabon v. Rowan Memorial Hospital*,[50] considered a towering model of jurisprudence, which overturned precedent to abolish charitable immunity for hospitals.[51] The plaintiff, a textile worker named Homer D. Rabon, had gone as a paying patient to Rowan Memorial Hospital, where a nurse had negligently injected a drug into or adjacent to the radial nerve in his left arm, resulting in permanent paralysis. Under the well-established doctrine of charitable immunity in North Carolina, the hospital could not be held liable. Manning recalled that Justice Sharp asked him to draft an opinion affirming the trial court's dismissal, saying, "Henry, I think North Carolina is pretty clear on this. . . . You might even do it per curiam."[52]

Manning, however, was struck by arguments in his research that supported overturning the doctrine of charitable immunity, and he asked Justice Sharp to look at an abstract he had done on the issue before she committed herself. A few days later, she told him that she was intrigued by the abstract. The doctrine had made sense when small charitable hospitals depended on donations and could not afford to have them applied to damage claims. But this argument was less persuasive in modern times when hospitals were big business with multiple sources of revenue and had access to liability insurance. In addition, the doctrine was judge-made law, more susceptible than statutory law to judicial reversal. But for a court so wedded to precedent and averse to "legislating from the bench" to decree the old doctrine invalid would be exceptional in the extreme. There was even in North Carolina a case explicitly upholding the doctrine and concluding that overturning it would constitute judicial legislation.[53] "I mean, there was no question about it, we were going to change the law," Manning said.[54]

Justice Sharp told Manning, "I'm going to give you this for a project," allotting him the next couple of weeks to work on it.[55] Fully aware of the odds against the court overturning such established precedent, she called on Shakespeare and told Manning that if they were going to shoot at the king, they had to have all the bullets because they could not afford to miss.[56] Manning produced a mountain of legal research in support of eliminating charitable immunity for hospitals, as well as a cross-country survey revealing that eighteen of the thirty states that did not recognize such charitable immunity had abandoned the doctrine by judicial decisions overturning precedent.[57] It was not until the following year that Justice Sharp could obtain a majority by creating a hybrid prospective application in which the opinion applied only to Homer Rabon and future plaintiffs. But it was Manning's enduring pride that he had played such a large role in her landmark decision.

Personal Relationships

Despite her formidable presence, Justice Sharp's clerks found her to have a warm personality and a sparkling sense of humor. To the extent her workload permitted, she took an interest in them, their families, and their futures. With some of her clerks, particularly those from her early years on the court, she established a personal relationship that would last long after their clerkship years.

Andy Vanore, the first clerk Justice Sharp selected after Dick Jones, whom she had inherited from Chief Justice Winborne, spent so much time with her that he came to feel almost like a son. He was then unmarried, so he was available to keep up with her grueling hours. It was very unusual for them to leave the office before seven or eight o'clock at night, and he early on offered to walk her back to the Sir Walter Hotel, where she had rooms for nearly fourteen years before she found time to move into an apartment. Often they would have supper together at the S&W cafeteria. And they worked many weekends. They maintained a close friendship over the decades.[58]

Henry Manning was another of those for whom the professional attention she offered grew into a lifelong friendship. To a young lawyer, "to be given more, to be listened to as somebody whose ideas are worth listening to," meant a great deal. "Now I wasn't a child, I had been in the Navy and come back and gone to law school," he said. "So I wasn't—but I sure was in awe of Judge Susie Sharp."[59] Beyond that, however, she was close enough to become the godmother to Manning's only child, Allen, to whom "Sharp, J." used to sign her birthday cards "Sharp, G. M.," for Godmother.[60]

After his clerkship, Manning maintained contact with Justice Sharp until close to the end of her life, visiting her several times a month in her office until she retired. He and his wife also saw her socially, often along with former chief justice William H. Bobbitt, with whom she had a "special friendship" for many years. One time, after the two justices had attended a cocktail party at the Mannings' home, a freshly laundered and starched linen napkin arrived in the Mannings' mail. Justice Sharp later inquired if Manning had received it, whispering that Justice Bobbitt could not bring himself to confess that he had stuffed it in his pocket and walked out with it. "So I helped him get it laundered and mailed it to you."[61]

For Jim Billings, her interest in his future likely prevented him from an unfortunate career error. At the time, before he became a United States senator known for his right-wing views, Jesse Helms was a high-profile radio and TV commentator in Raleigh, whose daily conservative on-air editorials expressed views on race and other subjects that Billings found offensive in the extreme. He decided he was going to write Helms a letter, word of which soon reached Justice Sharp, who summoned him into her office. As Billings recalled it, she said, "Jim, I hear you're getting ready to write Jesse Helms a letter." "Yes, ma'am, I am," he said. Justice Sharp said, "Well, I'm not trying to tell you what to do." But the message she got across was, "Jim, if you do it, he'll find out some way to hurt you. You're a young lawyer, you're just starting out in your career, and that would not be a wise thing for you to do. I understand your feelings, and you feel strongly, and I admire and respect you for being willing to stand up to somebody like that in a powerful position. But I'm just mighty afraid if you do that, that it will come back to haunt you."[62] Billings took her advice and was glad of it when a few years later he received a job offer from a prominent law firm in which some of the senior partners had a close association with Helms. In her later years, Justice Sharp would have a cordial relationship with Senator Helms, but clearly she perceived him as a person of vindictiveness with a long memory and a willingness to use whatever power he had at his disposal.

There were other examples of the interest Justice Sharp took in her clerks, among whom it was difficult to know how to express one's respect and appreciation. David Orcutt[63] liked to recall the special gift he had given her. Since her father's death in 1952, she had assumed the role of head of her large family, including her six siblings, their spouses and children, and especially her mother, who still lived in the old, cherished home place in Reidsville, North Carolina. Justice Sharp returned home to Reidsville every weekend until her mother died in 1971, to deal with problems ranging from management of her late father's farming operation to home maintenance to family upheavals of whatever sort. Orcutt contrived to get a photograph of the home place and had it decoupaged onto the lid of a small box, which he presented her. He felt that she really treasured it. "You know, it was something that made me feel good," he said. "I mean, what can a law clerk give a justice of the supreme court that has any meaning?"[64]

Lasting Impact

What Justice Sharp gave her clerks is easier to describe. Some stayed in touch, while others went on to jobs in other parts of the state or simply drifted away from their clerkship connection. But almost without exception, she left them with the enormous respect she had earned, along with an appreciation for just how hard a person can work, and a memory of the genuine warmth behind her imposing facade.

Notes

Unless otherwise identified, materials referenced are in the Susie Marshall Sharp Papers in the Southern Historical Collection, housed in the Wilson Library at the University of North Carolina at Chapel Hill.

1. Amend. 1945, I. See Act of March 15, 1945, ch. 634, 1945 N.C. Sess. Laws 875.

2. Terry Sanford, interview by author, June 12, 1995.

3. Andrew A. Vanore Jr. (clerk 1962–63).

4. Andrew A. Vanore Jr., interview by author, July 31, 1998.

5. E. Richard Jones Jr. (clerk 1961–62).

6. Susie Marshall Sharp, "Common Errors in Appellate Practice—The Mechanism by Which the Court Hears Appeals" (speech, Institute on North Carolina Appellate Practice and Procedure, North Carolina Bar Association, October 1965).

7. E. Richard Jones Jr., interview by author, July 1, 1998; Susie Marshall Sharp, letter to John Kesler, June 15, 1962.

8. Jones, interview.

9. Ibid.

10. Thomas J. Bolch, interview by author, August 7, 1998.

11. Susie Marshall Sharp, letter to Evelyn Ripple, June 19, 1962.

12. Henry Stancil Manning Jr. (clerk 1965–66).

13. Henry Stancil Manning Jr., interview by author, August 12, 1998.

14. Susie Marshall Sharp, letter to John Kesler, June 20–21, 1962.

15. Vanore, interview. Interestingly, in 1928 when Justice Sharp took the bar exam, there was a similarly shocking failure rate. See "Out of 181 Candidates for Bar 104 Pass

Test and 77 Fail to Survive," *Greensboro (N.C.) Daily News,* August 24, 1928. Susie Sharp, however, was not among the failures, passing on her first try.

16. William D. Kenerly (clerk 1973–74).

17. William D. Kenerly, interview by author, November 3, 1998.

18. Robert W. Sumner (clerk 1970–71).

19. Robert W. Sumner, interview by author, October 13, 1998.

20. William H. Sturges (clerk 1978–79).

21. William H. Sturges, interview by author, December 14, 1998.

22. Elizabeth Cochrane (later Bunting) (clerk 1974–75).

23. Susie Marshall Sharp, Journal, October 15, 1973.

24. Ibid. From Naomi Morris's appointment as chief judge on December 1, 1978, until Chief Justice Sharp's retirement on July 31, 1979, North Carolina had the distinction of being the first and only state whose supreme court and court of appeals were both headed by women.

25. Ibid.

26. Ibid.

27. Elizabeth Cochrane (later Bunting), interview by author, November 30, 1998.

28. Ibid.

29. Ibid.

30. Ibid.

31. Manning, interview.

32. Gary D. Chamblee, interview by author, December 22, 1998.

33. Joe Doster, "Appeals Court Has Speeded Up Process of Justice in N.C.," *Winston-Salem Journal-Sentinel,* August 2, 1970; handwritten tally attached to "Information on Intermediate Court of Appeals" [1965] (showing 379 written opinions for fiscal year 1962–63, and 181 motions).

34. Untitled, undated typescript, labeled "Montague" by hand ("An appeal may be taken") [1965]. Bert Montague was administrative assistant to the chief justice. See also handwritten tally attached to "Information on Intermediate Court of Appeals" [1965] (showing 473 written opinions for fiscal year 1964–65).

35. See, e.g., *Gideon v. Wainwright,* 372 US 335 (1963) and *Miranda v. Arizona,* 384 U.S. 436 (1966).

36. *Raleigh (N.C.) Times,* September 10, 1966.

37. The number of North Carolina Supreme Court opinions dropped to 162 in 1968. Doster, "Appeals Court."

38. Manning, interview.

39. Gary D. Chamblee (clerk 1978–79).

40. Chamblee, interview.

41. Ibid.

42. Clarence Hatcher Pope Jr. (clerk 1972–73).

43. Clarence Hatcher Pope Jr., interview by author, October 27, 1998.

44. Joseph W. Eason (clerk 1977–78).

45. Joseph W. Eason, interview by author, November 24, 1998.

46. James G. Billings (clerk 1969–70).

47. James G. Billings, interview by author, September 2, 1998.

48. Eason, interview.

49. Other examples of opinions demonstrating Justice Sharp's willingness to devi-ate from strict adherence to precedent in order to move the law forward include the following: *Terry v. Double Cola Bottling Co.*, 263 N.C. 1 (1964) (Sharp, J., concurring) (arguing for elimination of the privity requirement when a consumer purchased a food product in its original container); *Booker v. Medical Center*, 297 N.C. 458 (1979) (expanding coverage under workers' compensation); *Leatherman v. Leatherman*, 297 N.C. 618 (1979) (Sharp, C.J., dissenting, joined by Huskins, J.) (leading to enactment of equitable distribution in divorce cases in North Carolina).

50. *Rabon v. Hosp.*, 269 N.C. 1 (1967).

51. Ibid., 3. The doctrine of charitable immunity was well established in North Car-olina and provided that "a charitable institution may not be held liable to a beneficiary of the charity for the negligence of its servants or employees if it has exercised due care in their selection and retention."

52. Manning, interview.

53. *Rabon*, 269 N.C., 13.

54. Manning, interview.

55. Ibid.

56. Ibid.

57. *Rabon*, 296 N.C., 16–20.

58. Vanore, interview.

59. Manning, interview.

60. Ibid.

61. Ibid.

62. Billings, interview.

63. David S. Orcutt (clerk 1967–68).

64. David S. Orcutt, interview by author, September 8, 1998.

KIRSTEN D. LEVINGSTON

California's Technicolor Clerkship
Rose Bird and Her Clerks

B arbara Olshansky sat outside the imposing oak doors of Chief Justice Rose Elizabeth Bird's chambers, awaiting her interview. She had not planned to clerk for a judge after law school. When her public interest job fell through during her third year, however, one of her Stanford professors suggested she contact Bird, who happened to be filling a vacancy. Olshansky thought a clerkship out of reach—after all, "I had that C+ in Torts," she acknowledged—but applied anyway. When she was getting dressed for the interview, Olshansky accessorized her plain blue suit with "angelfish earrings, the size of drink coasters."[1] Her boyfriend disagreed with the style choice, urging her not to wear them. "I have to be able to be me when I practice law. I have to be honest," she told him.

As she waited to be called in, she saw a tall, elegant woman walking down the hall toward her. The woman's distinctive purple suede boots, made Olshansky think to herself, "Wow, the judge has an amazing assistant." Then the woman spoke, "Barb, it's nice to meet you, I'm Rose. Great f—g earrings. Come on in."[2] "It was truly an amazing experience working for her," Olshansky recalled years later. "She made me understand that the law could really be a force for positive social change in a very concrete way. I'll never forget the day that she pulled out her chair at the head of the [conference room] table and said, 'Sit down. You could sit here one day and make a difference in the world. And I expect you to.'"[3]

Rose Bird had outsized expectations for herself, achieving ambitious goals she set out to accomplish as well as some she had not planned to pursue. She also had high expectations for her law clerks. Bird led the California Supreme Court for nine years, through a dramatic and tumultuous time of deep change in the law, in society, and in the court itself. At the state and federal levels the judiciary was extending greater constitutional protection to individuals, refining the admissibility of illegally seized evidence, shaping the contours of affirmative action and busing to counter racial discrimination and segregation, and ruling on the constitutionality of the death penalty. Across the country grassroots movements for jobs, housing, and the environment brought people into the streets. America was changing, with California on the vanguard of that social and political transformation.

When Governor Jerry Brown appointed Bird to the California Supreme Court in March 1977, no woman had served as a justice—chief or otherwise—on the court. At the time of her appointment, California was only the third state in the country to have a female chief justice. Lorna Lockwood became the nation's first chief justice in 1965, when she assumed the center chair on the Arizona Supreme Court. A decade later, Susie Marshall Sharp of the North Carolina Supreme Court became the second woman to hold such a position. Today female chief justices preside over twenty-four state supreme courts, including Chief Justice Tani Cantil-Sakauye of the California Supreme Court—only the second woman and the first person of color in that position.

Governor Brown and Bird met while studying at the University of California, Berkeley in 1960. Later she volunteered to chauffeur Brown around during his 1974 gubernatorial campaign. He liked her directness and honesty, a contrast to those around him seeking only to please. When he won the race, Brown made Bird his secretary of agriculture. With the appointment, Bird became the first woman to serve in a California governor's cabinet. Bird spent approximately two years in the position before Brown appointed her to the California Supreme Court.

At the time of her appointment, commentators cheered and jeered Bird's historic appointment—sometimes for the same reasons. She was a she, she was young (only forty years old), and she was liberal, no surprise given the fact that the governor who tapped her was nicknamed "Moonbeam." Some complained Bird had a set of attributes that made her ill-suited for the position, such as no judicial experience—a trait she shared with men who served on both the California and the United States Supreme Courts. And both friends and foes said Bird could be difficult, some called her vindictive, but traditionally neither of these traits had disqualified men from assuming positions of authority. On the positive side of the ledger, Bird was universally praised as being intellectually gifted, if not a genius.

Opinions about Bird were strong and deeply held. The moment she was nominated, plotters began hatching plans to remove her from the court. The most potent opposition came from interests concerned about her many years fighting for people on the margins—such as the farmworkers she protected as secretary of agriculture and the people charged with crimes she represented as a public defender.

Bird knew what life on the margins was like. Born in 1936, she and her family lived on a chicken farm outside Tucson, Arizona. Her dad was a salesman who abandoned the family when Rose was five years old. A few months later bombers arrived at Pearl Harbor, drawing the United States into World War II. War presented employment opportunities, and Bird's mother Anne secured a job installing windows on air force transport planes. While she worked, the kids took care of themselves, except when a Native American woman sometimes looked after Rose.

When U.S. soldiers returned home, war machine manufacturing wound down, and men replaced women in the workforce. Out of work, Anne took in laundry and cleaned houses until 1950, when she moved the family to her home state of New York. There she found steady work at a plastics factory and settled in Sea Cliff, Long Island.[4]

Bird biographer Kathleen A. Cairns describes Sea Cliff as "virtually all white and middle to upper-middle class, with a smattering of wealthier and poorer residents. The former live in large homes with expansive gardens, and the latter reside in a small number of rental apartments."[5] Anne was divorced, single, and a renter, an atypical Sea Cliff mom who raised an atypical Sea Cliff kid. Politically active, teenage Rose knocked on doors for Democrats in her overwhelmingly Republican community. The year the United States Supreme Court ruled racial segregation in schools unconstitutional in *Brown v. Board of Education*, Rose graduated from high school. In her Sea Cliff yearbook she appeared in a photograph with her arm draped around one of the few African American girls in her class.[6] "It was in Sea Cliff," Cairns writes, "that Rose Bird began to reveal a set of values that would come to shape her life and worldview: an intense dedication to hard work, a fierce independence, and a highly developed sense of outrage at what she perceived as injustice."[7]

At a memorial service for Chief Justice Bird in 2000, former law clerk Scott Sugarman shared his personal observations about Bird's judicial philosophy:

> Maybe because she was the first woman to serve as a law clerk in the Nevada Supreme Court, or because she was the first woman to serve as a deputy public defender in Santa Clara County, or because she was the first woman to serve as a cabinet officer in the State of California, or because she was the first woman to serve on the California Supreme Court, Chief Justice Bird was keenly sensitive to the struggles of the outsider and the dispossessed, of

the power exercised by the "haves" on the "have nots," of the power used by government agents and officers on those who are powerless.[8]

Shortly before joining the California Supreme Court, Bird learned she had breast cancer. Over the next two decades the disease would recur four times, with Bird enduring multiple surgeries—including removal of both her breasts. The diagnosis afforded Bird perspective later in her life when she would be fighting for both her life and her seat on the court.

Despite the controversy swirling around her—perhaps because of it—dozens of passionate men and women flocked to Bird to serve as clerks, interns, and staff. Working for her, they came to appreciate how the job of chief justice encompassed three distinct roles–overseeing administration of the largest state judicial system in the country, serving as one of seven jurists tasked with interpreting the law, and retaining one's seat on the court.

Arriving at the court, Bird had to make immediate administrative decisions. One of her fellow justices had lost the cognitive capacity to serve, and she had to facilitate a graceful exit for him. Bird trimmed the administrative budget by selling the court's limousine—she had a car and planned to drive herself around—and requiring judges to opt for more moderate accommodations when attending conferences and traveling for court business. Some court personnel bridled at some of Bird's early decisions, resenting her rearrangement of the way things had always been done.

Loyalty was important to Bird, and she sought to surround herself with people she could trust. That may be why she drew many clerks from Stanford Law School and public defender offices, familiar institutions to which she had deep personal connections. Bird joined the Santa Clara County Public Defender's office directly after her Nevada Supreme Court clerkship. After eight years representing people charged with crimes who were unable to afford a lawyer, she advanced to head the appeals division. At the same time she taught in the clinical program at Stanford Law School, the first woman to teach there. An outdated 1972 marketing video called "Stanford Lawyer" includes an interview with the legendary anti–death penalty champion Anthony Amsterdam, then head of Stanford's clinical law program and Bird's teaching partner. Amsterdam sits before the camera, a cigarette burning nearby, as he describes Bird's contributions to the clinic. Notably neither the lens nor the microphone ever captures Bird's voice or image, save a quick shot of the top of her head.

Scott Sugarman first met Bird when he took her clinical seminar on criminal procedure. He remembers the class being challenging, and Bird being one of the best teachers on the faculty "because of her remarkable devotion to her students, her insight and intelligence, and her commitment to teaching law students to be real lawyers."[9] Later, Sugarman accepted Bird's invitation to serve as her supervising research attorney. From 1977 to 1980 he was responsible for researching and drafting opinions for the chief justice and supervising the preparation of opinions and memoranda by other law clerks. "She continued to be my teacher and mentor, as she was a mentor to all the law clerks who worked with her. And, for the years that followed my clerkship, until the day she died, she was my friend."[10]

Stephen Buehl also met Bird while a Stanford law student. He was the first to participate in an externship program she created between the law school and the Santa Clara Public Defender's office. Buehl spent over a decade of his career at Bird's side, first serving as her deputy at the Department of Agriculture (1975 to 1977) and, when she became chief justice, serving as her executive assistant and special counsel (1977 to 1987). Bird "loved to be in relationship with her clerks. They were giving her great work product, she was giving them a great experience," Buehl recounted.[11]

One article dubbed Buehl Bird's "guardian angel," describing him as "a combination of adviser, aide-de-camp and bodyguard, [who] screens Bird's telephone calls, travels with her, carries her tickets and money, and scours menus to make sure restaurants can accommodate the vegetarian diet the chief justice has followed since recovering from her last bout with cancer."[12] The article continued, Buehl "began martial-arts training to be ready for any physical attack that might be made on his boss." The possibility was a frightening reality. Threats against Bird increased during her years on the bench, with people writing to say they hoped she would be raped or die.

Before joining Bird as clerks, Kathy Kahn and Paul Fogel had been in the trenches, working in the state office of public defense handling appeals for people convicted of crimes who were unable to afford a lawyer. By then George Deukmejian had succeeded Brown as governor—and had cut funding for the state public defense office, necessitating layoffs. Bird put out the word that she would welcome clerkship applications from lawyers there. During her interview, Kahn confessed she "fell madly in love" with the chief justice, her warmth, kindness and humor.[13] Kahn subsequently clerked for Bird from 1983 to 1986, while Fogel clerked from 1983 to 1987.

Of course, people arrived in Bird's chambers via other routes as well. After graduating from University of California, Berkeley, Law School, David Oppenheimer started clerking in the summer of 1978. He was "excited and proud to work for this heroic figure," who at that point had been on the court for just over a year.[14]

Oppenheimer saw a unique side of Bird one evening, when she revealed to him she had asked Governor Brown not to make her chief justice. Oppenheimer had dinner with Bird and Buehl at a Mexican restaurant in Los Angeles. Though neither Oppenheimer nor Buehl recalls where they ate, it could have been Bird's favorite restaurant, El Cholo, which first opened in L.A. in 1923. Over chips, and possibly mariachi music, Bird told Oppenheimer that when Brown broached the possibility of her becoming chief justice she asked him to instead appoint her to the California Court of Appeals or Supreme Court as an associate justice so she could gain judicial experience.

"Why don't you make Matt Tobriner the chief justice—he will step aside for me whenever you're ready—he adores you," Oppenheimer recalled Bird saying.[15] The suggestion made sense. Brown's father, former California governor Pat Brown, had appointed Tobriner to the supreme court, and Jerry Brown clerked for him after graduating from Yale Law School. When Bird's predecessor stepped down, Tobriner became acting chief justice. But the governor held firm to his plan, telling Bird "I want you to shake things up."[16]

Stephen Gorski worked as an extern for Bird in 1979, during his final semester at the University of San Francisco Law School. Gorski said his university wouldn't sponsor his externship application because his GPA was .5 points lower than the school's grade cutoff for applicants. He persisted, successfully. Sitting in a bullpen area filled with desks, Gorski reviewed court filings and used carbon paper to draft memos on typewriters. Intimidated when his externship began, Gorski said Bird put him at ease—inviting him to her chambers to talk about his career plans and stopping in the court hallways to ask how he was doing. Four decades later he described his time with Bird as one of the best professional and personal experiences of his life.[17]

With her tripartite role—jurist, administrator, and candidate—it is not surprising that Bird would be a demanding boss. "Her work ethic was extraordinary, and she inspired and valued that level of dedication to excellence in those who worked with her," Buehl explained.[18] Sugarman's first day illustrates the point.

I drove from the East Coast to San Francisco, to begin my clerkship with the Chief Justice. I reached my destination on a Thursday evening. On Friday morning, I called her to tell her that I had arrived and she told me to meet her later that day. We spoke in her chambers about the vacation which I had just concluded, which, I must note, turned out to be the last vacation I would have for some time. At the end of our talk she told me that three days later, on Monday, the Supreme Court would commence its fall calendar. The court would hear oral arguments in 25 or so cases during that week. She then pointed to a three-foot-high stack of documents sitting on the corner of her desk—the court memoranda and briefs for that week's calendar. Could I, she asked softly, review all of those cases and discuss them with her on Sunday afternoon, two days later?

Sugarman counteroffered—he'd review the cases throughout the week and meet with the chief justice each morning to discuss them. She accepted.[19]

Working nights, weekends, and holidays was the norm, and Bird knew her clerks were making sacrifices to serve her, to serve justice. One New Year's Eve Kahn was working her usual late hours when she received a call instructing her to report to the chief's chambers. She entered to find Bird sitting at her conference table with a pastry sitting on the table in front of her. Not only was it New Year's Eve, it was also Kahn's birthday, and the chief took a break to mark the occasion. Kahn remembers it as "a genuine effort [by Bird] to be nice and concerned and connected, to show she was paying attention [to me]." As the women enjoyed their cake, Kahn had a revelation—"it became clear to me neither one of us had a date."[20]

"From the same place inside her from which came her passionate commitment to justice came her enormous caring and compassion for the men and women around her. Not a birthday, anniversary, or holiday came which she did not remember with a personal card or gift," Sugarman shared at Bird's memorial. "For each staff member, she obtained an individual memento or gift, tailored to his or her traits. She never bought 20 identical pens or pet rocks, but spent the time and effort to find some gift that would fit the recipient. And, at Thanksgiving or the New Year, she would send flowers to our homes."[21]

Bird officiated the marriage ceremonies of both Paul Fogel and Stephen Gorski. Bird went to Gorski's house for his wedding, afterward gathering all the children together and asking them what they wanted to be when they grew up. Gorski remembered her paying particular attention to the girls, telling them *she* was the top judge in the state of California and *they* could be whatever they wanted to be when they grew up.[22]

Bird's clerks both revered and feared their chief's intensity and certitude. For Buehl, Bird was "a tough, but fair critic."[23] For others she was more intimidating. "When you got a call saying the Chief would like to see you it was like going to the principal's office. You shook in your boots," Kahn confessed.[24] "If she perceived you had done something against her, you were on her shitlist for life," Fogel said.[25]

Bird was often standoffish in professional settings and expected her clerks to act more standoffish than they actually were, Kahn recalled. Other justices on the court at the time complained they had to make appointments to see Bird, rather than stop by unannounced. Kahn had a theory about the different styles. "As an old man you can be nice—be paternal, make jokes, pat your clerks on the head, and say 'good job.' Those people were so secure in their positions in the world, and she was not secure."[26] Bird biographer Cairns writes, "She sometimes waxed wistful about her desire to be depicted in more 'human' terms, but she seemed incapable of following a course designed to accomplish that goal."[27]

For some clerks, at least some of the time, Bird's process for engaging around cases was quite open. Each week the chief met with them for confidential discussions about requests for court review and pending cases. Former criminal appellate lawyer Kahn enjoyed these gatherings. They allowed her to gain exposure to a variety of legal issues and perspectives. Bird encouraged her clerks to speak up, to challenge her.

Fogel did just that, disagreeing with the chief on a parental rights case, *In Re Baby Girl M.*[28] In this case, not until two people ended their relationship did the woman learn she was pregnant. The mother did not tell the father about the pregnancy, had the baby, and put the child up for adoption. After the father's rights were eventually terminated and another family adopted the child, the father sued, claiming he had been wrongly denied the chance to seek custody.

By the time the case arrived at the California Supreme Court, the child had been with the adoptive parents for over three years. Still, the court reversed termination of the father's custodial rights because he had not been given notice of the hearing that terminated his parental rights. Bird and her colleagues sent the case back to the trial court for further consideration. Fogel, whose wife had recently had a baby, could not imagine the court ruling in favor of the father, telling Bird, "You can't yank this child from the adoptive parents and disrupt their lives." To which, she responded: "You know what Paul, fathers have rights too."[29] For Fogel the case was classic Bird, emblematic of her reverence for procedural due process as a bulwark, essential for protecting individual rights.

One of Bird's most significant opinions had no effect on the outcome of the case, but to Sugarman it represented her approach to judging and to working with clerks. In 1978 California voters enacted a ballot measure known as Proposition 13, or the People's Initiative to Limit Property Taxation, which amended the state constitution to limit increases in property taxes to a maximum of 2 percent per year. Under the referendum tax assessors were to use the value of the home in 1975 as the basis for the tax, unless a home was sold or underwent construction, in which case a new base assessment would be made based on the value of the property in the year those events occurred. Bottom line—Proposition 13 would substantially reduce the flow of tax dollars in to government coffers.

"Predictably," Sugarman explained, "within days of its passage, challenges to Prop. 13 from cities, counties and others throughout the state poured into the court. . . . Once the briefs were in, the Chief's instructions to her law clerks were simple: Read all the petitions and evaluate the best arguments that could be made about the constitutionality of Proposition 13. No prejudgment, no stacking the deck. . . . She did not want law clerks who were compliant, who would only mirror what she wanted to hear. She asked for, and got, our independent views."[30]

Sugarman continued:

After she personally reviewed the briefs and applicable precedents, she told us that, on reflection, she was deeply troubled by the fact that homeowners sitting side by side, with homes of the same value, would be required to pay very different amounts in taxes to the state for the same public services. Chief Justice Bird concluded that making those homeowners pay different taxes violated the equal protection clause of the United States Constitution. She held strong views about the importance of equal treatment in our society and, in her view, Proposition 13 treated identically situated individuals differently.[31]

The court upheld Proposition 13, with Chief Justice Bird writing separately to lodge the sole dissent.[32] "Each of the six other judges on the Supreme Court . . . concluded that the initiative was constitutional. It is little short of astounding that she was willing to stand alone in opposition to Proposition 13 just two months before her first confirmation election in 1978," according to Sugarman. "It would have been easy to join the court's six-member majority and stay silent. Her vote could not alter the court's decision to uphold the constitutionality of Prop. 13. However, she believed that to abandon her true understanding of the mandate of the Constitution would betray her core responsibility as a judge. While she understood that her expressed opinion might cost her the election and her office as Chief Justice of California, she would not bend to adopt a course she believed was contrary to her duty."[33]

California governors appoint individuals to serve as justices of the California Supreme Court, and those appointees must be confirmed by the Commission on Judicial Appointments. Following appointment and commission

approval a justice takes his or her seat on the bench. During the next gubernatorial election, voters also decide whether the justices stay—voting "yes" or
"no" on retention. Sitting justices also face a retention vote at the end of their
twelve-year terms. Because of the timing of her appointment, however, Bird
faced two retention votes in nine years. Brown tapped Bird in spring 1977, eighteen months before California's 1978 gubernatorial race, where she and three
other justices stood for retention. In addition, Bird stepped in to a term on the
court set to expire in the fall of 1986.

November 7, 1978, was election day, and it got off to a rocky start for Bird and
her supporters. Californians woke to an explosive frontpage headline in the
Los Angeles Times, carried on front pages of papers across the state: "Supreme
Court Decision to Reverse Gun Law Reported; But Sources Say Ruling, Completed by Justices Several Weeks Ago, Has Not Been Made Public." The lead
reported:

> The California Supreme Court has decided to overturn a 1975 law that
> requires prison terms for persons who use a gun during a violent crime,
> but has not made the decision public, well-placed court sources said Mon-
> day. The decision in *People v. Tanner,* is certain to anger law enforcement
> officials around the state. The court sources said the decision was reached
> on a 4–3 vote, with Chief Justice Rose Elizabeth Bird, whose name goes
> before voters today, among the majority.[34]

This November surprise notwithstanding, Bird kept her seat, squeaking
by with 51.7 percent of the vote. To celebrate, Oppenheimer and other clerks
hosted a post-election party in chambers, complete with sparkling cava and
a song—"Congratulations to you. Congratulations to you. Congratulations
dear Chief Justice. Congratulations to you." When the serenade stopped, Bird
responded, "So I see some of you weren't singing." Oppenheimer chuckled at
the remark.[35] While he heard dry humor in her response, others on her staff
heard a threat.

The election-day story in the *Los Angeles Times* troubled Bird on multiple
levels. It suggested improper communication between court personnel and the
press. Moreover, it impugned the ethics of her court, which Bird knew would
never delay an opinion for political purposes. Bird believed it was important
for an objective arbiter to convey that message to the public. Without consulting her fellow justices, she wrote a letter asking for an "impartial and complete
investigation by the Commission on Judicial Performance" into the newspaper's claim. This unilateral act angered her fellow justices. Even her friend

and former law professor Justice Frank Newman told her, "I think its terrible judgment that you've decided all by yourself without consulting us."[36]

As the commission's year-long investigation—some called it a spectacle—unfolded on both live television and behind closed doors, justices, court clerks, and staff were called in to testify. Bird, Sugarman, Buehl, and Oppenheimer were among those questioned by the commission. When Oppenheimer was asked what he knew about the *Tanner* case, he told his interrogators, "I knew we were holding for *Tanner*."[37] When shocked commission staff excitedly leaned in to hear more, Oppenheimer realized they had misconstrued his statement. Quickly he explained that the court was holding *other* cases that *Tanner* would affect until after the court decided *Tanner*, not holding *Tanner* itself. Oppenheimer remembers Chief Justice Bird being amused when he explained that his answer had created a momentary stir among the commission staff.[38]

Gradually the commission process receded from public view, with the panel completing its work in private. Its final "report" was a mere two and a half pages long and 443 words deep. In what one commentator called a "whimpering conclusion" the commission announced that the evidence presented did not support the filing of formal charges against anyone on the court.[39]

By the time of Bird's second retention vote in 1986, the chief's opponents had honed their message, raised money, and organized the voters. "Californians to Defeat Rose Bird" and "Crime Victims for Court Reform," folksy-sounding operations run by elite political consulting firms, formed an alliance to take out the chief, amassing a campaign war chest that covered, by one estimate, $5.5 million in activities. Financial supporters included oil and gas companies, car dealerships, police associations, banks, real estate firms, and agribusiness interests. And they portrayed Bird as an out-of-control liberal who placed personal views above the law. As Exhibit A they pointed to her handling of death penalty cases, claiming she had singlehandedly stopped all executions in California.

As momentum grew, the emboldened anti-Bird campaign broadened its reach. It also targeted two associate justices on the ballot that year, Joseph Grodin and Cruz Reynoso. Governor Deukmejian was himself running for reelection, and he began to forcefully speak out against Bird, Grodin and, Reynoso. "A thorough review of the opinions and votes cast by Justices Bird, Grodin and Reynoso on death penalty cases indicates a lack of impartiality and objectivity," he claimed.[40]

Bird's supporters rose to her defense, including Stanford Law School professor Barbara Babcock—the first tenured female professor at the law school. Babcock challenged what she claimed was a mischaracterization of Bird's record on the death penalty. "The chief justice's opinions in death penalty cases, like her other opinions, are legally creditable. Her main concern has been that no one should be executed if the conviction or death penalty was the result of a serious malfunction in the judicial process. Her opponents cannot deny that procedural malfunctions have taken place. Rather, they may be willing to tolerate errors given the heinous crimes involved."[41]

To many, a focus on the death penalty obscured a broader agenda. As *New York Times* columnist Tom Wicker wrote: "Don't believe for a moment that the campaign to oust Chief Justice Rose Bird from the California Supreme Court is a spontaneous public uprising. . . . Don't believe either that the effort . . . is nonpartisan. . . . Don't believe, finally, that the anti-Bird campaign is about the death penalty. . . . [T]he death penalty is only the trumped up excuse for the anti-Bird campaign—the actual purpose of which is clearly to put a conservative majority on the California Supreme Court."[42]

Kahn recalled that the chief justice scrupulously separated clerks from campaign activities. To the chagrin of friends and supporters, who wanted Bird to punch back, the chief justice resisted campaigning. The clerks kept abreast of what was happening through television, radio, and print news reports. One early poll showed that 57 percent of voters planned to reject Bird. In the final weeks of the campaign, Bird released a series of television ads focused on issues that mattered to her, such as judicial independence and fairness. Her supporters rightfully feared that her outreach to voters was too late in the day to sway people—even those who shared Bird's values. As expected, voters ousted Bird—66 percent voted against her retention. That was the "darkest day of the California judiciary," Fogel recalled, with Bird out, and Grodin and Reynoso "caught in the crossfire" of attacks on the chief.[43] Rose Elizabeth Bird's tenure was finished.

Life went on. Bird's clerks felt her influence in their careers and lives. Gorski represented consumers in personal injury cases against negligent companies, a career path Bird helped him identify, a way to "ride the white horse" without being a criminal defense attorney.[44] Troubled by the media's mishandling of judicial issues, Kahn took a sabbatical to go to journalism school, where she wrote about her law clerk experience.[45] "I don't think I would have practiced law after law school if I hadn't clerked for her," Olshansky said.[46] Years after clerking Olshansky helped litigate *Rasul v. Bush,* the U.S. Supreme Court case establishing that American courts have jurisdiction over claims brought by Guantánamo Bay detainees who are foreign nationals, the first major test of whether the executive branch had exceeded its powers in asserting Guantánamo was outside the jurisdiction of any court.

Governor Arnold Schwarzenegger appointed Fogel to the Superior Court bench in Alameda, California. After two years he returned to his global law firm, where he has led the appellate practice. After his clerkship Sugarman devoted himself to criminal defense, first in the Alameda County Public Defender office before hanging his own shingle, where he has been practicing for three decades.

A decade after the chief justice left the California Supreme Court, Death Penalty Focus honored Bird at their annual gala. Thirty-seven of the chief justice's former colleagues placed an advertisement in the program, which read: *To the Chief with much love, affection and admiration. From your former law clerks and staff.*[47] The Reverend Jesse Jackson and actor Sean Penn, who had recently starred in the film *Dead Man Walking,* were also honored that night. Director Oliver Stone's program ad read: *Congratulations and best wishes to Sean, Jesse & Rose. Three tough MFs.*[48]

After leaving the bench, Bird pursued other passions. Drawing on her undergraduate interest in journalism, she engaged in political punditry—working briefly as a commentator for local television stations in California and penning commentaries and opinion pieces from time to time. In one piece she supported the jury decision in the O. J. Simpson case, arguing that the prosecution had failed to prove its case and bemoaning that interracial relationships still touched a raw nerve in white America.[49]

For a university lecture series she partnered with Judge Robert Bork, the conservative U.S. Supreme Court nominee whose controversial nomination failed in the Senate. The chief justice returned to the classroom, teaching at the University of Sydney in Australia as well as other law schools.

Bird also continued serving people experiencing hardship. She cared for her ailing mother Anne until her death in 1991. She volunteered at a food pantry and read to people who were blind. When Bird arrived at the East Palo Alto Community Law Project office to lend a hand, she introduced herself as a housewife from Palo Alto. Not recognizing who she was, the legal staff asked her to make copies, which she was happy to do. It wasn't until a law school dean called the office to tip them off that the former chief justice was volunteering with them that the lawyers made better use of her skillset.

In March 2000, current and former members of the California Supreme Court memorialized Rose Bird in the San Francisco courtroom where she had presided for close to a decade. The black-robed justices sat aligned on the bench, as if ready to hear from litigants. There was no dispute that day, only praise for the chief. Scott Sugarman was the only former clerk to speak, the only person to speak who was not a justice, and the last person to speak. With his young son seated in the courtroom audience, Sugarman ended his reflection on his friend and mentor by quoting from a speech she had delivered at the January 1987 Annual Law School Deans' Luncheon. It was her final speech before leaving the bench. And Sugarman gave Chief Justice Rose Elizabeth Bird the final word at her memorial:

> If we judges and lawyers are not to be popular, let it be because we are standing on the forefront of protecting people's rights during a time of transition. Let it be because we have the courage to represent unsympathetic individuals and make difficult rulings in order to give life and breath to our constitutional guarantees.
>
> Let it be because we have the integrity to do justice, even though such actions may be met with criticism and disapproval. Let it be because we see our role from the perspective of its noble traditions, not from the pressured viewpoint of the moment.
>
> Let it be because we stand up for a just society and stand firm for the rule of law.[50]

Rose Bird's story is often offered as a cautionary tale, a warning to politicians who want to shake things up, and to elected judges whose rulings frustrate powerful interests. Yet her life is an archetypal American tale—a Great Depression baby, raised by a single mother and factory laborer, who worked hard, scaled walls, stayed true to her values and principles, and made history again and again.

Notes

1. "Olshansky to Share Expertise in International Human Rights," *Create Change,* Public Interest newsletter of Stanford Law School, John and Terry Levin Center for Public Service and Public Interest Law (Spring 2007), 7.

2. Ibid.

3. Ibid.

4. Kathleen A. Cairns, *The Case of Rose Bird: Gender, Politics and the California Courts* (Lincoln: University of Nebraska Press, 2016) 11–15.

5. Ibid., 13.

6. Ibid., photographs between pp. 140 and 141.

7. Ibid., 13–14.

8. Scott Sugarman's reflections are drawn from a eulogy he gave at a Memorial Service for Rose Bird on March 6, 2000, held at the Supreme Court of California in San Francisco, http://www.cschs.org/history/california-supreme-court-justices/rose -elizabeth-bird/.

9. Ibid.

10. Ibid.

11. Stephen Buehl, interview by author, April 3, 2017.

12. Frank Clifford, "Rose Bird's Guardian Angel," *Los Angeles Times*, October 5, 1986.

13. Kathy Kahn, interview by author, July 19, 2017.

14. David Oppenheimer, interview by author, February 6, 2017.

15. Oppenheimer, interview.

16. Ibid.

17. Steven Gorski, interview by author, June 5, 2017.

18. Buehl, interview.

19. Sugarman, eulogy for Bird.

20. Kahn, interview.

21. Sugarman, eulogy for Bird.

22. Gorski, interview.

23. Buehl, interview.

24. Kahn, interview.

25. Paul Fogel, interview by author, June 19, 2017.

26. Kahn, interview.

27. Cairns, *Case of Rose Bird*, 191 (citing Frank Clifford, "Campaign against Bird Grows Louder," *Los Angeles Times*, September 15, 1985, A1).

28. 37 Cal. 3d 65 (1984).

29. Fogel, interview.

30. Sugarman, eulogy for Bird.

31. Ibid.

32. *Amador Valley Joint Union High Sch. Dist. v. State Bd. of Equalization*, 583 P.2d 1281, 1302 (Cal. 1978) (Bird, C.J., dissenting).

33. Sugarman, eulogy for Bird.

34. William Endicott and Robert Fairbanks, "Supreme Court Decision to Reverse Gun Law Reported," *Los Angeles Times*, November 7, 1978, A1.

35. Oppenheimer, interview.

36. Cairns, *Case of Rose Bird*, 126 (citing Frank Newman, oral history interview conducted by Carole Hicke, 1989–1991, Regional Oral History Office, University of California, Berkeley, for the California State Archives State Government Oral History Program, 161–173).

37. Oppenheimer, interview.

38. Ibid.

39. For detailed discussions of the dramatic events surrounding the Commission on Judicial Performance's creation, investigation, and hearings see Betty Medsger, *Framed: The New Right Attack on Chief Justice Rose Bird and the Courts* (New York: Pilgrim Press, 1983); and Preble Stolz, *Judging Judges: The Investigation of Rose Bird and the California Supreme Court* (New York: Free Press, 1981).

40. Cairns, *Case of Rose Bird*, 213.

41. Barbara Allen Babcock, "Rose Bird under Attack for Results, Not for Court's Judicial Reasoning," *Los Angeles Times*, August 31, 1986, 3.

42. Tom Wicker, "In the Nation; A Naked Power Grab," *New York Times*, September 14, 1986.

43. Fogel, interview.

44. Gorski, interview.

45. Kahn, interview.

46. "Olshansky to Share Expertise."

47. Death Penalty Focus of California, 6th Annual Awards Dinner, April 29, 1997, Dinner Program.

48. Ibid.

49. Rose Elizabeth Bird, "The Jury Did Its Job: Put Blame Where It Belongs," *Los Angeles Times*, October 18, 1995, A12.

50. Sugarman, eulogy for Bird.

RONALD K. L. COLLINS

Hans Linde

And So He Stands among the Last of the Great State Judges

P ortland, Oregon. It came as the leaves of his life continued to turn brown. There he stood peering out at the crowd of well-wishers who gathered at the Sentinel Hotel to honor him. Eleven days earlier, on April 15, 2017, the Berlin-born jurist turned ninety-three. Only a month before, he tripped and broke his hip; thus the walking cane. Yet that Wednesday evening was a festive occasion layered with collective affection. Among others, Judge Henry Breithaupt and Governor Kate Brown spoke fondly and sincerely about the revered honoree who had been named the 2017 Jonathan U. Newman Legal Citizen of the Year. For one who had long been at the forefront of defending civil liberties as a judge, it was fitting that he receive the award named after the Oregon judge who played a key role in desegregating Portland schools nearly four decades earlier.

The irony: The honoree, though appreciative, was not one for fanfare. He shunned tags such as "hero"; he was not one who sought the limelight; and he abhorred the excesses of idle flattery. He saw his lifework in humble terms: he did his job as skillfully and as faithfully as he could. It was that simple. Still, it was also true: he "put Oregon's top tribunal on the map."[1] And so, judges, lawyers, educators, journalists, students, and former law clerks came together to pay tribute to the man who left a lasting mark on the law.

His name: Hans Arthur Linde (pronounced "Lindy").

A Brief Biography

The Linde family left Germany in 1933 and moved to Denmark, where Hans grew up (1933–1939).[2] His father, Bruno C. Linde (a judge), then took the family to Portland, Oregon.[3] Hans attended Lincoln High School, where he was one of the editors of the school paper (the *Lincoln Cardinal*). It was there that he met his wife-to-be, Helen Tucker. They went to their high school prom together. Thereafter, when Helen told him that she expected to go Oregon State College (there was no Portland State then), Linde replied "that with her mentality she might better go someplace more like Reed, and that is what she decided to do. I bought a friend's 1933 Plymouth coupe, and we commuted to Reed for our freshman year, until I was drafted. When Congress enacted the educational benefits of the G.I. Bill of Rights, Helen joined the WAVEs and was stationed at the Norfolk, Virginia naval air station. We expected to marry after the war."[4]

When the war in Europe ended in 1945, Linde's division was among the first to be sent back to the states, presumably for some potential use against Japan. His division was allowed several weeks' home leave, as were married service women whose husbands came home on leave. In light of that, Hans and Helen planned for her to come home on ordinary leave and apply for an extension after getting married.

As Linde recounted: Helen "hitched a ride west in the back of a small Navy bomber, and when this seat became hot in the summer sun, she tried to open an air hatch as advised by the pilot. Instead, the seat's plastic canopy flew off. Fortunately, she could push herself back into the belly of the plane, where she remained for the rest of the flight to Los Angeles, followed by another flight to Portland. We made it to the chambers of a judge who was waiting for us, and then headed, in my father's car, toward Victoria, B.C., for a few days' 'honeymoon'—or our properly extended marriage leave."[5]

Regarding his military service, here is how Linde remembered it when asked in the summer of 2017:

As for my time in the military, it fortunately was unheroic: Basic training at Camp Roberts in California, then an uncomfortable winter at Fort Sill, Oklahoma, supposedly to study maintaining armored force communications equipment that in fact was never repaired in the field but simply replaced. I was then assigned to the C Battery of the 414th AFA Battalion of the 20th (and last) armored division, which eventually was sent to Germany and rolled up the Rhine Valley from north to south without firing a shot in combat. Not surprisingly, when we stopped rolling (near the Mattsee in the south), I was assigned to be an interpreter for the battalion command (still as a PFC). When combat ceased, the division soon was returned north and shipped back to the U.S.[6]

Once back home and a civilian again, Linde attended Reed College[7] and subsequently went to Berkeley's Boalt Hall Law School (as it was then called).[8] Linde was thereafter selected to serve as a law clerk to Justice William O. Douglas.[9] "When I went to Washington to clerk for Douglas," Linde recalled, Helen "first studied at George Washington University and later became a second secretary for W.O.D., mainly to help prepare the typescripts of some of the books he wrote at that time."[10]

After that, Hans delighted in finding work at the State Department as an adviser to the U.S. Delegation to the U.N. General Assembly (1951 to 1953). Later, Linde served as a legislative aid to Oregon Senator Richard Neuberger (1955 to 1958). Though he had hoped to continue with a career in the State Department, it did not play out that way. Instead, Linde began his career as a law professor at the University of Oregon (1954, 1959 to 1977).[11] Originally, the dean wanted him to teach federal income tax, but soon enough he took to teaching federal constitutional law, legislative and administrative law, and torts.[12] And then came his next calling: he served as an associate justice on the Oregon Supreme Court from January 3, 1977, to January 31, 1990. True to his scholarly side, Hans Linde also served as a member of the Council of the American Law Institute and a fellow of the American Academy of Arts and Sciences.

There is, of course, more, some of which can be found in a book on Linde[13] and in various symposia[14] on him as well as in tributes to him.[15] Though a full biography has yet to be undertaken, for now this detailed sketch for a portrait of the justice must suffice.

Nuance, Foresight, Self-Reliance & Scholarship

He does happen to look at things in ways that are different.
Rex Armstrong (former Linde law clerk)

What is the measure of the man?

Nuance. Start there. Both in thought and writing, Hans Linde was careful, measured, and highly attentive to importance of parsing a phrase so that it had rational staying power. He did not deal in hyped rhetoric; ideas (coherent and cogent) were his stock and trade. It was that frame of mind that drew him away from legal catch phrases (e.g., "void for vagueness"[16]) that, when scrutinized, were often bereft of any clear and precise meaning. As Judge David Schuman (a former Linde clerk) has observed: "[Linde] demonstrated to us that intellectual rigor is more important than expedience. He urged us, not so much to question authority, but to question unexamined presumptions."[17] Consistent with that observation, while he respected Justice Oliver Wendell Holmes Jr.'s thought, Linde was not one charmed by Holmesian metaphors, even though the realist in him understood their role in the scheme of judicial decision-making. Were Linde opinions sometimes demanding? Yes. But they were not crafted in the name of pretense; rather, they were constructed in the name of precision. Take, for example, his opinions for the court in cases involving torts,[18] municipal government powers,[19] home rule,[20] criminal law,[21] pretrial detainment,[22] free speech,[23] state constitutional privileges or immunities,[24] prisoners' rights,[25] and a governor's veto power[26]—none made for easy reads. So, too, with Linde's scholarly writings such as his "Constitutional Rights in the Public Sector,"[27] his "Without 'Due Process,'"[28] his "Who Is Responsible for Republican Government?,"[29] and his "'Clear and Present Danger' Re-examined"[30] articles. None contained that in-a-nutshell closing paragraph that allowed one to sidestep the rigorous reasoning that had gone before. Linde made a bargain with his readers: if they read his works with the time, thought, and nuance he gave to his writings, then they could reap the benefit of his learned insights, which could prove most important to the attentive jurist or lawyer.

Foresight. That is another word linked to Linde's mindset. For Linde, law, at least for a high court jurist, was as much about tomorrow as it was about today. True, the particular case or controversy and the parties before the court were all important, and justice must be meted out to them according to the rule of law. That said, the rule of the case extended beyond them, to future cases in need of some larger principle. Whether in torts[31] or administrative law[32] or search and seizure law,[33] among other areas, his writings bore the stamp of a man with his eye on future facts, future scenarios, and potential future conflicts stemming from judicial precedents and/or public policies. Antithetical to Linde's approach was some cut-and-paste product slapped together by a law clerk to coincide with the preferences of the jurist assigned to a case. Never!

Self-reliant. Hans Linde was someone who did not rely much on others; he did his own work, pounding away on the keys of his old Underwood typewriter. While Linde was attentive to recommendations made by law professors he knew or knew of, he was the one who interviewed and selected potential law clerks. No delegation on that score. Consistent with such self-reliance, if one applied for a Linde clerkship and knew anything about the Judge, there could be no serious expectation of writing one of his opinions. To the best of my knowledge, none of his law clerks ever wrote one of his opinions, or even a portion of one. Law clerks provided research and proofed drafts; beyond that, not much. But there was this: sometimes as Linde worked through the logic of an opinion he would bounce ideas off a law clerk.

Being a Linde law clerk was demanding. First of all, he had but one clerk, so all the work was on you. Second, the clerks in the other chambers were of little help since their work demands were considerably different than those of Linde clerks. Hence, sometimes, especially at the outset of one's clerkship, it was best to telephone a former Linde clerk for advice. Third, Linde would often send a clerk a memo or note asking about this or that conceptual point. Before responding to such queries, one had to first *understand* them, which could be a challenge in itself. That is, you had to first see the problem before venturing into the arduous process of trying to research it, let alone resolve it.

Once such a memo was done and submitted, Linde would occasionally discuss the matter with the clerk in his chambers. "I'm curious," he might say, "as to why you said X. Tell me, why do you think that?" And so the Socratic process would begin. Dialogue mattered; it generated thinking, hard thinking.

Though it was a difficult conceptual game to stay in, if one endured it there was the delight of seeing the master's mind at work, the wheels turning with synchronized precision. In that sense, Linde continued to be a *teacher*. Thus, it is impossible to imagine any Linde law clerk leaving his or her clerkship without a bevy of new insights into the law. For myself, I learned more from the man in a single year than in all the years of my legal education. Not surprisingly, some of his clerks went on to become professors (Jennifer Friesen,[34] Ross Cheit,[35] and David Schuman[36]) and appellate judges (Rex Armstrong and David Schuman).

Scholar is yet another word that comes to mind.[37] Justice Linde was a scholar's jurist, both in his legal opinions and in his extra-judicial writings. Consider, for example, his judicial opinions with extended discussions of the law of contracts,[38] torts,[39] criminal law,[40] unemployment law,[41] insurance law, [42] the law of legislative reapportionment,[43] and the law of remedies.[44] When it came to his extrajudicial writings, Linde was the scholars' scholar as revealed by his "Due Process of Lawmaking"[45] and "Courts and Censorship"[46] articles, among others.[47] True to his scholarly credentials, Linde delivered the Oliver Wendell Holmes Devise Lecture[48]; coauthored a seminal casebook on the legislative and administrative processes[49]; and published learned pieces in the *Harvard Law Review*,[50] *Stanford Law Review*,[51] and *Yale Law Journal*.[52]

In all of these ways and others,[53] Linde approached the law as if it were a puzzle to be solved, duly mindful of the text and history of the law as well as its logic. By and large, such scholarly attention to his work made Linde stand out among his state court counterparts. We live in an era when the reign of great state jurists seems to have passed or been eclipsed by an obsession with the work product of federal appellate judges. The likes of Lemuel Shaw (Massachusetts), Oliver Wendell Holmes Jr. (Massachusetts), Benjamin Cardozo (New York), and Roger Traynor (California), among others, have no heirs, or so it seems. Hans Linde is a modern-day exception—a state court jurist of national renown.[54] Still, time takes its toll, even in Oregon.[55]

Affable. Notwithstanding his serious side and work ethic, Hans Linde could be very sociable. From time to time, he invited his clerks to spend a delightful evening with him and Helen at their Salem home perched on a hill with a long view of the Willamette Valley.[56] Such evenings were rich in conversation. Occasionally, a clerk would bring one of Hans's favorite German pastries (*Sachertorte*, a delicious and dense chocolate cake), which set the stage for yet more Germanic delights: music from the *Three Penny Opera*. In the midst of such moments, Linde's personal charm was almost magical. And though he was not, if you will, a "warm and fuzzy" sort of person, he could be quite engaging and considerate. For example, at the end of my clerkship term he gave me one of his neck ties (a "Roosternit" tie), one that several months earlier I had complimented him on.

My own relationship with the Judge was perhaps somewhat different from that of other clerks, at least in a few ways. Why? Because we were so different. Maybe that explains why I was not his first choice—that offer went to a Stanford law student who could not accept his offer in a timely manner since she hoped to secure a federal appellate clerkship. Where I was California in mindset, he was all Oregon. Where I was passionate, he was composed. Where I was interested in federal constitutional law, he set his sights on the state charter. Where I fixated on answers, he preferred questions. Where I was charmed by style, he was committed to substance—"spare me the fanciful words," he might say. Still, it made for a wonderful experience, which would have been impossible save for his mentoring ways. Over the years, our bond grew ever stronger, probably because I became more like him than vice versa.

One other point: most of Linde's clerks were progressive, or so I assume. We were ACLU, public defender, public interest, or environmental types. While the Judge certainly respected such work, he also thought it important for those of us with progressive stripes to seek work in government, for example, in a prosecutor's office, a city attorney's office, or the office of the state attorney general. In fact, he would encourage that. If you wanted real change, you had to work both within and outside of the system. You had to understand how the world looked from the government's point of view. David Schuman (who died in 2019) put that counsel to exemplary use.

In these and other ways, Linde invested in his law clerks. Yes, he befriended them, but he also inspired them to value the rule of law, in all its dimensions. No exaggeration; it's true!

It's also complex, much as the man is. Pick a label, almost any one, and chances are it really won't capture Linde: the jurist, the man, and the scholar. Unless, perhaps, the word is *rigorous,* or *serious,* or *curious,* or *meritorious.* He valued clear thinking; he invited open-mindedness; and he cared less about the "politics" of any legal issue than the soundness of the argument tendered. This is not to say that he was insensitive to the plight of the litigants before him, for he was not. But they had to make their case in law, in law buttressed with something more than sentimentality or ideology. In this way and others, he was radically different from his own boss, Justice William O. Douglas. On that score, it would not be uncommon for him to say (replete with accent) something like: "Ron, you can't just create this stuff out of thin air, like Bill Douglas. What is the *basis* for what you're saying other than it's the 'right result' in your judgment?"

Authorized by Law: A Principle of Constitutional Government

> With law shall a land be built. . . . But no law is so good to follow as the truth; where one is in doubt about the truth, there law shall find what is right.
>
> From a poster commemorating seven-hundredth anniversary of the Danish version of the Magna Carta

First as a naturalized American citizen, then as a law professor and jurist, Hans Linde had a profound commitment to and interest in constitutional government—to understanding it, teaching it, and applying it. That "it" was *law*—local, state, and federal—as formally constituted, legislatively authorized, administratively implemented, and judicially interpreted.

Central to Linde's jurisprudence is the maxim that government can only do what it is properly and specifically *authorized* to do. Hence, the first duty is upon lawmakers; they must work within state and federal constitutional parameters. This point was key to Linde's constitutionalism. Contemporary constitutional law, he argued, was obsessed with questions of the "legitimacy" of judicial review. But that mentality posed a problem: "If the premises of constitutional law are wholly indeterminate apart from one or another theory of judicial review, then constitutional law addresses no meaningful norms directly to public officials."[57] Practically speaking, the preoccupation with judicial review as the focal point of constitutional legitimacy left legislators free to act as they wished, unrestrained by the constitutional dictates. Their attitude: if they exceed their powers, courts can always attend to the matter after the fact. Of course, when they do so, lawmakers are among the first to condemn the courts—their rulings are "illegitimate" is their mantra.

In this regard, Linde's mission was to bring constitutional law (state and federal) down from the lofty realms of Supreme Court decision-making and back to the arenas in which laws are first made and then enforced. Among other things, that means that lawmakers cannot delegate legislative powers to either executive officials or judges. And perhaps more importantly, legislators ought not to abdicate their legislative responsibilities by entrusting any variety of issues to lawmaking by popular initiative.[58] In all of these ways, Linde's constitutional jurisprudence, unlike that of many of his contemporaries, was not court-centric.[59] By that same logic, his jurisprudence also focused heavily on those who implement the law[60] (e.g., administrative agencies, police officers, or even college administrators[61]); they, too, must operate within the realm authorized by statute, and neither short of it nor beyond it. "Unconditional delegation of open-ended lawmaking power to a single executive, elected or not," he wrote in 1999 in the *Cardozo Law Review*, "amounts to legislative abdication. It is the essence of modern dictatorships and incompatible with a republican form of government."[62]

Linde's dissent in *State v. Tourtillott* (1980)[63] illustrates his thinking on such matters. The case involved a roadblock overseen by an officer of the State Game Division. The roadblock was set up to check hunters' compliance with the game laws, to check hunting licenses, and to gather statistics on hunter success on the opening day of deer hunting season. When the defendant, Donna Tourtillott, was stopped, an officer asked for her driver's license. She responded that her license had been suspended. The defendant was thereafter arrested. On appeal she argued that the stop violated a state statute and was likewise unconstitutional under the search and seizure provisions of the state and federal constitutions. The majority denied her claims and Linde (joined by Chief Justice Denecke and Justice Lent) dissented.

The constitutional process: "Certain postulates are not in dispute," Linde wrote. "It is common ground between the majority opinion and this dissent that the question of state law governing this case is antecedent to the question whether defendant was "seized" in violation of the federal fourth and fourteenth amendments. As recent decisions of this court have repeatedly held, a court's obligation in a case that involves potential statutory and constitutional challenges to governmental action is to determine, first, whether the action is authorized by law; second, whether it is limited by the same or another law; third, whether it is limited by the state constitution and, if the action passes these tests, whether it contravenes the federal Constitution."[64] Applying those criteria, Linde concluded that the game officials had exceeded their authorized powers:

[1] "[T]he state has not demonstrated that defendant was stopped pursuant to a properly authorized administrative program designed for preventive or wildlife management purposes and including the necessary safeguards described in this opinion.

[2] Nor was the stop in this case authorized by [the relevant Oregon statute] as a law enforcement stop on reasonable suspicion of crime. Since the stop itself was not shown to have been lawful, there is no need to consider defendant's further argument that a stop [that] might be properly made for the administration of the game laws cannot be used for an inquiry into the driver's licensing laws.

[3] Under [the governing state statute], once the stop itself was unjustified, the subsequently discovered evidence of defendant's traffic offense should have been suppressed."[65]

Linde's *Tourtillott* dissent exemplifies his approach to constitutional law, both as to questions of what is duly authorized under law and how matters of state law must be resolved antecedent to questions of federal constitutional law. His *Tourtillott* opinion was designed in important part to remind executive officials that they cannot exceed the limits of what the law authorized them to do—this quite apart from what the Fourth Amendment as interpreted by the United States Supreme Court does or does not require. The problem with the *Tourtillott* majority opinion, then, was that it equated constitutional legitimacy with federal constitutional norms instead of focusing on constitutional authority as mandated by state constitutional and state statutory norms.[66] In the majority's rush to resolve the former, it paid inadequate attention to articulating the parameters of the latter.

State Law First: An Old Idea in a New World

It surely raises no federal concern if a state court decides a legal dispute that a federal court would not entertain, when the decision rests on state law.

Hans Linde, "The State and the Federal Courts
in Governance: Vive La Difference!"

As indicated by the preceding section, Linde's state-law first legal mindset traced back in time long before the Burger Court began to deconstruct the civil liberties edifice of the Warren Court. His devotion to state law, including state constitutional law, would have played out the same way even if Hubert Humphrey had defeated Richard Nixon, thus allowing Humphrey four liberal appointments to the Supreme Court.

Fall, 1961: that was *before* the Warren Court handed down *Gideon v. Wainright*,[67] *New York Times v. Sullivan*,[68] *Miranda v. Arizona*,[69] and *Griswold v. Connecticut*.[70] At a time when so many felt that the Warren Court was satisfying all their constitutional desires, a group of eighteen thinkers came together under the umbrella of the Oregon Constitutional Revision Commission. Their mission: to examine, discuss, hold hearings, and propose changes to the *state* constitution. Hans Linde was one of those members—one of its more active ones.[71] In other words, Linde's interest in state constitutions as independent limitations on government powers predated by sixteen years Justice William Brennan's call to state judges to "rediscover" their state charters in order to provide rights denied by the Burger Court.[72] Thus, Linde's interest in state constitutional law[73] long antedated what came to be known as the "New Judicial Federalism"[74] and state courts' use of their constitutions to circumvent unfavorable Burger Court rulings.

Even before Linde was elevated to the Oregon Supreme Court, he articulated his state-law-first thinking in an amicus brief he authored on behalf of the Oregon Environmental Council, this in the case of *American Can Co. v. Oregon Liquor Control Commission*.[75] In his brief to the Oregon Court of Appeals, Linde organized state law claims antecedent to any federal claims. In that regard, Linde as lawyer wrote: "Plaintiffs-Appellants state only perfunctory claims under the Oregon Constitution at the end of their brief.... They are placed first here because, if the Act violated the Oregon Constitution in any respect, the federal claims would not be reached."[76]

In another amicus brief, this one filed on behalf of the Oregon Newspaper Publishers Association, then-professor Linde wrote: "simply as a matter of logic, if Oregon law protects plaintiff's claimed right, then Oregon cannot be held to have abridged his liberty in violation of the 14th Amendment."[77] When the Oregon Supreme Court handed down its opinion, it echoed Linde's words: "if we hold that either of these provisions of the Oregon Constitution are violated by the statutes in question, it would not, then, be necessary to discuss the effect of the federal constitution (First Amendment) because in such case it would not come into play."[78] Again, all of this occurred *before* Hans Linde took his seat on the state high court. Hence, Justice Linde's state-law-first juris-prudence must be understood against this historical backdrop. That is, it was neither reactionary[79] in its approach nor criteria-dependent[80] on invoking state law prior to or independent of federal law.

That theory was put into practice once Linde donned his judicial robes. Whether the issue was free speech,[81] equality of treatment,[82] search and sei-zure,[83] or the treatment of prisoners,[84] the state-law-first maxim was central to Linde's judicial philosophy. Though he had not sought it, that principle of decision-making won him wide acclaim as the "intellectual godfather"[85] of the revival of interest in state constitutions as protectors of liberty. That reputation in turn attracted considerable attention among scholars, judges, and practic-ing lawyers intrigued by the "New Judicial Federalism" movement. As Linde viewed it, however, reliance on state law was less about a new movement than it was a forgotten principle of constitutional government. For Linde, that prin-ciple made sound constitutional and practical sense.[86]

Judicial Elections: Principle vs. Populism

> The system of electing judges calls into question what it means to be a judge.
> Hans Linde, "The Judge as Political Candidate"

If a state-elected judge[87] stands on principle, he or she had best be prepared to be punished for doing so—crass populism detests elevated principles.[88] By that measure, to defend constitutional rights is to risk arousing factional fury. This is especially so in the context of the rights of the criminally accused. Unlike some justices in other states,[89] Justice Linde declined to temper his constitu-tional principles in order to curry favor with a vocal segment of the populace as the time for judicial elections neared. Even so, he was not unmindful of the realpolitik consequences: "If one accepts legal realism not only as an observer's stance," he wrote, "but as demanding a legislative style of opinions, based on the judges' views of societal facts and desirable social consequences, weighing and balancing 'factors' and finding interests more or less 'compelling,' it should come as no surprise when society feels invited to express disagreement with those views by choosing some new judges."[90] That is to say that there is a dif-ference, an important one, between a judge acting on constitutional principles and a judge acting on his or her personal predilections. Of course, to the extent that judicial decision-making is politicized, that distinction vanishes . . . and with it any meaningful notion of the rule of law as legitimately constituted.[91]

Oregon is one of fourteen states that hold nonpartisan judicial elections. In 1984, Linde came up for reelection. In so many ways he was unsuited for the rough-and-tumble and pledge-and-promise of a political election. He was too scholarly, too judicious, and too quiet. And he had a German accent. It all made for a bad formula if the race was a contested one. As it turned out, it was a *hotly* contested and *highly* political race.

In 1984 (an Orwellian year) a campaign was waged to unseat Justice Linde. A thirty-year-old local prosecutor[92] and a middle-aged state trial court judge[93] opposed him. The campaign raised fundamental questions about the "tension between judicial institutions and popular passions,"[94] the clash between minority rights and majority rule, the conflict between judicial accountability and the politicization of the judicial process, and the independent role and rule of a state constitutional system and its bill of rights. As one involved as a volunteer in the campaign, I will not repeat my extended observations of that election[95] other than to highlight a few points.

On the one hand, a young Lane County deputy assistant district attorney joined with other prosecutors and so-called anti-crime groups to paint a portrait of Linde as someone whose criminal justice jurisprudence was insensitive to the victims of crimes and oversensitive to the alleged perpetrators of such crimes. In one of his many such charges, the vociferous prosecutor alleged that "we're dangerously close to a vigilante response because generally speaking the people have lost confidence in the criminal justice system." He continued, "time and again we felt one man was responsible for a lot of the bad decisions."[96]

Though irresponsible and unfounded, such wildly exaggerated claims (and others) became standard fare in the print press and electronic media. It made for eye-catching headlines; so much so that the *New York Times* carried a news story entitled "Law-and-Order Groups Opposing Re-election of a Justice."[97] With enough such stories, and Linde's refusal to publicly engage his opponent, the impetuous prosecutor's hope was that the charges would stick and thus pave the path to his victory.

On the other hand, there was a sitting circuit judge whose campaign strategy was to cast himself a restrained moderate—a centrist who avoided the judicial "excesses" of Linde and likewise shunned the rhetorical excesses of the young prosecutor. Nonetheless, he could not resist the occasional temptation to echo the anti-Linde line: "I disagree with his liberal policies; his opinions are not understandable and he's made it difficult for police to seize and search for property."[98] His hope was that he would surface as victor in the battle between the "soft-on-crime" justice and his brash opponent.

Linde's reluctance to enter into the political fray by way of promises or countercharges greatly worried his supporters, even if his reasons for doing so were principled. I know that his reluctance worried me, which is why I left Southern California to work on his campaign for a few months. Several Oregon-based Linde clerks—Rex Armstrong, David Schuman, and Theodore Falk, among others—felt likewise and joined in the campaign. The fear was that if Linde continued his silence, he would soon become a victim of the campaign to unseat him. "I think Hans Linde has a real chance of losing his seat,"[99] is how one newspaper publisher put it at the time.

Always busy, always thinking, the jurist who had successfully orchestrated a 1978 election campaign moved slowly, silently, and systematically. A "Committee to Re-Elect Justice Hans Linde" was formed; it consisted of prominent and powerful Oregonians. Fundraising plans were put into motion. The committee prepared mass mailings and radio and television spots. Additionally, a former Linde law clerk (Ted Falk) and a University of Oregon law professor (James O'Fallon) prepared a "national law professors" network letter. Among others, Harvard law professor Laurence Tribe, Stanford law professor Gerald Gunther, and former federal circuit judge Shirley Hufstedler signed the letter. Although things were starting to look up for Linde, the aggressive prosecutor's broadsides continued to draw widespread attention. Hence, something bolder needed to be done. Silence was no longer a viable option.

If there was a single turning point in the campaign, it came on the afternoon of April 23, 1984, when the Lane County Bar Association hosted an exchange between Hans Linde and the assistant district attorney. For tactical or other reasons, Linde's trial-judge opponent was absent. Though much can and has been said about the exchange between the two candidates, suffice it to say that the prosecutor hurled one charge after another against Justice Linde: he legislates "through the judicial branch"; he "decides cases on issues not raised"; "he's extremely slow" in deciding cases; and "he has greatly expanded the rights of criminal defendants." When Linde rose to reply, he was calm, measured, and firm. "One of my opponents says that I do not express myself plainly. [Pause] I shall speak plainly." With that Linde delivered a short but direct point-by-point response, at once both emphatic and professional in its defense of the integrity of the judicial system and the Oregon Supreme Court as a whole.[100]

The organized effort paid off, and Fate smiled, or at least partially so. In the few weeks that followed, numerous editorial endorsements came Linde's way. While they were enough to garner the most votes (45 percent) on election day, they were not enough to prevent a runoff between Linde and his trial-judge opponent, who secured slightly more votes (29 percent) than the arrogant prosecutor (25 percent).[101] Though Linde had to endure another campaign, time, money, and momentum were on his side: when the general election came around, he won it easily.

Adherence to Law

Twenty days before he retired, Justice Linde released his last opinion; it came in *State v. Wagner II,*[102] a death penalty case. *Wagner II* marked the end of a judicial career in which Linde had tried, often with success, to chart out a course of decision-making that was principled in process and at the same time protective of constitutional rights. Such concerns explain his *Wagner II* dissent, an atypically passionate one for a typically dispassionate jurist.

"Today's decision will not mark a proud day in the history of this court," he declared. "It comes at the beginning of a new decade in which many societies are turning in revulsion from regimes that were too ready to put people to death. While Western nations among whom we claim leadership continue to reject the death penalty even for heinous crimes, this country is rapidly accumulating the largest number of persons sentenced to death and awaiting execution in the world."[103] Law seemed to be taking a back seat to vengeance: "there is no legal reason why Oregon must add its share. To the contrary, today's majority opinion displays the extraordinary gymnastics required to salvage the unconstitutional 1984 measure."[104]

"Then why is this not done?"[105] he asked. His reply: "that remains for others to explain. If Oregon historians in the coming century take any note of the state's and this court's recent experiences with the death penalty, they may note that the current murderous ferocity of criminal behavior has called forth a ferocious popular demand for equivalent retribution against the guilty, to the point of initiating repeal of major constitutional guarantees in such cases."[106] Thereafter, his words grew sterner: "It is our duty not to extend the death penalty law beyond its exact terms. This is not due to sympathy or concern for a defendant. . . . The popular demand for retribution may run wide, but it is not unanimous. For many Oregonians, maybe hundreds of thousands, execution of a death sentence by state officials acting on behalf of the citizens of Oregon implicates them in a morally repugnant act. They may not be the majority, but they too are entitled to adherence to the law."[107]

Stop there, with *adherence to law*, and you will understand much about the man who strove to make that ideal a reality. And that is one important reason why so many gathered that April evening in Portland to pay homage to Justice Hans Linde.[108]

Click: Surrounded by his law clerks and friends, the elderly jurist stood up (bent over a bit) to be honored yet again. He smiled as the cameraman took farewell shots of him. Thus this sketch for a portrait of Hans A. Linde, among the last of state judges worthy of the label "great."

Notes

This essay is dedicated to the memory of David Schuman. Justice Linde reviewed a draft of this essay in the spring and summer of 2017. Oregon Supreme Court Justice Robert D. Durham (ret.) kindly offered a number of constructive comments.

1. Maureen O'Hagan, "It's Free Speech, Stupid," *Willamette Week* (Salem, Ore.), February 3, 1999, 23. See also David Margolick, "State Judiciaries Are Shaping Law That Goes beyond Supreme Court," *New York Times*, May 19, 1982, A1; and Jeffrey Toobin, "Better than Burger: States' Rights Even a Liberal Can Love," *New Republic*, March 4, 1985, 10. Cable TV appearances of Justice Linde can be found on C-SPAN: "Conference of Chief Justices," November 14, 2003 (with Chief Justice William Rehnquist, among others), https://www.c-span.org/video/?179264-1/conference-chief-justices, and "Federal Courts: Progress & Prospects—Bicentennial Conference on the Judiciary Act of 1789," September 22, 1989 (with Justices William Brennan and Antonin Scalia, among others), https://www.c-span.org/video/?9114-1/federal-courts-progress-prospects.

2. The Lindes had previously vacationed in Denmark on Bornholm Island in the Baltic Sea. In 1933, they returned to Bornholm and, as it turned out, remained there for the summer. Worried about developments in Nazi Germany, Hans's father, Bruno ("BC"), urged his wife (Luise) and two sons (Hans and Peter) to move to Copenhagen, where they lived for several years. Meanwhile, Bruno went back and forth between Copenhagen and his law office in Berlin. Hans Linde, interview by author, Portland, Ore., April 26, 2017.

3. Bruno Linde left Berlin in 1937 and then lived in Copenhagen for a while. In 1938 he secured an immigration visa and lived with friends and relatives in New York City. The following year, he returned to Copenhagen, this time to gather his family and move to New York, where they remained through the summer of that year. After he bought a 1931 Buick (for $65), "BC" and family ventured West on Highway 30. It took them some nineteen days to get to Portland. Sometime later, Bruno attended night school at the Northwestern Law School (later Lewis and Clark), where he received a law degree and then passed the Oregon bar. Linde, interview.

4. Hans Linde, e-mail message to author, July 20, 2017.

5. Ibid.

6. Ibid.

7. His senior thesis was titled "State, Sovereignty, and International Law—A Study of Three German Legal Theories," 1947 Senior Thesis, Reed College (available at Reed

College Library). Helen typed the 141-page senior thesis (an original and six carbon copies). Linde, e-mail.

8. Linde was the editor-in-chief of the *California Law Review* (1949 to 1950) and published two students' Notes. See Hans Linde, "Criminal Law: First Degree Murder: Discretion of Jury to Choose between Life Imprisonment and Death Penalty," *California Law Review* 36, no. 4 (1948); "Corporations: Elimination of Dividend Arrearages on Cumulative Preferred Stock by Amendment of the Articles of Incorporation," *California Law Review* 37, no. 1 (1949).

9. Among other cases, that term the court decided *Dennis v. United States,* 341 US 494 (1951), the controversial Smith Act free-speech case in which Justice Douglas authored a dissent. See generally John P. Frank, "The United States Supreme Court: 1950–51," *University of Chicago Law Review* 19, no. 2 (1952).

10. Linde, e-mail.

11. Among other things, during that period Linde authored an amicus brief on behalf of the Oregon Newspaper Publishers Association in the case of *Deras v. Myers,* 535 P. 2d 541 (1975) (issue: "whether the state may prohibit expenditures to be made on political advocacy in an election beyond a permitted formula for such expenditures, in the face of constitutional guarantees of freedom to speak and to write, freedom of the press, and freedom to assemble, to consult for the common good, and to petition for a redress of grievances"). He also wrote an amicus brief for the Oregon Environmental Council in *American Can Co. v. Oregon Liquor Control Comm'n,* 517 P. 2d 691 (1973). See also David B. Frohnmayer and Hans A. Linde, "State Court Responsibility for Maintaining Republican Government: An Amicus Curiae Brief," *Willamette Law Review* 39 (2003) (brief of Linde & Frohnmayer as amici curiae in support of the petition for certiorari, *cert. denied, Sawyer v. Or. ex rel. Huddleston,* 118 S. Ct. 557 [1997]).

12. Though Linde also taught as a visiting professor at Boalt Hall (Berkeley) and Stanford Law Schools, his passion for Oregon always brought him back to the Pacific Northwest. At Stanford, Linde forged a lasting friendship with the famed constitutional law professor Gerald Gunther, who first brought Linde to my attention when I was a teaching fellow there in 1980. Later that year, I applied to Linde for a clerkship and was selected.

13. Robert F. Nagel, *Intellect and Craft: The Contributions of Justice Hans Linde to American Constitutionalism* (Boulder, Colo.: Westview Press, 1995).

14. See *Symposium on the Work of Justice Hans Linde, Oregon Law Review* 70 (1991): 679–1007; New York University, School of Law, *Annual Survey of American Law* (Dobbs Ferry, N.Y.: Oceana, 1984); *Symposium: Unparalleled Justice: The Legacy of Hans Linde, Willamette Law Review* 43 (2006).

15. See, e.g., John P. Frank, "A Tribute to Justice Hans A. Linde," in New York University, *Annual Survey of American Law* (1984), xxi.; Alfred Goodwin, "A Tribute to Hans Linde," in New York University, *Annual Survey of American Law* (1984), xv.; Abner Mikva, "Hans Linde: Hard to Bluff," in New York University, *Annual Survey of American Law* (1984), ix.; Robert Summers, "Hans A. Linde as Seen by a Junior Colleague—

A Personal Tribute," in New York University, *Annual Survey of American Law* (1984), xi; Dave Frohnmayer, "Foreword, Hans Linde: Architect of Democratic Institutions," *Texas Law Review* 70 (1991); Patricia M. Wald, "Hans Linde and the Elusive Art of Judging: Intellect and Craft Are Never Enough," *Texas Law Review* 75 (1996): 215.; and Sanford Levinson, "Tiers of Scrutiny—From Strict through Rational Basis—and the Future of Interests: Commentary on Fiss and Linde," *Albany Law Review* 55 (1992): 745.

16. See *Megdal v. Oregon State Bd. of Dental Examiners*, 605 P. 2d 273 (1980). ("Petitioner's brief cites no clause of either constitution for his assertion that 'unprofessional conduct' is so vague as to be 'constitutionally impermissible.' Possibly the seductive alliteration 'void for vagueness' is thought to have achieved constitutional status on its own, judging by how often it is invoked. Actually, 'vagueness' in a statute, ordinance, regulation, decree, order, or other legal rule is a fault for reasons which differ with the function of the rule at issue, and which must search for footing in still unsettled constitutional premises").

17. David Schuman, "Unpublished Remarks" (speech, Portland, Ore., March 22, 2017, American Constitution Society Annual Dinner). As noted in the text, Schuman died two years later—he was perhaps closest to the Judge, both in personal contact and in his professional application of Linde's lessons.

18. *Top Serv. Body Shop, Inc. v. Allstate Ins. Co*, 582 P. 2d 1365 (1978). See also *Norwest v. Presbyterian Intercommunity Hosp*, 652 P. 2d 318 (1982).

19. *Defazio v. Wppss*, 679 P. 2d 1316 (1984).

20. *City of La Grande v. Public Emp. Retirement Bd*, 576 P. 2d 1204 (1978), *aff'd on rehearing, City of La Grande v. Public Emp. Retirement Bd*, 586 P. 2d 765 (1978).

21. *State v. Cloutier*, 596 P. 2d 1278 (1979). See "Sentencing the Multiple Criminal Defender," *Oregon Law Review* 59 (1980): 339.

22. *Haynes v. Burks*, 290 Or. 75, 80, 619 P.2d 632 (1980).

23. *State v. Robertson*, 649 P. 2d 569 (1982). See generally Rex Armstrong, "Free Speech Fundamentalism—Linde's Lasting Legacy," *Oregon Law Review* 70 (1991).

24. *State v. Clark*, 630 P. 2d 810 (1981).

25. *Sterling v. Cupp*, 625 P. 2d 123 (1981).

26. *Lipscomb v. State Bd. of Higher Ed*, 753 P. 2d 939 (1988).

27. *Washington Law Review* 34 (1964): 4 and *Washington Law Review* 40 (1965): 10. (The title in the text was the subtitle; the title to the articles was "Justice Douglas on Freedom in the Welfare State").

28. "Without 'Due Process,'" *Oregon Law Review* 49 (1970): 125.

29. Hans A. Linde, "Who Is Responsible for Republican Government?," *University of Colorado Law Review* 65 (1994): 709. In a May 19, 1990, personal letter to the author, Linde wrote: "By the way . . . if you look for *State v. Montez* [309 Or. 564, 789 P.2d 1352, 1377 (Or., 1990)], you will find that the Oregon Supreme Court acknowledged that it could decide a 'republicanism' challenge to an initiative, though it did not do so in that case" (on file with the author).

30. "'Clear and Present Danger' Re-examined," *Stanford Law Review* 22 (1970): 1163 (the article's subtitle was "Dissonance in the Brandenburg Concerto").

31. See, e.g., *Koos v. Roth*, 652 P. 2d 1255 (1982) (discussing strict liability).

32. See, e.g., *Megdal v. Oregon State Bd. of Dental Examiners*.

33. See Linde's opinion in *State v. Lowry*, 667 P. 2d 996 (1983).

34. Professor Jennifer Friesen, who was in Linde's constitutional law class at the University of Oregon, authored a major treatise on state constitutional law titled *State Constitutional Law: Litigating Individual Rights, Claims, and Defenses*, vol. 2 (Newark, N.J.: LexisNexis, 2006).

35. Ross E. Cheit teaches political science and international public affairs at Brown University, where he has been a professor since 1987. Among other works, he is the author of *The Witch-Hunt Narrative: Politics, Psychology, and the Sexual Abuse of Children* (New York: Oxford University Press, 2014) and *Setting Safety Standards: Regulation in the Public and Private Sectors* (Berkeley: University of California Press, 1990).

36. In 2017, University of Oregon law professor and retired judge David Schuman received the Hans Linde award from the state chapter of the American Constitution Society.

37. See Richard Kipling, "A Scholar Named Mr. Justice Linde," *Western Law Journal*, March–April 1980, 1 (then published by *Los Angeles Daily Journal*).

38. See *Kabil Developments Corp. v. Mignot*, 566 P. 2d 505 (1977) (discussing objective versus subjective intent in the law of contracts).

39. See *Donaca v. Curry County*, 734 P. 2d 1339 (1987) (discussing duty owed in negligence cases); *Koos v. Roth* (discussing strict liability); and *Nearing v. Weaver*, 670 P. 2d 137 (1983) (discussing statutory duties of police that give rise to liability for injury to citizens). See also Hans A. Linde, "Courts and Torts: Public Policy without Public Politics," *Valparaiso University Law Review* 28 (1994): 821.; Caroline Forell, "Replacing Pragmatism and Policy with Analysis and Analogy: Justice Linde's Contribution to Oregon Tort Law," *Oregon Law Review* 70 (1991): 815; and Wayne V. McIntosh and Cynthia L Cates, *Judicial Entrepreneurship: The Role of the Judge in the Marketplace of Ideas* (Westport, Conn.: Greenwood, 1997), 79–85 (discussing Linde's influence on tort law).

40. See *State v. Boots*, 780 P. 2d 725 (1989) (discussing aggravated murder statute).

41. See *McPherson v. Employment Division*, 591 P. 2d 1381 (1979) (discussing meaning of phrase "good cause" in unemployment compensation statute).

42. See *A-1 Sandblasting & Steamcleaning v. Baiden*, 643 P. 2d 1260 (1982) (discussing insurance claim and defense of "against public policy").

43. See *McCall v. Legislative Assembly*, 634 P. 2d 223 (1981).

44. See *Cole v. State by & through Or. Dept. of Rev*, 655 P. 2d 171 (1982) (noting the difference between state constitutional remedies clause and due process clause); and Hans A. Linde, "Without 'Due Process': Unconstitutional Law in Oregon," *Oregon Law Review* 49 (1970): 125.

45. "Due Process of Lawmaking," *Nebraska Law Review* 55 (1976): 197. For a thoughtful commentary on the scope of Linde's thinking in this article, see Philip P. Frickey, "Honoring Hans: On Linde, Lawmaking, and Legacies," *Willamette Law Review* 43 (2007): 157.

46. "Courts and Censorship," *Minnesota Law Review* 66 (1981): 171. See also Hans A. Linde, "Fair Trials and Press Freedom—Two Rights against the State," *Willamette Law Journal* 13 (1977): 211.

47. See, e.g., Hans Linde, "Moving Goods inside a Continent-Wide Common Market," in *Courts and Free Markets: Perspectives from the United States and Europe*, vol. 2, edited by Terrance Sandalow and Eric Stein (New York: Oxford University Press, 1982), 139–73.

48. Hans A. Linde, "Due Process of Lawmaking," *Nebraska Law Review* 55 (1976): 197 (Oliver Wendell Holmes, Jr., Devise Lecture for 1975).

49. Hans Linde and George Bunn, *Legislative and Administrative Processes*, University Casebook Series (Foundation Press, 1976, 1982). See also Donald W. Brodie and Hans A. Linde, "State Court Review of Administrative Action: Prescribing the Scope of Review," *Arizona State Law Journal* 1977, no. 3 (1977): 537–68.

50. Hans A. Linde, "Hercules in a Populist Age," *Harvard Law Review* 103 (1990): 2067.

51. Hans A. Linde, "Clear and Present Danger Reexamined: Dissonance in the Brandenburg Concerto," *Stanford Law Review* 22 (1970): 1163.

52. Hans A. Linde, "Judges, Critics, and the Realist Tradition," *Yale Law Journal* 82 (1972): 227.

53. On a few rare occasions, Linde floated his ideas in newspapers. See Hans Linde, "The Press & Rights," *New York Times*, April 27, 1979.

54. See Nagel, *Intellect and Craft*. Other notable state judges include Justice Mathew Tobriner of the California Supreme Court, Chief Judge Judith Kaye of New York's High Court, and Chief Justice Shirley Abrahamson of the Wisconsin Supreme Court.

55. Consider in this regard what Judge David Schuman (a former Linde law clerk) said: "It appears to me that the Oregon Supreme Court has embarked on a relentless de-Lindeification process. I mentioned to Hans at one point that I was thinking about writing a law review article exposing and lambasting this process, and calling it 'Worst Things First; The Decline and Fall of the Oregon Supreme Court.' Hans's response was, 'And what do you hope to accomplish by that?' and I had no satisfactory answer. The only answer that I could come up with was that the article would give me a chance to ventilate. Law review articles are not a good forum for ventilation." Schuman, "Unpublished Remarks."

56. The home was located at 2545 Birds Hill South in Salem. It was an old but charming farmhouse, constructed around 1908. The interior, however, was more modern and Scandinavian in style.

57. Hans A. Linde, "E Pluribus—Constitutional Theory and State Courts," in *Developments in State Constitutional Law: The Williamsburg Conference*, edited by Bradley D. McGraw (St. Paul, Minn.: West, 1985), 275.

58. See Hans A. Linde, "Who Is Responsible for Republican Government?," *Colorado Law Review* 64 (1994): 709.

59. In this regard, consider what Linde said in his 1982 remarks at an American Association of Law Schools panel discussion on "Teaching Constitutional Law":

"Constitutional law courses assume that their given subject is the work of one institution, the Supreme Court of the United States. . . . [M]y basic thesis is that the design of constitutional law courses and the next generation of books for these courses should abandon the assumption that a course in constitutional law and a course on the Supreme Court are one and the same. . . . As a body of substantive knowledge, constitutional law is not reasonably a single subject at all. . . . In short, constitutional law should be the primary course about the law governing the government of the republic." Hans A. Linde, "Unpublished AALS Teaching Panel Memorandum" (lecture, January 8, 1982), 1–5 (on file with the author).

60. See, e.g., Hans A. Linde, "Replacing a President: Rx for a 21st Century Watergate," *George Washington Law Review* 43 (1974): 384.

61. See Hans A. Linde, "Campus Law: Berkeley Viewed from Eugene," *California Law Review* 54 (1966): 40.

62. Hans A. Linde, "Structures and Terms of Consent: Delegation, Discretion, Separation of Powers, Representation, Participation, Accountability," *Cardozo Law Review* 20 (1999): 823. See also G. Edward White, "Hans Linde as Constitutional Theorist: Judicial Preservation of the Republic," *Oregon Law Review* 70 (1991): 707.

63. *State v. Tourtillott*, 618 P. 2d 423 (1980) (Linde, J., dissenting).

64. 618 P. 2d. at 436.

65. 618 P. 2d. at 448. Linde was also critical of the majority opinion's use of Fourth Amendment "balancing test." He wrote: "The majority believes that it can escape the burdens of rigorous analysis by simply invoking the magic term 'balancing.' The 'balancing' that follows may perhaps say something about the adequacy of that contemporary formula as a guide to courts that are called upon to translate constitutional law into operational rules." Ibid., 441.

66. As Linde admonished law professors the following year: "A generation of lawyers bred on recent constitutional doctrines completely misses the importance of sub-constitutional issues. Because they are taught criminal procedures from Supreme Court cases, they assume that anything is legally authorized that the Constitution does not forbid." Hans A. Linde, "Unpublished AALS Teaching Panel Memorandum," 13 (on file with the author).

67. *Gideon v. Wainwright*, 372 US 335 (1963).

68. *The New York Times Co. v. Sullivan*, 376 US 254 (1964).

69. *Miranda v. Arizona*, 384 US 436 (1966).

70. *Griswold v. Connecticut*, 381 US 479 (1965).

71. See *A New Constitution for Oregon: A Report to the 52nd Legislative Assembly by the Commission for Constitutional Revision*, December 15, 1962. In February 1999, Rex Armstrong kindly provided me with the records of the commission's minutes, which are quite revealing and thus lend themselves to future and extended scholarly commentary. Years later, Linde returned to the subject of the Oregon Constitution and how it might be revised. See Hans A. Linde, "Future Directions in State Constitutional Reform," *Oregon Law Review* 67 (1988): 65.

72. William J. Brennan Jr., "State Constitutions and the Protection of Individual Rights," *Harvard Law Review* 90 (1977): 489. See also Project Report, "Toward an Activist Role for State Bills of Rights," *Harvard Civil Rights–Civil Liberties Law Review* 8 (1973): 271.

73. See Hans Linde, "1959 Annual Survey of Oregon Law," *Oregon Law Review* 39 (1960): 161.

74. See A. E. Dick Howard, "State Courts and Constitutional Rights in the Day of the Burger Court," *Virginia Law Review* 62 (1976): 873; and Robert F. Williams, *The Law of American State Constitutions* (New York: Oxford University Press, 2009), ch. 5. See also Hans Linde, "Does the New Federalism Have a Future?" *Emerging Issues in State Constitutional Law* 4 (1991): 251.

75. *American Can Co. v. Oregon Liquor Control Comm'n.*

76. Oregon Environmental Council amicus brief in ibid., 3.

77. Oregon Newspaper Publishers Association amicus brief in *Deras v. Myers*, 7.

78. Ibid.

79. See Ronald Collins, "Reliance on State Constitutions—Away from a Reactionary Approach," *Hastings Constitutional Law Quarterly* 9 (1981): 1.

80. See Robert F. Utter, "Swimming in the Jaws of the Crocodile: State Court Comment on Federal Constitutional Issues When Disposing of Cases on State Constitutional Grounds," *Texas Law Review* 63 (1985): 1027–30.

81. See, e.g., *State v. Robertson.*

82. See, e.g., *State v. Clark.*

83. See, e.g., *State v. Lowry.*

84. See, e.g., *Sterling v. Cupp.*

85. Jeffrey Toobin, "Better than Burger," *New Republic*, March 4, 1985, 10–11.

86. See Hans A. Linde, "First Things First," *University of Baltimore Law Review* 9 (1980): 379; and Hans A. Linde, "E Pluribus—Constitutional Theory and State Courts," *George Law Review* 18 (1984): 165.

87. See Hans A. Linde, "Elective Judges: Some Comparative Comments," *Southern California Law Review* 61 (1988): 1995.

88. Even so, the federal Constitution places an important limitation on the use of the initiative process. See Hans A. Linde, "When Initiative Lawmaking Is Not Republican Government: The Campaign against Homosexuality," *Oregon Law Review* 72 (1993): 19; and Hans A. Linde, "State Courts and Republican Government," *Santa Clara Law Review* 41 (2001): 951.

89. See, e.g., Bob Egelko, "Bird Court's Major Death Penalty Ruling Reversed: Intent to Kill Not Necessary," *Los Angeles Times*, October 13, 1987 ("Justice Stanley Mosk, who had voted with the majority in the 1983 [death penalty] decision, voted today to overturn that decision. Mosk said the court had erred four years ago"). See also Jacqueline Braitman and Gerald Ulmen, *Justice Stanley Mosk: A Life at the Center of California Politics and Justice* (Jefferson, N.C.: McFarland, 2013), 217.

90. Linde, "Elective Judges."

91. Here is how Linde once put it: "legislation is legitimately political and judging is not. Unless a court can attribute public policy to a politically accountable source, it must resolve novel issues ... within a matrix of [statutory and constitutional] principles without claiming public policy for its own decision." Hans A. Linde, "Courts and Torts: Public Policy without Public Politics," *Valparaiso University Law Review* 28 (1994): 855.

92. David M. Nissman.

93. Albin W. Norblad.

94. Hans A. Linde, "Hercules in a Populist Age," *Harvard Law Review* 103 (1990): 2069.

95. See Ronald Collins, "Hans Linde and His 1984 Judicial Election: The Primary," *Oregon Law Review* 70 (1991): 747.

96. "Candidate Says Lack of Faith in Courts Leads to Vigilantism," *Register Guard* (Eugene, Ore.), March 23, 1984, B-4 (quoting David Nissman).

97. *New York Times*, April 2, 1984, A 17.

98. O'Connor, "Court Candidate Trods Campaign Trail in KF," *Herald & News* (Klamath Falls, Ore.), April 18, 1984, 2 (quoting Judge Norblad).

99. Robert Chandler, "Court/Tough Fight for Linde," *Bulletin* (Bend, Ore.), April 8, 1984, 10.

100. Collins, "Hans Linde and His 1984 Judicial Election: The Primary," *Oregon Law Review* 70 (1991): 774–82.

101. Ibid., 788–89.

102. *State v. Wagner*, 786 P. 2d 93 (1990) (Linde J., dissenting). In an earlier appeal in this aggravated murder case, the Oregon Supreme Court affirmed, over Linde's dissent, the defendant's death sentence. *State v. Wagner*. The defendant then petitioned the Supreme Court for a writ of certiorari. The Supreme Court vacated the judgment and remanded the matter to the state high court "for further consideration in light of *Penry v. Lynaugh*, 492 U.S. 302 (1989)." *Wagner v. Oregon*, 492 U.S. 914, 109 S. Ct. 3235, 106 L. Ed. 2d 583 (1989).

103. 786 P.2d at 111 (Linde, J., dissenting).

104. Ibid.

105. Ibid.

106. Ibid.

107. Ibid.

108. David Linde (the Judge's son—a famous movie producer) was also there that evening. At the time, David Linde was the CEO of Participation Media, a cinematic venture committed to social and environmental justice.

HENRY M. GREENBERG

"Lawyer Heaven"
Clerking for Judith S. Kaye

F rom the summers of 1988 through 1990, I had the privilege of serving
as a law clerk for Judith Smith Kaye, the thirty-seventh chief judge of
New York State's highest court, the Court of Appeals. She was the first
woman associate judge and chief judge of the court. She was the longest serving chief judge in the court's history.[1] She authored some 622 judicial opinions,
many of them landmarks.[2] She was a trailblazing court administrator.[3] In short,
Judith Kaye was chief among chief judges of her generation.[4]

The New York Court of Appeals

For a quarter century—from 1983 to 2008—Judge Kaye sat on the Court of
Appeals.[5] "This," in her words, "is the court of Benjamin Cardozo and other
luminaries of the common law."[6] The court consists of a chief judge and six
associate judges, each appointed by New York's governor for fourteen-year
terms.[7] Reflecting its historical purpose,[8] the court's primary role is to "be the
final arbiter of state-wide rules of law which would serve as a guide to the conduct of the general population."[9] It is almost entirely a "certiorari" court, meaning that it hears most appeals by its own permission, granted upon civil motion
or criminal leave application.[10] "Limited only by the human imagination," the
court's docket—roughly 60 percent civil and 40 percent criminal—is extraordinarily diverse.[11] "Lawyer Heaven" is the phrase Judge Kaye often used to
describe the experience of deciding the novel and challenging issues that came
before the court.[12]

Judge Kaye's Life and Career—In a Nutshell

Judith Kaye's life and career is a testament to the American Dream. Born on August 4, 1938, she was the daughter of Jewish immigrants from Eastern Europe who came to America fleeing religious persecution.[13] She was raised in a village located at the foothills of New York's Catskill Mountains and for a time attended a one-room school house.[14] A gifted student, she skipped two grades, graduating high school at age fifteen.[15] She continued her education at Barnard College, preparing for a career in journalism.[16] Following graduation she took a job with the *Hudson Dispatch* in Union City, New Jersey.[17] Like many women in a male-dominated field, however, she was assigned to the society page.[18] To enhance her chances of one day covering hard news, she worked as a copy editor for a news service during the day and attended New York University Law School at night.[19] She graduated in 1962, one of 10 women in a class of 290, ranking sixth in her class.[20]

Her first legal job was with Sullivan & Cromwell, an elite white-shoe firm in Manhattan.[21] There, she met and fell in love with a colleague, Stephen Rackow Kaye, whom she married in 1964.[22] Their forty-two-year marriage produced a daughter, two sons, and seven grandchildren.[23] Stephen Kaye was a high-powered litigator, who became a partner and chair of the litigation department at Proskauer Rose Goetz & Mendelsohn, another large Manhattan firm.[24]

After two years at Sullivan & Cromwell, Judge Kaye joined the IBM legal department.[25] From 1965 to 1969, through the births of her three children, she worked part-time as an assistant to the NYU Law School dean.[26] She then joined Olwine, Connelly, Chase, O'Donnell & Weyher, a midsize Manhattan firm, where, in 1975, she was named its first female partner.[27] Over the next several years she made a mark as a distinguished commercial litigator.[28]

In 1983, Governor Mario Cuomo appointed Judith Kaye to the Court of Appeals, making good on a campaign pledge to name the first woman in the high court's history.[29] Coming to the bench directly from private practice, she spent her first years on the bench transitioning from the "fundamentally different roles" of lawyer to judge, advocate to arbiter.[30] She once joked that "[f]or a long time after my appointment to the Court of Appeals I marked every passing week as a triumph of survival—my own as well as the law of the State of New York."[31]

Judge Kaye's self-deprecating humor notwithstanding, she quickly mastered the craft of judging, writing opinions for the court in high-profile cases, such as one striking down New York's mandatory death penalty for murder committed by an inmate already serving life imprisonment.[32] Additionally, through opinions and scholarly articles, she earned a national reputation as a forceful advocate for independent state constitutional adjudication—the doctrine that state courts should look to their own constitutions instead of limiting their decisions to analysis under the U.S. Constitution.[33] In *Immuno A.G. v. Moor-Jankowski*,[34] for example, she held that the New York State Constitution provided protection for speech greater than the minimal protections required under the U.S. Supreme Court's interpretation of the First Amendment.[35]

In 1993, Judge Kaye was appointed chief judge, in the wake of the tumultuous and sudden departure of her immediate predecessor, Sol Wachtler.[36] Now, in addition to being chief judge of the Court of Appeals, she assumed what amounted to a second full-time job—chief judge of the State of New York.[37] In that capacity, she was responsible for overseeing the state's judicial branch of government and setting priorities for "one of the largest, busiest and most complex judicial systems in the world."[38] She quipped that she had two jobs, and "each . . . took 80 percent of my time."[39] Under her leadership as chief executive of the court system, New York "became a laboratory for innovation, generating many important reforms that changed the way justice is delivered in the twenty-first century."[40]

At the same time, in her judicial role, she was first among equals on the Court of Appeals, respected as an intellectual leader and consensus builder.[41] Through "elegant, well-reasoned opinions" she "indelibly shaped the law of the State" in many critical areas.[42] These included seminal rulings recognizing adoption rights of same-sex couples[43] and insuring that all public school students—rich and poor—had "the opportunity for a meaningful high school education" that would prepare them "to function productively as civic participants."[44]

Among Judge Kaye's most memorable writings was a prophetic dissent in *Hernandez v. Robles*,[45] decided her last year on the court in 2008. A four-judge plurality held that same-sex couples had neither a constitutional nor a statutory right to marry.[46] Judge Kaye could not disagree more strongly. She wrote: "While encouraging opposite-sex couples to marry before they have children is certainly a legitimate interest of the State, the exclusion of gay men and lesbians from marriage in no way furthers this interest. There are enough marriage licenses to go around for everyone."[47] Vindication was not long in coming. In 2015, the U.S. Supreme Court in *Obergefell v. Hoges*[48] required all fifty states to recognize same-sex marriage, following a slew of lower court decisions (many citing Judge Kaye's dissent in *Hernandez*) striking down bans on same-sex marriage across the nation.[49]

In the 1990s, Judge Kaye rejected overtures by the Clinton administration to move to Washington, D.C., and become U.S. attorney general or a justice of the U.S. Supreme Court.[50] She never regretted those decisions. She and her husband adored New York City, and, save only her family, she loved nothing more than being on the Court of Appeals. She served as chief judge until 2008, when she reached the mandatory retirement age of seventy.[51] She then joined the international law firm Skadden, Arps, Slate, Meagher & Flom, where she focused on arbitration and projects that improved the lives of underprivileged children. After a lengthy battle with cancer, she died at her home in Manhattan on January 7, 2016, at age seventy-seven.[52]

The Kaye Clerks

The modern clerkship model took root at the New York Court of Appeals in the late 1920s, when then–associate judge Irving Lehman[53] began hiring graduates from Ivy League law schools, for stints of two to four years. Initially, not all of the judges of the court emulated Lehman's practice, relying instead on permanent "law secretaries." By the 1950s, however, judges regularly hired clerks on a rotating basis.

Judith Kaye had a profound appreciation for the importance of law clerks to the court's work. Twice (in 1990 and 1997) she published a booklet, entitled *Counsel to the Court: Law Clerks and Court Attorneys of the Court of Appeals of the State of New York*. It listed the names, addresses, and dates of service of current and former law clerks, and the judges with whom they served, going back to the Cardozo era.[54]

During her twenty-five years on the Court of Appeals, Judge Kaye had thirty-nine law clerks, most serving for one or two years.[55] She was entitled to two clerks as an associate judge, and added a third when she became chief judge, and later a fourth. She did not believe in hiring law clerks fresh out of law school, preferring young lawyers with real-world experience. Typically, a Kaye clerk spent at least a few years practicing law in the private or public sector. Many came from the litigation departments of large New York City firms, although she also drew from district attorney's and legal aid offices. A couple had prior clerkship experience.

Judge Kaye's taste in law schools was eclectic. Nine clerks attended her alma mater, New York University Law School, and a number graduated from other top-tier law schools, such as Columbia, Cornell, Georgetown, Harvard, Michigan, Pennsylvania, and Yale. Still other clerks attended Albany, Brooklyn,

Cardozo, Fordham, Houston, Kansas, Seton Hall, and Syracuse. Naturally, she was gender-blind in her hiring practices, with the division between men and women clerks almost exactly 50/50.[56] She also hired clerks who were of color and openly gay. Many clerkship candidates came to the Judge's attention on the recommendation of personal and professional friends. Her husband's law firm served as a farm team, too, providing a training ground for a number of clerks.

My own journey to Judge Kaye's chambers was unusual. The first time she and I spoke was in August 1987, when I was a litigation associate at a Manhattan law firm. The Court of Appeals had extended me an offer to join its Central Research staff, which performs legal research to aid the judges in considering motions and jurisdictional issues. The law firm was reluctant to have me leave at just that moment. But Judge Kaye, who then oversaw Central Staff, intervened with the firm and facilitated my arrival at the court.

Soon thereafter, Judge Kaye asked Central Staff to provide the court with a background paper on critical legal studies (CLS)—a radical movement in the 1980s with a seemingly growing following in legal academic circles. The movement's adherents produced scholarly books and articles and sponsored well-attended conferences. None of the judges on the court held a candle for CLS, which rejected any distinction between law and politics and argued "that all judicial efforts at principled decision-making are necessarily doomed to failure."[57] Nevertheless, Judge Kaye, who maintained connections to the legal academy,[58] wanted to know what all the fuss was about with the "Crits" (as they were commonly known).[59]

I had a preexisting interest in legal philosophy and volunteered to work on the CLS project. When I submitted my report in late November 1987, Judge Kaye thanked me and remained "curious" about the Crits' "apparent ascendency today." "What's good about them?" she asked. Next to nothing, I answered, predicting (correctly as it turned out) the movement had no future. My work must have made an impression. A few months later she agreed to participate in an academic conference on contract theory at which a prominent Crit would be making a presentation, and she asked me to help her prepare a rebuttal. I leaped at the opportunity, sending her four memos over the next several weeks. She peppered me with questions and asked for my opinion. She also took me along to the conference, where I watched her vivisect an earnest but benighted professor who touted the CLS party line that "law is really nothing at all."[60] The entire experience was exhilarating.

The next time Judge Kaye was in the courthouse she summoned me to her chambers. Without forewarning, she asked a question that changed my life:

Would I be her law clerk? "Yes," I said instantaneously. I was at once shocked, overwhelmed, and overjoyed.

This was just the first of many surprises Judge Kaye sprang on me over what ripened into a friendship spanning three decades. The next one came shortly before my clerkship began. Judge Kaye called to talk about my start date, in the course of which she asked where I was going to live in New York City. Her home chambers were located in the Helmsley Building on 200 Park Avenue. I told her that my apartment search had not yet begun, but, rest assured, it would soon. Unconvinced, she took matters into her own hands. Soon she called with amazing news: she found for me a studio apartment, with affordable rent, in an upscale neighborhood, located four blocks from her chambers!

The Work of a Kaye Clerk

The work of a judge's clerk at the Court of Appeals varies depending on whether or not the court is in session at Court of Appeals Hall in Albany—the seat of state government. During my clerkship, the court held eight sessions a year, each usually lasting two weeks, when the judges heard oral argument and conferenced cases daily.[61] A typical session was an intense, fascinating, grueling experience. The court's seven judges decided about three hundred appeals a year in published writings and more than four thousand requests for appellate review.[62] Given this enormous caseload, session days for a clerk began at about 7:30 a.m. and lasted until midnight.[63] The long hours provided no cause for complaint, though; Judge Kaye was invariably at her desk around 5:00 a.m.[64]

The court processed appeals through a "hot bench" system that required all of the judges to carefully prepare every case before oral argument. Writings were assigned by a random draw. As Judge Kaye explained it, "after oral argument . . . the judges picking in order of seniority from among index cards, each bearing a case name, which were arrayed face down on a table."[65] Each judge assigned a case delivered an oral report about it at the court's conference the next morning, with a recommendation (affirm, reverse, modify) and an explanation.[66] This was followed by commentary from each of the other judges, sitting around a circular conference table, in inverse order of seniority.[67] Ordinarily, if the reporting judge carried a majority, he or she would write the opinion for the court. Otherwise, the junior judge in the majority would take the writing.[68]

Immediately after drawing a case, Judge Kaye came back to chambers and began preparing her report for conference. Sometimes she would "go back and forth" (as she put it) on how to vote. As she weighed the merits of the case, she was always willing to listen to her clerks' views. But once her mind was made up, that was it—she was unmovable. Nor was there any doubt who made the decision or determined the rationale for it. Some clerks may believe they influenced how the judge voted on cases. But I'm not one of them. Judge Kaye knew her own mind and had vast experience in life and law. She hardly needed a law clerk to think for her.

In deciding cases, Judge Kaye had no agenda or fixed ideology. She understood the limits of the judicial function and honored the principle of stare decis. In hard cases, where precedent did not compel a particular outcome, she developed legal principles through the common law case-by-case approach. Her instincts were pragmatic.[69] She asked herself and her clerks whether a new rule or potential result made sense.[70] And, in answering that question, she brought to bear the full measure of her life's "experience ... [and] moral core."[71] She was no judicial sentimentalist. But, as one former clerk observed, she "never lost sight of the lives behind each case."[72] A marriage between "head and heart" sums up the process of decision for Judge Kaye.[73]

The court's conferences began at 10:00 a.m. sharp. As soon as Judge Kaye left for conference, I joined clerks from other chambers in a room in the courthouse where coffee and crackers were available. The clerks discussed and debated the cases on the calendar, current events, and anything else that piqued our interest. These "coffees," as the clerks called them, were fun, providing an opportunity in an informal setting to socialize and, occasionally, pick up intelligence about what the other judges (or at least their clerks) thought about the cases.

After conference, Judge Kaye returned to chambers, where my co-clerk and I eagerly awaited hearing how the court voted in response to her case report. We then went over the cases on the calendar that day. Oral argument began at 2:00 p.m., and 1:00 p.m. on Fridays, and consumed the afternoon. The judges would then go out to dinner together at a local restaurant. Afterward, Judge Kaye came back to the courthouse and spent the balance of the evening preparing for the morning conference.[74] This cycle repeated itself day after day until the session was completed, and I was finally able to get a good night's sleep.

Albany sessions were usually followed by three weeks in "Home Chambers," each judge having chambers near their residences located throughout the state.[75] The judges and their clerks used the intersessions to draft opinions, study briefs for upcoming cases, review requests for permission to appeal in civil and criminal cases, and decide occasional orders to show cause for emergency relief.[76] The judges also fulfilled other judicial and professional responsibilities.[77]

A "thunderous quiet" prevailed in Judge Kaye's home chambers in Manhattan.[78] We were a small group—the Judge, two clerks, and a secretary. There was so much work to do that we didn't have much time for small talk and idle chatter. But the Judge's door was always open. She not only welcomed hearing what was on my mind, she insisted on it. Every day—sometimes multiple times a day—she came into my office to see how I was progressing on whatever was on my desk. She often treated my co-clerk and me to working lunches, setting a table in the conference room for the three of us to eat and talk about the cases.

Opinions

Most of a clerks' intersession was spent working on draft opinions. Judge Kaye would have her clerks prepare a first draft, providing guidance about the line of reasoning she wanted to take in the opinion. While always polite and considerate (she never raised her voice), she had high expectations for our work product. Clarity of expression, cogent analysis, and technical proficiency were a sine qua non for the first draft. But she wanted more than that—especially in terms of the thoroughness of our research. The cases and other authorities cited in litigants' briefs were only a starting point. Frequently she had me do a deep dive into treatises, law review articles, legislative history, and case law from other state and federal courts.[79] She looked to law review articles for "the newest thinking on the subject, for a sense of the direction of the law and how the case before us fits within it, for a more global yet profound perspective on the law and its social context than any individual case presents."[80] Illustrative of her propensity to rely on secondary authorities was a 1990 opinion involving lawyer regulation that cited ethics advisory opinions from sixteen states other than New York, fourteen federal court decisions, six law review articles, five treatises, and state court decisions from California, Illinois, and Washington.[81]

After receiving a first draft of an opinion, Judge Kaye took control of the writing process. She viewed each opinion assigned to her as an opportunity to paint a masterpiece. Her attention to detail was incomparable; nothing escaped her attention. She was hyper-intelligent and intellectually rigorous. She composed in longhand; a beautiful cursive that flowed out of a blue felt pen held in her left hand. She wrote with astonishing speed, making prodigious use of dashes.[82] Widely regarded as one of the finest legal writers of her generation, her prose was concise, precise, dazzlingly graceful, and always unmistakably hers, and her opinions could educate, inspire, instruct, or obscure, as the occasion warranted.[83] Then, as now, the court sometimes decided cases without a full written opinion, using instead a short unsigned memorandum. But anyone familiar with Judge Kaye's distinct writing style could easily spot an unsigned memorandum opinion written by her.[84]

When Judge Kaye gave me back a marked-up first draft, I often could see little of my original text. It was now buried underneath her edits and interpolations, accompanied by inserts written on separate sheets of paper. I would prepare a second draft, incorporating her revisions and proposed tweaks of my own. This resulted in a third draft, and a fourth, whatever it took to get the opinion just right. In the process, we exchanged ideas and talked about language and cases to cite or distinguish, as the case may be. Lawyer Heaven indeed.

Bench Memos

During home chamber intersessions, I spent a significant amount of time preparing bench memos for upcoming cases. The Judge let my co-clerk and me divide-up among ourselves the cases on the calendar. Once one of us took a case, we were then responsible for drafting a bench memo for it and doing whatever else Judge Kaye required until the case was finally resolved. A typical bench memo would summarize the facts, questions presented, lower court decisions, the parties' argument, and applicable law, and offer a recommendation on how the case should be decided. For each session day, Judge Kaye put together a three-ring binder, with a tab for each case scheduled for oral argument. The bench memos were placed in the binder behind the corresponding tabs, along with copies of the lower court decisions and relevant case law, statutes, and regulations. The Judge would take the binder with her, along with the parties' briefs, when she went on the bench to hear oral argument.

Extrajudicial Articles

Judge Kaye provided me with several opportunities to work on extrajudicial writings and speeches. Notwithstanding the demands of her position as an associate judge, she diligently kept abreast of emerging trends in society and the law. One way she did this—and in the process help shape the path of the law—was by researching and writing articles for law reviews and other professional publications. While a judge of the court she published over two hundred articles[85]—on a "kaleidoscopic range of topics"[86]—"confront[ing] as educator, scholar and advocate many of the most important issues facing our country."[87]

The articles on which we worked covered a wide range of subjects, including the role of academic law review writing in judicial decision-making,[88] constitutional common law,[89] and the value of amicus briefs in appellate litigation.[90] I provided research assistance, served as a sounding board, and offered constructive criticism. Unlike an appeal, where the Judge was constrained by the record and applicable law, the articles allowed her to experiment with new ideas. She took obvious delight in these projects, and her enthusiasm was infectious. Working on articles and speeches provided a welcome respite from the ceaseless flow of appeals and motions that came before the court.

Requests for the Court to Grant Leave to Appeal

Although the court decided thousands of civil and criminal requests for leave to appeal (the equivalent of a motion for certiorari at the U.S. Supreme Court), I spent little time assisting Judge Kaye with this important work. Once in a while she would ask me for my opinion about whether the court should take a case. But that was usually the extent of my participation. There were a few reasons for this. First, the court's Central Staff did a superb job of researching and writing reports for the judges on civil motions for leave to appeal, and there was no point having a chamber's clerk, like me, cover the same ground as a Central Staffer. Also, two of my co-clerks were former prosecutors, and the Judge would turn to them for assistance on criminal leave applications. Most of all, the Judge had a keen grasp of the type of legal issue that warranted Court of Appeals review. So she could quickly size up a case and determine whether it was "leaveworthy" (in the court's parlance).

The Relationship between Judge and Clerk

Judge Kaye had a unique personality and commanding presence. She stood tall, 5'10" or 5'11"; spoke in a melodic voice; and was always meticulously dressed, wearing colorful blouses and red shoes (which later became her trademark).[91] Warmth, dignity, elegance, gravitas, rectitude, and high intelligence exuded from her every word and movement. She was always composed, always appropriate, and never spoke ill of others (at least to her law clerks). Some clerks found her intimidating,[92] but she had deep empathy for people and never forgot from whence she came. Nor did she stand on ceremony. Telephone callers to chambers were often surprised to discover the person answering the phone was not a receptionist, but rather the Judge. Time and again, she intercepted calls for me from my father (who was a lawyer) and regaled him with exaggerated descriptions of my prowess as a clerk.

Judge Kaye had a wonderful sense of humor and quick wit, which she deployed regularly.[93] She spoke freely about the things outside of work that gave her joy, especially her family[94] and love of opera and theater. She had a lovely singing voice and, every once in a while, burst into an aria she heard the night before at the Metropolitan Opera House, where she and her husband had season tickets.[95] When Andrew Lloyd Webber's latest musical opened on Broadway in 1990, she saw it multiple times and took me to see it near the end of my clerkship. Similarly, when a hero of hers, U.S. Supreme Court Justice William J. Brennan Jr.[96] came to Manhattan to receive an award, she took my co-clerk, his girlfriend, and me to the private reception and dinner honoring him.

Many a clerk forged strong personal bonds with the Judge. Sometimes her interest in a clerk's welfare and personal life was akin to a doting mother. Of this, I have firsthand knowledge. She had heard through the grapevine that for a long time I had been dating a woman who clerked for another judge on the court, but that we were not engaged to be married. The Judge was displeased. Whereas, in her politics, she was a staunch Democrat with progressive views on social issues,[97] in her personal life, she was a traditionalist, with conservative values.

So, one day, the Judge walked into my office, with a frown on her face, and asked how long my girlfriend and I had dated. The question startled me. But I collected myself and replied, "about six years." The Judge then went where few employers dare go: "Do you intend to marry her?" "Well, I suppose so," I answered. She shot back, "Well, why don't you get to it!" and left the room. The next day, the Judge handed me a piece of paper, with the name and phone number of a jeweler on it. She said, "Call that number." I dutifully complied, met with the jeweler, purchased an engagement ring, and proposed to my girlfriend, who (thank heavens) accepted. Judge Kaye attended our wedding and, with tears in her eyes, watched my wife and I exchange vows. After twenty-seven years of marriage, and three beautiful children, I can truthfully say that Judith Kaye was the proximate cause of my family.

The end of a clerkship with Judge Kaye often marked the beginning of a lifelong relationship. Former and current clerks periodically got together with her at reunions. The most memorable of these was held in 2003, to celebrate her twentieth anniversary on the Court of Appeals and tenth anniversary as chief judge. We gathered at the John Jay Homestead in Katonah, New York, and the theme of the evening was "From Jay to Kaye." Jay was the first chief judge of New York's court system and the first chief justice of the U.S. Supreme

Court. With characteristic attention to detail, Judge Kaye had transported to Katonah the portrait of John Jay that hangs above the chief judge's chair in the courtroom at Court of Appeals Hall.[98]

Judge Kaye took great pleasure watching her former clerks find fulfilment in their personal and professional lives. Behind her desk, she kept pictures of her clerks' small children, which occupied increasing amounts of shelf space, as families grew. Many of her clerks have gone on to brilliant careers, becoming judges, partners in prestigious law firms, law professors, and senior officials in the federal and state government. Representative of such success stories were the three individuals whose clerkships overlapped with mine. Laura Johnson (1988–90), a graduate of Barnard College and Columbia Law School, is a Civil Court judge in Manhattan. Dierdre Roney (1990–92), a graduate of Harvard University and Columbia Law School, is general counsel at the Massachusetts State Ethics Commission. And Michael J. Garcia (1990–92), valedictorian of his class at Albany Law School and a former U.S. attorney for the Southern District of New York, is an associate judge of the Court of Appeals.

Judge Kaye was a master at the art of keeping in touch. Every year I received in the mail a birthday card and gift (usually a tie). We talked often about extra-judicial projects on which she was working, and we would catch up over lunch in her chambers. When she became chief judge, she appointed former clerks to serve on professional committees and bodies, providing further opportunities to get together.

My relationship with the Judge came full circle near the end of her life. After she stepped down from the bench, she became chair of the New York State Commission on Judicial Nomination, which nominates candidates for the Court of Appeals. In 2013, I was appointed counsel to the commission[99] and, in a sense, reprised my role as her law clerk. During the two and a half years we worked together on the commission, my esteem for her (already immense) grew into awe.

Despite the cancer spreading through her body, she discharged the responsibilities of commission chair with consummate skill and diligence. Her final public act was sending to Governor Andrew Cuomo the commission's recommendations for a vacancy in the office she graced for nearly sixteen years: chief judge of the Court of Appeals and the State of New York. She was in pain, coughing, and weak. But nothing could stop her from making sure that the state's judicial branch would be left in good hands, which it was when the governor appointed Janet DiFiore chief judge. In her final days, Chief Judge Kaye entrusted her black robe to Chief Judge DiFiore, who wore it proudly upon taking the oath of office during her investiture ceremony.[100]

In 1886, Oliver Wendell Holmes Jr. gave a lecture to college students on the "Profession of the Law," closing with these stirring words: "I say—and I say no longer with any doubt—that a man may live greatly in the law as well as elsewhere; that there as well as elsewhere . . . [he] may wear his heart out after the unattainable."[101] Holmes did not envision a world where women were full-fledged members of the bar and bench. But his words aptly describe Judith Kaye's career. No state court jurist lived a greater life in the law than she. Future generations will see in her a singular example of how a person born without advantages can rise to greatness and a lawyer can make the world more gentle and just.[102] She was a chief judge for the ages.[103]

Notes

1. See New York State Court of Appeals, "Statement on the Passing of Former Chief Judge Judith S. Kaye from Acting Chief Judge Eugene F. Pigott, Jr.," press release, January 7, 2016, https://www.nycourts.gov/ctapps/news/PressRel/01-07-16-CJ-Kaye.pdf ("Chief Judge Kaye passed away last night. She was the first woman Judge and Chief Judge in Court of Appeal's history. She was the Court's longest serving Chief Judge. She served tirelessly and compassionately for over 25 years. The Court of Appeals and the entire New York State Court System is saddened by her loss. She has been an inspiration to all of us who were privileged to know her and she will be greatly missed").

2. "Judith Kaye's opinions on the Court of Appeals span a quarter century, from 1983 through 2008, and about 50 volumes of the New York Reports, from 60 N.Y.2d through 10 N.Y.3d." Janet DiFiore, "A Tribute to Chief Judge Judith S. Kaye," *Brooklyn Law Review* 81 (2015): 1379–80. She wrote "some 522 majority and over 100 concurrences and dissents during her time on the bench." Trevor W. Morrison and Julie B. Ehrlich, "Chief Judge Kaye as Model," *New York University Law Review* 92 (2017): 2.

3. See Jonathan Lippman, "Chief Judge S. Kaye: A Visionary Third Branch Leader," *New York University Law Review* 84 (2009): 661 ("During nearly sixteen years at the head of the New York State courts, Judith Kaye virtually rewrote the script for how a twenty-first century chief judge can lead the courts in delivering justice in ways that are relevant and responsive to the evolving needs and expectations of our citizenry. Her jurisprudential and administrative achievements have left an imprint on New York State history."); Jonathan Lippman, "Chief Judge S. Kaye: A Visionary Third Branch Leader," *New York University Law Review* 84 (2009): 648–49 ("Chief Judge Kaye has spearheaded numerous administrative reforms, all of which have made the New York courts fairer and more effective. . . . Essentially, Judith Kaye's tenure as Chief Judge has seen more than twenty-five years of human concern, imagination, and effective action, all harnessed in the interest of an improved state justice system").

4. See Randall T. Shepard, "Judith Kaye as a Chief among Chiefs," *New York University Law Review* 84 (2009): 821; see also Jonathan Lippman, "Judith S. Kaye: The Great

Reformer," *New York University Law Review* 92 (2017): 86–92 ("She is clearly one of the most influential jurists of her generation, a brilliant legal scholar with a distinctive, clear writing style. She grappled with the most significant, complex legal issues, and, in the process, contributed her singular humanity and erudition to the evolution of the common law and state constitutionalism").

5. See Sam Roberts, "Judith S. Kaye, First Woman to Serve as New York's Chief Judge, Dies at 77," *New York Times,* January 7, 2016.

6. Judith S. Kaye, "The Importance of State Courts: A Snapshot of the New York Court of Appeals," *Annual Survey of American Law* (1994): xiii. As I have written elsewhere, Judge Kaye "idolized Cardozo—indeed, she personally identified with him—and was a scholar of his life and works." Henry M. Greenberg, "The Making of a Judge's Judge: Judith S. Kaye's 1987 Cardozo Lecture," *Brooklyn Law Review* 81, no. 4 (2016): 1365. See, e.g., Judith S. Kaye, "Cardozo: A Law Classic," review of Cardozo, Andrew L. Kaufman, *Harvard Law Review* 112, no. 5 (1999): 1026–29 ("I occupy Cardozo's desk in Albany Chambers and his center chair at the Court's daily conferences and oral arguments, his spittoon at my feet [confident that neither of us would dream of using it for its intended purpose]. My home is a mere five blocks from his, on the Upper West Side of Manhattan. My husband and I are long-time members of the Spanish and Portuguese Synagogue—his congregation—and friends of Cardozo family members").

7. See New York Constitution art. XIX, § 2(b) ("The court of appeals . . . shall consist of the chief judge and . . . six . . . associate judges[.] . . . The official terms of the chief judge and the six associate judges shall be fourteen years").

8. The Court of Appeals was created by the New York State Constitution of 1846 "to bring harmony and unity into the law." Stuart M. Cohen, 1997 Annual Report of the Clerk of the Court to the Judges of the Court of Appeals of the State of New York 2 (1998) (quoting Historical Resume of the Judiciary Article, Problems Relating to Judicial Administration and Organization, vol. 9, 1938, New York State Const. Conv. Comm., at 6).

9. Alan D. Scheinkman, "The Civil Jurisdiction of the New York Court of Appeals: The Rule and Role of Finality," *St. John's Law Review* 54 (1979): 446.

10. John P. Asiello, 2016 Annual Report of the Clerk of the Court to the Judges of the Court of Appeals of the State of New York 2 (2016) (hereinafter Asiello, 2016 Annual Report).

11. Kaye, "Importance of State Courts," xiv.

12. Judith S. Kaye, "My Life as Chief Judge: The Chapter on Juries," *New York State Bar Association Journal* 78 (2006): 10–11.

13. See Steven C. Krane, "Judith Smith Kaye," in *The Judges of the New York Court of Appeals: A Biographical History*, edited by Albert M Rosenblatt (New York: Fordham University Press, 2007); Steven C Krane, "Dedication to Judith S. Kaye," *Albany Law Review* 70 (2006): 808; Roberts, "Judith S. Kaye."

14. Krane, "Judith Smith Kaye."; Krane, "Dedication to Judith S. Kaye," 808; Roberts, "Judith S. Kaye."

15. Ibid.

16. Judith S. Kaye, "Reflections on Opportunity in Life and Law," *Brooklyn Law Review* 81 (2015): 384.

17. Krane, "Judith Smith Kaye," 806; Krane, "Dedication to Judith S. Kaye," 808.; Roberts, "Judith S. Kaye."

18. Ibid.

19. Ibid.

20. Ibid.

21. Ibid.

22. Krane, "Judith Smith Kaye," 806.; Krane, "Dedication to Judith S. Kaye," 808.

23. Associated Press, "Stephen R. Kaye, 75, Litigation Lawyer. Dies," *New York Times*, November 3, 2006.

24. Ibid.

25. Krane, "Judith Smith Kaye," 806; Krane, "Dedication to Judith S. Kaye," 809; Roberts, "Judith S. Kaye."

26. Ibid.

27. Ibid.

28. Ibid.

29. Krane, "Judith Smith Kaye," 806–7; Krane, "Dedication to Judith S. Kaye," 809.; Roberts, "Judith S. Kaye."

30. Judith S. Kaye, "My Freshman Years on the Court of Appeals," *Judicature* 70 (1986): 166.

31. Judith S. Kaye, "A Five-Year Retrospective," Address at New York State Family Court Judges Conference, September 24, 1988, 10.

32. *People v. Smith,* 63 N.Y.2d 41, 468 N.E.2d 879, 479 N.Y.S.2d 706 (N.Y. 1984), *cert. denied,* 469 U.S. 1227 (1985).

33. See Ruth Bader Ginsburg, "In Praise of Judith S. Kaye," *New York University Law Review* 84 (2009): 653–54 ("[Judge Kaye] ... understood that New York's constitution and common law had important roles to play in the protection of fundamental human rights. On her watch, the state's constitution and laws were read to advance due process, freedom of expression, freedom from unreasonable searches and seizures, and genuinely equal opportunity. The U.S. Supreme Court's sometimes constricted reading of parallel provisions of the Federal Constitution did not overwhelm her judgment"); Vincent Martin Bonventre, editor's foreword to *Albany Law Review* 70 (2007): 795 (describing Kaye as the "leading authority on state constitutional law" and a "thoughtful proponent of independent state adjudication").

34. 77 N.Y.2d 235, 567 N.E.2d 1270, 549 N.Y.S.2d 906 (N.Y. 1987).

35. Ibid., 249; 567 N.E.2d, 1277; 549 N.Y.S.2d, 913. Judge Kaye explained: "This State, a cultural center for the Nation, has long provided a hospitable climate for the free exchange of ideas. That tradition is embodied in the free speech guarantee of the New York State Constitution, beginning with the ringing declaration that '[e]very citizen may freely speak, write and publish ... sentiments on all subjects.' Those words,

unchanged since the adoption of the constitutional provision in 1821, reflect the deliberate choice of the New York State Constitutional Convention not to follow the language of the First Amendment, ratified 30 years earlier, but instead to set forth our basic democratic ideal of liberty of the press in strong affirmative terms."

36. Krane, *Judith Smith Kaye*, 811–12; Krane, "Dedication to Judith S. Kaye," 810. On November 6, 1992, Wachtler was arrested for allegedly having harassed and threatened a former lover and her young daughter. Four days later, he resigned as chief judge and eventually pleaded guilty to a felony charge, serving eleven months in federal prison.

37. Helaine M. Barnett, "Chief Judge Kaye's Legacy of Innovation and Access to Justice," *New York University Law Review* 92 (2017): 6.

38. DiFiore, "Tribute to Chief Judge Judith S. Kaye," 1379.

39. Roberts, "Judith S. Kaye"; see also Susan N. Herman, "Portrait of a Judge: Judith S. Kaye, Dichotomies, and State Constitutional Law," *Albany Law Review* 75 (2011): 1991–92 ("When you factor in the amount of time that it consumes to be chief judge of all the courts of New York State as Chief Administrative Judge and to have the full workload of a judge on the Court of Appeals, it is nothing less than astonishing that Judge Kaye managed during that same period of time to publish over two hundred articles").

40. DiFiore, "Tribute to Chief Judge Judith S. Kaye," 1379–80. Specifically, Chief Judge Kaye "transformed and modernized the entire court system, with a special focus on serving the needs of families and children, reforming the jury system, and establishing Community Courts, Drug Treatment Courts, Domestic Violence Courts, and Mental Health Courts to deal more effectively with the modern-day societal problems swelling our court dockets." See also Judith S. Kaye, "Delivering Justice Today: A Problem-Solving Approach," *Yale Law & Policy Review* 22, no. 1 (2004): 143–45 (discussing establishment and progress of problem-solving community, domestic violence, and drug courts); Lippman, "Judith S. Kaye: The Great Reformer," 86–92 (summarizing court reforms instituted by Judge Kaye as chief judge of the state of New York); Krane, "Dedication to Judith S. Kaye," 811–13.

41. See Albert M. Rosenblatt, "Judith Kaye: Beyond Scholarship, to the World of Style and Mirth," *New York University Law Review* 92 (2017): 97 ("As Chief, Judge Kaye generated collegial qualities that set the right tone. This did not happen by accident. She worked at it. . . . She sought consensus whenever possible"); Richard C. Wesley, "A Portrait of Judith S. Kaye," *New York University Law Review* 84 (2009): 678 ("In the conference room, Judith was always prepared. She listened carefully to the views of her colleagues, and she conducted the business of the court with fairness and dignity. Judith set the tone; Judith guarded the flame").

42. DiFiore, "Tribute to Chief Judge Judith S. Kaye," 1380.

43. *Matter of Jacobs*, 86 N.Y.2d 651, 660 N.E.2d 397, 636 N.Y.S.2d 716 (N.Y. 1995).

44. *Campaign for Fiscal Equity, Inc. v. State of New York*, 100 N.Y.2d 893, 908, 801 N.E.2d 326, 332, 769 N.Y.S.2d 106, 111 (N.Y. 2003).

45. 7 N.Y.3d 338, 55 N.E.2d 1, 821 N.Y.S.2d 770 (N.Y. 2006), *abrogated by Obergefell v. Hodges*, 135 S. Ct. 2584 (2015).

46. *Hernandez v. Robles,* 7 N.Y.3d at 357–379, 55 N.E.2d at 5–22, 821 N.Y.S.2d at 774–791.

47. Ibid., 391; 855 N.E.2d at 30, 821 N.Y.S.2d at 799 (Kaye, C. J., dissenting).

48. *Obergefell v. Hodges,* 135 S. Ct. 2071 (2015).

49. See Roberta A. Kaplan, "The Dissent That Paved the Way to Equal Dignity: Chief Judge Judith S. Kaye's Dissent in *Hernandez,*" *New York University Law Review* 92 (2017): 62. ("There can be no question that Chief Judge Kaye's *Hernandez* dissent had a significant impact in paving the way towards marriage equality. To date, Chief Judge Kaye's dissent has been cited at least 116 times, in 16 cases and 150 law review articles. It was cited explicitly in at least seven state court decisions (California, Connecticut, Maryland, New York, New Jersey, Iowa, and Montana, and two federal marriage equality decisions in the Ninth and Tenth Circuits"). The author of this article, Roberta A. Kaplan, graduated from Harvard University and Columbia Law School and clerked for Judge Kaye from 1995 to 1996. She successfully argued before the U.S. Supreme Court on behalf of her client, Edith Windsor, in *United States v. Windsor,* 133 S. Ct. 2675 (2013), a landmark decision requiring the federal government to recognize same-sex marriages.

50. See Krane, "Dedication to Judith S. Kaye," 807–8 ("She turned down offers to become a justice of the Supreme Court of the United States and our nation's Attorney General, deciding instead to devote her efforts to the courts of the State of New York, serving as our Chief Judge for the past 14 years, longer than any of her 21 predecessors."); see also Stephen Labaton, "Clinton Nears Choice for High Court Nominee," *New York Times,* May 20, 1993, 17, http://www.nytimes.com/1993/05/20/us/clinton -nears-choice-for-high-court-nominee.html (noting that "Judith Kaye, the chief judge of the New York Court of Appeals, withdrew from consideration" for the vacancy on the United States Supreme Court created by the retirement of Justice Byron R. White"); Neil A. Lewis, "Clinton Expected to Name Woman Attorney General," *New York Times,* December 9, 1992 (stating that Judge Kaye was a finalist to serve as U.S. Attorney General).

51. The New York State Constitution forbids a judge of the Court of Appeals from serving past age seventy. See N.Y. CONST. art. VI, § 25(b) ("Each judge of the court of appeals . . . shall retire on the last day of December in the year in which he or she reaches the age of 70").

52. Roberts, "Judith S. Kaye."

53. For a short biography of Lehman, see Henry M. Greenberg, "Irving Lehman," in *The Judges of the New York Court of Appeals: A Biographical History,* edited by Albert M. Rosenblatt (New York: Fordham University Press, 2007), 451–67.

54. The last project Judge Kaye assigned to me as her law clerk was updating the 1990 version of this booklet.

55. This figure includes those attorneys of whom I am aware who served more than six months with Judge Kaye.

56. Twenty of her clerks were men; nineteen were women.

57. Girardeau A. Spann, "A Critical Legal Studies Perspective on Contract Law and Practice," *Annual Survey of American Law* (1988): 225.

58. Robert F. Williams, "Tribute to Judge Judith Kaye: A Renaissance Lawyer," *Annual Survey of American Law* (1994).

59. Judith S. Kaye, "Commentary on a Critical Legal Studies Perspective on Contract Law and Practice," *Annual Survey of American Law* (1998): 266 ("The movement has scholarly books, scholarly articles, annual conferences and a seemingly growing following in academic circles. These facts give me real pause. I say to myself, there just has to be something here for all the rest of us. I just can't seem to find it").

60. Spann, "A Critical Legal Studies Perspective," 257.

61. Judith S. Kaye, "The Importance of State Courts: A Snapshot of the New York Court of Appeals," *Annual Survey of American Law* (1994): xii.

62. Donald M. Sheraw, 1990 Annual Report of the Clerk of the Court to the Judges of the Court of Appeals of the State of New York 3 (1991) (stating That Court Decided 287 Appeals In 1990); Donald M. Sheraw, 1989 Annual Report of the Clerk of the Court to the Judges of the Court of Appeals of the State of New York 4 (1990) (stating That Court Decided 295 Appeals In 1988); Donald M. Sheraw, 1988 Annual Report of The Clerk of the Court to the Judges of The Court of Appeals of the State of New York 3 (1989) (stating That Court decided 369 appeals in 1988). In 1990, for example, the court decided 967 civil motions for leave to appeal, and 3,066 applications for leave to appeal in criminal cases were assigned to individual judges, with each judge receiving an average of 438 applications.

63. Kaye, "Importance of State Courts," xii n.3.

64. Rosenblatt, "Judith Kaye," 98.

65. Kaye, "Importance of State Courts," xii n.3.

66. Ibid.

67. See Rosenblatt, "Judith Kaye," 97 ("After oral argument and round the conference table, the deliberative process began with a presentation by the judge who 'drew' the case, out of the hat so to speak, and never by assignment. It is a random draw, sometimes followed by cries of delight or pain. This initial presentation included a recommendation [affirm, reverse, modify, and why], followed by commentary from the other six judges in inverse order of seniority. By this inversion, the newer judges speak first, so as to be uninfluenced by their 'elders,' with the Chief Judge going last").

68. Kaye, "Importance of State Courts," xii n.3.

69. See Helen Hershkoff, "Chief Judge Kaye's Dynamic Legacy," *New York University Law Review* 92 (2017): 43 ("Whether writing for the court or in dissent, Kaye never strayed from the shrewd institutional realism that informed her work as an administrator. She saw the courts as partners with the legislature in the enforcement of rights, and appreciated that each played a distinct role subject to important and traditional boundaries. Moreover, her opinions and extra-judicial writing never succumbed to the nirvana fallacy; she resisted ascribing heroic capability to judges or disparaging elected

officials as inept or myopic. Rather, her pragmatic, functional approach kept her clear-eyed about shared institutional limits, but optimistic about possibilities for reform and adaptation").

70. See Krane, "Dedication to Judith S. Kaye," 810 ("Many commentators have tried to analyze her judicial philosophy, or to detect patterns or trends in her decision-making over the passage of time, and it is doubtless that her writings will be the subject of scholarly debate for decades to come. At bottom, however, Kaye's judicial opinions can be harmonized under a single theme, indeed, a single question: "Does it make sense?" That mantra, coupled with an abiding respect for stare decisis and the stability of the law, are the overarching principles that can be extracted from the jurisprudence of Judith Kaye").

71. Only a few years after she was appointed to the court, Judge Kaye expressed the idea that informed her decision-making over the course of her long career on the bench: "The danger is not that judges will bring the full measure of their experience, their moral core, their every human capacity to bear in the difficult process of resolving the cases before them," she said. "It seems to me that a far greater danger exists if they do not." Judith S. Kaye, "Human Dimension in Appellate Judging: A Brief Reflection on a Timeless Concern," *Cornell Law Review* 73 (1987): 1015.

72. Kaplan, "Dissent That Paved the Way," 60; see also Roberta A. Kaplan, "Tribute to Judith S. Kaye," *Albany Law Review* 70 (2006): 801 ("Chief Judge demonstrated 'an ever-present awareness that cases involve human beings and that the role of the courts is to balance a respect for abstract principles with an appreciation for the fact that in the real world, there is no such thing as an abstract principle since the application of a rule or precedent in any particular situation necessarily has an impact on peoples' lives'").

73. Judith S. Kaye, "State Courts at the Dawn of a New Century: Common Law Courts Reading Statutes and Constitutions," *New York University Law Review* 70 (1995): 2.

74. Kaye, "Importance of State Courts," xii n.3.

75. Ibid. at xiii.

76. Ibid.; Asiello, 2016 Annual Report, at 2.

77. Asiello, 2016 Annual Report, at 2.

78. Kaye, "My Freshman Years on the Court of Appeals," 166.

79. See Judith S. Kaye, "One Judge's View of Academic Law Review Writing," *Journal of Legal Education* 39, no. 3 (1989): 319 ("It is hard to think of completing an opinion without venturing into the literature, and ideally I like starting an opinion with good briefs and [law review] articles").

80. Ibid.

81. *Niesig v. Team*, 76 NY 2d 363 (1990).

82. See Rosenblatt, "Judith Kaye," 98. ("Judith . . . used dashes almost as her trademark. She was the queen of the dash, and it worked to perfection, as a stylish substitute for the comma").

83. Renowned legal writing teacher Bryan Garner is reported to have considered Judge Kaye among eighteen legal writers who are worth emulating. Dan Slater, "Tress and the Law, Judge Kaye's Last Legal Issue," *Wall Street Journal*, December 31, 2008.

84. See, e.g., Craig R. Levine, Joseph Lee Matalon, Mary C. Rothwell, Wendy H. Schwartz, and Elise A. Yablonski, "In the Matter of the Honorable Judith S. Kaye," *Annual Survey of American Law* (1994): xliii ("It's easy to spot a memorandum opinion drafted by Judge Kaye [memoranda are unsigned]. Look for concise, precise and graceful language").

85. For a partial list of Judge Kaye's published articles, see Krane, "Judith Smith Kaye," 821–24.; Herman, "Portrait of a Judge," 1983.

86. See Krane, "Judith Smith Kaye," 821–24.

87. Sandra Day O'Connor, "A Distinguished Path in Public Service," *New York University Law Review* 84 (2009): 663.

88. Kaye, "One Judge's View of Academic Law Review Writing."

89. Judith S. Kaye, "Common Law and State Constitutional Law as Full Partners in the Protection of Individual Rights," *Rutgers Law Journal* 23 (1991): 727.

90. Judith S. Kaye, "One Judge's View of Friends of the Court," *New York State Bar Journal* 61 (1989): 8.

91. See Wesley, "A Portrait of Judith S. Kaye," 679 (describing famous photograph taken of Judge Kaye by Annie Leibowitz and published in *Vanity Fair* magazine in 1998, showing the judge wearing her "trademark red shoes"). See also Jeffrey Toobin, "Special Kaye," *New Yorker*, December 15, 2008 ("Kaye's passion for clothes prompted the New York State Bar Association to designate her 'chief shopper,' and she retains an endearing vanity about her appearance").

92. See Levine et al., "Honorable Judith S. Kaye," xl ("Her breadth and depth of knowledge—about law or life—is intimidating to those [such as law clerks] trying to catch up").

93. See Rosenblatt, "Judith Kaye," 95 ("Judith could be howlingly funny"); Levine et al., "Honorable Judith S. Kaye," xlii ("she has a delightful sense of humor and quick wit").

94. See, e.g., Levine et al., xliii ("While her achievements as a lawyer and judge are well known, one cannot spend a day in Judge Kaye's company without realizing that her highest priority is her family, and how much support, dedication and love they receive from her, and she from them").

95. See ibid., xlii ("She attends the Metropolitan regularly; several opera-related posters adorn her Manhattan chambers; and one [applicant for a clerkship] . . . was treated to a judicial rendition of the Tosca aria E Lucevan during the interview").

96. See David H. Souter et al., "In Memoriam: William J. Brennan, Jr.," *Harvard Law Review* 111, no. 1 (1997): 14. See also Greenberg, "Making of a Judge's Judge," 1365–66 (discussing Justice Brennan's influence on Judge's Kaye's view of independent state constitutional adjudication).

97. See Toobin, "Special Kay," 97 ("In her politics, Kaye has reflected the liberal views of Mario Cuomo, the governor who, in 1983, when she was a Manhattan litigator, plucked her from the ranks to make her the first woman on the Court of Appeals").

98. Krane, "Judith Smith Kaye," 820.

99. See N.Y. State Commission on Judicial Nomination, "The Commission on Judicial Nomination Appoints New Counsel," press release, June 12, 2013).

100. See DiFiore, "Tribute to Chief Judge Judith S. Kaye," 1381 ("I was the beneficiary of many kind words and supportive gestures from Judith Kaye—but none more special than her final ones. On February 8, 2016, during my formal investiture ceremony in the magnificent courtroom in the Court of Appeals, I took the Oath of Office before the Governor and other State officials, my colleagues on the bench and at the bar, and every New Yorker, wearing Judith Kaye's black robe. She entrusted it to me in her final days, assuring me with her typical thoughtfulness and grace that it was only fitting that I should wear her robe while publicly pledging my own commitment to administer justice and discharge the duties of the office of Chief Judge. Needless to say, I was moved and honored beyond words").

101. The lecture is reprinted in Max Lerner, *The Mind and Faith of Justice Holmes: His Speeches, Essays, Letters, and Judicial Opinions* (New York: Routledge, 2017), 31.

102. See Krane, "Dedication to Judith S. Kaye," 814 ("Generations of lawyers will continue to look to her as a role model, the archetype of what can be made of a life in the law, and a stunning example of how a single individual from modest beginnings can, with perseverance and determination, realize her full potential and achieve greatness and immortality").

103. See Henry M. Greenberg, "Judith Smith Kaye: A Chief Judge for the Ages," *Albany Law Review* 79 (2015): 1249 ("We live in a cynical age. Displays of respect for public service and public servants are rare. The coarsening of public discourse quickens. Judith Kaye is our answer to the cynics. She was a miracle, the best of the best— a perfect blend of brilliance, compassion and practicality. Our state has produced many of America's greatest jurists. But none stood taller than Judith Kaye").

II Clerking for Federal District Court Judges

POLLY WIRTZMAN CRAIGHILL

Clerking for the Honorable Burnita Shelton Matthews

A Southern Gentle Woman

On July 26, 2016, I was in a hotel room in Reykjavik, Iceland, watching Hillary Rodham Clinton accept the Democratic nomination for president of the United States. A vision of Judge Burnita Shelton Matthews flashed in my mind. I saw the twinkle in her eye and the wry smile cross her lips. The Judge would have had the same smile and appreciation for the event that occurred in 2008 when Barack Obama was nominated for president. Politics aside, those two events and what I think would have been the Judge's reaction to those events so perfectly personify her. She was a great advocate of women's rights and a daughter of the Confederacy who believed in equal rights and equal justice for everyone.[1]

Burnita Shelton Matthews was an exceptional person. Her accomplishments by today's standards are inspiring. However, putting her life in historic context illustrates how impressive she really was.

The Judge was born in 1894 (almost a century before we began talking about a "glass ceiling") in Copiah County, Mississippi. She took over the motherly responsibilities of her four brothers at the age of sixteen when her mother died. In an interview with Amelia Fry she described her father as a "planter." I believe he actually had a plantation. Her father was the tax collector and clerk of the Chancery Court in Copiah County. Because she spent time in court with her father, she developed an interest in the law and felt comfortable in court.

Expectations for her, as a southern woman, were limited to being a gracious wife and mother. She honored the expectations to be "gracious," but she was unstoppable in what she succeeded in accomplishing. She worked while going to law school at night, because she knew her father, who had paid for her brothers to go to law school, would not do the same for her. When she graduated from law school she applied for a job as a lawyer at the Veterans Administration. The agency told her that it would never hire a woman in the legal department, so she opened her own law office.

Judge Matthews graduated from the National University Law School in 1919 (now George Washington University School of Law). She received her master of laws in 1920. When she passed the District of Columbia Bar in 1920, she was admitted to practice, but the DC Bar Association returned her application and the check for her dues. She kept that check and donated it to the Schlesinger Library at Harvard along with other papers. Despite the obstacles she faced, she always retained her positive attitude and never lost sight of her goals.

The Judge participated in the push for women's suffrage in the 1910s. In 1919, she was among several dozen women who regularly picketed the White House on Sundays on behalf of women's suffrage. "You could carry a banner," she recalled in a 1985 interview, "but if you spoke, you were arrested for speaking without a permit. So when they asked me why I was there, I didn't answer." She felt the Nineteenth Amendment did not go far enough. After women got the vote in 1920, she shifted the focus of her activities to secure equal rights for women in other areas. For instance, she worked for giving women the right to serve on juries, to do away with discrimination against women with reference to the guardianship of their children, to strengthen the laws on descent and distribution, and many other issues that would insure that men and women had equal rights.

She became the lawyer for the National Woman's Party, which was trying to persuade state legislatures to lift legal barriers to women. Judge Matthews researched state laws and drafted proposed bills. The National Woman's Party owned the property across the street from the Capitol, where the Supreme Court building is now located. In the 1920s, when Chief Justice William Howard Taft proposed acquiring the land for the court, she went to the chief justice's home to try to persuade him to look for another site. Her efforts failed, but she represented the party in the condemnation proceedings and won a generous settlement for it.

In 1949, when President Truman appointed her to be the first woman to serve on a United States district court, the appointment (while an honor) was also an adjustment. She was given the worst assignments, the heaviest caseload, and the least amount of collegial support. She handled the difficulties with her usual grace and dignity, determined not to complain and to do her best. She often recounted her early years on the bench to her law clerks as a way of emphasizing how we should focus on doing our best work no matter the circumstances. As Chief Judge John Sirica said when her portrait was presented to the court in February 1973, "She was a working Judge and in those days of the master calendar she took cases as they came, whether difficult or routine, asking no favors and offering no excuses."

Her work ethic, along with her formidable intellect, won Judge Matthews the admiration and respect of her fellow judges. She had the highest rate of affirmances by the United States Court of Appeals of any district court judge. The regard in which she was held was confirmed when she became a senior judge in 1968 (approximately twenty years after her appointment). She was repeatedly asked to serve as a senior judge on the Court of Appeals. She twice sat on the United States Court of Customs and Patent Appeals (the first woman to do so in the history of that court).[2]

The office atmosphere in her chambers was one of quiet grace, where guests were greeted with warm southern hospitality. The Judge was always gracious, but also very, very private. Yet her convictions were discreetly evidenced even by the décor in her workspace.

For instance, she loved to regale guests with tales of Judge Andrew Wylie, whose portrait hung in the outer office. When asked to choose a portrait of a federal judge to hang in her chambers, she initially selected the portrait of Andrew Wylie because she liked his face. Afterward though she learned that Judge Wylie was the judge who heard the writ of habeas corpus filed by Frederick Aiken, attorney for Mary Surratt.

Mary Surratt was the first female executed by the federal government; as a civilian, she was tried by a military tribunal under questionable circumstances. Judge Matthews had always believed in Mary Surratt's innocence. Handsome face or not, Judge Wylie's portrait was not going to be in her chambers until she did more research and learned that, in fact, Wylie had granted the writ (which had been set aside by President Andrew Johnson). Thus the portrait of Judge Wylie went up on her wall. Wylie was the hero, not the villain.

When Judge Matthews served on the bench, judges had one law clerk, a secretary, a messenger, and a United States marshal.[3] The Judge's criteria for hiring law clerks were gender-specific. She felt that none of the other judges hired women, so she would. The Judge relied on recommendations of former clerks as being able to recognize candidates who would be a good fit. I had the good fortune to have the Judge's first law clerk, Ellen Lee Park, as my mentor. Looking back after fifty years and meeting some of the other people who applied for the clerkship, I think Ellen Lee Park's recommendation had a great deal to do with my being selected. But I also think when the Judge interviewed me she saw my passion for equal rights and fairness. I brought to the office the idealism of a first-generation American.[4]

A federal clerkship is one of the best jobs a young lawyer can get upon graduation. It was my good fortune to spend the first two years of my professional career in the federal judiciary family under the tutelage of a truly remarkable human being.

My office as a law clerk was the biggest office I had ever seen. To this day I joke that it was the best office I had throughout my legal career. The office was at least twenty feet by ten feet. It was furnished with Persian rugs, a leather chair, a brass table, and other memorabilia that the Judge and her husband, Colonel Percy Matthews, had acquired on their travels. The office was lined with bookcases on three sides. The bookcases were filled with leather-bound volumes of the *Federal Supplement,* the *Federal Reporter, American Jurisprudence, West Law,* and the *Supreme Court Reporter.*

I loved to show off my office. My parents visited Washington often and always stopped by to talk to the Judge. On one occasion my uncle Nat was with them. Uncle Nat was born in 1898 in a small village in northeastern Romania. He loved books and spent time each day in the public library. He came into my office, admired the décor, and ran his fingers over the spine of those leather-bound books. "Just think," he said, "in Romania we couldn't even vote."

I would like to think that the criteria for selecting a law clerk also included the ability for critical legal thinking and clear writing. I know many law clerks claim authorship for their judge's opinions. I would never have the temerity to say that I authored any of the Judge's opinions.

Judge Matthews's work belonged to her and only to her. She was painstaking in her decision-making and oh-so-careful in her writing. I was always asked to proof her opinions and check citations. On some rare occasions I got to try my hand at a first draft. I'm not sure the final product ever resembled the first draft. The Judge was a wonderful teacher in many ways. She taught me a great deal about legal writing and about appreciating the political, social, and economic issues surrounding each case. She also taught me how to be a lady in a man's world. During my two-year clerkship, I came to learn that the side to which she gave the most leeway in court was the side that was going to lose. Judge Matthews was careful to give everyone an opportunity, but especially the side she felt had the weakest case.

The Judge's door was always open. And it was always open and welcoming to me and my enthusiasm for whatever issue was topmost in my mind. In the 1960s, Washington, D.C. had three daily papers.[5] Bar exam results were published in the paper before letters went out to the candidates. The "scoop" on the candidates passing the bar was rotated among the three papers, and as a courtesy, the paper that got the news first informed the judge if their law clerk passed. Judge Matthews's chambers were in the corner on the fourth floor of the United States Court House at 3rd and Constitution Avenue, NW. The press office was across the hall from her chambers.

When the bar results came out in November 1966, I went across the hall to find out if I passed. My excitement on learning I had passed was beyond description. I ran down the back hall, got on the judges' elevator, went to the sixth floor, burst into the judges' dining room, and announced to everyone that I had passed. When I didn't see Judge Matthews there, I ran out the door, jumped back on the elevator, ran down the fourth-floor corridor and in the back door of my office with a clear path to the Judge. Her eyes sparkled as she smiled at my announcement. "Yes, I know," she said. "I never doubted you would pass."

When Judge Matthews went on the bench, the United States District Court for the District of Columbia was a general trial court. Both civil and criminal cases were filed in the district court. The court had jurisdiction over almost every legal matter in the city with the exception of some misdemeanors and minor traffic cases. The law clerks were responsible for a number of duties, including drafting jury instructions and preparing motions. Friday was Motions Day at the court. The law clerks went down to the clerk's office late Wednesday or early Thursday to pick up the motions assigned for their respective judge to hear on Friday. It was our job to review the motions, research both sides, make a recommendation, and draft a preliminary order.

One such motion involved a group of Black Muslims incarcerated in the D.C. jail who claimed the kitchen in the jail put ham hocks in the soup, which violated their religious tenets not to eat pork. I was going to recommend that the Judge dismiss the motion for lack of standing. I went to meet Judge Robinson's law clerk for lunch and while I was waiting I was looking through *Federal Reporters* trying to figure out what to recommend on this particular motion. Judge Robinson walked in and asked what I was doing. I told him and then said, "What judge gave them standing to sue in the first place?" "Your judge," was Judge Robinson's reply. It was, in fact, Judge Matthews who presided over a suit brought by the Black Muslims for the right to conduct religious services in prison.[6] That decision illustrates the Judge's passion and belief that all people should be treated equally and with respect.

In addition to the suit brought by the Black Muslims, the Judge presided over a number of major trials, including a passport dispute for singer Paul

Robeson and a criminal trial of Jimmy Hoffa, leader of the Teamsters in 1957. The case received wide press coverage and reports appeared daily in the *Washington Post*.

While I clerked, all of the law clerks traditionally ate together in the Judges' Dining Room at least once a week. We discussed upcoming motions and cases and, of course, exchanged gossip. The Judge almost always ate in her chambers. She awaited my return from these lunches with the "boys" and delighted learning the latest gossip when I came back from my lunch. We, Judge Matthews's law clerks, were affectionately called the "girls."

The Judge was always proud of her "girls." Her pride (to quote Betty Poston Jones) was "well-founded." Her "girls" included Ellen Lee Park (1950–1956), assistant chief of the Civil Division of the United States Attorney's Office; Sylvia Bacon (1956–1957), judge of the Superior Court of the District of Columbia; Mary Margaret Burnett (secretary, 1960–1963; law clerk, 1963–1964), private practice; Bonnie Lewis Gay (1964–1966), Office of the General Counsel, United States Treasury; Barbara Yaffe (1965–1966), private practice; Polly Wirtzman Craighill (1966–1968), senior counsel, Office of the Legislative Counsel, United States Senate; and Betty Poston Jones (beginning in 1968). Mary Giove Seaton served as the Judge's administrative secretary beginning in 1966. Margaret A. (Peggy) Deeds was never on the Judge's staff but was a court reporter assigned to the Judge. She studied law at night and eventually became the first deputy in the Office of the Register of Wills. Peggy was considered part of the "girls."

The Judge always took an interest in what we (the "girls") were doing personally and professionally. At least once a year she wrote us each a letter expressing pride in our accomplishments. For her "girls," the Judge was not just a role model, but a mentor. We all met with the Judge at least once a year, usually for a luncheon.

When Judge Matthews decided to become a senior judge, she was determined that a woman be named to succeed her on the District Court for the District of Columbia. She urged all the organizations with which she was involved to campaign and lobby the White House to fill her vacancy with a woman. During the last few months of my clerkship, I was tasked with monitoring the progress of the campaign. I spent many hours at the National Woman's Party headquarters, which was housed in the historic Sewall-Belmont House. The Honorable June L. Green was appointed by President Lyndon Johnson to fill the vacancy, and Judge Matthews administered the oath of office.

Clearly the accomplishments of Burnita Shelton Matthews as a jurist are significant regardless of her gender. But her leadership in securing suffrage and women's equality cannot be underestimated. She paved the way for professional women by her quiet grace and hard work.

When I walk through George Washington University Law School, I stop by the Judge's picture on the first floor of Lerner Hall. How thrilled she would be by the many women who pass through these halls today, and how proud she would be at the many accomplishments women have had in law and in other fields.

One of my most vivid images of the Judge is seeing her with her white lace collar and cuffs poking out of the neckline and sleeves of her black robe. It was her usual attire on the bench, and a tradition that Justice Ruth Bader Ginsburg continued. Justice Ginsburg delivered the tribute in memory of the Honorable Burnita Shelton Matthews at the District of Columbia Circuit Judicial Conference in Williamsburg, Virginia, in May 1988. Justice Ginsburg said: "Burnita Shelton Matthews graced the bench of the United States District Court for the District of Columbia for three decades and more. She was a southern gentle woman of bright mind and indomitable spirit, a 'role model' before that term was coined."[7]

Notes

1. The Judge was a staunch independent. Although she had many friends who were politically active, she claimed she was not registered as either a Democrat or Republican.

2. The United States Court of Customs and Patent Appeals was a federal court that existed from 1907 to 1982. In 1982, the United States Court of Customs and Patent Appeals was abolished and its jurisdiction transferred to the United States Court of Appeals for the Federal Circuit.

3. The United States marshal assigned to Judge Matthews from 1966 to 1968 was Charles Wright. In addition to his regular duties, he was charged with seeing that the Judge and I made it home safely in 1968 when riots broke out in the District after the Martin Luther King assassination. The rioting had reached 7th and Pennsylvania Avenue, NW, just a few blocks from the United States Court House.

4. Betty Poston Jones described her interview for the position of law clerk. "When in 1968 I interviewed for the position of law clerk, I met Judge Matthews for the first time. Although I knew her by reputation, I was hardly prepared for the warm and gracious lady who welcomed me into her chambers. We chatted the better part of an hour. Because there emanates from her such a sincere interest in the person she is talking with, her involvement converted an otherwise stereotype interview into one of the most delightful hours I've spent. I remember thinking afterwards that whatever the outcome, I would always treasure that hour."

5. The *Washington Post,* the *Washington Evening Star,* and the *Washington Daily News.*

6. See Ruth Bader Ginsburg and Laura W. Brill, "Women in the Federal Judiciary: Three Way Pavers and the Exhilarating Change President Carter Wrought," *Fordham Law Review* 64, no. 2 (1995): 281.

7. It is not possible to overstate Judge Matthews's achievements and how much she advanced women's rights. Several noteworthy articles include "Burnita Shelton Matthews: The Biography of a Pioneering Woman, Lawyer and Feminist, 1894–1988," by Christine L. Wade, Women's' Legal History Biography Project, Stanford Law, Spring 1996; "Burnita Shelton Matthews: Pathfinder in Legal Aspects of Women," Interview Conducted by Amelia R. Fry, Suffragists Oral History Project, Calisphere, University of California; "The Little Bronze Button," by Chief Judge Edward Curran as part of his "America's Old Bailey Series: An Anecdotal History of the United States District Court for the District of Columbia," *Journal of the Bar Association of the District of Columbia* 23, no. 5 (May 1966): 236–40. The article is about Judge Matthews granting the motion to dissolve the Grand Army of the Republic.

MITCHELL A. LOWENTHAL

Edward Weinfeld

Steadfastly Principled Judge and Warmhearted Teacher

There already is a considerable and rich body of literature on Judge Edward Weinfeld, who was appointed to the Southern District of New York in 1950 by President Harry S. Truman. Beyond the scholarly biography prepared by noted legal historian and former Weinfeld law clerk Professor William Nelson,[1] there are numerous essays in law reviews, tributes by the bar (in addition to the volume published by the Federal Bar Foundation[2]), and other papers. In Bill Nelson's biography there is a chapter on the Judge's fifty-five law clerks, and the Federal Bar Foundation's 1998 tribute to him contains remembrances from almost two dozen of them.[3] In this essay, I describe my experience as his law clerk. The following is what I recall about the most special year of my professional life, one filled with warmth, happiness, awe, and much learning.

I first met Judge Weinfeld early one morning in late May 1981. The Judge was then, and remained until the end, an active member of the court, never having taken senior status. I was interviewing for clerkships at the time—a phrase with which the Judge always took issue: *he* was interviewing *me*, he regularly enjoyed pointing out. His chambers, room 2204, opened to a room with a large couch (and lined with bookshelves) where visitors would wait. The first door off of that room, to the right, led to a smaller room with desks for each of the two law clerks. It was also lined with bookshelves and had a small college dorm–sized refrigerator and a well-worn coffee maker.

The clerk's room had a second door that led to the office of the Judge's secretary, Marie Vollrath. In addition to her desk, that room had a book shelf with a typed copy, chronologically organized in binders, of every opinion the Judge had ever issued, many file cabinets filled with the Judge's jury instructions organized by subject and statute,[4] and a file cabinet containing the papers relevant to all matters—motions, appeals from bankruptcy and other courts, and trials—requiring opinions. The inventory of matters needing opinions was, usually, quite limited.

By far the most formidable feature of Marie's office was Marie herself. She had a tough, seen-it-all-before exterior, had the answer to every question we were too timid to ask the Judge directly (and, undoubtedly, many others), and was never parsimonious with her opinions. On the inside she was warm, caring, and utterly devoted to the Judge.

Marie's office also had a door that led to Judge Weinfeld's inner chambers. Those chambers had three desks: a long table where conferences could be held, a small desk abutting a window where he did virtually all of his work, and an enormous desk filled with photos and other mementos (including a wood cutting with the inscription "Order in the Court, Gramps"), which he used for the interview. It began on a formal note. We discussed his judicial approach, what he expected from his clerks, and similar subjects.

He then turned to more personal matters. He asked about my family—my parents, who lived in Monticello, New York (where he had relatives), and my wife—discussed his recent trip to Jamaica when hearing that my family was planning to go there, and made clear his very evident interest in me as a person. He was courteous, warm, and bursting with energy. He had just celebrated his eightieth birthday, was the oldest person with whom to that point I had ever spoken, and seemed like a character right out of the Bible.

After meeting the Judge, I spent some time talking with his clerks. They let me know what I could look forward to: cutting grapefruits (including "sectioning") five days a week at 7:30 a.m.,[5] on Saturdays buying double toasted bagels wrapped in tin foil to keep them hot, requests for a variety of salads from several local groceries for lunch, supplying blueberries when they were in season (especially when baked in a blueberry muffin), and serving "a spot" of black coffee on virtually a nonstop basis.[6] They also said that the hours would be as long as I had ever worked before, and longer, and that the Judge would always work harder.

I flew back to Ithaca that afternoon to begin preparing for the wedding of close friends the next day and graduation from law school the day after. Judge Weinfeld called before 7:30 the next morning to give me the good news. Needless to say, I was ecstatic—because I would be spending a year with him, and because (truth be told) I did not answer the phone in an inappropriate way at the audacity of a caller phoning that early in the morning. I promptly phoned

Judith T. Younger, one of the Judge's clerks who was on the Cornell Law School faculty. She, however, already knew; he had already called to tell her. I got the message then that the Judge's morning started quite a bit earlier than did mine.

The Judge regularly referred to the joy he received from his work, and it was evident that he thoroughly enjoyed what he did. That does not mean his work did not exact a toll; it did, and the toll was considerable. His hours, for example, were legendary. I was never there to greet him, but when he said he arrived in chambers at 4:30 a.m. Monday through Saturday, I had no doubt that he did. I can attest that he was there before 7:30, which is when Nina Gilman, my co-clerk, and I arrived. We spent long hours drafting memoranda describing motions, preparing drafts of jury charges and opinions, and summarizing testimony. As hard as we worked, though, the Judge never asked more from us than he did from himself.

I started my clerkship in early August 1982 and learned more about the Judge's approach to his work. The rules in chambers were strict. Extended telephone calls with lawyers were prohibited, as were ex parte calls of any length. Whatever lawyers had to say on the phone could be put in writing, and the Judge would read whatever they wrote. There were oral arguments on all motions, and they were held on Tuesday afternoons at 2:15 p.m. On Monday evening the motion papers were left in a row on one of the Judge's three desks, and almost invariably by 8:00 the next morning he had read all the parties' papers and a bench memo prepared by a law clerk, had written in longhand a tentative decision on each motion (often six to ten each motion day), and was working on something else. As a result, litigants frequently obtained resolutions of motions on the day they were argued.

Trial began each morning at 10:00. As with oral arguments, the Judge always (or nearly always) arrived *promptly*. Once, because of an errantly locked door, he was late for the 10:00 a.m. beginning of a trial day. That was in 1964, a story regularly repeated only because of its exceptionalism. The affected law clerk, Frank Tuerkheimer, went on to a distinguished career that, in addition to private practice, included serving as an assistant United States attorney in the Southern District of New York, as a member of the Watergate Prosecution Team, and as the United States attorney for the Western District of Wisconsin. He was subsequently appointed to the University of Wisconsin law faculty, teaching courses in criminal law and evidence, and writing many scholarly works. Yet, decades later, he still vividly recalled the fateful day when the Judge was late:

During the clerkship, I occasionally had to perform bailiff duties. One of those was assisting the Judge in the robing room with his robe. Once he was ready, I was to knock hard on the door (to alert the persons in the courtroom so they could stand) and then open it to let the Judge in.

One morning I helped him on with his robe. As the [bells of the nearby] church began [their ten-chime cycle], I opened the door to the courtroom to let the Judge in. Obviously, this simple three-step task was beyond my abilities. Just as I opened the door, I realized that I had neglected to knock. Therefore, I closed it so I could knock hard on the stationary door. It seemed, however, that the piece of rubber used to keep the door from locking slipped when I opened it, so that when I closed the door the door was locked. After knocking, I tried to open the door, but couldn't. I then grabbed my keys and, in panic, tried the first key that came to my fingers. It didn't fit.

In the meantime, the church bells continued their ominous chiming as the Judge's consecutive day record of prompt appearances, then of 14 years' duration, began to slip away. I tried another key; it didn't fit. The Judge then let me know something which I would otherwise not have guessed. "Frank," he said, "I'd like to get in there." I tried another key; it didn't work. By this time, there was silence.

In the calm of the deafening silence that followed the tenth church bell, I looked at my keys carefully, found the right key, knocked hard, opened the door and the Judge came onto the bench—late.[7]

If a lawyer was late to trial, it only happened once. Someone arriving after 10:00 a.m. would find the Judge on the bench, the jury seated, a witness in the box, and everyone else in their place. The Judge issued no words of reprimand, but there was no doubt in anyone's mind who was responsible for the delay in the proceedings.

Lawyers were advised to be well prepared in oral arguments and trials. An oral argument in an admiralty case was typical of the Judge's preparation. One side wanted an attachment but had cited no legal precedent for obtaining such provisional relief on the facts alleged in that case. The Judge mentioned that there was no authority cited by either side, but said he recalled a district court case in which such relief had been granted, citing the case by name (I was amazed by the Judge's recollection and chagrined that I had missed the case when preparing his bench memo). The movant seized the moment, agreeing with the Judge's recollection of the case, and apologizing for not citing it. In fact, the Judge went on, your firm was involved in that case. Yes, said the lawyer (I knew then that things did not bode well for that lawyer). And the case was reversed by the Second Circuit, said the Judge, denying the motion without further comment (he also never questioned me why I had failed to mention the Circuit opinion in my bench memo, which I appreciated to no end).

At other times, he could be much less forgiving. Once, he had a particularly strong reaction to an early use (an abuse, he thought) of the civil RICO statute, and at argument on a motion to dismiss said that he was considering speaking to a disciplinary committee about the pleading. The lawyer withdrew the claim on the spot, eliminating my opportunity to work on a Weinfeld opinion that might have helped shape the civil RICO statute.

While some have said that he could be short with lawyers at times, Judge Weinfeld was invariably courteous and respectful to jurors and litigants. I will never forget the early days of the Brinks criminal proceedings, where the robbery of an armored car in Westchester led to several deaths. The courtroom was packed with marshals, the press, and supporters of the defendants. Although the defendants claimed they were political revolutionaries whose defense included the illegitimacy of the U.S. government, every time the Judge walked into the courtroom they stood up in respect.

There is a similar story about the respect shown to the Judge by Anthony "Tony Ducks" Corallo, who was sentenced by the Judge in a celebrated corruption case in the early 1960s that involved a state judge (the brother of a powerful congressman), an acting U.S. attorney in the Eastern District of New York, and accusations of fixing cases.[8] Years later, after Corallo's release from prison, he was indicted for other crimes, and the case was assigned to Judge Weinfeld. The Judge offered to recuse himself, but Corallo declined (he was convicted again and sentenced to another prison term by Judge Weinfeld). Former U.S. attorney and Manhattan district attorney Robert Morganthau once described this incident as evidence that Judge Weinfeld's reputation for fairness was as well known on Mulberry Street as it was on Wall Street.[9]

In fact, Judge Weinfeld's reputation extended beyond those streets— including to Pennsylvania Avenue in Washington, D.C. As Frank Tuerkheimer recounts,[10] staffers on the Senate Select Committee on Presidential Campaign Practices (the "Ervin Committee") learned in the summer of 1973 from Lt. General Alexander Butterfield that there was a taping system in the Nixon White House, a fact that became public on July 16, 1973, when Butterfield testified before the Ervin Committee. Special Watergate Prosecutor Archibald Cox obtained a grand jury subpoena for nine tapes a week later.

During that week-long gap, President Nixon discussed with his counsel, Leonard Garment, whether the tapes could be destroyed. Garment researched the issue and came upon *United States v. Solow*,[11] where Judge Weinfeld held that the destruction of evidence that the defendant *believed* would be sought by a grand jury subpoena constituted obstruction of justice under 18 U.S.C. § 1503. While many Nixon advisers, including Secretary of State Henry Kissinger and Secretary of the Treasury John Connally, urged that the tapes be destroyed, Garment told his client it was "plain" that, under the circumstances, even in the absence of a subpoena, the tapes had to be preserved: "the key decision, *United States v. Solow*, had been written by one of the most respected jurists in the country . . . and there was no court holding to the contrary. So the tapes could not be destroyed."[12]

Of course, President Nixon did not destroy the tapes. Instead, he moved to quash the subpoena. The motion was denied, and the Court of Appeals for the District of Columbia affirmed that ruling. At that point, President Nixon sought a compromise with Cox by which he would produce transcripts of the tapes and allow Senator John Stennis to listen to the tapes and confirm the accuracy of the transcripts. The verified transcript would then be given to Cox, on condition that he not seek any further tapes. Cox rejected this proposal and was fired in what is now known as the Saturday Night Massacre.

Cox's successor, Leon Jaworski, eventually obtained an indictment against several Watergate figures. The grand jury unanimously voted to include the president among the known conspirators in a charge alleging obstruction of justice. As that criminal case was approaching trial, Jawarski issued a trial subpoena pursuant to Rule 17 of the Federal Rules of Criminal Procedure for additional tapes. President Nixon moved to quash that subpoena and lost. He appealed, and the appeal went directly to the U.S. Supreme Court.

Writing for a unanimous Supreme Court (with Justice William H. Rehnquist abstaining), Chief Justice Warren Burger—after ruling that federal courts had jurisdiction to hear a dispute between two persons in the executive branch—addressed the validity and scope of the subpoena. In doing so, he noted that "as both parties agree[d] cases decided in the wake of *Bowman [Dairy Co. v. United States*,[13] which set very general principles governing a Rule 17(c) subpoena] have generally followed Judge Weinfeld's formulation in *United States v. Iozia*, 13 F.R.D. 335 (S.D.N.Y. 1952), as to the required showing."[14] Relying on *Iozia*, and applying the test *Iozia* established, the Supreme Court affirmed the denial of the motion to quash, requiring the tapes to be produced.[15]

One of the tapes included a recording of President Nixon agreeing with his chief of staff, H. R. Haldeman, to order the FBI to abandon its investigation of the Watergate break-in. This tape became known as the "smoking gun." It was publicly released on August 5, 1974; President Nixon resigned three days later. As Frank Tuerkheimer notes, President Nixon had been reelected overwhelmingly in 1972, and the Saturday Night Massacre "stands as a pivotal point in the Watergate saga, a turning point that could only exist if there were tapes in existence that could be the subject of litigation. Both at this turning point and in the final denouement of the Nixon presidency, Judge Weinfeld's decisions are the hidden player."[16]

Judge Weinfeld's devotion to individualized justice was a, if not the, hallmark of what made Edward Weinfeld the judge he was. He famously and repeatedly said that "every case is important," and that "no case is more important than any other." He labored to reach a just result in each case and to express clearly why the result was just. Opinions often went through many drafts until they finally met his standards. Even the form his opinions took—heavy with footnotes citing to cases and statutes, almost never to other sources, such as law reviews—were designed to convey that these *were* the facts and this *was* the law, not just the opinion of one person.

The Judge also took pains to explain and dignify the legal process to litigants. The one occasion that stands out most strongly in my mind involved an unfair competition claim in which both parties were in the construction business, and the defendant was a subsidiary of a huge developer. Both had "Grenadier" in their corporate names, and the plaintiff claimed to be losing business because his customers thought he was affiliated with the defendant's parent corporation, which was one of their competitors. Near the end of the trial, after the rebuttal testimony was completed, the Judge asked the plaintiff's CEO (whose surname was Grenadier) whether he would be satisfied if the defendant was required to publish a prominent disclaimer disavowing any relationship with the CEO's company. "I would not be satisfied," he said, "but I understand that you have to reach some sort of compromise." "No," the Judge immediately responded, "I do not reach compromises. I must reach a judgment."[17]

The Judge had strict rules on how his law clerks worked. For the motions not resolved at oral argument, he would give us the entire file, and we were to draft an opinion. When we were finished, all the papers, except our draft, were laid out in a defined order on the Judge's conference table. He would then review them at his small desk and draft his own opinion. When he was finished, he would ask to see our draft. Once he had read that, he would call the author in to discuss how to proceed. Only then did we learn what his views were, and what we had missed. I asked him once why he did not just tell us up front what his views were, so our draft would at least reach the conclusion he thought correct. He answered with a question: "If you knew how I was leaning, how often would you come out differently?" He wanted to know what we thought, not how well we could say what he wanted.

Judge John Koeltl, a Weinfeld clerk, has recounted an early experience he had with Judge Weinfeld's opinion-writing process:

> In the first week that I clerked for Judge Weinfeld, the Judge left me a draft of an opinion that he had written, and he asked me to cite-check it and get it ready for issuance. I worked on the opinion and left it for the Judge, but I was not completely satisfied with the resolution of one issue. When I arrived in Chambers at seven o'clock the next morning there was a revised opinion on my desk. The revised opinion resolved the issue that had troubled me. I went into the Judge's office and explained—somewhat amazingly to me in retrospect—that I had reviewed the prior opinion and tried to edit it. I explained that I had done what I could, but there was something that was still "not quite right." I told the Judge that the new opinion had solved the problem and was really very good. I beamed in my brashness. The Judge responded with one of the few cold comments I can recall in the course of the clerkship: "Don't ever, ever, let me do something that's not quite right."[18]

Needless to say, there was always some anxiety in chambers whenever we knew the Judge had finished his draft and was about to read ours. But once we reached the stage of working together on an opinion, the process was exhilarating. The attention the Judge paid to the facts, to reading cases carefully, to stating rules narrowly, sufficient only to resolve the issues presented and no further, were lasting lessons.

I remember only one disagreement of any substance I had with the Judge about an opinion. In the Brinks case, two defendants faced criminal charges arising out of the 1981 killing of a private security guard and two state troopers in Nanuet, New York. The defendants moved to dismiss the indictment based upon alleged grand jury abuse, arguing that the grand jury had been told an informant had given an extensive written statement incriminating the defendants, but was not told that the informant had recanted (the informant claimed his original statement had been coerced). Separately, the defendants moved to suppress evidence derived from wire taps that were authorized in part on the basis of the informant's original statement.

In response to the motion to dismiss, the government submitted grand jury testimony from Mark Pomerantz, an assistant United States attorney who had been a Weinfeld clerk and went on to a distinguished career in private practice and in leadership roles in the Southern District U.S. Attorney's Office. The defense then moved for recusal, based upon the relevance of Pomerantz's grand jury testimony to the suppression motion, even though the government had not submitted it in connection with that motion. There was no doubt that the grand jury was informed that the informant had recanted; Pomerantz's testimony unambiguously confirmed that. But his grand jury testimony also cast very substantial doubt on the informant's coercion allegation.

The Judge was acutely aware of the burden his recusal would have on one of his colleagues, and he was initially of the view that he could decide the suppression motion without taking Mark's testimony into account, making recusal unnecessary. My draft concluded that recusal was warranted. We exchanged competing draft opinions. Ultimately, he completely redrafted the opinion and granted the recusal motion, concluding that "his ability to be impartial in fact, was equally important as the appearance of impartiality." "The issue is not the Court's own introspective capacity to sit in fair and honest judgment with respect to the controverted issues," he wrote, "but whether a reasonable member of the public at large, aware of all the facts, might fairly question the Court's partiality." He added that his relationship with Pomerantz "is so intimate and my esteem for him so high, as it is for all my many former clerks through the years," that the average person on the street might reasonably question whether his testimony in fact would play no role in the decision on the suppression motion.

One word in the penultimate draft was deleted from the final opinion in *United States v. Ferguson*.[19] By pointedly noting his close relationship with all of his *former* clerks, I asked if he was intending to suggest that Nina and I had fallen short. From the final opinion, the Judge struck the word "former."

The Judge's exacting standards and his extraordinary devotion to work suggested to many that working for him must have been quite stressful. At times, particularly in the beginning of the clerkship, it was. But that evaporated very quickly. Although perfection was obviously the goal, we knew our limitations. We also knew that the Judge would carefully review everything we did and correct whatever needed fixing. As renowned corporate lawyer Martin Lipton, a Weinfeld clerk, put it at the Judge's funeral service:

However careful and thorough we thought we were, the Judge was more careful and thorough. Good was never good enough. Great was not great enough. Perfect was the goal. No one was more realistic about the impossibility of perfection, but no one worked harder to achieve it.[20]

Indeed, very little slipped by his scrutiny. Some cases, because of their complexity, may have demanded more of his time. No case, however, was not given his full attention. His close friend, Judge Henry Friendly, once summed up this aspect of Judge Weinfeld's judicial philosophy:

> The essence of Judge Weinfeld's greatness is not the high degree to which he has won affirmances, but the quality of the attention he has given not only to every case but to every issue. He once expressed deep indignation to me over an opinion of one of my colleagues which had begun "This is an ordinary criminal case." For him, no case can be "ordinary" when liberty is at stake.[21]

Despite the exacting standards Judge Weinfeld applied to each case pending before him, he often expressed doubts when his opinions were being considered by the Court of Appeals, pointing out in discussions with us the weaknesses in his arguments and the strengths in those of the other side. As far as I could tell, however, he was not disturbed when the inevitable happened and he was reversed.[22]

Early in my term, the Second Circuit unanimously reversed a decision by the Judge interpreting the derivative works exception under the Copyright Act. It was a case of first impression, and the Judge and one of my predecessors spent a great deal of time on the opinion. And the appellate process itself was historic: the oral advocates were both former members of the Southern District (Harold Tyler for the appellant and Marvin Frankel for the appellee), a first according to the circuit judge who presided over the Second Circuit panel. When the panel's unanimous decision of reversal was announced, the Judge discussed its reasoning with Nina and me at a Saturday morning breakfast and took responsibility for not giving sufficient weight to the points stressed by the Circuit. Then he quickly moved on to other matters. He exhibited the same dispassionate reaction near the end of my term with him, many months later, when the Supreme Court (5–4) reversed the Second Circuit, reinstating his original opinion.

While Judge Weinfeld's record on appeal was well known to members of the New York legal community, I was surprised to learn how far beyond that community his record on appeal had spread. One incident stands out: an obviously troubled pro se litigant had filed a complaint asserting that the government of Mexico had stolen money from his bank accounts. The government's motive and ability to accomplish this theft was left to the imagination, and in due course the Judge dismissed the complaint. Week after week, it seemed, the plaintiff moved for reconsideration, eventually prompting the Judge to issue an order precluding the clerk's office from accepting further reconsideration motions. The plaintiff remained undaunted, and the direction to the clerk's office notwithstanding, soon thereafter another reconsideration motion came in, this time accompanied by a phone call from the plaintiff asking if the Judge would hear him. I decided to confront the issue (and violate a rule of chambers) by speaking ex parte with the plaintiff and asking if he knew about the Court of Appeals. He responded that he did; that its role was to correct the errors of the district judges. "Well," I asked, "you believe Judge Weinfeld made a mistake in your case?" "Yes," he responded, "I do." "Then, shouldn't you file an appeal?" To which he responded: "Don't be ridiculous. Everyone knows the Second Circuit never reverses Judge Weinfeld."

Judge Weinfeld believed that the law was fundamentally fair, and that doing justice turned more on carefully and thoroughly finding the facts. He did not desire to make new law; rarely did he feel the need to do so. For example, in one case the Judge was confronted with the practice of the then-Manhattan U.S. attorney (who later became the mayor of New York City) of interviewing defendants after they were arrested, rather than immediately taking them to be arraigned (where they would be assigned, or advised to retain, counsel). No other U.S. attorney followed this practice, and the Judge thought it was an unprincipled, strategic end-run around the defendant's right to counsel. Vicki Been, now on the New York University Law School faculty, clerked for the Judge at that time and worked with him on that matter. She wrote about the experience:

> I poured my soul into a full attack on the constitutionality of the practice. He took one look at the draft, patiently explained that he was a district judge, not the Supreme Court of the United States, and sent me back to write about the facts of the delay and leave the law and the appropriateness of the practice to "higher authorities." [A second draft led to further significant editing by the Judge.] After some back and forth, he agreed to address the law in one footnote that cited Judge Friendly [who had sharply criticized the practice] as obviously and incontrovertibly right, and distinguished all the (many) cases cited by the prosecution.[23]

Judge Weinfeld suppressed the confession obtained after the unreasonable delay in presenting the defendant to a magistrate arraignment, but his opinion simply assumed that he had the authority to do so (which he explained in a footnote), and he noted in another footnote (which Been mentions in her note above) that whether the U.S. attorney's practice of interviewing defendants before arraignment was per se unlawful "involves a policy decision as to judicial supervision of the administration of criminal practice in the Federal Courts [that] should be left for determination by higher authority."[24]

His ruling was appealed, and the U.S. attorney himself argued the appeal, urging reversal. The Circuit Court affirmed, noting that "Judge Weinfeld was convinced that the DEA Agents had no legitimate excuse for not arraigning Perez [the defendant] promptly. Certainly, we have no 'firm conviction' that any of his findings of fact were erroneous. Moreover, the district court correctly concluded that the government's decision to ignore Perez as he was waiting in his DEA holding cell justifies suppression of Perez' confession."[25] As Vicki notes, "the Court went on to strike a serious blow at the practice itself by requiring district courts to rule on the reasonableness of any pre-arraignment delays exceeding six hours (the time deemed reasonable by the applicable statute)."[26]

Close attention to the facts in every case was one of the Judge's precepts. Higher courts could correct errors of law (or change the applicable law). But failing to get the facts straight was unforgivable: because appellate courts generally cannot alter the facts found by the trial court (unless the finding was clearly erroneous), Judge Weinfeld felt that he had to get the facts right. Moreover, the Judge believed that close attention to the facts would lead to the just result.

Even though the Judge thoroughly immersed himself in work, there was always time for frank discussions with friends about the issues of the day. Chambers saw almost a parade of judges, close friends, and family stopping by. Often, at least once a week it seemed, there was an early morning breakfast or lunch guest. Other judges of the court or visiting judges would invariably stop by to converse with him and discuss problems. The most frequent visitors were former law clerks, each of whom would regale the current clerks with their own stories of the Judge's career and their time clerking.

Saturday mornings were the most special time of the week for the clerks. First, the day did not officially begin until 8:00 a.m.—a half-hour respite. Second, and more importantly, breakfast meant sitting with the Judge and listening to stories about his life and professional experiences. He talked about his early career as a solo practitioner, handling criminal and civil trials and appeals (for almost two decades before the Federal Rules of Civil Procedure were adopted and *Erie Railroad Co. v. Tompkins* was decided). He also talked about his political career as a district captain in the days of Tammany Hall, which led to his involvement in the 1938 New York State Constitutional Convention, and about many of his earlier cases. We also learned about his service as housing commissioner of New York, the housing projects he built, his interactions with "Power Broker" Robert Moses and New York City mayor Fiorello LaGuardia, and his close relationship with "the Governor," Herbert Lehman.

Those breakfasts often went on for several hours, but never long enough. When they ended, as they had to, back to work we would go. As Saturday evening came, the Judge would walk into our room to say good night and wish us a good "weekend" (that was his word for Sunday). At first, his actual salutation on Saturday evenings was "Good night, boys," after which Nina and I would look at one another and smile. I mentioned to the Judge one day that it was really not accurate to say "Good night, boys" to us. The next Saturday he again stopped in and wished us well—and, with his own smile, said, "Good night, children."

Judge Weinfeld's warmth was not restricted to Saturday mornings. Despite the austere seriousness with which he approached his work, the lighter side of Edward Weinfeld sometimes shined through in his opinions and elsewhere. One case I remember well involved a *Baker v. Carr* challenge to the constitutionality of the method of electing representatives to the Sullivan County Board of Supervisors, the county's legislative body. The residents of larger townships claimed that their votes were worth "less" than residents of smaller townships because the board's rather complicated weighted voting system allegedly disfavored them.

Aside from intrinsic interest in the subject, I particularly enjoyed the case because I was born and raised in Monticello, the county seat. In rejecting some of the technical points the plaintiffs raised, the Judge wrote that "these matters cannot be determined with mathematical exactitude." In a later draft, however, and ultimately in the published opinion, the Judge added the phrase "or the fine balance of an apothecary's scale" to the sentence.[27] Weinfeld opinions were not long on such phrases, so I inquired why he had made this edit. In a tone indicating I should have known better, he said, "out of respect to your father," who he knew was a pharmacist.

I also fondly remember the celebration of the Brooklyn Bridge's one hundredth birthday. Chambers had a marvelous view of the bridge, which figured prominently in Judge Weinfeld's life; his lunch-time walks across the bridge, for example, were well known. As the evening grew near, visitors started pouring in. By the time the fireworks started, there were over forty people in chambers, including members of the Judge's family, my family, friends, and other members of the court. The Judge greeted everyone and told stories late into the night about the bygone days of New York City. Well after midnight the crowd finally dispersed; the Judge stayed in chambers all night, and was still bubbling the next morning over the excitement of the evening.

For the law clerks, the highlight of the year—every year, for many years—was the law clerks' annual surprise dinner for the Judge held in late May or early June. The current clerks were charged with the task of making the arrangements and working with the Judge's wife, Lillian, and his secretary, Marie, to lure him to a restaurant. Invariably, the Judge would walk into the room, hear a shout of "Surprise" from those assembled, and then hit his head with his hand, announce how he must be the most naive person in the world to have been truly surprised at yet another annual dinner, and hug everyone. That claimed confession of surprise always brought a round of laughter, particularly since the dinners came every year at about the same time.

The evenings proceeded with everyone catching up on the past year's events, toasts, speeches, often a gift for the Judge, and then a speech from him. We all knew what he would say, and it meant so much to each of us. The law clerks were part of his family, he always said, and he would thank us all for easing his burdens and sharing the joy of judicial life. He would also try to persuade us that he was truly surprised that year (a singular example of an argument Edward Weinfeld never won) and called his wife and secretary the "co-conspirators" for having successfully "deceived" him once again.

Nina and I hosted our surprise dinner for him in June 1983, as our clerkship term was coming to a close. The next day he sent us the following note:

> I did not believe that another surprise party could be achieved. But I underestimated the imaginative genius of that prime conspirator, my bride of 54 years, to act in concert with you as accomplished co-conspirators. There was no way I could possibly have suspected the event.... It is another treasured experience to add to my store of happy memories. It was a great gathering of all of you who mean so much to me.

This expression of warmth was an endearing aspect of Judge Weinfeld's character. His clerks were always encouraged to visit him in chambers and to keep him informed of the developments in our lives. He took pride in our accomplishments and shared our disappointments. In words and deeds, he consistently demonstrated the strong, almost filial, affection he had for each of us.

In August 1983 I returned to Cleary Gottlieb, where I remained for my professional career. Shortly afterward, while I was waiting my turn for what I was sure would be an unpleasant time in a dentist's chair, the receptionist told me I had a call. Somehow, the Judge found out where I was and called to ask if I would agree to serve as a temporary receiver for a brokerage firm the SEC has asked him to shut down. I agreed. A few weeks later, the brokerage was placed in a SIPC liquidation, the trustee hired Cleary Gottlieb to represent him, and I accordingly had the pleasure of experiencing what it was like to appear as an advocate before Judge Weinfeld.

That experience is difficult to describe. He had a physical presence that created an unmistakably powerful atmosphere. His features embodied the law in an almost biblical sense. Short, balding, a furrowed brow with bushy eyebrows above dark eyes, an ever-present bow tie, and spry even into his eighties, he took the bench with a solemnity that was both a reflection of the seriousness with which he approached his duties and the importance his judgments had on the lives of the people who had matters before him. With the characteristic three knocks on the door of the courtroom, the deputy's announcement for all to "please rise" was almost surplusage—all *did* rise. He was, as the *New York Times* understatedly said in the July 11, 1950, editorial praising President Truman for nominating Weinfeld to the district court, "a man of warm sympathies, of fairness and of high personal integrity."

For trials, Judge Weinfeld regularly read both the official transcript prepared by the court reporters and a summary of the prior day's testimony prepared by a law clerk. He was similarly well prepared for oral arguments, having read the papers submitted by the parties and a bench memorandum from a clerk and, often, having done some research on his own. Each motion day began with the declamation from the bailiff: "All persons appearing before the United States District Court for the Southern District of New York draw near, give your attention, and you shall be heard. Edward Weinfeld presiding."

He was an active participant in those arguments but listened carefully to what the advocates had to say. As a law clerk, and as an advocate, I felt that each side left Weinfeld arguments feeling that they *had,* as the bailiff promised, been heard—particularly when they lost. Instilling that feeling in litigants and lawyers who appeared before him was, I believe, of foundational importance to Judge Weinfeld: in doing justice, it was of course important to reach the just result, but it was no less important to leave both sides with the confidence that their arguments had been carefully considered.

The Judge battled cancer for more than a decade and fell seriously ill in the fall of 1987. One measure of the gravity of his illness at that time was his withdrawal from a case, a complex criminal tax trial, just as the lawyers were about to sum up and the jury to be instructed. As John Koeltl explains:

Unbeknownst to the lawyers, the Judge was dying, but his mind and work habit [had, until then] remained unaffected. Finally, however, he explained to the lawyers that he could not continue the case because he was going into the hospital. He offered to have any other judge of the court complete the trial because he was confident that they would do that for him. The lawyers for all parties said that they were prepared to adjourn the trial until the Judge returned. The Judge responded that they did not understand—he was never coming back. The lawyers taped the summations so that the Judge could listen to them in the hospital.[28]

Around this time Marie told the law clerk family that the situation was grave and encouraged us to visit the Judge. When my wife and I did so, in addition to an emotional and inadequate thank-you, we were able to convey very happy personal news. Despite his obviously grave condition, his reactions were as warm and engaging as were his comments when I first met him. He demanded details, broadly smiled, and glowingly spoke of the future.

A few weeks later, on the day of his funeral, the *New York Times* published an editorial aptly captioned "The Devotion of Judge Weinfeld."[29] It spoke about his sense of fairness, his commitment to doing justice, and his deep study and conscientious preparation, and it noted Justice Brennan's distillation of Judge Weinfeld's career as one "distinguished by the purity of its devotion and its quiet dedication to the business of judging." The editorial mentioned that the Judge had delivered more than two thousand opinions and highlighted one that captured not only his devotion to the law and the legal process, but why they took precedence over even his own deeply felt personal views on a matter. In that opinion, Judge Weinfeld wrote that a judge's personal views "must yield to a higher authority—the majesty of the law. A cardinal principle of our system of justice is that not only must there be the reality of a fair trial and impartiality in accordance with due process, but also the appearance of a fair trial and impartiality."[30]

Edward Weinfeld rarely spoke for public consumption outside of his judicial opinions. The June 9, 1986, memorial service held at the Association of the Bar of the City of New York in honor of Henry J. Friendly was one of those rare occasions. There he discussed the close relationship he had with Judge Friendly and how it formed—asking how it was that two men of such different backgrounds had grown to have such an unusually close relationship: an intellectual admiration, a personal affection, and an enduring friendship.

There was a similar relationship between the bench and bar, on the one hand, and Judge Weinfeld, on the other. It is a relationship that surely had at its core the awe in which Judge Weinfeld was held by his colleagues on the United States District Court for the Southern District of New York—the "greatest court in the country, bar none" as Judge Weinfeld almost lovingly referred to it—on which he served for thirty-seven years. In November 1985, for example, thirty-four members of the Southern District of New York joined Chief Judge Constance Baker Motley in nominating Judge Weinfeld for an award, describing him as a "friend, a colleague, and a mentor," and noting that "no one has labored as long or as hard in the service of justice as has Judge Weinfeld."[31] "While his contributions to the administration of justice have been great on many levels," it continues, "the greatest is the personal example he has set for all those who know him or know of him," and adds:

> What makes him great is the spirit and dedication that have marked his work and his life. All of us know, at least as an intellectual matter, the qualities that the ideal judge should have. The judge must of course be fair, and must take each case as he finds it. He must be patient, and hard-working. He must be sensitive to the impact that his judgment will have upon those litigants who appear before him, for his decision will profoundly affect their property, their reputations, and often their very liberty. He must pride himself not as a master of men but as their servant. He must not seek thanks; rather, he must be thankful for having been given the opportunity to sit in judgment of his fellows. But, though all of us know this credo, few among us can say that we lived up to it, day after day. And no-one has lived up to it as long or as faithfully as Judge Weinfeld.[32]

Similarly, Judge Morris Lasker, speaking on behalf of his colleagues of the Southern District of New York, spoke these words at Judge Weinfeld's January 17, 1988, funeral service:

> Your colleagues on the court—that court which you have made known as the greatest trial court in the country "bar none"—have been enriched beyond telling by your friendship, your guidance and your wisdom. To many of us you have been both father and brother, and none of us has, before today, ever served on the court without you. . . .We commit ourselves to live and act by your standards, because the proudest boast any of us can ever make will be that we served with Edward Weinfeld.[33]

Litigants and lawyers revered him not just for the enormous intellect he applied to the problems placed before him, but also for the Herculean efforts he made to understand them and the pristine majesty with which he resolved those problems. Whatever his judgment—and that is what he reached; there was no room for compromise or short cuts in the Weinfeld repertoire—those who appeared before him knew they had received the best the administration of justice had to offer. As Justice Brennan said at the 1983 dedication of a professorship of law in Judge Weinfeld's name at NYU Law School, "there is general agreement on bench and bar throughout this nation that there is no better judge on any court in the country."[34] He continued:

> In a sense, it would be easier to salute him if he had been more noisy, if he had laid claim to some innovative legal philosophy or sought attention through great opinions or monopoly of important cases. He has had his share of these, of course, but in truth, no more than his share. For important cases go as they come, and most are forgotten. Even the greatest decisions are worn away by the usage of time. [T]he lesson I take from the life of Edward Weinfeld is, to paraphrase Learned Hand, a lesson that we have never quite learned but neither have we wholly forgotten, that judges should be more patient than quick, more ready to learn than to teach and, at the last, prepared to instruct more by personal example than by pious pronouncement.
>
> What there is about Judge Edward Weinfeld that we have found impossible to ignore, although first it was known only within [New York] [C]ity and only later as the ripple spread throughout the nation, is the day-by-day living example that he has given us of what we want our judges to be.[35]

In his biography of the Judge, Bill Nelson asks: "Will Edward Weinfeld leave a timeless legacy? Will Weinfeld's distinctive style of judging be important in the future?"[36] More time must pass before these and other searching questions Bill poses can be answered fully. Without doubt, though, the men and women who were privileged to serve as his law clerks will never forget him.

Notes

1. William Nelson, *In Pursuit of Right and Justice: Edward Weinfeld as Lawyer and Judge* (New York: New York University Press, 2004).

2. Federal Bar Foundation, *Edward Weinfeld: A Judicious Life* (New York: Federal Bar Foundation, 1998) (coauthored by the Honorable P. Kevin Castel, Barry H. Garfinkel, the Honorable John G. Koeltl, Professor William Nelson, Amy Weinfeld Schulman, Whitney North Seymour, Jr. and the author of this essay; hereinafter *Judicious Life*).

3. *Judicious Life*, 89–129.

4. During my clerkship, I had the pleasure of photocopying every one of his jury charges for what I recall being told was a book project. Judge Weinfeld's accumulated

jury instructions became the foundation of *Modern Federal Jury Instructions,* the leading treatise on jury instructions in the Second Circuit.

5. In an October 9, 2014, argument in the U.S. Supreme Court considering whether federal labor laws required compensating employees for time spent in security screenings, Justice Elena Kagan asked the following question: "Can I give you a different hypo, which is similar to some of the ones that have been floating around in a brief, but it's actually based on real life circumstances. There was a judge ages ago in the Southern District of New York who had his clerks—all that they did was help him with his opinions and his cases and that was their principal activity, but had his clerks come early in order to cut his grapefruit and otherwise make breakfast for him. And would that be compensable?" Observers understood that she was referring to Judge Weinfeld. With due respect to Justice Kagan, however, "ages ago" seems a bit strong to me, and while they immeasurably benefited by their clerkship experience, Weinfeld clerks were not paid by the hour.

6. While they were the subject of jokes over the years, I never heard a law clerk complain about performing these tasks. Having spent years working as a busboy in a Catskills resort, moreover, serving food and cutting grapefruits were among the tasks I felt confident I could perform without disappointing the Judge.

7. *Judicious Life,* 96–97.

8. That trial is the subject of an article cowritten by two former Weinfeld clerks. See John Koeltl and Frank Tuerkheimer, "Judge Weinfeld and the Criminal Law: The Keogh-Kahaner Trial—A Case Study in Criminal Justice," *New York University Law Review* 50 (1975): 1008 (hereinafter "Keogh-Kahaner Trial"). Affirming the convictions in that case, Judge Friendly wrote for a unanimous Second Circuit: "Absolute perfection in trials will not be attained so long as human beings conduct them; few trials of this length and difficulty can have been so nearly free of error as this one." *United States v. Kahaner,* 317 F.2d 459, 485 (2d Cir. 1963). James Keogh, a Kahaner codefendant, subsequently filed a Section 2255 petition, which Judge Weinfeld denied. Judge Friendly sat on the panel that heard the appeal from that denial. In all respects but one, the denial was affirmed. *United States v. Keogh,* 271 F. Supp. 1002 (S.D.N.Y. 1967), *aff'd in part and vacated in part,* 391 F. 2d 138 (2d Cir. 1968). See "Keogh-Kahaner Trial," 1045–47. Shortly after the circuit's opinion was released, Judge Friendly wrote to Judge Weinfeld that he was "sorry we could not affirm your fine opinion 100 percent—I came the closest that I could." Four days later, Judge Weinfeld responded: "It was so nice of you to write. As I often told you before, to a soldier in the ranks it is all part of the day's work."

9. *Judicious Life,* 61–62. See "Keogh-Kahaner Trial," 1049–50.

10. Frank Tuerkheimer, "Judge Weinfeld and Watergate: The Critical Connection," *Federal Bar Council Quarterly* 20, no. 3 (Spring 2013): 13.

11. 138 F. Supp. 812 (S.D.N.Y. 1956).

12. Leonard Garment, *Crazy Rhythm: From My Journey from Brooklyn, Jazz, and Wall Street to Nixon's White House, Watergate and Beyond* (Cambridge, Mass.: De Capo Press 2001): 278–79.

13. 341 U.S. 214 (1951).

14. *United States v. Nixon,* 418 U.S. 683, 699 (1974).

15. Ibid., 699–702.

16. Tuerkheimer, "Judge Weinfeld and Watergate," 20.

17. See *The Grenadier Corp. v. Grenadier Realty Corp*, 568 F. Supp. 502, 507 (S.D.N.Y. 1983).

18. John Koeltl, "Reflections on Judge Weinfeld," *Judicature* 100 (October 2012): 13.

19. 550 F. Supp. 1256 (S.D.N.Y. 1982).

20. *Judicious Life*, 56.

21. Henry Friendly, "The Ideal Judge," *New York University Law Review* 50 (1975): 977, 978.

22. While this may well be apocryphal, the story has been repeated enough to make it fact: at one point in the mid-1970s, one of the clerks attempted to track the outcome of the Judge's decisions on appeal. Out of some 1,500 opinions, the Judge had been reversed fewer than two dozen times by the Second Circuit, and his opinion was reinstated by the Supreme Court in about half of those.

23. *Judicious Life*, 119–20.

24. *United States v. Toney*, 579 F. Supp. 652, 655 n.4 & 657 n.11 (S.D.N.Y. 1984), *aff'd*, 733 F.2d 1026 (2d Cir. 1984).

25. 733 F.2d at 1035.

26. *Judicious Life*, 120.

27. *Greenwald v. The Board of Supervisors of the County of Sullivan*, 567 F. Supp. 200, 210 (S.D.N.Y. 1983).

28. Koeltl, "Reflections," 13.

29. "The Devotion of Judge Weinfeld," *New York Times*, January 19, 1988.

30. *United States v. Ferguson*, 550 F. Supp. 1256, 1260 (S.D.N.Y. 1982).

31. *Judicious Life*, 42.

32. Ibid., 42–43. A few days later, Judge Weinfeld wrote this response, which he addressed to his "beloved colleagues." "Last night I saw for the first time the nomination submitted by you to the Devitt Committee. It was not only touching, but without embarrassment it moved me to tears. It is really difficult to give adequate expression to how deeply stirred I was by your overgenerous evaluation of my service in our noble calling. The warmth of your sentiments means more to me than any decision that could be made by the Devitt Committee."

33. Ibid., 51.

34. Ibid., 38.

35. Ibid., 39. In November 1985, Chief Justice Warren Burger wrote privately to Judge Weinfeld to say that "almost any good lawyer can be an appellate judge but great trial judges, like great poets, are direct creations from the hand of the Lord. You are one such. Just the same, I wish you were here!" Ibid., 41.

36. Nelson, *In Pursuit of Right and Justice*, 223.

RUTH BADER GINSBURG

Remembrance of Judge Edmund L. Palmieri

In the last decade, the American public embraced Supreme Court Justice
Ruth Bader Ginsburg as a women's rights icon and pop culture celebrity.
There are documentaries and books on the justice's groundbreaking career,
socks and coffee cups bearing her likeness, and even Justice Ginsburg dolls and
finger puppets. This fandom is a phenomenon unprecedented in the history of
the Court.

Many accounts of the Justice's early days as a lawyer include the fact that
despite her sterling academic record at both Harvard and Columbia Law
Schools, Justice Felix Frankfurter rejected out of hand the idea of hiring Ginsburg as a law clerk. Historical explanations for Justice Frankfurter's decision
vary slightly, although they all relate to gender. Some accounts assert that Justice Frankfurter did not want to be the first justice to break the tradition of
hiring only male clerks, an explanation that rings hollow given the fact that
William O. Douglas hired the first female law clerk—Lucille Loman—in 1944.
Other accounts point to more blatant sexism, asserting that Justice Frankfurter was worried Ginsburg might wear pants in chambers (the Justice did not
approve of women in pants[1]) or be offended by his swearing.

Former Frankfurter law clerk Paul Bender (October term 1959) recalls
talking with the Justice about the prospect of hiring a female law clerk.

> One day during the term Justice Frankfurter comes into our office and
> announces "guess who Al Sacks wants to send me as a law clerk next
> year—Ruth Bader Ginsburg." My co-clerk and I told him that it was a
> wonderful idea, but Justice Frankfurter replied that "she has a couple of
> kids [Ginsburg only had one child at this time], and her husband has
> been ill, and you know that I work you guys very hard, and I do curse
> sometimes" as reasons why it wouldn't be a good idea. Well, that wasn't
> the case. We had the softest job of all the law clerks at the court—we

didn't work nights or weekends—and the Justice did not use four letter words. I concluded that the Justice wasn't comfortable with a female law clerk. This was odd since the Justice had strong intellectual relationships with a number of women, including the wives of some of his law clerks.[2]

Curiously, Second Circuit Court of Appeals Judge Learned Hand cited the same concern about swearing as the reason why he, too, would not consider hiring Ginsburg. On one occasion, Ginsburg had the opportunity to question Judge Hand about this rationale. Ginsburg was riding in the back seat of an automobile driven by Judge Edmund Palmieri. Judge Hand was in the front passenger seat. After Judge Hand uttered some blue language, Ginsburg inquired why the Judge was seemingly no longer concerned about cursing in front of a female. His response: "'Young lady . . . here I am not looking you in the face.'"[3]

As for Justice Frankfurter's decision, Justice Ginsburg later wrote: "I was disappointed but not surprised. There were no antidiscrimination laws on the books when I graduated from law school and men of a certain age were not accustomed to dealing with women in a work setting (except for secretaries). And being a mother of a four-year-old diminished my chances."[4]

Luckily for Ginsburg, she had a champion in Columbia law professor Gerald Gunther. The constitutional law professor was responsible for finding clerkships for Columbia law students, and Ginsburg stated that she was "his most challenging case" due to her gender and her young child. "In those now ancient days, a mother was more than legal employers would bargain for," explained Justice Ginsburg.[5]

Ginsburg was also lucky that Judge Edmund L. Palmieri of the Southern District of New York was one of the federal judges who received an inquiry from Gunther. Like Ginsburg, Judge Palmieri was a Columbia Law School graduate and a member of its law review. After graduation, Palmieri served as Charles Evans Hughes's legal secretary when the former and future Supreme Court justice was a member of the Court of International Justice at The Hague. Palmieri would subsequently work as an assistant United States attorney, as a law secretary to New York mayor Fiorello La Guardia, as a domestic relations court judge, as assistant corporation counsel to the city of New York, as a lieutenant colonel who received the Legion of Merit and two battle stars for his overseas service in the United States Army, and in private practice before being appointed to the federal bench in 1954 by President Dwight Eisenhower. Palmieri would be the first Italian American to serve in the Southern District.

Unlike many of his peers, Judge Palmieri did not disqualify law clerk candidates because of gender. "My father had the right mind set," explains his daughter, Marie-Claude Wrenn. "If you distinguished yourself academically and demonstrated writing skills, it did not really matter if you were a woman or a man."[6] In keeping with this philosophy, Judge Palmieri hired Yale Law School graduate Jeanne Ritchie Silver to serve as one of his first law clerks.

According to Professor Malvina Halberstam, Judge Palmieri initially resisted the idea of hiring a female clerk who was also a mother.

> Years later, I learned from Professor Gunther that even though Judge Palmieri was impressed by Ruth Bader Ginsburg's record, he was very reluctant to appoint her as his clerk, and did so only after a great deal of urging by Gunther, who knew him personally, and a written promise by a male student that if the appointment of Ginsburg did not work out he would leave his law firm to take over the clerkship.[7]

Wrenn carefully points out that any concerns her father had about hiring Ginsburg were related to motherhood, not gender. "Her status as a mother would have given my father pause," explains Wrenn. "My father would have been solicitous. He would have wanted to assure himself that everyone was happy and everything was under control" [in the Ginsburg household].

Judge Palmieri's fears of hiring a female law clerk with a young child were quickly allayed by Ginsburg's exemplary work. In fact, the Judge hired Professor Halberstam to succeed Ginsburg—thus hiring two female law clerks in a row.[8] In the next twenty years, the Judge would hire ten more female clerks.

Wrenn recalls the first time that she met Ruth Bader Ginsburg:

> She was pretty and small, quiet and serious. Because she was small, she looked younger than her age. When I walked into the law clerk's office in chambers and was introduced, I was stunned by her youthfulness. Who is this kid that my father hired? It did not strike me that she was female and my father never remarked on her gender. I don't think that she said anything. Little did I know at the time that it was a moment in history.[9]

Wrenn adds that Judge Palmieri and Ginsburg had much in common, including their Brooklyn roots and their love of opera. "My father always spoke about

Ruth in laudatory terms, impressed with her intelligence and abilities from day one. I think that he felt very lucky to have her."

What follows are the remarks that Justice Ginsburg prepared for Judge Palmieri's memorial service after his death in 1989.

In his extraordinary service on the bench, Judge Edmund L. Palmieri helped educate over thirty law clerks. I had the good fortune to be one of them. In the two years I worked in his chambers, from 1959 until 1961, I observed the work-ways of a wise and compassionate jurist, but I learned at least as much about the art of good living. Judge Palmieri loved beautiful sights, sounds, and tastes. On our late afternoon walks across the bridge to Brooklyn and back, he spoke of opera, art, and theatre, or of great books, architecture, scenic places, fine food and wine. To convey the spirit of this true gentleman, I will quote from some of our 1980s correspondence.

Soon after my appointment to the D.C. Circuit, Judge Palmieri wrote of his pride and pleasure. "One day," he said, "I hope to slip into your courtroom quietly to enjoy your presence on the bench."[10] My colleagues arranged, instead, for Judge Palmieri's service to our court as a visiting judge. He graced our bench in 1982, 1984, and again in 1988, and he regularly aided other circuits as well, including the Ninth and the Fifth. Judge Palmieri enjoyed being in D.C. in the cherry blossom season and on each visit, he and his beloved wife, Cecile Claude Verron Palmieri, planned something special—an afternoon touring Hillwood or attending a National Gallery exhibition. After his spring 1988 week with us, he wrote: "I hear from my friends in Paris that the Gaugin exhibition is now in full sway there, requiring at least two hours wait before admission. How fortunate we were to have been able to see it in Washington, D.C., in quiet, comfortable circumstances."[11]

In 1987, I wrote to Judge Palmieri about a conference I attended that winter in Paris at the French Sénat. He remembered things past: "The French Sénat building and the beautiful gardens it overlooks bring back a host of wonderful memories. I had the run of the building and the use of its splendid library when I was there as a young lawyer for several months in 1930 . . . And I never missed a chance to enjoy the gardens, especially after lunch at a superb nearby restaurant called Foyot."[12] (Judge Palmieri and his family spoke French at home, and he was equally fluent in Italian.)

Judge Palmieri stayed au courant with, and often applauded, the innovations of his colleagues. He wrote approvingly, for example, of Judge Pierre Leval's conduct of the Westmoreland trial: "With the right counsel and the right case,"

Judge Palmieri commented with enthusiasm, "his procedure should save lots of time and effort."[13] He also sought for his own endeavors the frank evaluation of others. In 1988, for example, he ruled that Congress could not require the Palestine Liberation Organization to close its observer mission to the United Nations; in a companion opinion, however, he concluded that the government could prohibit P.L.O. activities not connected to the U.N. mission.[14] "If and when you can get to it," he wrote soon after publication of the opinions, "I'd be grateful for your critical comment on my P.L.O. decision."[15]

Judge Palmieri had mastered the lawyer's craft, and he had uncommonly good sense, judicial instincts and insights. I recall how, on short notice, and without doing violence to 28 U.S.C. §2283,[16] he stopped a state court settlement that could have sheltered wrongdoing and wrongdoers associated with a swindler's schemes and manipulations. He was among the few judges in the 1950s ready to impose prison sentences on white-collar criminals—antitrust, securities, and tax law violators.

I recall only one case in which I seriously questioned Judge Palmieri's judgment. The issue, in an estate tax controversy, was whether the life tenant, a single woman in her forties at the time of the donor's death, was then capable of having children (in legal terms, whether the possibility of issue was so remote as to be negligible). Impossible for her to have a first child at that overripe age I insisted. More experienced in the world than his twenty-six-year-old law clerk, Judge Palmieri firmly but kindly disagreed and ruled for the Commissioner. He said I would come to understand. He was right.

His caring for his former law clerks was remarkable. When one of my predecessors, for years a law teacher, received a visiting appointment at a D.C. law school, Judge Palmieri wrote: "It would make me very happy" if you could be in touch with him during his stay.[17] In my daughter's first year on the Columbia law faculty, he corresponded: "I am happy to hear good things about the new member of the Columbia Law School faculty. You must be very proud of Jane. So am I."[18]

Judge Palmieri was indeed a family man. He so loved his children, son Alain, daughters Marie-Claude and Michelle. I believe his hopes and expectations for them account in large measure for his willingness to entertain my application. In the 1950s, few judges would even interview women for law clerk positions. (Judge Palmieri's most excellent and cherished friend, Judge Learned Hand, for example, wanted no woman as a law clerk in his chambers and did not hesitate to say so.) In my case, there was some hesitation on Judge Palmieri's part. I was a woman, and that was not a problem for him. But I was also the mother of a four-year-old child. To my great good fortune, upon the urging of one of my teachers at Columbia Law School, Judge Palmieri decided to take a chance on me. He thereafter engaged other mothers, content that they could do the job.

A reporter, in 1983, asked several of Judge Palmieri's former law clerks if we knew why the judge "hired female clerks at a time when it was not the thing to do."[19] We all had the same suspicion. Judge Palmieri wanted his own children to enjoy equal opportunity, to be judged on the basis of their merit. As one of the former clerks said: the judge "always realized professional ability had nothing to do with sex," and "maybe it was because of his attitude that his two daughters became professionals,"[20] one a physician, the other a writer and lawyer. Judge Palmieri wrote that he found the law clerks' conclusion about his motivations "most gratifying."[21]

In the last letter I received from him, in the winter of 1989, Judge Palmieri wrote: "I have just tried two criminal cases with juries. They have left me rather tired. One of them is now engaging me with a motion for a new trial. It is all grist for the mill and I am not complaining. I expect to take some time off, however, before the increased activity of the spring term."[22] Judge Palmieri's illness stopped his plans for the spring term. He served his court and his country, almost until the end of his life. He was, as his revered colleague Judge Learned Hand wrote of him, "a just and proficient judge, a charming and entertaining companion, a warm and generous friend." He taught his law clerks, by his example, to strive for what one believes to be right, to be gentle and compassionate, and to enjoy life in full measure.

Notes

1. David Margolick, "Trial by Adversity Shapes Jurist's Outlook," *New York Times*, June 25, 1993.

2. Paul Bender, interview by Todd C. Peppers.

3. Margolick, "Trial by Adversity."

4. Ruth Bader Ginsburg, letter to Todd C. Peppers, October 13, 2016.

5. Ruth Bader Ginsburg, "Memories of Gerald Gunther," *Stanford Law Review* 55 (December 2002): 639.

6. Correspondence between Todd C. Peppers and Marie-Claude Wrenn.

7. Malvina Halberstam, "Ruth Bader Ginsburg: The First Jewish Woman on the United States Supreme Court," *Cardozo Law Review* 19 (March 1998): 1441, 1443.

8. Ibid., note 4.

9. Correspondence between Todd C. Peppers and Marie-Claude Wrenn.

10. Edmund L. Palmieri, letter to Ruth Bader Ginsburg, October 22, 1980.

11. Edmund L. Palmieri, letter to Ruth Bader Ginsburg, January 30, 1989.

12. Edmund L. Palmieri, letter to Ruth Bader Ginsburg, April 29, 1987.

13. Edmund L. Palmieri, letter to Ruth Bader Ginsburg, April 7, 1987. To keep the jury on track during the course of a long and complex libel trial, Judge Leval allowed counsel to make brief interim summations from time to time as the case unfolded. He also put a limit on the total number of hours each side could use to present its case. See Leval, "From the Bench: Westmoreland v. CBS," 12 *Litigation* 7 (1985).

14. *United States v. Palestine Liberation Organization,* 695 F. Supp. 1456 (S.D.N.Y. 1988); *Mendelsohn v. Meese,* 695 F. Supp. 1474 (S.D.N.Y. 1988).

15. Edmund L. Palmieri, card to Ruth Bader Ginsburg, August 29, 1988 (from a Swiss village near Montreux).

16. The statute prohibits federal court stay of a state court proceeding "except as expressly authorized by Act of Congress, or where necessary in aid of [the federal court's] jurisdiction, or to protect or effectuate its judgments." 28 U.S.C. §2283 (1982).

17. Edmund L. Palmieri, letters to Ruth Bader Ginsburg, August 3 and August 15, 1983.

18. Edmund L. Palmieri, letter to Ruth Bader Ginsburg, April 7, 1987.

19. *New York Law Journal,* June 13, 1983, at 1.

20. Ibid. at 4.

21. Edmund L. Palmieri, letter to Ruth Bader Ginsburg, June 20, 1983.

22. Edmund L. Palmieri, letter to Ruth Bader Ginsburg, January 30, 1989.

RONALD J. JOHNSON

John H. Wood Jr.

Mentor, Friend, and Hero

From August 14, 1978, to May 29, 1979, I had the honor to serve as a law clerk to the Honorable John Howland Wood Jr. My clerkship was cut short on the morning of May 29, when Judge Wood was assassinated in the driveway of his San Antonio home. In this short essay, I discuss my clerkship with this remarkable jurist and mentor.

Judge Wood was born in Rockport, Texas, on March 31, 1916, into a family steeped in Texas history and tradition. His great-great grandfather was Colonel John H. Wood, a New York native who traveled to Texas to fight in the Texas Revolution. Colonel Wood received a grant of land for his service, and he subsequently became a rancher and founded the cities of Rockport and Woodsboro. The Judge's father was an attorney, and the Judge attended the University of Texas School of Law and briefly entered private practice with the law firm Birkhead, Beckmann & Standard before serving in the U.S. Navy during WWII. After the war, the Judge returned to the law firm, where he remained for the next two decades, being named counsel in over two thousand civil cases.[1]

In October 1970, the Judge was nominated by President Richard Nixon to serve as a federal district court judge in the Western District of Texas. The district included the cities of El Paso and San Antonio, which were considered the front lines of the Department of Justice's efforts to stop the importation of illegal drugs. Judge Wood's criminal docket had a large number of drug trafficking cases, and the Judge quickly developed a reputation for imposing long sentences on drug dealers. The nickname of "Maximum John" was bestowed on Judge Wood, a nickname that the law clerks despised—responding that the Judge "frequently agonized over 'taking away a man's freedom'"[2]

Judge Wood selected me as a law clerk in the summer of 1978, shortly after my graduation from St. Mary's School of Law. While my law school grades were acceptable, I had not considered pursuing a clerkship with Judge Wood. As I prepared to graduate from law school, a prominent Texas trial lawyer named Harold D. Putnam Sr. told me that I had an interview with the Judge.

Harold, the father of a college roommate, had become a surrogate father to me after the premature death of my dad in the fall of 1967. I loved, respected, and obeyed Harold. As an attorney, Harold had litigated cases against the Judge, and the two men shared many of the same interests—the value of hard work, a dedication to the law, and a love of hunting, fishing, young retrievers, and good whiskey. Harold had steered me toward law school. Now he not only arranged for an interview with Judge Wood, but he also wrote a letter of recommendation. I believe that it was Harold's recommendation, combined with the fact that my brother Ed had previously clerked for the Judge, that got me the interview.

The door to Judge Wood's office was open when I arrived for the interview. Judge Wood greeted me, and we initially talked about Harold Putnam and the court battles we both enjoyed with each other. Judge Wood asked about my hobbies and took a special interest in the fact that I had acquired a new Labrador puppy from another mutual friend. As the interview finished, the Judge asked his secretary, Mrs. Krause, to call the dean of the law school. The Judge subsequently requested that the professor teaching the last course required for my August gradation to be kind enough to grade my final examination no later than Saturday, August 14, and verify that I had passed, so the Judge could subsequently give me my oath of office. The grade arrived, the oath of office was administered, and by the following Monday I was in El Paso—attending a session of court with the Judge.

The bar results were subsequently mailed to Mr. Putman's office. When he received my confidential envelope from the Texas Bar Association, he immediately opened the envelope, read my bar grade, and called Judge Wood's El Paso chambers. I was with the Judge when he answered his phone. He expected that the telephone call was from his wife, and he excused me from his office before finishing his conversation. Nothing was said to me about the nature of the telephone call. When the court opened, however, after the lunch break, the Judge surprised me by asking me to rise and announcing to those assembled in the courtroom that I had made an 89 on the Texas Bar Examination. The Judge immediately gave me my oath as a Texas lawyer.

A short celebration was held in Ciudad Juarez, Mexico, that evening. And with that, I became a law clerk to Judge Wood.

Judge Wood always employed two law clerks.[3] The senior clerk handled the civil docket, while the junior clerk handled the criminal docket. The senior clerk that year was Donald Clayton Reser, a bright young lawyer who received a B.A. in economics from Stanford University, an M.B.A. from the University of Texas, and a J.D. from the University of Houston Law Center. An avid tennis player who was the master of the backhand drop shot, Don and the Judge played tennis at the Midland Country Club when we went to Midland for the monthly docket.

Besides handling the civil docket, Don tracked motions and hearing dates. Together, we coordinated the settings for the criminal and civil cases as well as the necessary rulings on those contested motions that needed to be heard and decided in order to move cases toward a final resolution.

My primary responsibility as the junior clerk was the criminal docket. I reviewed motions that affected excludable time for cases in which defendants were not on bond for speedy trial calculations, reviewed and summarized motions, and scheduled motion dockets, trial dockets, and sentencing dockets in the El Paso, Midland, and San Antonio Divisions of the United States District Courts for the Western District of Texas. The clerk's office staff sent the notices to the parties and lawyers, the jury summons, and made arrangements for staffing. I reviewed the coming week's dockets with Judge Wood at the conclusion of each week, and we determined how many cases he would be able to hear that week. Most cases settled, and I would then call the lawyers for a "trailing docket" and told them to be ready for trial if the case was to be heard before their clients' case(s) settled. While Judge Wood considered the relief requested in the motions, we would discuss motions that were not routine motions and the effect of his rulings in complicated drug cases with multiple defendants and a large number of lawyers representing the defendants. After we discussed the motions, Judge Wood instructed me to his written rulings, as per his findings.

Here are a few observations about the faith and trust Judge Wood placed in his law clerks. Judge Wood was randomly assigned a case in which the defendant was charged with thirteen counts of distribution of heroin. Defense counsel was Gerald "Jerry" Goldstein, a former president of the National Association of Criminal Defense Attorneys. Jerry was a gracious, intelligent, and resourceful lawyer whose beliefs in the rights of a criminal defendant to bail were the direct opposite of Judge Wood's. Jerry was appalled by the sentences imposed by Judge Wood for narcotics convictions and took this particular case for the express purpose of obtaining an opinion from the Fifth Circuit Court of Appeals that bail decisions by Judge Wood on defendants convicted of selling narcotics were excessive, cruel, inhumane, and unconstitutional punishments.

After reviewing and researching cases on the right to bail, and distinguishing facts for hours, I was uncomfortable with the detailed findings we drafted, which seemed to be explanations more than findings. I worked into the night and the next morning to polish and refine an order. At 5:00 a.m., I woke up and realized the order and its findings were an apology and an explanation of why Jerry Goldstein was wrong, not why bail was being granted or denied, which is the only question the court should decide.

I drafted a two-sentence order for Judge Wood to review, finding that public records showed the defendant was born in Mexico, resided within one mile of the Mexican border, had relatives on both sides of his family who resided on both sides of the border, was fluent in Spanish, had prior convictions for narcotics, was charged with selling heroin within a mile of elementary schools, and had been indicted for twelve separate offenses. Faced with the prospect of a minimum sentence of 60 years in prison, and the possible sentence of 144 years in prison, the defendant, in the court's opinion, was a flight risk, and for those reasons, bail was to be denied. Judge Wood was going on the bench when I handed him the order and told him I wanted to explain why I changed directions on him as he reviewed the order. At the end of the day we talked, and he told me less is often more and that a judge is very rarely reversed for something not said in an order. He signed the order, as drafted.

That weekend, the Judge told me I did not have to explain myself to him. He told me never to back down before the court when I believed I was right, but to start and end with the words "respectfully" and "in deference to this Court, may I say" and then pause, when addressing a judge who was not receptive to what I was going to say. After making eye contact, resume and state you believe that both attorneys and judges are governed by requirements of respect, candor, and courtesy.

In my subsequent legal career, I have been threatened with contempt—but I have never had a court hold me in contempt. I have taken some licks, but I have never failed to address a court when I felt the court was in error, as courts are rarely wrong, when the issues are properly addressed.

All in all, I served as the Judge's law clerk from August 14, 1978, to May 29, 1979. On what would prove to be the final morning of my clerkship, the Judge called to tell me that he was running behind schedule because of a flat tire. The Judge was waiting for a service vehicle, and he declined my offer to come assist him. The Judge added that when he arrived at chambers, we would review the docket and pending motions before turning to more important matters— a fishing trip that we were planning.

When the chamber's telephone rang again, my world changed forever. On the other end of the line was a neighbor of the Judge's, who told me that the Judge had been shot and was lying in the driveway next to his vehicle. The Judge was struck in the back by a bullet fired from a rifle, and he died by the time he reached a local hospital. He became the first federal judge to be assassinated in the twentieth century.

Six months prior to the Judge's death, local assistant United States attorney James Kerr had survived a similar assassination attempt. In response, the Judge was assigned a protective detail by the U.S. Marshal's Service. The Judge had also been assigned bodyguards in 1974, after receiving a death threat. The Judge was angered by the attempted killing of Kerr. In a letter to a member of Congress, Wood wrote: Words cannot express the depth of my feelings of outrage at the attempt to intimidate the prosecution of criminal cases by such threats on the lives of the members of the federal prosecutors and the courts."[4] In the weeks prior to his own death, however, the Judge declined further protection— telling a federal marshal that "'if someone really wants to kill me, all the protection in the world would not prevent it."[5] He privately told me that he had a job to do, and that he couldn't do that job if his movements were limited.

After receiving word of the shooting, I immediately called the U.S. Marshal's Service, the DEA, and the FBI. After telling the Judge's secretary to stop crying, to call the Judge's children, and then to call his church and ask the parish priest to be prepared to administer the last sacraments. I then called my wife and wept for a long time.

Months later, we learned the assassination was planned by Jamiel Chagra, a defendant charged with the distribution of narcotics under what was to become the "kingpin" statute—which provided discretion of life imprisonment if convicted. The trigger man was identified as Charles Harrelson, an assassin who had been charged with at least two previous murders in Texas. Harrelson and members of the Chagra family were indicted and charged with conspiracy to commit murder; after Harrelson was sentenced to life in prison, his son, Woody Harrelson, spent a great deal of time and money seeking hearings or rehearings filed in San Antonio in hopes of obtaining his father's release. His son's efforts were not successful, and Harrelson died in prison in 2007.

The Judge's death made national headlines, and it was met with outrage and shock. President Jimmy Carter publicly remarked that the Judge's murder was an assault on our very system of justice,"[6] while Attorney General Griffin Bell—himself a former federal judge—declared that "we cannot have a country where federal judges are assassinated or killed," while promising that investigators would leave "no stone unturned" in their search for the killer.[7] The local

Texas legal community contributed to the search by quickly raising a $100,000 reward for information leading to the capture of the unknown assassin.

At the office the day after his death, I answered Judge Wood's phone. An employee of the United States Federal Court's Administrative Office called and identified himself, and he asked that Judge Wood's last check be returned, as he had not worked the entire month. I was not surprised by the phone call, having learned during my clerkship that the Administrative Office put form over substance. I assured that civil servant that I would take care of the matter immediately.

I immediately called Mrs. Krause and asked in which drawer she kept Mrs. Wood's bank deposit slips; I called Mrs. Wood and told her I was very sorry to disturb her, but the government needed a few minutes of our time. She graciously told me to come over right then, while her family was present, and told me I was welcome. After her son-in-law, Jeff Moorman, answered the door, she endorsed the Judge's check, which I deposited into Mrs. Wood's account. Later, I assisted her in preparing various forms for submission to various federal agencies and handling other matters related to the Judge's retirement and reimbursement of contributions to the judicial retirement system. In short, I did what I believed Judge Wood would have done for my wife had I died.

Judge Wood's funeral mass was held on May 30, 1979, at Our Lady of Grace Catholic Church—the same parish church in which his daughters were married and his grandchildren baptized. A rosary had been held at a local funeral home the night before. The funeral was attended by four hundred mourners, including thirteen federal judges who were purposefully scattered through the audience and watched over by a protective force of twenty federal marshals, FBI agents, and state police troopers. Another one hundred mourners gathered on the lawn in front of the church, unable to find seats inside the small stone building. At the front of the church was the Judge's brown wooden coffin, covered with red roses and surrounded by large arrangements of white daisies. In his eulogy, Monsignor Martin lamented the loss of his close friend and reminded the audience that the Judge's "work against the power of evil, whatever shape, must go on with greater vigor than ever."[8]

Judge Wood's former and present law clerks served as pall bearers and accompanied the hearse and immediate family to the private interment in a family cemetery in his hometown of Rockport, Texas. My wife, Sasa, and I rode to Rockport with former law clerks Ronald Hornberger and Marshall Steves and their wives. We shared a cup of kindness before the bitterness of laying Judge Wood down in the cold ground.

The law clerks would again gather for the dedication of the Judge John H. Wood, Jr. Federal Courthouse in San Antonio, a building originally constructed as a theater for the 1968 World's Fair. A year later, the clerks gathered for a dinner hosted by Mrs. Wood at the San Antonio Country Club. Sadly, Mrs. Wood would pass away within a few years after the Judge's murder.

Until his death, I rarely considered the relationship we enjoyed. There are many memories when I look back, especially those occasions when our wives would come out to El Paso over the two-week tours of duty, and we would all go out together. One memory that stands out is the "ultimate" hunt in January 1979, when the federal courthouse closed because of snow and ice while quail, dove, and duck seasons were all open. The Judge, his Brittany spaniel, Beauregard, and I left for Kinsbury, Texas, in a four-wheel drive Jeep CJ-5 convertible with a tear in the driver's side front door screen (my co-clerk Don lived in dread of duck hunting trips and did not join us). The Judge and I hit the ultimate hat trick that day, and we each got complete limits of the three species—ten Blue Wing Teal, twelve Mourning Doves, and fifteen Bob White quail.

It rained on the way home, and the wool trousers I had on over my insulated boots froze around my left ankle in the thirty-degree chill. When we got out at Judge Wood's house, his wife, Kathryn (Katy), told me to get my frozen boots and pants off and get in the house and in the shower, immediately—all while berating "John H." (his nickname) for "freezing the poor boy." There was a robe when I got out of the shower. We drank hot buttered rum, cleaned the game we had killed that morning, and laughed about the best ending to the best hunt ever. Judge Wood told me that when we were hunting and not working, I could now call him "John H." because we were friends.

The remaining weeks of my clerkship were spent in the chambers of the Honorable Adrian A. Spears, chief judge, United States District Court for the Western District of Texas. I received two gifts from Katy Wood—a picture of Judge Wood and a sterling silver water pitcher, inscribed with the words "His Dear Boy, Friend, and Lawyer, in Life and Death." Not a hunt or a fishing trip has gone by that I do not miss Harold and John H. and their warmth, friendship, and wisdom.

Almost forty years later, I am unable to express exactly how devastating Judge Wood's death was. I cry every time I think about it. My daughter, Allyson, will complete her internship for the Honorable David R. Jones, chief bankruptcy judge for the Southern District of Texas, this spring. Life is coming full circle. Perhaps now I can deal with the Judge's death and regain the faith in humanity that I lost when John H. was assassinated.

The world and the United States courts have changed, and not for the better. Judge Wood was a remarkable man. He was not insensitive or damned obstinate, but he knew what he could do and what he would not do under the law. He was a lawyer, a judge, a mentor, a husband, a father, and a dear and treasured friend. Judge Wood has an indelible place in history and in my heart.

Notes

1. Joseph C. Elliott, "In Memory of the Honorable John H. Wood, Jr., United States District Judge," *St. Mary's Law Journal* 11 (1979): xi; "Judge Wood Brings 30 Years of Experience to El Paso," *El Paso Herald-Post,* December 23, 1970, 10.

2. Kemper Diehl, "U.S. Judge, Known for Severity in Drug Cases, Is Slain in Texas," *Washington Post,* May 30, 1979; John M. Crewdson, "Federal District Judge Assigned to Drug Trial Is Shot in Texas," *New York Times,* May 30, 1979, 1.

3. Judge Wood's law clerks included Joseph C. Elliott, Edward M. Johnson, Howard "Howie" Newton, Marshall T. Steves III, Clayton Trotter, and Donald Clayton Reser.

4. William J. Choyke, "Judge Voiced 'Outrage' at Intimidation," *Austin-American Statesman,* May 31, 1979, A1.

5. Associated Press, "Top Detective Called into Slain Judge Case," *Press and Sun Bulletin* (Binghamton, N.Y.), May 30, 1979, 6C.

6. Associated Press, "U.S. Judge Is Slain in San Antonio, *Baltimore Sun,* May 30, 1979, A1.

7. Associated Press, "Agents Search for U.S. Judge's Assassin," *Paris (Tex.) News,* May 30, 1979, A1.

8. Associated Press, "Reward Money Offered for Judge's Assassin: Mourners Gather for Judge John Wood's Funeral Mass," *Paris (Tex.) News,* June 1, 1979, 4A.

LYNN E. BLAIS

Learning to Be a Lawyer for Justice

An East Texas Clerkship

The life of the law has not been logic; it has been experience.... The law embodies the story of a nation's development through many centuries, and it cannot be dealt with as if it contained only the axioms and corollaries of a book of mathematics.

Oliver Wendell Holmes Jr., *The Common Law* (1881)

There was a particular breed of federal judge in the south in the latter part of the twentieth century that history has fairly recorded among the heroes of the civil rights movement.[1] These judges were known for their passion for social justice and their steadfast commitment to enforcing the promise of the Civil War amendments and the recently enacted civil rights statutes in recalcitrant southern states. Judge William Wayne Justice was one of these heroic judges. During his tenure on the federal bench—which ranged from 1968 until his passing in 2009—Judge Justice stood up to injustice in every instance in which it was presented in his courtroom. During that time, he ordered the state of Texas to end racial segregation in public schools,[2] forced state officials to rehabilitate the Dickensian state penal system,[3] required officials to rectify ongoing racial segregation in public housing communities,[4] invalidated a policy requiring undocumented school children to pay tuition to attend public schools,[5] and mandated drastically needed improvements in juvenile detention centers[6] and institutions for persons with intellectual disabilities.[7] And while this list reads to most like a lifetime of accomplishments, it represents just a portion of Judge Justice's important decisions during his time on the bench.

Judge Justice entered these sweeping and transformative orders in what was, essentially, hostile territory. When Judge Justice took the bench in 1968, East

Texas, like many other areas in the Deep South, had not yet fully emerged from the Jim Crow era. In Tyler and surrounding areas, public schools were still predominantly segregated, as were public housing projects and private neighborhoods. Notwithstanding federal public accommodations laws, public nightlife in Tyler was also entirely segregated. Many East Texas counties were dry counties, meaning that retailers could not sell alcohol by the bottle, and only "private clubs" could sell drinks by the glass. Because they were private, these clubs were essentially self-segregated.

De facto segregation even extended as far as the renowned social event of the year—the fair. Although state officials had outlawed the practice of setting aside one day per week for people of color to attend statewide and regional fairs in the mid-1950s, during my clerkship in 1988 everyone in town knew that Thursday was "Negro Day" at the East Texas State Fair. In these and many other ways, Tyler was a harsh and unforgiving city for people of color and undocumented aliens in 1968, and the white business and social leaders of the city were comfortable with the status quo.

As a result, in response to Judge Justice's early controversial rulings (the school desegregation case was decided in 1970), denizens of Tyler's white "society" were openly hostile to Judge and Mrs. Justice. The Justices were no longer included in the elaborate social events that characterize southern society, and they were often subjected to rude and hostile remarks when in public. Notwithstanding this substantial personal sacrifice, the Judge kept his eye on the prize and his focus on the law.

This combination of a progressive, heroic judge in a conservative and hostile community set the tone of our clerkships with Judge Justice. The Judge's law clerks were young, idealistic recent law school graduates who came to Tyler eager to work hard and "do right." Most of us came from elite East or West Coast law schools, and many of us had not spent meaningful time in the south before starting work in the Judge's chambers. But I suspect we all had a similar vision of what we were getting into: we had signed on to work for a legal legend, a larger-than-life hero who fearlessly stood up for justice notwithstanding the great personal sacrifice this caused he and Mrs. Justice in a community that overtly rejected the values that he, and we, held so dear.

Ultimately, however, in the day-to-day operations of this humble federal judge's chambers we learned that heroes aren't always larger-than-life, and heroism isn't always flashy and showy. The Judge's particular brand of heroism was simply doing the right thing—over and over and over again, day in and day out, when people were watching and especially when they weren't, when easier alternatives presented themselves, and the right thing was the hard thing, when standing up for the underdog meant sacrificing your family's social standing, and when the problems to be addressed seemed never to end. Clerking for Judge Justice was a master class in quiet heroism.

In December 1994, in anticipation of the Judge's seventy-fifth birthday, his law clerks at the time, Eric Albritton and Reid Wittliff, solicited one-page letters from his former staff and law clerks to be combined into a book of tributes and remembrances for the Judge. This book, which is now a part of the Judge William Wayne Justice Papers in the Tarlton Law Library at Texas Law, is a treasure trove of stories and memories.[8] Several common themes are woven throughout these letters, and I have chosen to organize this essay around them.

Clerking for a Progressive Judge in a Conservative Town

Judge Justice had a novel interview technique. Because few of his clerkship applicants had ever been to Tyler before their interview, the Judge took the opportunity to introduce them to the character of the town on their first visit. He did this by meeting the applicant at his or her hotel at 6:15 a.m. and driving them to a greasy spoon named D's Royal Coffee Shop for breakfast. According to the Judge, having breakfast at a diner full of local residents was the best way for an applicant to get a sense of Tyler and of East Texas culture. Most of the other customers at the diner would recognize the Judge when he walked in with an applicant. Some would nod hello, others would glare, and still others would turn to their tablemates and start into a heated discussion of the Judge's most recent, or most controversial, ruling. By 7:00 a.m. the applicant generally had a pretty good idea of what they would be getting into if they accepted an offer to clerk for the Judge.

After breakfast at the coffee shop, the Judge would deliver the applicant to chambers, and the rest of the interview would take place there. The applicant would meet with the current law clerks and again with the Judge in a more formal office interview. But perhaps the most important meeting was with the Judge's two long-serving secretaries—Marcelle Simmons and Debbie Magee. If the Judge was the intellectual and moral head of the chambers, Marcelle and Debbie were its warm beating heart. They both were fiercely protective of the family-like atmosphere in chambers and were committed to making sure that future law clerks would fit in. So several times during the long day of interviews the applicant would sit in the secretaries' office chatting with Debbie and Marcelle—ostensibly waiting for their next interview but actually being scrutinized for collegiality, graciousness, sense of humor, and other qualities that Debbie and Marcelle felt were important to a smoothly operating, supportive, and fun work environment.

The Judge's interview strategy worked. Law clerks came to Tyler aware of the Judge's role in the broader community and prepared to embrace and enhance the close knit community within chambers. In my case, in fact, the Judge's lesson from D's Royal Coffee Shop was reinforced on the flight home after my interview. I had accepted the Judge's offer of a clerkship, and I made the long drive back to Dallas thrilled with my good fortune. The Judge seemed brilliant and kind and witty and hard-working, and my time spent with his current clerks and staff made clear that they loved him and loved their jobs.

I was still reveling in my good fortune as I took my seat on the Southwest Airlines flight back to Boston. In those days, at least some Southwest planes had an unusual seating configuration at the bulkhead in which two seats faced backward and thus four passengers were essentially sitting knee-to-knee during the flight. I was in such a seat, sharing this space with three middle-aged men in business suits. We exchanged pleasantries for a while, until one man ask me, "What brings you to Texas?" I replied, probably gushing, about my visit with Judge Justice and my acceptance of a job in his chambers. Our little seating area went silent. The men exchanged glances. Finally, one of them said, quietly, "You do know that everyone in Texas hates him, don't you?"

Of course, not everyone in Texas hated Judge Justice, but Tyler was a lonely place for him and Mrs. Justice and, albeit to a lesser extent, for his staff and law clerks. Perhaps for that reason, life in the Judge's chambers offered something of a surrogate family and social life for the Judge, his staff, and his law clerks. Work days started early in the Judge's chambers, when the Judge and his staff and clerks gathered in the breakroom for breakfast. Some people just had coffee, while others stored cereal or other breakfast food in the breakroom and tucked into a full breakfast every morning. Breakfast in the breakroom was a casual time for catching up on everyone's lives and discussing politics and current events, followed by a rundown of the day's business in chambers.

At lunchtime, the Judge would often go out for lunch, but law clerks and staff generally gathered again in the breakroom to eat a lunch brought from home and to play very competitive rounds of dominos. Clerks who didn't have southern roots or who had not grown up playing dominos were at a severe disadvantage—the Judge's staff was full of dominos ringers!

Shared weekend outings were also common. The Judge loved movies and often sought a law clerk or two to accompany him to weekend matinees. And he loved BBQ, especially the BBQ at Pat Gee's—a classic East Texas BBQ joint located disconcertingly close to a cow pasture. Saturday morning lines outside Pat Gee's often left groups of the Judge's staff and clerks standing next to the cows—the pungent fresh air of an East Texas ranch competing with the smells from the BBQ pit for our olfactory attention. I was a vegetarian while I was clerking for Judge Justice, but the Pat Gee trips were as much for camaraderie as for good food, so I spent many a Saturday morning eating white bread and pickles at Pat Gee's. And when we were not socializing with Judge and Mrs. Justice, law clerks and court staff often gathered at one or another's house on weekends for dinner or drinks.

It is not uncommon for law clerks to feel a special kinship with their judge, co-clerk(s), and the judge's staff. In fact, it is probably a common element of most successful clerkships. But clerking for a progressive judge in a deeply conservative small city far from home presents distinctive pressures that serve to crystallize the importance of the chambers' family. As Jackee Cox said, "We needed the sense of family that you created in your chambers, because Tyler was a strange and foreign land for clerks who came from everywhere but there."[9] The clerkship with Judge Justice was an entrée into a close-knit chambers family, which included not just Judge and Mrs. Justice, but the entire court staff and all the current and former law clerks.

The Importance of a Hard Day's Work Done Well

Judge Justice worked hard. When he was sworn into the United States District Court for the Eastern District of Texas in 1968, two judges were responsible for covering the entire Eastern District.[10] At that time, the six divisions of the Eastern District encompassed forty-one counties, ranging from Cooke County in the northwest to Jefferson County in the southeast—a distance of approximately 350 miles. Joe Fisher was chief judge at the time, and he assigned Judge Justice responsibility for all of the cases filed in four of those six divisions (Marshall, Paris, Sherman, and Tyler) and one-third of the cases in the fifth (Beaumont). Chief Judge Fisher handled all the cases in the Texarkana Division and two-thirds of the Beaumont cases. Trying cases in five of the six divisions kept Judge Justice and his clerks and staff on the road for as many as twenty weeks a year.

On the Sunday night before a travel week, he and his clerks and staff would pack up everything they needed to hold court in another courthouse in their various cars and drive off to Sherman or Paris or Lufkin to set up the courtroom for the week. In those days, "everything they needed to hold court" included boxes and boxes of files, as well as typewriters and the court reporter's equipment. The Judge helped load the cars along with everyone else, and then they would drive off and settle into a local motel. The pace of work was hectic during these weeks on the road, because the Judge would try to resolve as many motions and hold as many trials as he could squeeze into the week. And his clerks often worked late into the night researching legal issues that had arisen during the day and drafting jury charges for the following day. And when they all packed up again at the end of the week and returned to Tyler, the work of the Tyler docket seemed to have expanded exponentially while they were gone.

Over time, additional judges joined the Eastern District, and Judge Justice's travel schedule became more manageable. But the Judge's workload did not diminish appreciably. As the Judge gained a reputation for paying careful attention to progressive legal challenges, civil rights lawyers worked hard to find ways to file claims in his court. As a result, during his first several years on the bench Judge Justice issued sweeping orders or accepted comprehensive agreed settlements compelling state officials to reform major state institutions in several cases. In some of these cases, the Judge had appointed monitors to oversee the state's compliance efforts, and the Judge and his clerks worked closely with the monitors—all while managing a docket that often had more than seven hundred active cases.

Then came *Ruiz v. Estelle*.[11] Beginning in 1972, when Judge Justice assigned his law clerks the task of reviewing the hundreds of prisoner petitions, the massive prison reform litigation threatened to overwhelm the Judge and his law clerks. They were instrumental in orchestrating the development of the case, from securing excellent representation for the plaintiffs to ordering the United States Department of Justice to appear as amicus curiae (after discussing it with the DOJ and being assured that the department was interested in being involved), so it could undertake the investigation that the plaintiffs and their lawyers could not afford to do. And state officials objected strenuously at virtually every step.

Eventually, the Judge set *Ruiz* for trial. The state filed a motion to transfer the trial to Houston because so many of the inmate witnesses were incarcerated in or near Houston (and, most likely, in an effort to secure a different judge for the trial). Judge Justice agreed that Houston would be a more convenient venue and also a safer one for the inmates, so he granted the motion to move the trial. Typically, when a case is transferred to a different federal judicial district, it is assigned to a new judge in that district. But Judge Justice felt that he "couldn't in good conscience transfer a case of this magnitude without making an offer to follow it," so he told the chief judge of the Southern District that "if he felt any injustice would be done to his judges, [Judge Justice] was perfectly willing to follow the case and try it."[12]

Thus began an extraordinary 161-day trial in Houston. Most weeks during the trial the Judge and his staff and clerks would travel two hundred miles from Tyler to Houston on Sunday evening and check into a Holiday Inn, hold court for the next five days, and then battle Friday afternoon traffic in Houston to get back to Tyler for the weekend. At the conclusion of the trial, the Judge returned to Tyler and to the backlog of motions and trials waiting for him on his Tyler docket. For the next eighteen months, while working through that backlog, the Judge and his law clerks evaluated the voluminous record, researched the complex constitutional claims, and drafted the 249-page *Ruiz* opinion.

The *Ruiz* case—the trial in Houston, the research and drafting of the opinion, and the posttrial compliance phase working with the Special Master—likely sets the high-water mark for how demanding a clerkship with Judge Justice could be. But throughout his tenure on the bench the Judge demonstrated the importance of a hard day's work done well, and he expected as much from his law clerks.

Learning to Be a Lawyer

Judge Justice was a lawyer's lawyer, and clerking for him offered an intense and comprehensive education on the art and science of the practice of law. The Judge ran his courtroom with a precision reflective of his time in the military. Early in his judicial career, the Judge adopted a demanding docket and courtroom management protocol that he implemented to move cases through his court. There would be no languishing lawsuits on his watch. In an early pretrial conference for every case, the Judge would set a strict timeline for pretrial discovery and motions, and then he would hold the lawyers to it. The Judge took pretrial motions seriously and would not shy away from granting summary judgment when warranted; he often mentioned his experience as a lawyer, when he thought some judges denied motions for summary judgment just because it was the easier course of action, with little downside risk if the judge was wrong. Judge Justice never took the easy way out. Law clerks were informed that every motion for summary judgment was to be reviewed carefully and with an open mind toward granting. The Judge would not force lawyers to try an issue that should have been settled as a matter of law.

And if a case did go to trial (more cases did in those days), the Judge refused to preside over trials by ambush. At the final pretrial conference in each case, the Judge required the parties to work together to prepare a joint pretrial order that set out all the uncontested and contested facts and issues of law, and lists of witnesses and exhibits from both sides. Clerks were deeply involved in every stage of the pretrial process, and the Judge's efficient and expedient case management system provided clear instruction in how to proceed with our own cases when we became lawyers.

Once a trial was underway, the lawyering lessons continued. Judge Justice was an active participant in voir dire and often did most of the questioning. Lawyers knew they had to be particularly well prepared to try a case in the Judge's courtroom, because he was always exceptionally well prepared and thinking two steps ahead of the lawyers. So direct examinations were usually crisp and sharp, and cross-examinations generally cut right to the point. For a law clerk, this was quite a show, and many of us saw some of the best lawyers in Texas do their best work in the Judge's courtroom.

Of course, not all of the lawyers in Judge Justice's courtroom were highly skilled, and sometimes the lessons we learned were how *not* to practice law. As Amy Johnson recounted, the times when Judge Justice relaxed his tight control over the courtroom just enough to give a lawyer enough rope to hang himself were instructive as well:

> I learned about "the record" in an employment discrimination case. A black man brought suit after being fired for dating a white woman. When white witnesses testified about the plaintiff, they referred to him as "Jim Bob," but they called the white people by their surnames. Before that time, Judge had always required witnesses to refer to people in his court by their last names. But he later explained that the record itself would show the prejudice that pervaded the workplace.[13]

The best (or at least the most fun) lawyering instructions the Judge gave his law clerks were delivered in his scrawling handwriting on torn slips of paper. During trials, the law clerk assigned to the case would sit at a little desk to the side and below the Judge, and while the trial was proceeding the Judge would often slip that clerk handwritten notes. Some of the notes were requests for books that the Judge wanted to consult while on the bench or for quick research on a legal issue that had piqued his interest. But many of the notes were observations about the lawyers—what they were doing right and what they were doing wrong. The Judge was an astute observer of people, and he would offer insight about which of a lawyer's strategies or actions were working and which were not.

Maybe a lawyer was going on a little too long in a closing argument and was losing the jury's attention. Or maybe another lawyer's questions to a witness during cross-examination were too strident, and several jurors were visibly upset. Or maybe a lawyer was posturing, but the Judge could tell that the jury could see right through it. These notes were invaluable lessons in the human aspect of the practice of law.

But every now and then one of the notes would contain a joke. It would be a dry, wry observation that was so spot-on that it would be all the law clerk could do to stop herself from bursting out in raucous laughter right there in the courtroom. And a sidelong glance to the Judge would reveal him sitting quietly on the bench, stone-faced, with a brilliant twinkle in his eye.

The Awesome Authority of the Federal Court

Judge Justice was a realist. He knew that many of his decisions challenged a cherished way of life for some Texans, and he was well aware of the fundamental lack of enforcement mechanisms that characterize our federal judiciary. So he ran a very formal court. According to Judge Justice, he wanted the essential nature of the power of the federal courts to permeate his courtroom. He insisted that men wear coats and ties in his courtroom, and if a man arrived without one, the Judge had extras on hand for him to borrow. Lawyers stood when they addressed the bench, and if the Judge was addressing a litigant (usually a defendant), he or she would stand to listen. Every aspect of a hearing or trial in the Judge's courtroom was a carefully choreographed production intended to impress on the parties the awesome authority of a federal court.

To this end, the Judge had his law clerks "knock him in" and "cry open" each session of court. Before he entered the courtroom, one clerk would stand with him at the door that led from chambers to his bench and bang the knocker three times—issuing three firm and deliberate knocks that reverberated throughout the courtroom. Judge Justice would then enter the courtroom behind his bench, while another clerk stood beside the bench and cried: "Hear ye, hear ye, hear ye! All persons having business before the honorable, the United States District Court for the Eastern District of Texas, are admonished to draw near and give attention, for the court is now in session. God save the United States and this Honorable Court!"

The Judge considered the cry-in a crucial ritual that transformed a mere room in a federal building into powerful apparatus of the civilized state. So new clerks practiced the cry over and over, with the Judge standing in the back of the courtroom, until they captured just the right tone of fearsome sovereignty that the Judge was looking for. Sometimes, however, even that level of command was not enough for the Judge if he perceived one (or more) of the parties before him to be insufficiently impressed with the authority of the rule of law. Jim Tourtelott related one such time from his clerkship year:

> One day we were having a hearing in the Harris County jail case.... The county defendants were being fairly obstreperous, as was their wont. That morning in the break room, Judge gave Jim Wooten and me our marching orders. "Tourtelott," he said, "I want you to cry at the opening louder than you've ever cried before." [I will say without false modesty that asking for that meant Judge was asking for one hell of a noise.] "Wooten, when you knock me in I want that knocker to sound like the hammer of Hell. *I want these sons-of-bitches to know that they are in court.*"[14]

Compassion: Everyone Counts and Everyone's Problems Are Important

By far the most common theme of the law clerks' remembrances was the lesson of compassion and consideration that Judge Justice set for us. Judge Justice was constitutionally inclined to attend to the concerns of the poor, the powerless, the disenfranchised, and the oppressed as carefully as he would consider the polished pleadings of powerful clients with fancy lawyers. Or perhaps with more care, since important legal claims might be hidden in unsophisticated pro se pleadings. Fritz Byers captured this quality eloquently:

> The Judge infused all of [the work], every single inch of the office, every word of the writing, every thread of the thinking, with his singular inspiring mien: every person, every party, every participant, was important, worthy of respectful treatment and careful attention. I have never met anyone else who so thoroughly and constantly conveyed, in words and in deeds, a principled rejection of the great American star machine, by which we segregate luminaries and bit players.[15]

Sandi Zellmer described how the Judge conveyed the importance of this approach to her one day:

You had received numerous letters from a certain inmate of TDCJ, alleging one thing or another. I'd processed one too many and summarily rejected the inmate's allegation that his unit refused to find him some decent shoes. I drafted up a very brief order finding the claim to be frivolous and dismissing it. You sat me down and illustrated, in no uncertain terms, how the lack of decent shoes could truly be a cruel and unusual thing for an inmate who had to work outside in Texas in the winter, and I realized that there could be something there. Indeed, maybe the wardens felt as I initially did that the guy was a crackpot, and gave him ill-fitting shoes in retaliation for all his prior complaints. In the end, I will never forget your way of looking beyond the pleadings at the equities of the situation and people who are affected by your rulings.[16]

In fact, the Judge's insistence on giving every complaint a fair reading was instrumental in the development of the aforementioned prison reform case, *Ruiz v. Estelle*. As I described in an earlier tribute to Judge Justice:

> [The *Ruiz*] case did not arrive fully constructed in the Judge's court, with elegant pleadings laying out alleged constitutional violations. Rather, it grew out of the Judge's attention to the myriad pro se petitions, mostly scrawled, some illegible, that were sent to the judges in the Eastern District by state prisoners complaining about the conditions of their incarceration. He read each letter carefully as it arrived, always concluding that the individual missive did not adequately state a legal claim, but troubled by the patterns and persistence of the letters. So he assigned to two law clerks the task of reading and rereading the letters, to see if a pattern of unlawful conduct could be discerned. The clerks identified four categories in which the allegations could mostly be placed: brutality by staff and other inmates; inadequate medical care; lack of due process for prisoner complaints; and overcrowding. The Judge then consolidated several representative pro se petitions for trial, and requested that William Bennett Turner, a first class prison reform advocate, handle the cases.[17]

Work-Life Balance and the Importance of Having Fun

Judge Justice and his law clerks worked hard, but the clerkship was far from all work and no play. To the contrary. Perhaps because he worked so hard and demanded such hard work from his staff and clerks, the Judge knew that it was important to balance the stress of the job with healthy habits and a healthy dose of fun. Judge Justice became committed to health and fitness when he was in his late thirties, and over the years he adopted a series of different exercise routines. For many years he jogged regularly after work. Later, he took up weightlifting and joined Reuland's Gym, which Feriale Abdul described as a "smelly, loud, clanging gym . . . full of serious weight-lifting types."[18] Eventually, the Judge began to study karate, which he found exhilarating and demanding and an excellent stress reliever.

The Judge encouraged his law clerks to stay physically active as well, and he had a particular way of reminding us that it doesn't do any good to try to work around the clock. Each evening as the Judge was leaving for his daily workout, he would step into the law clerks' shared office to say goodnight. As he left, he would close by quoting Matthew 6:34: "sufficient unto the day is the evil thereof." We clerks came to learn that the Judge interpreted this phrase—or, rather, the entire verse—as an admonition to attend diligently each day's work, but not to delude ourselves into thinking that we could ever really get fully caught up with all the work. The Judge knew that more cases would always be filed, and there would always be injustices and inequities to be remedied in his courtroom, and that only by carving out time for rest and revitalization would he have the stamina for a long tenure on the bench.

One particular way that the Judged liked to revitalize his soul was by driving fast cars. For years he drove some version of the latest, fastest sports car. His first sports car was an XK-150 rag-top Jaguar that he bought for three thousand dollars in the mid-1960s, and at various times after that he owned a yellow Camaro, a silver Datsun 280z, and a black Mitsubishi Starion. The frequent road trips of his early years on the bench provided the perfect opportunity to test the outer limits of these cars' performance, and at times he tested them in comparison to a law clerk's sports car. Which is not to say that he was racing on the roads, necessarily, but if you have ever been to rural East Texas, you know that in many areas you can travel for a very long distance without seeing another car, or a state trooper. No one but the Judge and the clerks involved really know what sort of contests occurred during those road trips, but the birthday letters to the Judge reveal lingering rivalries many years after the fact.

Conclusion

Judge Justice's law clerks traveled to Tyler to clerk for their hero. We expected to work hard and to do good. We knew that we might encounter resistance, and perhaps even hostility, from local residents due to our work. But we could not have known that our time in Tyler would change us forever, in ways we could not have predicted. In their birthday letters to Judge Justice, his former clerks told him different versions of the same sentiment: that their clerkship was "one of very few true watershed events of my life," "a turning point in my life," "a pivotal point in my life," "the greatest opportunity in my professional life," and "the best job I will ever have." We had the great privilege of working side by side with a quiet hero, and we will never be the same.

Notes

1. See, e.g., Jack Bass, "John Minor Wisdom and the Impact of Law," *Mississippi Law Journal* 69 (1999) (discussing the social justice impact of the judicial careers of John Minor Wisdom, Elbert P. Tuttle, John R. Brown, Richard Taylor Rives, Frank M. Johnson, and J. Skelly Wright); Keith P. Ellison, "William Wayne Justice," *Texas Law Review* 89 (2010).

2. See *United States v. Texas*, 321 F. Supp. 1043 (E.D. Tex. 1970), supplemental opinion, 330 F. Supp. 235 (E.D. Tex. 1971), aff'd with modifications, 447 F.2d 441 (5th Cir. 1971), stay denied, 404 U.S. 1206 (1971), and cert. denied, 404 U.S. 1016 (1972); *United States v. Tatum Indep. Sch. Dist.*, 306 F. Supp. 285 (E.D. Tex. 1969).

3. See *Ruiz v. Estelle*, 503 F. Supp. 1265 (E.D. Tex. 1971).

4. See *Young v. Pierce*, 544 F. Supp. 1010 (E.D. Tex. 1982).

5. See *Doe V. Plyler*, 458 F. Supp. 569 (1978).

6. See *Morales v. Turman*, 364 F. Supp. 166 (E.D. Tex. 1973).

7. See *Lelsz V. Kavanagh*, 807 F. 2d 1243 (1987).

8. I would like to thank the professional staff of the Tarlton Law Library, especially Elizabeth Hilkin, for facilitating my access to these papers. And thanks also to Michael P. O'Reilly, Judge Justice's first law clerk, for providing me with a copy of the compiled letters even before I found them in the library's collection.

9. Jackee Cox, letter to William Wayne Justice, February 6, 1995, included in the Seventy-Fifth Birthday Book.

10. Before penning this essay, I reread Frank R. Kemerer's thorough and insightful judicial biography of Judge Justice. Many of the historical and factual statements about Judge Justice's career are drawn from that work. While I have not footnoted each of them in this essay, to facilitate the flow of the story, the essay is deeply indebted to Professor Kemerer's careful chronicle of the Judge's career. See Frank R. Kemerer, *William Wayne Justice: A Judicial Biography* (Austin: University of Texas Press, 1991).

11. The discussion of the *Ruiz* litigation in the following paragraphs is drawn largely from chapter 15 of Kemerer, *William Wayne Justice*.

12. Kemerer, *William Wayne Justice*.

13. Amy Johnson, letter to Judge William Wayne Justice, February 3, 1995, Seventy-Fifth Birthday Book.

14. Jim Tourtelott, letter to Judge William Wayne Justice, undated, Seventy-Fifth Birthday Book.

15. Fritz Byers, letter to Judge William Wayne Justice, February 7, 1995, Seventy-Fifth Birthday Book.

16. Sandi Zellmer, letter to Judge William Wayne Justice, February 13, 1995, Seventy-Fifth Birthday Book.

17. Lynn E. Blais, "William Wayne Justice: The Life of the Law," *Texas Law Review* 77 (1998).

18. Feriale Abdul, letter to Judge William Wayne Justice, undated, Seventy-Fifth Birthday Book.

JEREMY MALTBY

Eugene H. Nickerson

A Tribute

I first met Judge Nickerson in a setting that can sometimes produce awkwardness and even stress—a job interview. He conducted that interview in a way that exemplified his manner in all things—with grace, humility, and an abundance of cheeriness and laughter. He greeted me with a warm smile and a handshake and led me into his bright, sun-filled office. My résumé advertised fluency in Italian, and the Judge seized upon this detail to put me at ease, explaining that one of his daughters and her family lived in Venice and that he was in the midst of learning Italian. His funny, self-deprecating way of describing his efforts made me feel comfortable immediately.

Though the Judge was doubtless using the interview to evaluate me, it felt only like a very enjoyable conversation. We exchanged ideas about a variety of topics, from Italy to the New York Rangers to my law review note, and the Judge told me stories about his experiences on and off the bench. The Judge then gave me a sketch of life in chambers, counting off the duties of his law clerks: drafting opinions, jury charges, and bench memos; rigorously observing the rules of Strunk and White; watching proceedings in court; interviewing jurors after trials; and joining him for lunch several times a week. At the end of this list, the Judge paused. "Of course," he said, "the most important thing is that we like to have a lot of laughs in chambers."

As I left, I knew that I would be lucky to spend a year with the Judge. That initial impression proved correct. As the Judge had promised, my year in his chambers was full of laughter. It also gave me an opportunity to watch and learn from a man who was a rare combination of brilliance, compassion, and basic goodness. The Judge was a teacher, a friend, and a shining example of how to be not only a good lawyer but also a good person.

The Judge as Teacher

The Judge ran chambers like a school for his law clerks but managed to make us think that we were indispensable to its operation. He allowed us to spend as much time as we wanted in the courtroom, but he did not require us to be there. This arrangement let us watch and learn about trials but also gave us ample time to draft opinions, jury charges, and bench memos. When the Judge was alone in court and saw a lawyer performing exceptionally well or badly, he would use the ancient intercom to call us into the courtroom. Through the crackle of the tinny metal speaker affixed high up on our wall, we would hear his disembodied voice: "Cristine, Jeremy, come into the courtroom—there is something you should see." In this way, the Judge made sure that we did not miss any valuable real-life demonstrations of how to act—or not to act—in the courtroom. After we watched lawyers at work, the Judge would always ask what we thought of their performance and discuss what he thought was effective. In this informal way, he shared his vast experience about courtroom lawyering.

The Judge taught us how to write. Left to himself, he could have disposed of motions in civil cases very quickly, either by delivering quick rulings from the bench or by taking care of first drafts on his own initiative. When the Judge was not presiding over a trial and found himself with free time because we had not given him a draft to edit, he would ask us for a "little" motion on which to work. When he did so, he would take the pleadings, filings, and exhibits to his office, spread them out on his desk, and begin immediately to dictate into a little tape recorder. In a remarkably short time—usually after just a couple of hours—he would emerge from his office and present his secretary, Alice, with a tape containing a complete draft to be transcribed. After a few intensive rounds of editing, the Judge had a complete opinion, ready to go. Had he drafted all his opinions in this way, he doubtless could have dealt with his motion practice far more expeditiously. But the Judge wanted his clerks to have the chance to learn by drafting from scratch, so he would give us some guidance and then put us to work.

There were a few basic ground rules. We were not to succumb to writer's block. To help us avoid this pitfall, the Judge suggested a basic template for our drafts. First, identify the parties and their claims. Second, recite the relevant facts. Third, set forth the applicable legal principles. Fourth, apply the facts to the law. The Judge also gave us rules of style. He preferred short sentences and insisted upon the active voice, unless some rare circumstance called for the passive. The Judge categorically forbade split infinitives and the use of footnotes—if an idea was important enough to appear on the page at all, it was important enough for the body of the text.

These rules flowed in part from the Judge's own aesthetic of writing, but more from his view of the role of the judiciary. He believed that the law should be transparent and wanted his opinions to be simple enough for an intelligent sixth grader. By imparting these rules, and by rigorously editing drafts prepared by his clerks, the Judge maintained a consistent Nickersonian voice in all his opinions. As a result, his opinions are easy to recognize. Never longer than necessary, they have short, crisp sentences, with few commas, and a simple, flowing structure. Though their language is typically spare, the Judge knew the power of forceful prose. When he wanted to drive home a point, he could always unleash a rhetorical flourish—a little bit of "purple prose," as he called it.

The Judge imparted his most important lessons during the editing process. I produced my first draft opinion in a case about kippers. The government had seized several crates of imported kippers and mushrooms at the border and had made a convincing demonstration that they contained some particularly nasty toxins. The government wished to destroy these dangerous products and claimed the Food and Drug Act authorized it to do so. The importer argued that the statute conferred no such authority, and it demanded that the government return the kippers and mushrooms, presumably so that it could sell them elsewhere. The applicable statutory scheme was a tangled mess, and my draft began by trying to untangle it, by setting forth the various provisions seriatim. After laboring over the draft long and hard, I finally left it on the Judge's couch for his review. A few days later, the Judge called me into his office to discuss the draft. As we sat side by side at the large table in his office, he produced my draft, marked up with an alarming amount of red ink. The Judge went over all the changes carefully, but emphasized his central message repeatedly: "Jeremy, you have to tell a story!" The Judge showed me how to move away from the intricacies of the statutory scheme and to cast the case as a compelling narrative about poisonous kippers. His approach highlighted the important policy question at the heart of the case, presented an interesting statutory question, and, most important, made for an interesting read. The Judge taught me that a good "story" lies at the heart of all good legal writing.

My second draft opinion addressed claims of a civil rights conspiracy. Though the plaintiff had counsel, his complaint was rambling, vague, and conclusory. After a considerable struggle to understand and characterize the claims and allegations, and to construe them in the plaintiff's favor, I produced a convoluted draft that was almost as long as the thirty-page complaint, and probably not much clearer. The Judge proposed a more elegant solution. In an opinion of only a few pages, he dismissed the complaint without prejudice for failure to comply with Rule 8's requirement of a "short and plain statement of the claims," but he noted some of the complaint's more egregious mistakes and provided a guide for a better complaint. The Judge's approach in this case exemplified his broader view that "no souls are saved after the first five minutes" and that a "little jewel" of an opinion is sometimes more effective than a lengthy discourse. More important, it gave the attorney a gentle reproach but did not punish the client for that attorney's poor effort.

The Judge emphasized the importance of grounding precedents in their specific facts. My first few drafts inevitably included extensive quotations of the applicable legal "rule," as uttered by other courts. When I quoted such a rule, or brought "great language" to the Judge's attention, he would invariably ask, "But Jeremy, what were the facts of that case?" With this gentle guidance I soon came to appreciate the Judge's view about the proper use of precedent in common law judging. Language and quotations are all very nice, but they mean precious little when divorced from the facts that give rise to them.

On a daily basis, the Judge taught the importance of rigorous editing. When I gave him drafts, he would return them full of red ink, and the revisions would come back with similar markings. Time and time again, the Judge honed the opinions, making the language ever crisper and the analysis ever sharper. This treatment might have been disheartening, but the Judge treated his own writing in exactly the same way. When Alice gave him a typed copy of an opinion that he had dictated, the Judge would hack away mercilessly at his own writing. When she gave him the revised version, he would do the same thing again. The Judge edited his own material several times, constantly restructuring and refining it, and accepting proposed edits willingly. Watching the Judge treat his own writing this way softened the impact of seeing him edit my drafts and also instilled an abiding sense that great writing is the product of hard work and intense editing.

The Judge was particularly diligent about eliminating from his opinions any language that might appear less than humble. On a few occasions, I added concluding language along the lines of: "After careful consideration, the Court concludes ... " or "Upon thorough examination of the record, the Court sustains. ..." Such drafts inevitably returned to me with words such as "careful" and "thorough" stricken from the text, with an explanatory parenthetical remark like "Too self-serving" or "Too self-congratulatory."

After every jury trial, the Judge sent us to interview the jurors. He told us first to ask about their experiences—to ensure that they had been treated nicely, that the courtroom had been comfortable, and that their needs had otherwise been satisfied. We were then to ask about the case, to find out what they had thought about the attorneys, the witnesses, the jury charge, and about his running of the case. (We never got to ask that final question, because the jurors always started off by volunteering how much they loved the Judge—he was so witty, so charming, so kind, they said.) After the interview in the jury room, we would return to his office to relate what we had learned.

This exercise had a number of purposes. First and foremost, the Judge wanted to be sure that jurors in his courtroom had a positive experience while discharging their civic duty. Second, he was genuinely curious to hear what the jurors thought about the trial and to see how their impressions compared with his own. When we returned from the interview, he was full of eager questions: What did the jurors think about lawyer X? What did they think about a particular piece of evidence? What about witness Y? Did they like the closing argument by the defense? Third, the Judge saw those interviews, and our discussions of them, as a learning experience for the law clerks. This was the chance for us to hear what the jurors thought was effective, and also for us, as a chambers, to talk about effective trial advocacy. These informal conversations were full of laughter, but were also an education in how to try a case.

The Judge as Judge

Judge Nickerson was good to everyone who entered his courtroom. He welcomed jurors, lawyers, litigants, and all court personnel with a warm greeting and treated them all with profound respect. He let lawyers make their arguments and listened politely to everything they said; his rare impatience was evident only to those very familiar with his ways. He maintained order in his courtroom, not by bullying those who appeared before him, but by showing them good manners and setting an example of exquisite courtesy. If one attorney spoke before an adversary had finished, the Judge would remark, "Please don't interrupt. I'll listen to you when he [she) has finished."

If an attorney went on too long in making a legal argument, the Judge might interject, "I understand your argument." Some took this cue and went quickly to the next point. When others missed the hint, the Judge did not castigate them; he simply let them say their piece. If a lawyer dwelled too long on a particular line of questioning, the Judge would simply say, "Move along." The Judge would also "sustain" evidentiary objections that the opposing lawyer failed to make. If an attorney was behaving in a particularly theatrical manner during a bench trial, the Judge might remind him that there was no jury.

When selecting a jury, the Judge would ask prospective jurors a range of questions about their backgrounds. He inevitably asked about their families and their interests and hobbies. On one occasion, an elderly widower told the Judge that his hobby was ballroom dancing. A few minutes later, a widow told the Judge that she belonged to a group that practiced line dancing on Saturday nights. Puzzled, the Judge asked, "What's line dancing?" As he listened intently to the juror's description of her hobby, the Judge's face brightened. "Perhaps you could bring Mr. Byrne [the widower] along with you some time."

The Judge showed concern for everyone who came into his courtroom. This solicitude manifested itself most frequently with smokers. If the Judge noticed that a juror, attorney, court security officer, or other court employee was a smoker, he would remind that person of the dangers of that activity. The jurors, who had to tolerate these gentle admonitions for a couple of weeks at most, took them in the spirit in which they were offered. Some of the court employees seemed to tire of them. A court security officer once told me, "I love Judge Nickerson, but he's driving me crazy, always busting my chops about smoking." When the Judge's tact prevented him from expressing his concerns directly, he would air them in the privacy of chambers. I often heard him fret that a lawyer had put on too much weight and really needed to exercise more regularly.

During my clerkship, an assistant United States attorney (AUSA) tried his first case before the Judge. After four days of evidence, the jury retired to the jury room to deliberate. After a short time, the jurors sent a note asking to see the trial exhibits, and the government duly provided a cart containing all the exhibits. A few hours later, the jurors sent out another note informing the Judge that, along with the trial exhibits, they had received a set of binders marked "3500." After reviewing the binders, the jurors asked if there had been a mistake. The jurors had read the witnesses' out-of-court statements, and under those circumstances the Judge had no choice but to declare a mistrial. He immediately brought in the jury, explained the situation, apologized profusely, and dismissed them. The crestfallen AUSA, who had provided the exhibit cart without removing the 3500 material, turned ashen and stammered the beginning of an apology. Before he could get a word out, the Judge said, "You tried a very good case, and I look forward to seeing you at the retrial." Where some might have expressed anger at the waste of four days' work, the Judge, understanding the AUSA's pain and embarrassment, gave him some subtle encouragement instead of abuse.

In short, Judge Nickerson's courtroom was a place in which lawyers and litigants could make their arguments and present their evidence. The Judge dispensed justice, treated everyone with respect, and maintained proper decorum without raising his voice, by setting an example.

His Sense of Duty

The Judge went about his work in a selfless way, never passing his duties, even the unpleasant ones, on to others. After taking senior status, the Judge could have reduced his workload but chose not to do so, in part because he loved his work, but also because he knew that his colleagues would have to take on any cases that he discarded. For this reason, the Judge kept all his cases, even ones that he found particularly draining.

Shortly before my interview with the Judge, I read an article about several federal judges who, after taking senior status, had declined to preside over narcotics cases to protest the unfairness of the federal sentencing guidelines in such cases. During the interview, I asked the Judge if he had considered doing the same. The Judge said that he respected and sympathized with the judges who had taken that position, and that he found it very unpleasant to apply the guidelines in narcotics cases. He did not join the protest, however, because he realized that if he declined to take his share of the cases, the unpleasantness would simply fall to his junior colleagues. His conscience and sense of duty would not allow him to avoid that burden.

Towards the end of his career, the wheel that randomly assigns cases gave the Judge a series of high-profile, politically charged, and potentially explosive criminal trials. Presiding over these trials was a physically and emotionally exhausting task, yet the Judge never thought of transferring them to another judge. His sense of duty and fairness would not permit it.

The same sense of duty manifested itself in the Judge's treatment of cases filed by pro se litigants. All judicial opinions treating pro se claims cite the Supreme Court's decision in *Haines v. Kerner*,[1] which requires courts to construe pro se pleadings liberally. The Judge took *Haines* seriously and directed his law clerks to do the same. Early in the clerkship, he explained that he expected us, when reviewing the pleadings of pro se litigants, to act as their lawyers, scouring the facts for viable arguments and possible claims.

His Jurisprudence

One of my law school professors, Harold Korn, once told me that Judge Nickerson was a "big-hearted judge." That description is a perfect fit. The Judge went out of his way to understand what was at stake for the parties in every case before him and was particularly protective of those with less power. In one of his more famous cases, *Abel v. United States*, a challenge to the military's

"Don't Ask, Don't Tell" policy, the Judge wrote that "[a] Court should ask itself what it might be like to be gay."[2] This statement illustrates the compassion and empathy that drove the Judge's approach to the law and permeate his opinions.

Though accurate, the label of "big-hearted judge" only begins to capture the essence of the Judge's jurisprudence. His compassion should not obscure his diligence, creativity, analytical brilliance, and courage, all of which were equally characteristic of his judicial work. I saw his diligence firsthand when he was assessing whether a criminal defendant was competent to stand trial. In making that decision, the Judge painstakingly reviewed more than thirty years of medical records, extensive testimony and writings by medical experts, and voluminous descriptions of the defendant's conduct during the period in which he was said to have been suffering from mental illness. The opinions finding that defendant competent to stand trial exemplify the Judge's careful, methodical approach.

Judge Nickerson's judicial courage is apparent on the face of his opinions. It is well known that he anticipated the Supreme Court's decision in *Batson v. Kentucky*,[3] ruling for the first time that race-based peremptory challenges were unconstitutional. The Judge also went against the current of judicial opinion by ruling twice that the "Don't Ask, Don't Tell" policy was unconstitutional.[4] Although the Second Circuit disagreed with the Judge on both occasions, his opinions are meticulous and forward-looking. Though *Able* has been praised for applying enhanced scrutiny under the equal protection clause to classifications based upon sexual orientation, it can also be read in a different way. With his usual diligence, the Judge systematically refuted every single justification advanced on behalf of the policy. One could argue that this rigorous factual analysis established the irrationality of the policy. However one chooses to read the Judge's opinions in *Able*, they exemplify his care and his courage.

The Judge as Friend

Though the Judge took his judging and his teaching seriously, he did not lie when he promised a lot of laughs during the course of the clerkship. Indeed, as wonderful as it was to watch and learn from such an accomplished jurist, the human parts of the clerkship had the biggest impact on me. As the Judge had indicated, my co-clerk and I ate lunch with him regularly and took full advantage of his open-door policy in chambers. The time that we spent with him was precious.

Every Monday, Wednesday, and Friday, my co-clerk and I ate lunch with the Judge, usually at Celeste's, a greasy spoon around the corner from the courthouse. (On Tuesdays and Thursdays, the Judge lunched with his col-leagues in the Judges' Dining Room. Characteristic of his sociable nature, the Judge organized these lunches, too.) Lunch was a central "duty" of our clerk-ship. One day early in the year, when the Judge came through to get us for lunch, my co-clerk told him that because she had to leave early to take her daughter to the doctor, she thought that she should work through lunch. The Judge looked at her for a moment and then said, "Cristine, that would be fool-ish. You can leave early and still come to lunch. Get your coat."

The Judge's lunchtime diet was a constant—sardines on toast were his sta-ple, sometimes supplemented by Yankee bean soup. On the rare occasions that we convinced him to shift from Celeste's to Fortune House, a local Chinese restaurant, he would order steamed chicken and vegetables, without any sauce. The Judge always regarded my lunches—cheeseburgers with fries, chicken sha-warma, szechuan beef—with something between distaste and alarm. "I hope that you are keeping up with your exercise." Shaking his head, he often asked if I wouldn't prefer something healthier, and nodded with approval if ever I ordered a Greek salad.

Over lunch, we sometimes talked about the law, but more often we spoke about books, movies, and ideas. The Judge was interested in everything from history to sports to politics to art. With equal vigor and interest he discussed topics ranging from Vermeer to the Yankees, to Robert Caro's book about Lyn-don Johnson, to sleep apnea, to Warren Buffett's theory of investing, to *Seinfeld*, to neorealism in postwar Italian cinema, to Deepak Chopra. It must be said that the Judge had a special fondness for *Seinfeld*. Some part of Friday lunch was invariably devoted to analysis of the previous night's episode, with the Judge sometimes laughing to the point of tears as he remembered something that Kramer had done.

There was some tension about the topics for discussion at lunchtime. The Judge was always more interested in hearing about what we had been reading and thinking, while we wanted to hear his stories, of which there was an appar-ently inexhaustible supply. The Judge prefaced every story with the caution: "Now stop me if I have already told you this story." Over the year, we heard about the Rangers' previous Stanley Cup victory in 1940, the Judge's days as a law clerk for Judge Augustus Hand and Justice Harlan Fiske Stone, his tennis matches with Justice Hugo Black (of which Justice Frankfurter disapproved, for he thought Justice Black too old for such games), his argument before the Supreme Court (in which he resolved a disagreement with Chief Justice Vin-son about the meaning of a case—*Mahler v. Eby*[5]—by saying "Well, I guess,

Mr. Chief Justice, you will just have to read that case"), and about his days as Nassau County executive. Most of all, the Judge told us stories about his days on the bench, about the parties and the lawyers who appeared before him, and about his interactions with other judges.

The Judge's many stories had two things in common. First, they were hilarious. This was in part because the Judge had a marvelous sense of humor and a great memory, and thus he had a ready store of funny tales. The Judge was a natural comedian, with a great sense of timing, an elastic face that he could suitably contort, and impeccable delivery. Second, the Judge's stories were not exercises in self-glorification. Most of his stories involved things that he had observed or read. To the extent that the Judge figured in his own stories, he did so as a neutral figure, or as the object of amusement—as he was in the story in which he incurred the wrath of Chief Justice Vinson by suggesting that he had not read the case of *Mahler v. Eby*.

The Judge had a side that can only be described as silly. After lunch one day, I purchased from a gumball machine a small egg containing a blue, slimy substance known as "The Blob." When affixed to the ceiling, the Blob would gradually ooze down to the ground in a slow and disgusting fashion. The Blob fascinated the Judge, so we kept it in the small refrigerator in chambers for special occasions. The Judge once appeared at my door with one of his colleagues. "Jeremy, let's demonstrate the Blob for Judge Gleeson." With this prompting, we tossed the Blob to the ceiling, and had a good laugh as it gradually dripped down to the floor.

The Judge forged deep and lasting relationships with all of his clerks. Over the course of our clerkship, he learned all about our families, backgrounds, interests, and aspirations. My co-clerk's daughter Nina was one year old when our clerkship began, and the Judge followed her development carefully, insisting on regular updates. When Cristine brought Nina to chambers near the end of the year, the Judge insisted on placing her on his seat behind the bench. He did not forget what he had learned about his clerks. The Judge told countless stories of past clerks and amazed me with his detailed memory about each of them. Answering the telephone in chambers, I regularly fielded calls from former clerks seeking the Judge's advice or simply wanting to say hello. A steady stream of law clerks visited chambers throughout the year. When they did so, the Judge made a point of bringing us in to meet and talk with them. If they visited around lunchtime, they would join us at Celeste's. When we met our predecessors, the Judge told them about the cases that we had worked on and told us about the cases from their year as a clerk. Consciously or not, the Judge made sure that the different generations of law clerks knew each other, and he created a bond between them.

After my own clerkship year, the door to chambers was always open, and I suspect that I abused that privilege. I visited the Judge as often as I could, bending his ear about cases on which I had worked, seeking his advice about career decisions, and reminiscing about the year we spent together. On many of these visits, he had me to lunch with the present clerks, and made sure that I got to know all of my successors. His door always open, the Judge was a true friend, a dedicated mentor, and, as always, the most entertaining conversationalist that one could hope to find.

The Judge once told me a story about Judge Learned Hand visiting Justice Oliver Wendell Holmes Jr. at the Supreme Court in Washington, D.C. After the two completed breakfast at the Court, Holmes set off for the bench to hear that morning's argument. As he left, Hand called out to him, "Go do some justice this morning." Holmes responded to the following effect: "Oh, pshaw, Hand! I'm just doing my job." As the Judge recounted Holmes's response, he screwed his face up into a very sour look. As soon as he had finished uttering the words, however, he burst into a big smile and let out a hearty laugh.

Many of my postclerkship visits to chambers ended with the Judge putting on his robe and walking out to the courtroom to take the bench. On those occasions, I would bid him farewell by encouraging him to "do some justice in there." In response, he would screw up his face and say "I'm just doing my job." He would then smile, laugh, and hurry off to the bench. For the Judge, doing justice and doing his job were one and the same.

Notes

1. 404 U.S. 519, 520–21 (1972).

2. 968 F. Supp. 850, 861 (E.D.N.Y. 1997), vacated and remanded, 155 F.3d 628 (2d Cir. 1998).

3. 476 U.S. 79, 89 (1986).

4. See *McCray v. Abrams*, 576 F. Supp. 1244, 1249 (E.D.N.Y. 1983).

5. 264 U.S. 32 (1924).

Roger Traynor at his desk while a professor at the University of California Hastings College of Law. During his judicial career, Traynor was commonly referred to as the best American judge not sitting on the United States Supreme Court. (Traynor Archives, University of California Hastings College of Law)

The granddaughter of an Alabama slave and the daughter of schoolteachers, Juanita Kidd Stout was the first African American female to serve as a justice on a state supreme court. (*Philadelphia Inquirer*)

Chief Justice Susie Sharp was only the second woman to serve as the chief justice of a state supreme court. According to biographer Anna Hayes, the chief justice was a fair but demanding boss who carried a parasol to protect herself from the sun and a gun in her purse to protect herself from trouble. (North Carolina Supreme Court Historical Society)

Chief Justice Rose Bird at a press conference on November 4, 1986, where she conceded the results of the recall election against her. (AP Images)

Essayist Henry M. Greenberg with Associate Justice William J. Brennan Jr. and Chief Judge Judith Kaye of the New York Court of Appeals. The Chief Judge considered Brennan to be a "personal hero," and she introduced her then–law clerk Greenberg to him. (Photograph courtesy of the New York Court of Appeals)

In this photograph taken November 20, 2008, Chief Judge Judith Kaye listens to her last session of oral arguments. (AP Images)

A young Burnita Shelton Matthews, in her law office during the time she worked for the National Women's Party. Matthews would also join other party members in picketing outside the White House and demanding the right to vote. (Prints and Photographs Division, Library of Congress)

Judge Edward Weinfeld and his law clerks during one of his annual "surprise" dinners. Clerking for the Judge included not only legal research, but cutting up grapefruits and securing fresh bagels. (Photograph courtesy of Barry Garfinkel)

Justice Ruth Bader Ginsburg (*second from left*) at a party at her New York apartment in honor of Judge Edmund Palmieri (*far right*). (Photograph courtesy of Marie-Claude Wrenn)

Federal district court judge John Howland Wood Jr., one of only three federal judges to be assassinated in the twentieth century. (Getty Images)

Judge William Wayne Justice, his staff, and his law clerks outside of Pat Gee's Barbeque, a favorite haunt of the Judge's. Essayist and former clerk Lynn Blais describes it as "a classic East Texas BBQ joint located disconcertingly close to a cow pasture." (Tarlton Law Library, University of Texas School of Law)

Judge Jerome Frank (*far left*) with Judge Augustus Hand (*second from right*) at the wedding of their law clerks, Carmel "Kim" Prashker Ebb and Larry Ebb. Kim Ebb was the first woman to clerk for a federal court of appeals judge. Her husband would go on to clerk for Chief Justice Fred Vinson. (Photograph courtesy of the Ebb family)

Judge and Mrs. Elbert Tuttle at the wedding of former law clerk Alfred C. Aman. Tuttle agreed to officiate at the wedding, but only after first requiring Aman to prepare a legal memo showing that the Judge had the authority to do so. (Photograph courtesy of Alfred C. Aman)

Judge Frank M. Johnson, in chambers. In his essay on clerking for Judge Johnson, author Ronald Krotoszynski writes about the "state"—a "famous look of perturbation that Judge Johnson used with great effect as both a trial court and appellate judge." (*Birmingham News*)

Former law clerk and essayist Barry Sullivan, pictured with Judge John Minor Wisdom during a visit to the Washington and Lee School of Law. (Photograph courtesy of Patrick Hinely, Washington and Lee University)

Judge A. Leon Higginbotham Jr. with essayist and former law clerk Robert Kaczorowski. Kaczorowski writes that Higginbotham was a natural teacher and mentor, adding that he "learned more about lawyering in the sixteen months of my clerkship than I did in three years of law school." (Collection of Robert J. Kaczorowski)

Judge Damon Keith in chambers with law clerks Claude Bailey (*far left*), Renee Chenault, and Gerry Hargrove. Essayist and former law clerk Robin Konrad writes of the Judge's ability to bring people together through his kindness, generosity, and love. (Detroit Free Press via ZUMA Press)

Judge Jane Roth and her family of law clerks. Author Chad Oldfather (*kneeling in the front row and wearing bow tie*) writes that the Judge was an important role model to him. (Photograph courtesy of the chambers of Judge Jane Roth)

III Clerking for Federal Court of Appeals Judges

CARMEL "KIM" PRASHKER EBB

A Life of Legal Firsts

I graduated from Columbia Law School in 1945, twenty years before the Civil Rights Act made it illegal to discriminate in employment on the basis of sex. Although some eastern law schools—Yale and Columbia, but heavens, not Harvard—already admitted women, female graduates couldn't expect to be recommended as law clerks to sitting judges, no matter how well their records stacked up against their male classmates.

Being a law clerk was, and still is, a dream job. Back then, each judge had only one clerk—the chief justice of the U.S. Supreme Court was entitled to two. Clerks really got to know and work with their own judges and often the other judges on the court. They worked long and hard but earned the princely sum of $2,400 per year compared to the paltry $1,800 paid to first-year associates by prestigious New York law firms. And a clerkship on a well-regarded court was a sure path to desirable future employment.

So there I was, Carmel Prashker, in the spring of 1945, twenty-one years old (a product of the New York City school system's hurry-up philosophy of education and wartime 'round-the-calendar university scheduling), nearing graduation and contemplating the practical limits of my rather casually chosen profession. (My father was a professor of law; my beloved brother was in law school, and I was dating his roommate—remember dating?—so why not go to law school?) In 1945, the prospects for a female law graduate were pretty dismal. You might be hired to draw up wills in a law firm's back room, where no client would discover that a woman had done the work, or toil anonymously for some legislative commission, drafting revisions of dusty statutes. So I was delighted to read an article in the *Saturday Evening Post* by Judge Jerome Frank of the United States Court of Appeals for the Second Circuit, opining that women were as intellectually competent as men, and that there was no reason not to hire a woman to do what was traditionally a man's work.

The Second Circuit, which heard appeals from district courts in New York, Connecticut, and Vermont, generally was regarded as the best appellate court in the country. Its six members included the famous and uniformly admired Judge Learned Hand; his cousin Augustus Noble Hand (less famous but equally learned and eloquent); Thomas Swan and Charles Clark, both former deans of Yale Law School; and Harrie Chase, a distinguished attorney from Vermont, a specialist in the increasingly important field of patent law, and one of the few judges of his day who was really comfortable in the worlds of science and engineering.

And then there was Judge Jerome Frank: legal philosopher; former successful practitioner and chairman of the Securities Exchange Commission; unabashed iconoclast; and a man who with his poet wife was simply unable to exist on the relatively modest salary of a jurist on the second-highest court of the land (Chief Justice John G. Roberts Jr. is still complaining about insufficient pay for federal judges, but Frank somehow suffered more than most).

To help keep the wolf from the door, he supplemented his often lengthy and controversial legal opinions with short, witty articles on matters unrelated to current court concerns, for which magazines paid happily and well. Having read Frank's encouraging words, I wrote him a letter describing my credentials and ambitions (newborn after reading his article), and to my astonishment, I received an invitation to come talk to him. It was love at first encounter, and Columbia confirmed that I was qualified to be a law clerk, although it would never have proposed me.

The court heard cases from September through June—during "term time." Judges vacationed for the summer months, a relic of the days when they literally "rode circuit," not to mention the absence of air conditioning. In September 1945, I became the first woman to clerk on a federal circuit court and spent the term happily writing memos on legal issues and drafting occasional opinions in cases that really didn't interest my judge, such as matters involving the collision of two tugs in a New York harbor and arising under maritime law. I put a lot of effort into trying not to blush furiously at Learned Hand's mildly indecent jokes (I never succeeded, which pleased him to no end), and sometimes sewed on the buttons that often came loose from Frank's slightly shabby jackets, which his wife never thought to repair. I knew I would never settle for taking dictation, but I couldn't see any harm in sewing on buttons, which I actually did very well.

Near the end of that first golden year, I again tested the employment waters, with disappointing results. Although I now had Frank's introductions and endorsement, the war had ended and the veterans had returned. Not even Frank's good friends could see much reason to hire a woman to do a "man's job," although drawing up wills in the back room remained a possibility. Sad and defeated, I reported back to my sponsor, who as usual had a nontraditional solution. Although clerkships normally lasted for one term, we had had a wonderful run, and he suggested that I stay for another. By then, the log jam of job-seeking veterans might have loosened, and maybe, just maybe, hiring a woman might seem less of a leap. Needless to say, I joyfully agreed, and thereby hangs my tale.

My first year of clerking had offered limited romantic possibilities. The war dragged on, and four of the other law clerks were married. The fifth, Judge Chase's clerk, was mostly in Vermont, where the judge resided except when he was actually hearing cases. (The judges sat in panels of three, usually about one week in five.)

But the courthouse was also home to the U.S. District Court for the Southern District of New York and the offices of the U.S. attorney for the Southern District. In my spare time (what there was of it), I dallied with the assistant U.S. attorney in charge of the civil division—an Austrian refugee, a friend of Frank's twenty years my senior, and with male chauvinist leanings. Frank was mightily amused—and my parents were openly horrified—so of course I stubbornly persisted.

But another force was at work. In those days, judges not only were poorly paid, but they had no retirement or death benefits. So when U.S. District Judge Frank Coleman died suddenly in 1934, leaving his wife, Marjorie, and two small daughters with very little to live on, those wonderful men, Learned and Augustus Hand, set up a formal Second Circuit law library with Marjorie Coleman as its learn-on-the job librarian. I recall that during the first few years, the Hand cousins paid her salary out of their own pockets, but that eventually she was paid from federal funds.

Marjorie Coleman had been delighted by the advent of a female law clerk, but she shared my parents' disapproval of that assistant U.S. attorney. When a new crop of law clerks arrived in September 1946, she surveyed the field, made her selection, and invited us both to tea in her library.

Larry Ebb had recently graduated from Harvard Law School after four years in the Navy. He had been president of the law review, was now Augustus Hand's law clerk, and was slated to clerk for U.S. Supreme Court Chief Justice Fred M. Vinson the following year. He was thin as a rail (his natural tendency reinforced by four years in the Pacific), was smart as a whip, and had a nice dry sense of humor. Tea with Marjorie Coleman led to frequent meetings: in the library (where else should law clerks be?); at conferences when our judges were sitting on the same cases; on Saturdays when judges were home and law clerks were at work; and on the stairs between the twenty-third floor, where Judge Frank had his office; and the twenty-fourth floor, where the Hands held sway.

We thought we were being very discreet, but this was the first romance between law clerks, and the whole courthouse was greatly entertained. Thankfully unbeknownst to us, there was a pool as to how it would all turn out, in which even our judges participated.

By February, I had concluded that New York remained an employment wasteland and decided to try my luck in Washington. Larry was headed for Washington, and Frank had a lot of useful connections there. Never underestimate the importance of connections.

Still no luck at private law firms. But the federal government had become the employer of first resort for professional women. And thanks to Frank's introductions, I landed a job with the newly established Atomic Energy Commission, whose general counsel was willing to add a woman with good connections to his still-incomplete legal staff. It was another dream job, and chief among its pleasures was my assignment as counsel to the raw materials division (think uranium), headed by Virginia Jeffers's father, Jesse Johnson. Yes, it's a small world.

On my return to New York, I reported my success to Larry, who said, "Well, I guess we should get married." And I said, "I guess we should," as though the thought hadn't previously crossed my mind. We agreed that sooner was better—like tomorrow or the day after. We already were seeing each other seven days per week: at work, after work, and on our precious Sundays off. We saw no reason for a long engagement or for any engagement at all.

My mother had a different view. She had finally realized her lifelong dream of going to law school (everyone else in the family already had) and told us that she'd be ready to plan a wedding after the school year had ended. Would June do? No, June wouldn't do. We said that we'd manage the wedding, and she could just come as our guest.

There was another, more serious problem: the unwritten law that no law clerk ever married during term time. Term time was for working, and weddings were for later. But ours was the first law clerk romance, and we petitioned our judges for a waiver. Amused and indulgent (had they won the courthouse pool?), they told us that if we could find a week when neither judge was hearing cases and memoranda were under control, we not only could marry but could steal a week for a honeymoon.

We scoured the court calendar, and so it came to pass that on April 26, 1947, two law clerks married during term time, which had never happened before. We had a small, mostly family wedding. We planned it, and my mother came. Two weeks later, we had a large (for us) reception, attended by friends, our enabling judges, and, of course, Marjorie "Matchmaker" Coleman. My mother must have managed that one—we were much too busy playing catch-up at work.

Note

This essay first appeared as "A Life of Legal Firsts—Including Romance and Marriage," in the December 4, 2018, issue of the *ABA Journal*. It is reprinted here with permission.

ALFRED C. AMAN AND ANNE S. EMANUEL

Clerking for Judge Elbert Tuttle

A Privileged Witness

Alfred C. Aman, Law Clerk, 1970–1972

When I was a second-year student at the University of Chicago Law School in 1969, I applied for a number of federal clerkships. I had two primary criteria: I applied to judges whose opinions had inspired me and who sat in parts of the country I had never before visited. Coming from Rochester, New York, and not having traveled much at that point, the second criteria covered quite a wide area. As it turned out, however, most of my applications were with judges who sat in the Deep South or in the West.

One day I received a phone call from Judge Elbert Tuttle. He introduced himself and said he did not like to interview clerks in person if they had to travel long distances—it was costly for the applicants, and he could not accept everyone he interviewed, but could he speak to me by phone? Of course, I said. He noted that my hometown of Rochester had caught his eye—his daughter and her family had just moved there—and after a very pleasant conversation, he said that he would be happy if I were to be his law clerk for the coming year, but please, he said, feel free to take a few days before making my decision.

I thanked the Judge and went immediately to the office of one of my professors and recommenders, Owen Fiss. He had recently joined the faculty after a stint in the Department of Justice litigating civil rights cases throughout the South. He taught a wonderful course based on many of those cases called Injunctions, which I took. It was in that course that I read many of the Fifth Circuit's cases including, of course, Judge Tuttle's opinions. When I spoke with Professor Fiss, I noted that the Judge had recently taken senior status, and I wondered if he was, well, a bit old (the Judge was then as old as I am today!). Fiss, a very tall and imposing individual, stood up at his desk and walked with me to the other side of his office, where a picture of the entire Fifth Circuit hung. He pointed to Judge Tuttle and said, "Does that man look old to you?" "Well, no," I replied. He then gave me some of the best advice I ever received and in a form that was undeniable. He simply said, "If you don't go back to your room and call Judge Tuttle immediately and accept this job offer, you will be making the biggest mistake of your life."

I turned on a dime, went back to my room, and called the Judge back. I told him that I accepted his offer and looked forward to working with him in the coming year. Once again, Judge Tuttle said it was okay if I wanted to take a few days. "Oh no, Judge," I said. "I have made up my mind and am honored to accept." Owen Fiss was so right! The clerkship was an ongoing tutorial on law and life, as well as a friendship with the Judge and his family that continued for so many years thereafter. It was one of the high points of my life.

When I went to Atlanta to start my clerkship, I knew no one. I flew into Atlanta on a Sunday night before reporting for work on Monday morning. I took an airport shuttle to various hotels and got off at one that looked affordable. I met the Judge the next day. He was warm and welcoming. In commenting on why he usually tried to avoid, if possible, interviewing clerks who would have to travel long distances, he mentioned that he had learned long ago that he could get along with just about anyone for a year. That made me a bit nervous, but as it turned out, such concerns were unnecessary. I clerked for two years!

Though the times were demanding—the civil rights movement was still intense and controversial, and the Vietnam War raged on—Judge Tuttle was always calm and easy to work for. He was clear in what he wanted you to do and open at all times to deeper discussions about the cases he was working on. It became clear to me that senior status as a federal judge was an advantage from a clerk's point of view. The Judge could sit as much or as little as he chose, but since the caseload was so heavy and intense, Judge Tuttle sat as much as he did when he was chief judge. Only the administrative tasks he undertook as chief were no longer necessary.

Moreover, the Judge felt obligated, from time to time, to help out on other circuits as well. During my clerkship he sat for one week in Cincinnati with the Sixth Circuit and another time in Los Angeles with the Ninth. I accompanied the Judge on these trips, which were exciting. It was interesting not only to meet the judges on those circuits but also to experience what seemed like different circuit cultures as well.

Mrs. Tuttle always traveled with the Judge, but they never flew. Whether it was sitting the Fifth Circuit in Houston, New Orleans, or Jacksonville, or with the Ninth Circuit in Los Angeles, they always drove. The Judge did all the driving, and Mrs. Tuttle read aloud along the way. They were voracious readers. Normally I took a plane, but I once accompanied them on a car trip to Houston. It was a joy, and I got to read a chapter or two along the way.

In my first year with Judge Tuttle, I was his only clerk—that was typical at the time for senior judges. The clerk who preceded me was Bernard Parks, the first African American to ever serve as a law clerk on the Fifth Circuit. He prepared me well for my time with the Judge. In my second year, the Judge was authorized to hire two law clerks. John Barmeyer joined the Judge in 1971, and we had a very happy office. Lillian Klaiss was the Judge's secretary at the time. She had been with the Judge since he was first appointed in 1954. Needless to say, she knew the office routine and the Judge extremely well. It was like a small and very harmonious law firm.

Life in chambers revolved around sittings with the court and the opinions that the Judge agreed to write. The briefs and records for the cases to be heard showed up well in advance, and one of our tasks was to succinctly summarize the arguments made by the litigants. Judge added one additional requirement: he wanted to know how we thought that the case should be decided. For the Judge, having to take a position would sharpen our analysis of the arguments. And he was right.

Oral arguments were almost always illuminating, especially as you got to see who and what were effective or ineffective. In many of the arguments, especially those involving either complicated legal issues or confusing oral advocacy, the Judge would pick a crucial point and extend his right hand and arm—which were stiff as a cleaver—as if he were about to slice through a thick loaf of bread. He would then ask a question, and everyone knew that the answer to that question would decide the case. I would like to think that our bench memos had something to do with these questions, but that was rarely the case. The Judge could simply listen carefully to what the lawyers chose or did not choose to say, and then sum it all up in one great question. It was a true gift.

I once asked the Judge about a lawyer who argued often, and usually successfully, before the court. "What made him so good?" I asked. Judge Tuttle replied that it was the lawyer's ability to understate the case—that he got the court really interested in his argument and its implications, and that often worked to his advantage. Being a clerk to the Judge was like having a steady tutorial on so many aspects of the law, including advocacy.

Of course, opinion writing occupied much of the Judge's time in chambers. As a senior judge, Judge Tuttle would preside almost every time at oral arguments, except when sitting with the chief judge and, of course, when sitting en banc. The Judge would assign the opinions to be written by the judges on the panel. Because he believed he had a little more time as a senior judge, he invariably took the lion's share of opinions to write.

Judge Tuttle was incredibly efficient. He would often talk through his proposed opinions with his clerks and operated very much with an open-door policy in that regard. He was always interested in discussing the ins and outs of a tricky opinion, and as a clerk, I always knew that I could raise and discuss any possible argument. When the Judge was ready to write, he just picked up his Dictaphone and dictated the entire opinion—usually in one fell swoop. When Mrs. Klaiss typed it up, he rarely made significant changes. It was a skill he learned, the Judge said, when he worked for a newspaper and had to phone in his stories from the field.

The court had already changed while I was there—becoming much larger and, perhaps, a little less predictable in its outcomes. The Judge now dissented in some cases that he might have prevailed on when the court was smaller. In a prisoners' rights case, the Judge asked me to drop off a draft of his opinion to the chambers of one of the other sitting judges. That judge happened to be outside his office, conferring with his secretary, when I came in. He asked me for the name of the case and how Judge Tuttle came out on it. I summarized the opinion. He thanked me for the draft and replied that he would look at it closely, but then he added: "We should all remember that prisoners are the debris of society." I knew this was not remotely how Judge Tuttle approached this or any case.

That opinion became a dissent. The Judge, however, never lost faith in either his views or in the views of his fellow judges. He was convinced that the individual facts of particular cases would prevail in most cases, and the other judges would typically agree on the outcome. This attitude certainly put a premium on the care, skill, and accuracy with which we clerks prepared our memos.

Quite apart from life in chambers, there were moments in the Judge's home. Judge and Mrs. Tuttle often entertained judges who were sitting in Atlanta that week, and they occasionally invited the law clerks as well. It was a great opportunity to informally meet other members of the court. The visiting judges would often take me aside and say how much they admired Judge Tuttle and how lucky I was to be working for him. One of them, Judge Irving Goldberg, was especially demonstrative. He liked to call me "Red Fred"—nothing political, but descriptive, because of my red hair. "Do you know that you are clerking not only for one of the greatest judges of all time, but one of the greatest human beings too?" he would ask. I sure did.

Both during my clerkship and after, while I was a practicing attorney in Atlanta, I would be invited to the Tuttles' home for drinks. Those visits were an opportunity to learn more about the Judge and Mrs. Tuttle personally as well as to talk about the issues of the day. I usually made the drinks—an old-fashioned for Mrs. Tuttle and a ginger ale for the Judge. It is interesting that he did not drink—never had. When I asked him why, the Judge simply said that his mother told him not to.

On one of my visits, I introduced them to Carol Greenhouse—who was to become my wife in 1976. In fact, I eventually asked the Judge if he would be willing to marry us. In agreeing to do so, the Judge remarked that he had never performed a marriage before and that "there weren't many things you could ask an eighty-year-old to do for the first time!" The Judge did ask me to prepare a memo making sure he had the authority to do so. He subsequently married us in the District of Columbia in 1976.

Many years later, I mentioned to Professor Fiss that "but for" his sage advice many of these wonderful things might never have happened, including my marriage to Carol. The professor wrote a nice note back, saying that he was happy that it had all worked out so well, but that he could not take responsibility for what was not "foreseeable." But some things were, I believe, clearly foreseeable. Clerking for Judge Tuttle provided me with not only a very special legal education, but one that showed me what a person of great integrity, intelligence, and compassion could accomplish. The Judge's life was exemplary in so many ways. He was and remains a role model for me to this day.

Anne S. Emanuel, 1975–1976

I applied for a clerkship with Judge Tuttle in the spring of my second year at Emory Law School. Shortly after I mailed my application, I received a letter asking me to call his chambers and schedule an interview. Leaving the law school that afternoon I passed by Ellen Leitzer, whose roommate (Frank Hull) was clerking for Tuttle that year. When I told her that I was getting ready to call Judge Tuttle to arrange an interview time, her response surprised me. "Wonderful," she said. "You do know that he's liable to answer the phone himself." That stopped me in my tracks. Judge Tuttle was an icon, an Olympian—the thought of having him answer the phone was overwhelming. "You're kidding?" But no, she was serious. It was a small office, she explained—the Judge, his secretary, Mrs. Betty Keener, and two law clerks. If no one else was available, he answered the phone himself. I can't explain why having the Judge answer the phone was so much more intimidating than the interview itself, but the possibility all but paralyzed me. As it happened, Mrs. Keener answered when I finally made the call.

I arrived early for my 9:00 a.m. interview. I was sitting in a chair by Mrs. Keener's desk when the door opened and Judge Tuttle strode in. He was not a large man (5'9" and 150 pounds), but he walked with purpose. As the Judge passed by, he saw me out of the corner of his eye and called back, "You're early; that's good."

I didn't realize at the time that it was not only good, but likely critical. Judge Tuttle believed in timeliness—his friends joked that he ran his schedule on Naval Observatory time. He was not a complainer, but he did grumble on occasion about being kept waiting. "You just have to be on time yourself," he once explained, "even if you know the other fellow might not be, and even if you think your time might be more valuable than his." "Sometimes you know it is," his wife, Sara, interjected.

Despite my nerves, the interview went well. Judge Tuttle's polite and professional manner was calming. Although I realize now that law review articles are far too long, dense, and too much of an imposition on a judge's time to be used as writing samples, that is hindsight. I had included an entire article with my letter and résumé. Judge Tuttle had clearly read the article very carefully; we talked about the topic—whether class action lawsuits were viable under the ADEA (Age Discrimination in Employment Act)—and he also had a very particular query about grammar. At one point where the preceding text called for a singular pronoun, I had used *they*. As he started to ask why he caught himself and said, "Oh, I see why you did that." At that time, the pronoun of choice whenever the individual referred to was of indeterminate gender was *he*. I did not want to use *he*, and back then, in 1974, using *she* instead simply didn't occur to me.

A good deal of our conversation wasn't about law. Tuttle was intrigued by the fact that my husband was a sculptor. Marty and I had come to Atlanta in 1972 because I was accepted at Emory, and the Atlanta College of Art had offered him a position on the faculty. As Tuttle noted from my résumé, we had spent a year in Philadelphia. Had we visited the Barnes Collection, he asked. We had, and he had too, and so we talked for the most part about that extraordinary collection.

The school year ended, and I commenced work with the Atlanta law firm of Huie, Brown & Ide. In late June one of the receptionists found me in the library and told me I had a phone call. It was from Judge Tuttle's office. He had tried to call and I wasn't at my phone, and he simply intended to place the call later. Meanwhile he called Melissa Clark, who was clerking at a different Atlanta law firm for the summer, and offered her a position.

Frank Hull, who was Tuttle's first female clerk and who had cheered for me in the application process, was all but distraught. Word will get back to Anne that Melissa has a clerkship, she explained to the Judge. She'll think that since she hasn't heard anything she is not getting one. Let me call the firm and ask someone to go find her, she pleaded. She called, they found me, and Melissa and I were co-clerks in 1975 to 1976.

Judge Tuttle had been at the front of the curve when he hired Frank Hull two years earlier, but he was not alone. Other judges had female law clerks. But with Melissa and me on board, he was the first to have only female law clerks. Later that year, he came back bemused from the Fifth Circuit Judicial Conference. A colleague had asked him a question to which several judges were keenly interested in hearing the answer. "I've always considered you the epitome of a southern gentleman" preceded the query (Tuttle didn't bother to remind his colleague that he had been born in California and raised in Hawaii). "So I just wonder—now that you have two women as law clerks, do you feel like you have to keep your jacket on in chambers? And do you stand up every time they come into your office?" Tuttle told Melissa and me about the queries but asked us not to repeat the story; given that forty years have passed, I do not think he would now object. We shared a bittersweet laugh, recognizing that concerns like that adversely affected all too many women in the workplace.

Sometime during the first week of my clerkship, Judge Tuttle came back to my desk (I sat at the far end of the in-chambers library) to convey his office rules. First was a point of style: noting that we were almost always writing with reference to a lower court opinion, he said it was his custom not to use the judge's name, but instead to refer to either the "District Court" or the "trial court." He had a slight preference for the former. Second, he explained that he maintained a permanent recusal from any cases in which the law firm then known as Sutherland, Asbill & Brennan participated. He would not pretend any distance from the firm he had founded and in which his brothers-in-law Bill Sutherland and Mac Asbill and his beloved nephew Mac Asbill Jr. were still principals. Melissa and I were, therefore, expected to check every record carefully to make sure the Sutherland firm did not appear on any letterheads or in any pleadings.

Finally, if Sarah Tuttle called, and the Judge was in chambers, the call should be put through to him—no matter what he was doing or with whom he was engaged. That was the only rule that gave Melissa and me pause. One did not have to be in the office long to realize that conversations one would be loath to interrupt were not uncommon. And yet, the Judge insisted. It seemed that early in his career, when Sutherland was a young firm, Sarah had called the office one morning and asked for Elbert. "He's not available; may I take a message," the receptionist replied. "Why is he not available?" countered Sarah. "He's with the other gentlemen; they're having their drinks in the library" came the reply. Anywhere else she would have explained that they were having coffee, but this was Atlanta in the 1930s—in fact, Coca Cola was the beverage of choice. At any rate, when Elbert arrived home that evening he was met at the door by Sarah. She delivered her ultimatum before he entered: when she called her husband, she expected to be put through to him; and tell that young woman to stop saying you are having drinks. Hence the office rule.

As things turned out, it was never an issue. When Sarah called she invariably asked if the Judge was with anyone. If the answer was yes, she would ask that he be given the message that she had called as soon as he was free.

Those specific rules supplemented the overarching ones. In many offices there was only one—confidentiality. Virtually nothing could be said about what one was working on, not even the fact that one was working on any particular matter or issue. In chambers conversations were sacrosanct—not to be shared. Nothing—no comment, no outlook, no opinion or concern—was to be imputed to the judge. In Tuttle's chambers there was one more rule, one perhaps widely stipulated but definitely not widely enforced in other chambers. FTN stood for Federal Telephone Network, not Free Telephone Network.

From one perspective, long-distance calls on the office phones were free. No cost was reflected in the office budget. This was in an age when long-distance tolls were high enough to discourage most people from having all but the most critical conversations. Judge Tuttle took the more informed view. It was true that his office budget did not include a line item for long-distance calls—but the federal government did pay the carriers, and the amount paid was affected by the volume of calls. So the office phones were for official business only. Tuttle took the official business restriction seriously, to the extent that he thought it inappropriate when a colleague, realizing that they were sitting in Jacksonville at the same time, called to set up a golf game.

When Chief Justice Burger appointed Tuttle as the first chair of the newly created Advisory Committee on Judicial Conduct years later, Tuttle wryly suggested the chief justice chose him because of his reputation for being "persnickety" about ethics issues. It was not his favorite work because he often had to advise his colleagues they could not participate in events or accept honors or gifts. He did, however, enjoy calling it the "Dear Abby Committee."

By the mid-1970s, Tuttle ate lunch with his clerks in chambers almost every day. He sometimes went out to lunch—most often when judges from out of state were sitting on a panel in Atlanta, especially when Judge Irving Goldberg was among them. Effusive where Judge Tuttle was reserved, Judge Goldberg regularly embarrassed Tuttle with his unabashed declarations of affection and admiration. The two men shared jurisprudential values; they also shared a deep commitment to family. Judge Goldberg never tired of hearing the story of when Elbert Tuttle Jr., a nephrologist, dismantled his wife's dishwasher and made a portable dialysis machine using the stainless steel tub. And Judge Tuttle never tired of telling it.

Melissa and I usually brought our lunch; one of us would slip across the street and pick up a lettuce and tomato sandwich for the Judge. His private office included a bathroom; the chambers included a library with its own bathroom. We used the paper towels from the library bathroom for placemats and napkins and ate at one of the library tables. The three of us were sometimes joined by clerks from other chambers and former clerks, occasionally by other friends of the Judge, and on occasion by another judge.

Judge Wade McCree of the Sixth Circuit joined us for lunch in the library several days when he sat as a visiting judge for a week of oral arguments. Before he left he shared his rueful recollection of an applicant for a clerkship several years earlier. He had not hired her because his own chambers were in Detroit, which meant that, accompanied by his clerks, he regularly traveled to the headquarters of the Sixth Circuit in Cincinnati for oral arguments. The applicant, like Melissa and me, was a young white woman. He was the first black judge on the Sixth Circuit. He had feared, no doubt accurately, that hiring her would have proven racially inflammatory. Had so much travel not been involved, Judge McCree explained, he could have and would have hired her. And times were changing. And yet Judge McCree remained pained and frustrated. He still did not think it possible for him to hire a white female clerk without provoking a destructive firestorm of attention.

The conversation was usually light—about current books (the Judge and Mrs. Tuttle were voracious readers), or our social lives and plans, or whatever was in the morning paper (as long as it wasn't something likely to come before the court). Sometimes an abstract legal question would arise. More than once the conversation turned to Section 1983, which is shorthand for the federal statute that provides a cause of action for the deprivation of civil rights. As much as anyone, Tuttle had written the opinions that fleshed out the meaning and reach of Section 1983. One of his great lessons to the young lawyers around the table was how he approached questions about it; invariably he would say, "Let's get the book off the shelf and see exactly what it says." To parse a statute, he parsed a statute.

Lunch was the highlight of every day. The rest of the day was spent in relative isolation. Judge Tuttle's office, Mrs. Keener's office, and Melissa's office were at one end of the chambers. My desk was at the other end, capping a substantial library. Melissa and I were often both working in the library—either doing research (and yes, the exclusive method at that not-so-distant point in time was pulling books off shelves) or reading through records. We talked, but for the most part only when we needed to talk about an issue on which we were working. Our work day was relatively short—9 a.m. to 5:00 p.m.—but while we were at work, we were at work. Tuttle was not a task master, but he was a serious man who took his work and his responsibility very seriously. The mood in chambers was collegial and light, but never frivolous. If one were to do one's job well, there was no time to be lost.

Providing a first draft of an opinion was the easiest part of the job. By then the court had heard oral argument, and the judges had decided in conference how the case would be decided. In assigning a draft opinion to us, Judge Tuttle would explain the reasoning of the court. We simply had to first get it down on paper and find the appropriate citations to authority that supported the court's conclusions. Second, to check the record to make sure that every fact used in the opinion was supported by evidence that had been introduced at trial. And then to Shepardize every case to make sure it had not been overruled or questioned in a way that diminished its authoritativeness.

Bench briefs were often more difficult. For those we were on our own, tasked with condensing the briefs to a concise statement of the facts and the issues. Judge Tuttle, whose analytic mind was reflected in the relative brevity of his opinions, wanted, if possible, only one page. We realized that not all judges used that rule of thumb. Once Judge John Brown asked Tuttle if he could use his bench briefs for the cases before a panel on which they were both sitting. Tuttle, of course, agreed. Judge Brown thanked him somewhat profusely, and then, in a voice loud enough for Melissa and I to overhear announced, "Tell them I want bench BRIEFS. Not g— d— law review articles."

I remember only one instance in which Judge Tuttle was clearly irritated with me. A law school classmate, Judson (Jud) Graves stopped by chambers to say hello to me and to seize the opportunity to meet Judge Tuttle. I introduced them, and we had a pleasant conversation. When Jud left Judge Tuttle asked me what court Jud was on. I explained he wasn't on a court, he was a newly minted lawyer like me. Judge Tuttle shook his head; he kept up with the news and kept track of the bench, and he had spent the entire conversation racking his mind for a Judge Graves. He made it clear he wished I had made Jud's name more clear.

That is also the only instance in which I recall Judge Tuttle's age showing—part of the problem was his slight hearing loss. When I began my clerkship Judge Tuttle was seventy-eight. I did not think I suffered any bias about age. But as the weeks went on I realized I had carried an unconscious bias, an assumption that he would be mentally and physically adversely affected by his age. I came to realize that seeing his physical and mental stamina and his extraordinary mental acuity, I too often thought to myself how impressive he was "for a man his age."

No one has ever described Judge Tuttle better than Congressman John Lewis did in his eulogy. "This extraordinary man, so good and so decent, prevailed. He had an inner strength—a moral strength born of righteousness—that would not fail." Congressman Lewis was alluding to Judge Tuttle's leadership of the historic Fifth Circuit through the turbulent years of the civil rights movement. But in doing so, he delineated the character that Judge Tuttle exemplified in all of his life and work. Clerking for Judge Tuttle was an immeasurably great gift.

RONALD J. KROTOSZYNSKI, JR.

Judge Frank M. Johnson Jr. and His Extended Law Clerk Family

Reminiscences on Working for a Living Profile in Courage

Judge Frank M. Johnson Jr. was an iconic jurist. As a federal district judge sitting in Montgomery, Alabama, during the height of the civil rights movement, he issued rulings and orders that desegregated public institutions across the state. Moreover, he did so at great personal risk to himself and his family. George C. Wallace Jr., while running for governor in the 1960s, attacked Johnson by name in his campaign speeches. Wallace fulminated against him as an "integrating, scalawagging, carpet-bagging, race-mixing, bold faced liar" who "hasn't ever done anything for Alabama except to help destroy it"[1] and also suggested, on the public record, that what Judge Johnson really needed was "a barbed wire enema." [2] In 1967, the Ku Klux Klan, finding an entry for "Frank M. Johnson, Sr." in the local white pages, along with a residential address in Montgomery, bombed the home of Mrs. Alabama Long Johnson, Judge Johnson's mother. The bomb caused significant damage to her home— but miraculously, no physical harm to her.[3] Of Judge Johnson, the Reverend Dr. Martin Luther King Jr. said that he was a jurist "who gave true meaning to the word *justice*."[4]

After Judge Johnson's elevation to the U.S. Court of Appeals for the Fifth Circuit in 1979, he issued landmark rulings involving the rights of unpopular minorities, notably including his path-breaking opinion in *Hardwick v. Bowers*,[5] which held that the constitutional right of privacy encompasses the right of same-sex couples to engage in intimate acts free and clear of the threat of criminal prosecution by the government.[6] He also wrote the panel decision in *Doe v. Plyler*,[7] which invalidated a Texas state law that denied children of undocumented migrant farm workers free access to the state's public schools.[8] Unlike his opinion in *Hardwick*, however, the Supreme Court affirmed his decision in *Plyler*.[9]

Thus, although Judge Johnson is probably best known today for his bold civil rights rulings as a federal district court judge in the 1950s and 1960s, and for his creative use of injunctive relief to reform Alabama's state prisons and mental hospitals in the 1970s, his commitment to securing equal justice under law to all the litigants who appeared in his court did not wane with his elevation to the U.S. Court of Appeals. Throughout his tenure on the federal bench, Johnson was a fierce and unrelenting guardian of the Constitution, the Bill of Rights, and the Rule of Law.

Following my graduation from Duke Law School in 1991, I had the distinct privilege of serving as a law clerk to Judge Frank M. Johnson Jr. I can say without qualification or reservation that working for Judge Johnson as a law clerk was the best job I have ever had or ever will have. Moreover, this sentiment is widely shared among his former law clerks. Judge Johnson had a deep impact on all of us—although his example of doing the right thing under extraordinarily difficult circumstances can be more than a little bit daunting. Nevertheless, for his former law clerks, when faced with tough professional and personal decisions, we find ourselves asking, "What would Frank Johnson do?" and then take that course of action.[10]

Of course, it is not possible in this short chapter to provide a full and complete sense of the man and his unshakable commitment to securing constitutional values in a time and place where doing so was extraordinarily difficult—and, frankly, rather dangerous. Nevertheless, in addition to discussing how Judge Johnson selected and deployed his law clerks, I provide a more general sense of Judge Johnson's approach to his craft and his overall judicial philosophy. In my view, Judge Johnson's selection and use of law clerks reflected and incorporated some of the same legal, moral, and philosophical views that animated his work from the bench. In particular, Judge Johnson had a strong commitment to equality and fairness—and he expected those working in his chambers to embrace this ethic with brio. I begin with a brief introduction to Frank Johnson—the jurist, the boss, and the person.

To understand the Judge, one must begin with his ability to commit to a task and see it through to completion. He brought this ethic to the bench, to his fishing excursions, and even to his woodworking and rose gardening. In the professional context, Judge Johnson had an uncanny ability to do what he believed the law required—and an iron force of will to see right done no matter the obstacles that stood in the way. He was capable of being remarkably warm, friendly, and kind with his staff and clerks in one moment—but then changing tone and demeanor, seemingly on a dime, in order to dress down a government lawyer who had the temerity to offer specious arguments in his courtroom a few minutes later.

Frank Johnson also was a devoted husband and father—as well as, perhaps surprisingly, something of a practical jokester who always seemed to have a story or quip ready to hand. As an example, one weekend, when the Alabama Crimson Tide won and the Auburn Tigers lost, the Judge asked Mrs. Perry, his devoted and long-serving assistant and die-hard Auburn football fan—"Did you happen to catch that 'double header,' Mrs. Perry? How did you like it?" Mrs. Perry, perplexed, responded, "Oh, Judge, I didn't see the Braves this weekend. Did they win?" He replied, with a wry smile, "Oh, not baseball, Mrs. Perry, college football! Alabama won and Auburn lost—in my book that counts as a 'double header.' And, I for one thoroughly enjoyed *both* games!"

This provoked an "Oh Judge, really!" and reduced the law clerks to gales of laughter. I am quite certain that this performance was undertaken for our benefit. Moreover, I'm certain that for the lawyers who appeared before his bench, the idea that Frank Johnson was an avid Alabama college football fan, much less someone who would tease an Auburn fan over a critical SEC (Southeastern Conference) loss, would come as something of a shock. For the record, however, I also observed Mrs. Perry, later that season, pointedly ask Judge Johnson, "How did Alabama do this weekend? I missed the game," when the Crimson Tide had lost, a fact well known to Mrs. Perry.

Contrary to the impression he conveyed of being all work and no play, Johnson enjoyed several regular pastimes, notably including angling—primarily for redfish and speckled trout in the Gulf of Mexico, but also for bass in fresh water lakes and rivers. Sometimes he would go fishing with his law clerks or colleagues from the federal courts. But more often than not, Judge Johnson would go fishing with a rag-tag band of misfit "hillbillies" from Winston County, friends of longstanding who knew the Judge from his boyhood, rough but friendly fellows with whom Judge Johnson could let down his guard (something he almost never did when in Montgomery). Johnson was also an avid woodworker—he handcrafted beautiful pieces of furniture. Perhaps more surprising, the Judge had a green thumb and enjoyed growing roses in the backyard of his home on Old Farm Road.[11] I suspect that very few lawyers or judicial colleagues knew these sides of Frank Johnson—but his law clerks most certainly did.

In sum, Judge Johnson was not a marble statue brought to life; he was a complex and often enigmatic person. Essayist and journalist Hal Crowther gets is exactly right in observing that "Frank Johnson was Alabama to the bone," a "tobacco-chewing, bass-fishing, George B. Dickel–drinking country lawyer."[12]

Accordingly, "of all the abuse Johnson suffered, none was more unjust than the yellow-journalists' assertion that he was an unnatural native son, an alien creature of Northern institutions and Northern conspiracies."[13]

In the courtroom and in his judicial chambers, Judge Johnson displayed a strong and unwavering commitment to seeing justice done—and, more specifically, to ensuring that his rulings advanced the twin constitutional values of equality and fairness. To be clear, "equality and fairness" did not necessarily mean that the "little guy" would always win in Judge Johnson's courtroom— for Johnson, "equality and fairness" meant hewing to the letter of the Constitution and laws.[14] In some instances, this produced results that promoted the cause of social justice, but this was not an inevitability. Judge Johnson did not conceive of himself, or his role as a federal judge, as involving either activism or social engineering.[15] He firmly believed that "obedience to the laws we like and defiance of those we dislike is the route to chaos,"[16] and cautioned that "strong moral conviction is not all that is required to turn breaking the law into a service that benefits society."[17]

Accordingly, Judge Johnson followed established precedents carefully and would not attempt to stretch or bend the law to reach results that he found personally congenial.[18] But, by the same token, he would not hesitate to follow the logic of the law to conclusions that he had to know would be remarkably controversial and deeply unpopular. These decisions included his major desegregation and institutional reform litigation rulings—but they also include rulings involving the rights of sexual minorities,[19] undocumented children,[20] and religious dissenters.[21] Thus, when a litigant put forward a claim with merit in Judge Johnson's courtroom, he or she would not leave his court without an effective remedy.[22] He explained his approach in this way: "It is one thing for a judge to adopt a theory of political morality *because it is his own*; it is another for him to exercise his judgement about what the political morality implied by the Constitution is."[23]

The Judge was also remarkably conservative in his own personal attitudes, behavior, and mores.[24] To borrow an apt line that encapsulates his personality, "Frank Johnson was not your man to join hands and sing the anthems of Odetta and Joan Baez."[25] The Judge was a very formal man—for example, I do not recall anyone but Mrs. Johnson ever calling him by his given name. Certainly none of his law clerks, before or after their tenure, had the temerity to address him as "Frank." He was simply "Judge"—and for his former law clerks, always will be.

Understanding Judge Frank M. Johnson Jr.: "It's Hard to
Ostracize a Fellow Who Does His Own Ostracizing"

Judge Johnson was always something of an outsider in Montgomery, the city where he spent his entire judicial career. Montgomery's country club set never really warmed up to Frank Johnson—worse still, they did not limit their targeted snubs to the Judge but quite often extended them to encompass his family. The Judge's public response was always consistent and emphatic: "It's hard to ostracize someone who does his own ostracizing."[26] Although I am certain that the Judge was quite sincere in this sentiment, at least regarding himself, he deeply resented and sincerely regretted the toll that these targeted, repeated, and often highly public insults took on Mrs. Johnson and their young son, Johnny.[27] The Judge's attitude toward his own exclusion from Montgomery high society was largely a matter of supreme indifference because he would "rather be fishing for speckled trout and chewing tobacco and maybe drinking a beer than [be] at the Phantom Ball" (Montgomery's most prestigious Mardi Gras soirée).[28]

Johnson hailed from Winston County, Alabama, a hardscrabble county in northwest Alabama settled by Jacksonian populist immigrants from Tennessee in the early nineteenth century. The land in Winston County is not particularly good for farming—or really anything else. The place is quite different from the typical mental image most people have of Alabama, which quite often features resplendent antebellum Greek Revival mansions situated among seemingly endless cotton fields.

Prior to the Civil War, few white households in Winston County owned human chattel slaves. And loyalty to the Union ran deep in that part of the state—in fact, during the Civil War, Winston County declared itself to be "The Free State of Winston" and purported to secede from Alabama. The denizens of Winston County reasoned that although Alabama's secession from the Union seemed blatantly illegal, if this action was somehow legal, then by parity of logic, Winston County should be no less free than Alabama to declare its political independence. Even today, visitors to Winston County will see barns painted with the slogan "Free State of Winston," and for many years *The Incident at Looney's Tavern*, an outdoor musical drama celebrating Winston County's secession convention,[29] took place in the spring as part of the annual "Winston County Free State Festival."

Judge Johnson wore his Winston County roots on his sleeve and took his "hillbilly" heritage as a badge of honor. He did this in a place, Montgomery,

Alabama, that served as a center of plantation culture prior to the Civil War and retained a strong "Old South" identity well into the twentieth century. In consequence, the Montgomery elite were not at all pleased, or amused, when, in 1955, President Dwight D. Eisenhower appointed Johnson, who was then serving as the U.S. attorney for the Northern District of Alabama (based in Birmingham), to serve as a United States district judge for the Middle District of Alabama. From the perspective of the Montgomery elite, Frank Johnson was a backwoods parvenu who had "stolen" a judgeship that rightfully should have gone to someone local to the Middle District.[30] At thirty-seven, Johnson was the youngest federal judge in the country at the time of his appointment.

Johnson had been active in helping General Eisenhower secure the GOP nomination for president against Senator Robert A. Taft at the 1952 Republican National Convention; Johnson helmed "Veterans for Eisenhower" in Alabama and, in this capacity, got to know Ike's future attorney general, Herbert Brownell Jr., prior to the 1952 primary and general election campaigns. In fact, Judge Johnson's family had been prominent Alabama Republicans for many years. His grandfather served as sheriff, and his father served as both Winston County's probate judge and as the lone GOP member of the Alabama state legislature in the 1940s. One should keep in mind that at this time, Republicans in Alabama were "Lincoln" Republicans—not Goldwater or Reagan Republicans.

Because Alabama's congressional delegation, like those of the other "solid south" states, was composed entirely of Southern Democrats, President Eisenhower enjoyed a relatively free hand in naming judges to the lower federal courts in the region.[31] With Attorney General Brownell's active encouragement and assistance, Ike named a bevy of well-qualified, pro–civil rights judges to the lower federal courts in the states of the former Confederate States of America. These jurists, along with Frank Johnson, included judicial legends such as John R. Brown, Elbert P. Tuttle, John Minor Wisdom, and J. Skelly Wright.

The Southern Christian Leadership Conference's Alabama Project swung into high gear at almost the same moment Judge Johnson assumed the bench. In consequence, Johnson sat in judgment over many iconic civil rights cases, including *Browder v. Gayle*,[32] the Montgomery Bus Boycott decision; *U.S. v. Alabama*,[33] addressing the systematic and near-total exclusion of African American citizens in Alabama from exercising the franchise; *Sims v. Frink*,[34] involving the gross malapportionment of the Alabama state legislature; and *Williams v. Wallace*,[35] the Selma March case. From his courtroom in Montgomery, Johnson systematically desegregated virtually every public institution in the state—public schools, state-sponsored colleges and universities, libraries, parks, public transportation, and the state's civil service. He undertook this work under extraordinarily difficult circumstances—the state of Alabama, led by the virulent race-baiter governor George C. Wallace Jr., attempted to obstruct and impede the implementation of Johnson's remedial orders at each and every juncture.

Governor Wallace's efforts to block the disestablishment of apartheid in Alabama did not stop in the courtroom—he used his bully pulpit as governor to inveigh against Judge Johnson and the federal courts. He called for local and state officials to disregard federal court orders requiring the desegregation of public institutions. And he worked daily to demonize Judge Johnson and render him a social pariah within the state. In my view, Wallace's repeated and irresponsible jeremiads were in part responsible for the violent attack on Alabama Long Johnson's home. Not only Judge Johnson, but even his wife, Ruth, and son, Johnny, were objects of Wallace's poison tongue and demagoguery.[36] As one commentator aptly observes, "In a thirty year morality play with the soul of the South in the balance, Frank Johnson played the white knight and George Wallace wore black, and the issue decided between these onetime friends and law school classmates was arguably the most important issue America has resolved in our lifetime."[37]

Later, in the 1970s, Johnson oversaw and decided pioneering institutional reform litigation involving pervasive unconstitutional conditions in Alabama's prisons[38] and state mental hospitals.[39] Once again, and true to form, Wallace attacked Johnson's rulings and accused him of creating a "hotel atmosphere" and "vacation club" conditions for convicted felons.[40]

Through it all, however, Johnson persevered—he never wavered. He decided the cases that came before him according to law and precedent.[41] Judge Johnson also never hesitated to provide comprehensive remedial decrees for proven violations of constitutional or statutory rights—despite the radically unpopular nature of these decisions with many white Alabamians. His resolute commitment to the Constitution, the Bill of Rights, and the Rule of Law provides a clarion example of how one person, at the right place and the right time, can make a fundamental difference not only to his local community, but to the nation and world as well.

Judge Johnson, at the ceremony for the renaming of the Montgomery federal courthouse in his honor, observed:

The hallmark of any society that claims to be civilized has to be its ability to do justice—to apply rules with equal favor to both the privileged and the downtrodden. Impartial and consistent interpretation of the laws promotes faith and justice by the people of all stations in life, a faith which, in turn, safeguards the rule of law and thus the civility of our nation. The citizenry's confidence in justice is essential—is absolutely essential—to a government of laws.[42]

Moreover, he emphasized that "[a] judge fosters belief in the rule of law only by consistently protecting the law from the passions of the moment, from politics, from partisanship, from prejudices, from personal, local or sectional interests and unethical influences."[43] Over Judge Johnson's forty-year tenure on the federal bench, his rulings and behavior (on and off the bench) consistently embodied these judicial virtues.

Clerking for Judge Johnson: The Kabuki of the Unspoken Rules Governing "A Good Law Clerk"

Judge Johnson did not have a manual or written set of directives for his law clerks. Instead, the outgoing clerks would pass down words of wisdom to the new, incoming law clerks. The incoming clerks had to take it on faith that the outgoing clerks knew whereof they spoke regarding the Judge's expectations and workplace rules; we simply assumed that the received lore was more or less correct. Although the Judge personally welcomed us and gave us a short pep talk about the importance of the work, Judge Johnson never actually sat us down as a group and provided comprehensive marching orders to his law clerk team. In general, if we had doubts about what we were supposed to be doing, we took them to his long-serving and highly competent assistant, Mrs. Dorothy ("Dot") Perry.[44] Nevertheless, the outgoing clerks were careful to emphasize the importance of following the rules if we were to live up to the standards of our predecessors—and achieve the status of "good" law clerks.

What were these rules? For starters, a good and efficient law clerk would always arrive for work before the Judge. To be sure, this sounds like a simple rule—and a quite reasonable expectation. However, a significant catch applied: Judge Johnson was a very early riser and routinely came to work at 7:00 a.m. Accordingly, an efficient and reasonably diligent law clerk should be at work by approximately 6:50 a.m. This was an unexpected aspect of the job that the incumbent law clerks failed to mention when I interviewed for the position. I have never risen as early, as consistently, as I did when clerking for Judge Johnson.

On the other hand, Judge Johnson did not expect his law clerks to stay in the office beyond 5:00 p.m. Moreover, working during the weekends constituted a sign of a problem with workload management, rather than extraordinary diligence. A good and efficient law clerk should be able to keep up with the workload by working a regular day and work week—meaning Monday to Friday, 7:00 a.m. to 5:00 p.m., with a one-hour break for lunch around midday.

As for the workload, it was both predictable and quite manageable. A typical sitting for a panel of the Eleventh Circuit at that time involved approximately twenty cases to be argued over a three- or four-day period. With three law clerks in chambers, each clerk had to prepare six or seven bench memoranda for each sitting. The Judge was very clear in his expectations regarding bench memoranda—he wanted them to be comprehensive, well researched, well written, and not overwritten. They followed a set template: statement of the facts, summary of the ruling below, statement of jurisdiction, major legal issues presented, relevant statutory and case law regarding those issues, an analysis of the merits of those issues, and a recommended disposition of the major issues presented and the case as a whole. .

After oral arguments each morning, the panel members would privately conference in the afternoon to discuss the cases and take a preliminary vote on the disposition of each appeal. If Judge Johnson was in the majority and assigned an opinion, he would usually ask the law clerk who prepared the bench memorandum to take a first crack at drafting the opinion. These drafts were then circulated among the law clerks and, after revisions based on the observations and suggestions of one's fellow law clerks, would go to Mrs. Perry for a careful review of grammar, spelling, and syntax. Nothing got past Mrs. Perry's eagle eyes—no split infinitives, no dangling participles, and certainly no noun-verb number disagreements.

After the draft opinion had been revised once more, to correct for the technical writing errors that Mrs. Perry inevitably discovered—notwithstanding the law clerks' best efforts, there was always something that we missed—the draft went to the Judge for his consideration. In some instances, the Judge would significantly edit and revise a draft opinion; whereas in others, his edits were relatively modest. If there was a pattern to his practice of heavy or light edits of draft opinions, it eluded me.

Although I am not absolutely certain, my impression is that Judge Johnson's use of his law clerks with respect to drafting opinions evolved over time. Based on conversations with some of his early law clerks from his time on the district court bench in the 1950s and 1960s, I believe that the Judge tended to prepare initial drafts of opinions and orders himself more frequently when he first took the bench—and he shifted over time to having his law clerks prepare first drafts of opinions, orders, and sometimes letters to another judge's chambers. In fact, when he first took the bench, I understand that the Judge, who could type eighty words a minute,[45] would often type up orders on his own and was famous for rendering very fast decisions. Burke Marshall, head of the Civil Rights Division of the Department of Justice during the Kennedy administration, has observed that Judge Johnson enjoyed a strong reputation for issuing "clear, straight, and quick" decisions.[46]

Because the Judge did not always rewrite every draft opinion from soup to nuts, opinions from his chambers would sometimes read in slightly different voices. While clerking for the Judge, I recall being somewhat puzzled by this—and discussed it at the time with one of my co-clerks, John Hueston. John's theory—which, for the record, we never had the temerity to run by the Judge himself—was that Judge Johnson had come to conclude that what mattered most in an opinion was not the precise wordsmithing so much as getting the fundamentals right: the facts, the law, the legal analysis, and the outcome. If the fundamentals were correct, then the opinion worked—but if they were not, then it did not. To be sure, the details were not unimportant to him—again, and for the record, he actively edited and revised all draft opinions. That said, however, Judge Johnson seemed to place primary emphasis on an opinion's clarity of exposition, getting the law right in light of the governing legal rules and precedents, and rendering his decisions on a timely basis.

At this juncture in the narrative, it probably bears noting that Judge Johnson was never particularly fulsome with his praise—whether for a bench memorandum or a draft opinion. When he reviewed a bench memorandum, for example, he would usually simply note that he had reviewed it and deemed it acceptable by marking a check mark at the end in a dayglow lime green highlighter that he used to mark up the memorandum. If he was particularly pleased, a clerk might see a check mark with an addition sign (+)—this indicated "good job." On very few occasions, a lucky clerk might get a "good" or "good" augmented by an addition sign. Rumors of "excellent" notations existed within the realm of clerk lore, but none of my cohort managed final marks better than "good" (and those were sparingly bestowed). Accordingly, in Judge Johnson's grading system, a "good" law clerk was, by more generous metrics, an excellent law clerk.

I do remember my first draft opinion for Judge Johnson. It was for an ERISA (Employee Retirement Income Security Act of 1974) case that presented a fairly simple issue regarding whether a state law regulated an ERISA-covered plan and was therefore preempted. My draft opinion ran for dozens of pages and was festooned with almost one hundred footnotes. I tried to write a thorough, scholarly opinion that covered every issue, no matter how tangential, from A to Z (including all the letters in between).

My office phone rang. Mrs. Perry said, "Ron, Judge wants to see you now. Can you please come into his chambers?" (My office was one of two law clerks' offices just outside the main chambers door.)

I entered the reception area, and Mrs. Perry buzzed me into the inner sanctum—Judge Johnson's personal office. He looked up and smiled at me. I knew that was a bad sign—there was mirth in his eyes. He started flipping through the pages and counting off the page number and the running footnote count. "Page 38, up to 64 footnotes." "Let's see here. . . 39, 40, 41, 42—42 pages?!" He stopped, put the draft down, and gave me "the stare." This was a famous look of perturbation that Judge Johnson used with great effect as both a trial court and appellate judge.[47] I sat quietly, wishing I was anywhere—anywhere—other than where I presently was seated.

"Mr. Krotoszynski," he finally intoned. "This chambers does not write for the law reviews. Opinions should be direct, to the point, and written in a fashion that a reasonably intelligent layperson can understand and follow." I said, meekly, "Yes, Judge. Understood." I then offered to fall on my sword: "Would you like me to rewrite the opinion to make it shorter and plainer?" The Judge responded, "No. That will not be necessary. But, going forward, remember: This chambers does not write for law reviews. Make sure you remember that fact." He then picked up the draft, started flipping the pages again, and laughed at how marvelously overwrought it was. Judge Johnson did edit the opinion and reduced some of my more operatic verbiage—after Mrs. Perry incorporated his edits, it was sent out to the other chambers, and the concurrences came in without incident.

I told my co-clerks about my dressing down for drafting an overlong, overwrought opinion. One of my co-clerks asked the Judge a few days later, "Why didn't you make him totally rewrite the draft opinion if you did not like it?" My colleague reported that Judge Johnson responded, "Because I did not want to break his spirit—especially so early in his time with me." He added, "He heard me just fine—it won't happen again." And it did not.

Since my clerkship, I have learned that getting his law clerks to get to the point, and stick to the point, constituted something of an ongoing battle for the Judge with more than a few of his law clerks. For example, Pam Pepper (1989 to 1990), who currently serves as a federal district judge, recounts that she too "wrote *way* too much for him. His way of dealing with me about it, however, was gentle humor."[48] More specifically, Judge Johnson "would make jokes about how computers had done no favors to judges, because they allowed law clerks to write even longer bench memos (with pointed looks at me)." Years later, at a reunion of the Judge's former law clerks, this clerk prepared a celebratory song[49]—after which the Judge exclaimed, "That Pepper—even her *songs* are long!" Judge Pepper told me, "I'm not sure I've ever been able to be as concise to this day as he'd have wished, but he let me know I was too wordy without being mean about it, for which I always have been grateful."

Along similar lines, a law clerk in the mid-1980s reports that he came to Judge Johnson's chambers with a strong tendency to produce overwrought draft opinions glistening with obscure (and, therefore, in his view, learned) literary and philosophical references—as well as esoteric foreign words.[50] After reviewing this clerk's first draft opinion, Judge Johnson told him essentially the same thing he told me: Opinions should be direct, written in a style that a reasonably educated person could understand, and should not be needlessly complex or overlong. And, again, the Judge did not require the law clerk to completely rewrite the offending draft—because, as the Judge told the former clerk, he "did not want to break his spirit."

This clerk wrote a draft opinion using the term "bête noire"—which Judge Johnson edited out and replaced with "bugbear." He explained to this clerk that "bête noire" was too fancy and constituted purple prose of the sort he preferred to abjure. The draft opinion went out, and another judge on the panel came to see Judge Johnson and suggested that rather than "bugbear" the better turn of phrase would be "bête noir." Judge Johnson said he would consider it—and then called in the clerk to revel in his proof that "bête noire" went too far. The Judge disliked the writing style of this particular colleague, which he thought to be overwrought—bordering on pretentious.

We clearly benefited greatly from the Judge's efforts to make us clearer and more direct legal writers. As another former clerk, who, like me, had a tendency to write long bench memoranda and draft opinions, explains, "I just feel lucky to have been able to work with him, and he definitely made me a much better writer."[51] In this regard, the clerk notes, "I recall *lots* of heavy mark-ups but I did learn a lot—though this may have accrued more to [my law firm's] benefit than to his!"

Judge Johnson's dislike of overwritten judicial opinions was not limited to purple prose in draft opinions from his law clerks. He disliked opinions from his judicial colleagues that contained needless dicta and that sought to decide more than was necessary for the disposition of a case. From time to time, he did this in print by concurring in an opinion solely to disavow an opinion that he believed to be needlessly complex or overwritten.[52] The Judge explained in a law review article that "one of the worst characteristics of judges in particular, and the legal profession in general, is a penchant for dull or simply incomprehensible writing, a fact decried by the likes of Shakespeare, Swift, Bentham, and many others."[53] As he admonished his law clerks, including me, a well-crafted judicial opinion should be "accessible to the layman."[54]

Sound reasons existed for the Judge's very strong preference for concise, direct, and plainly written judicial opinions. During the height of the civil rights movement, when Judge Johnson was issuing opinions that were radically unpopular with white Alabamians, he would routinely answer letters that came in criticizing his rulings—explaining to the letter writer why the ruling was correct in light of the applicable laws and legal principles. Johnson would even take calls from the public to discuss his opinions. (The Judge sometimes would delegate the fielding of irate telephone calls and letters to his law clerks; responding to angry locals was not a task that we particularly relished, but we did as we were told.)

He believed that if ordinary people could understand the relevant legal rules and principles, they would come to agree with his court's rulings. He also believed that the vast majority of Alabamians were essentially law-abiding and fair-minded people—and, accordingly, if they could understand the relevant legal principles, they would accept the inevitably of his decisions requiring the end of state-enforced racial segregation. He complained privately, and sometimes publicly, about judicial opinions that he believed to be unduly complex, overwrought, or confusing.

As part of his public educational efforts, Judge Johnson often wrote for the law reviews himself during the 1960s and 1970s—to defend the work of the federal courts in securing constitutional rights and civil liberties.[55] He also accepted speaking invitations for a wide variety of groups—and his message was inevitably that a society committed to the Rule of Law is much to be preferred to a society in which government may violate constitutional rights with impunity.

Judge Johnson also took pains to emphasize that so long as the courts were open to hear and decide constitutional complaints, those suffering constitutional wrongs should seek relief through the judicial process rather than resort to various forms of self-help—notably including violent forms of protest. As he explained, "There is no legal or moral justification for the rioting, burning, looting and killing that have occurred in such cities as Los Angeles, Detroit, Chicago, Newark, Kansas City and Washington. Understandable, perhaps; justifiable, never."[56] For Johnson, self-help simply was not an option that the federal courts could countenance, and violence was never an appropriate means of seeking to vindicate federal civil rights.[57] Courts should provide reliable, effective relief when litigants established in open court that the government had failed to respect their rights; as Judge Johnson put it, "A judge cannot discharge his oath of office without seeing to it that relief is provided."[58]

Johnson always kept on his desk current lists of all pending cases on which he was the writing judge and on which he served on a panel. As opinions were sent to other chambers for concurrences and approved, he marked them off the lists. Woe unto the law clerk who took too long to draft an opinion for his review and submission to the other panel members for their consideration and, hopefully, approval. He believed that the litigants had a right to expect a timely decision from the Court of Appeals, and he found it embarrassing to have a case languish in his chambers. Of course, when he was not the writing judge, the timing of the opinion was beyond his control. But it frustrated him to have cases pending for inordinate periods of time.

There was a kind of rhythm to our work as clerks: cases would arrive from the clerk's office about six weeks before a sitting, the clerks would prepare bench memoranda, the panel would hear oral arguments and vote on a disposition of the appeal, and the law clerk would, as needed, assist with drafting an opinion, a concurrence, or a dissent. Usually, it was possible to be more or less current with one's work for the Judge. The chambers could not control the speed with which concurring votes arrived after Judge Johnson sent out a draft opinion, but to the extent it was within his power, he wanted to see appeals decided expeditiously—ideally within no more than sixty to ninety days after the oral arguments.

The Judge would routinely ask his law clerks to review draft opinions from other chambers and to review the drafts for consistency with the conference disposition—and the Judge's preferred outcome in the case. Occasionally, he would ask a law clerk to draft a letter to another Judge's chambers recommending an edit or an alteration to a draft opinion. However, he admonished his clerks never to "nit-pick" the work of other chambers—which he viewed as both unwarranted and unwise. Why antagonize a colleague over a point that did not really matter to the disposition of the case?

The Judge made it very clear to his law clerks that we were not to tell tales out of school; we were strictly admonished not to discuss the internal workings of Judge Johnson's chambers with the law clerks from other judge's chambers—whether in Montgomery or at a sitting elsewhere. To be clear, the Judge did not discourage us from meeting, getting to know, and socializing with the other law clerks—or their employers, the other federal judges serving in the Middle District and on the Eleventh Circuit. That said, however, informal communications about judicial business through a law clerk network was not within our job description. I am unaware of any of the Judge's law clerks ever breaching his trust by gossiping about his work in other chambers; such a course of action would have been unthinkable to us. As has probably become quite clear by this juncture, Judge Johnson inspired fierce loyalty in both his law clerks and staff. We knew that we were working for a great hero of the law and that we were incredibly lucky to play even a small part in his tremendously important work. None of us would ever have consciously taken any action that would have betrayed his faith in us.

Simply put, what went on in his chambers was not be discussed outside of them. Accordingly, any communications with other judges took place through formal rather than back channels. Given the blaze of intense scrutiny under which Judge Johnson toiled for so many years, it was not at all surprising to me that he ran his chambers, like his courtroom, strictly by the book.

The clerks also reviewed "screeners"—cases reviewed by staff attorneys in the Eleventh Circuit Clerk's Office and deemed not to raise any novel questions of law and, in light of this, suitable for summary disposition without oral arguments. The staff attorney would prepare a draft disposition (an order), a memorandum explaining the legal issues presented and why the appeal clearly lacked merit in light of the governing law, and a brief explication of the relevant statutes and precedents. The draft order and staff attorney memorandum were attached to the parties' briefs. Most screeners recommended summary affirmance of the district court's disposition of the case—a summary reversal, without a statement of reasons for the reversal, would have provided insufficient guidance to the district court judge on remand. More often than not, the screener panel would accept the staff attorney's recommendation for summary disposition. Even in 1991, most appeals in the Eleventh Circuit were considered and resolved in this fashion—oral arguments were the exception, not the rule.

Draft opinions from other panels circulated as preliminary slip opinions to the full court before being released to the public. This was so other judges could review the decisions and decide whether to pull the mandate and seek a poll of the full membership regarding en banc review of the appeal. I recall one instance in which a panel blatantly disregarded an opinion that the Judge had written involving an obscure copyright issue. I prepared a memorandum noting that the panel had, more or less, ignored the governing circuit precedent, authored by Judge Johnson, and recommending that he pull the mandate and ask for a poll of the full court on rehearing en banc.

The writing judge, who fancied himself a veritable Melville Nimmer, initially resisted this suggestion but ultimately agreed that his opinion departed from circuit precedent. The motion for en banc review carried.[59] In reviewing the work of other chambers, the Judge admonished us to look only for "serious problems" and not minor issues that did not merit the full court's attention.

The Judge received innumerable invitations to speak at various events: graduations, bar events, civic organizations. He would usually ask one of his incumbent clerks to prepare a first draft of the remarks—but he would inevitably revise the drafts so that they read in his own voice. For example, my friend and co-clerk, John Hueston (1991 to 1992), prepared a beautiful first draft of the Judge's remarks at the dedication ceremony for the Judge Frank M. Johnson, Jr. Federal Building and United States Courthouse, which took place on May 22, 1992. But, when one reads the remarks that the Judge delivered that day, they read entirely in his own voice. The draft was a starting point for his public remarks—never an end point. I think, given all the difficulties he faced, that when he spoke out as "Frank Johnson," he felt it essential to speak in his own voice.

The difficulties he faced also led him to have rules that, at the time, seemed somewhat idiosyncratic to me. For example, when we went to Atlanta for sittings, we would always drive rather than fly. Judge Johnson disliked flying, and he was also a fierce guardian of the U.S. Treasury. Why buy expensive plane tickets at the taxpayer's expense when he could drive up with a clerk or two in almost the same time and at very little cost? He expected his law clerks to dress up for the drive—a practice that always seemed rather odd to me (and one I resisted at the margins, getting away with a navy blazer and polo shirt rather than a suit and tie). In retrospect, I think that he took such pains with his public appearance, and the appearance of his chambers staff, because of the intense blaze of scrutiny he was under for so many years.

Judge Johnson also made clear that Montgomery was a small town and his law clerks should not expect to cohabitate without a marriage license—telling one incoming law clerk who had planned to have a live-in girlfriend with him during his clerkship year that "he should find a marriage license or a second apartment, I don't care which." The relationship, alas, came to an end before the clerkship began; accordingly, I cannot report on which choice this law clerk would have made. I am certain, however, that open and notorious cohabitation in defiance of the Judge's "advice" would not have constituted a well-informed choice. On the other hand, Judge Johnson played the matchmaker between a former law clerk and an incoming clerk—Peter Canfield (1979 to 1980) and Laurel Lucey (1983 to 1984). They are still married to this day.

If the law clerks were extensions of the public face of Judge Johnson, they were also afforded access to the Judge's private life as well. The Judge took law clerks on fishing trips and also initiated them to the joys of woodworking. One of the Judge's favorite pastimes was building handcrafted furniture. Many of his former law clerks have grandfather clocks that they built, side by side with Judge Johnson, in his backyard woodworking shop. At sittings, he always took the clerks to dinner with him and insisted that we all "Salute the Constitution"— meaning drink straight bourbon, ideally George Dickel white label (if available). He also initiated more than a few of us to "chew"—meaning chewing tobacco.

Seeking to show the Judge that I was an adventurous soul, I agreed, at the first sitting I attended with him, to try chew after dinner. I did not realize, however, that swallowing the juice was not recommended—and can essentially cause nicotine poisoning. I attempted to spit the juice in various flower pots, but the Judge, ever a prankster, admonished me "don't do that to the nice flowers!" So I swallowed the tobacco juice—producing one of the worst hangover-like experiences in my life.

The next morning, when I could not eat breakfast and appeared green, the Judge asked me, sternly, "Krotoszynski, did you go out and get drunk last night? Are you hung over?" I said, "No, Judge, I swallowed the tobacco juice from the chew." He laughed at me and said, "Well, you're not supposed to do that. You're supposed to spit the juice out." (One of our duties, at sittings, was to ensure that Judge Johnson had his spittoon available in the courtroom.)

Judge Johnson was not usually an active questioner at oral arguments. There were some exceptions. Nancy Olson, who clerked a year after me in 1992 to 1993, reported that at an appeal involving a Florida school district's effort to obtain "unitary status" and cease continuing district court oversight of its operations,[60] the Judge listened, with growing incredulity, as the lawyers for the school district argued that the district's efforts at desegregation were, to use a common turn of phrase, "good enough for government work." He abruptly cut off the public school district's lawyer midsentence: "Can we help you?" The lawyer, taken by surprise, paused, said nothing, and then indicated that he did not understand the question.

Johnson repeated himself: "Can we help you?" The lawyer, flummoxed, stammered, "Judge, I am just not following your question. Can you please elaborate?" The Judge smiled broadly and said, "Well, you've been trying to desegregate your schools for around twenty years now, and you've got precious little progress to show for it. And, now, you want to call it done. Seems to me you could use some help. We're here to help you get the job done." He then gave the lawyer his patented "stare." Stunned silence from the school district's lawyer. "Your client is having difficulties, obviously, and we can assist your client in addressing those difficulties. So, can we help you? You seem to need some help." At this point, the lawyer, realizing the train of the Judge's reasoning, stammered, "Um, no Judge, thanks, we're good—we appreciate the offer and all, but we don't need help."

Judge Johnson had made his point—the failure of the school district to make progress represented the kind of defiance of a federal court order that he had experienced as a district court judge. And, as a former district court judge, he viewed his role as an appellate court judge as working to facilitate good faith compliance with the desegregation order—which, in his view, had not yet occurred even though the district was now seeking the termination of the district court's ongoing remedial order.

Of course, many stories exist of Judge Johnson's ability to hold the attention of lawyers who appeared before him—perhaps most famously, the Judge's patented stare allegedly caused a young Department of Justice lawyer in his trial court to faint from fear.[61] Judge Johnson, particularly as a district court judge, had a reputation for being a strict and demanding judge, a judge who insisted on proper decorum in his courtroom. As a Montgomery legal journalist explained, "'It was terrifying for most lawyers, litigants, and reporters. Everyone was scared to death of the man—which is what I believe he wanted.'"[62] But, as this reporter noted to Jack Bass, "'he was usually kind to beginners.'"[63]

I personally observed this "kinder, gentler" approach to management of the court's business in action. In a routine criminal appeal in one of the innumerable drug-related cases that came before Judge Johnson, an assistant United States attorney advanced several arguments in the government's appellate brief that were very clearly not supported, at all, in the record. Nevertheless, I had to spend several hours chasing down the law and facts to swat these arguments away. As it became increasingly clear that the brief was almost completely lacking in merit, and in fact bordered on being intellectually dishonest, my mind turned down a vengeful path.

When, after the oral arguments in the case, Judge Johnson was assigned to write the opinion, overturning a federal drug conviction because of serious legal errors in the trial process, I dropped a footnote observing that the government's arguments not only lacked any support in the record but verged on the border of being sanctionable as frivolous. After the usual review by my co-clerks and Mrs. Perry, the draft opinion went to the Judge for his review.

When I received the revised draft opinion, I noted, unhappily, that the Judge had edited out that footnote—he had red-lined the whole thing with his pencil and marked it for deletion. After I had reviewed his other edits to the draft, I had the temerity to ask about only one edit: the redaction of my vengeful footnote. "Judge, if you don't mind, may I ask: why did you take out this footnote? The government's arguments were not borderline frivolous, they were frivolous— utterly without any legal merit." He stared at me, without smiling, and finally said "That young fellow, the government lawyer, is at the start of his career, and if that footnote stays in this opinion, then he won't have one. A legal career, that is. Anywhere. The arguments were frivolous, and he's losing the appeal and also the conviction. That will cause him problems enough professionally."

He then smiled at me and said, "It just wasn't a hanging offense." And he went into his chambers office and closed the door, audibly chuckling, having taught his overeager law clerk an important lesson about empathy and proportionality. Of course, the Judge was right—that footnote would have destroyed this lawyer's career in the United States attorney's office before it had really even begun.

There are so many stories about Judge Johnson being fierce to lawyers in his courtroom. And he was that—if they wished to waste the court's time or tested his patience, he would react swiftly and strongly to defend the dignity of the federal courts. But he was also capable of being empathetic and kind. In this instance, he had an overeager law clerk go a step too far—and he intervened because, as he explained to his overeager law clerk, one very bad brief should not be a career-ending offense.

Judge Johnson took the same approach when his own law clerks made the occasional mistake. For a law clerk, the idea of having to enter the boss's office and tell him, "Judge, I goofed" is a nightmare scenario—a scenario that fills any and every law clerk's heart and mind with abject fear and dread. And, of course, from time to time, law clerks, almost invariably newly minted lawyers just graduated from law school, make mistakes. Judge Johnson, however, accepted bad news with equanimity and, to the best of my knowledge, never expressed even mild anger when a clerk goofed. That said, however, I suspect it was because the Judge knew nothing he could say would make a law clerk feel any worse— or inspire them to do any better going forward.

One former law clerk recounts the following story involving a First Amendment case decided in the 1980s. Soon after the decision was published, Judge Johnson received a letter from a law professor; he called the clerk into his chambers, handed her the letter, and asked her to read it.[64] The letter started off promisingly enough: it "was very complimentary, praising the opinion." Alas, a bit further down, the letter noted that "a decision that I had cited in a footnote was no longer good law." Upon reading this, the law clerk "started to hyperventilate, and began babbling about how sorry I was and how I couldn't believe I'd missed it and how. . ." Judge Johnson cut off the law clerk; "he raised his hand, looked at me over the glasses, and said, 'Just wanted to show it to you.'" He then took the letter back. The clerk reports: "I walked out, and I spent the rest of the day (probably the week) trying to convince myself not to quit because I had failed him. Yet, he never mentioned it again. It was worse than getting excoriated—by a long shot. I had disappointed him." Having called the matter to the law clerk's attention, without comment or condemnation, he deemed the matter closed.

Other law clerks have similar stories about making mistakes and then having to own up to them. A former law clerk who worked for Judge Johnson when he served on the district court bench reports that just a few months into his clerkship with Judge Johnson, he "had prepared a memorandum and order for the Judge dismissing a case based on an Alabama statute of limitations having expired."[65] He adds, "The case was routine and, after the order dismissing the case was entered, the plaintiff filed an appeal with the 5th Circuit arguing the facts regarding when the time for filing should be measured."

However, there was then a twist in the plot:

> Several weeks later, my co-clerk and I were engaged in an after-hours bull session with the magistrate late one afternoon. The magistrate happened to mention that he had run across a bizarre tolling provision in the Alabama statutes that was not clearly indexed and was not anywhere near the section of the law to which it applied. As he continued to discuss it, my blood ran cold as I realized that the tolling statute applied to the case that the Judge had dismissed based on my research and recommendation.

The law clerk prepared to fall on his sword: "The next morning, I went to Mrs. Perry's desk and said I needed to see the Judge. She said, 'go on in.'"

Needless to say, this clerk was terrified of the Judge's potential reaction: "Nervous doesn't begin to describe how I felt. Terrified was more like it." He told the Judge that he "had made a mistake in the order to dismiss the case, explained how I had missed the existence of a tolling statute, and told him that the case was on appeal to the 5th Circuit." The Judge was unperturbed— entirely sanguine—and told the clerk, "O.K., we'll issue a *nunc pro tunc* order." And so, without any drama or shouting, the error was corrected without the intervention or assistance of the Fifth Circuit.

Of course, the law clerk had expected to be dressed down and was "completely taken aback by the Judge's calm demeanor, matter-of-fact response, and lack of criticism or even comment on my mistake." The Judge's example of how to handle a mishap provided a highly useful lesson: "Over the years, I had numerous occasions to recall that valuable lesson in 'fixing the problem and not the blame,' both applying it to those who worked for me and teaching it to others." Over a thirty-year career in the law, "I never found a more valuable management tool than the one I learned that day in the Judge's chambers."

Thus, although Judge Johnson had a well-deserved reputation for running a tight ship when presiding from the bench, he accepted his law clerks' occasional errors and snafus with a high degree of equanimity. I suspect that this was because he believed, quite correctly, that his law clerks gave him their best efforts. And he had the wisdom and perspective to realize that newly minted twenty-three- or twenty-four-year-old lawyers' best efforts would sometimes not quite measure up to the task at hand. Even though we expected and feared that the wrath of God would be brought down on our unworthy heads when we came up short, Judge Johnson was far more inclined to use humor than thunderbolts to bring a wayward clerk to book.

Judge Johnson's Law Clerk Hiring Practices

Judge Johnson would review clerkship applications himself but also would ask the incumbent law clerks to review the applications and recommend applications that seemed particularly promising. He sometimes credited the suggestions of his law clerks, and in other instances, he would strike out on his own and make hiring decisions without their input.

He was not inclined to follow hiring plans. The year I applied to Judge Johnson, 1990, featured an effort by Judge Harry T. Edwards, of the United States Court of Appeals for the District of Columbia, to rein in the practice of federal appellate judges selecting their law clerks at earlier and earlier time points. Before federal judges started racing each other to see who could hire the best law clerks first, most of them had hired their law clerks just under a year out before the hires' start date, that is, in the fall semester of the third year of law school. When I was applying for a federal judicial clerkship, the hiring timetable had accelerated to late January of the second year—and threatened to accelerate into the fall semester of that year. Judge Edwards, seeking to end this pattern of ever-accelerating clerkship hiring decisions, proposed a hiring plan that would establish a formal May 1 hiring date as the earliest point in time at which a "hiring plan" judge would extend an offer of employment to an applicant for a clerkship. Moreover, clerkship interviews were not to take place until March 1 of the second year.

When I interviewed with Judge Johnson, in his Montgomery, Alabama, chambers, I asked him if he planned to follow the hiring plan timetable. He responded, "No. I do not run a dog and pony show here with hiring my clerks; I will decide to make offers when I decide to make offers. Any more questions about my hiring schedule?" He added that, in his view, it was highly unseemly for federal judges to openly compete with each other for potential law clerks— he interviewed candidates, he would make offers on a rolling basis, as the interview process went forward, and I would hear from him relatively soon. He then asked me again, "Any more questions?" I responded that I did not have any additional questions—but it was very clear that May 1 was entirely irrelevant to Judge Johnson. He might make offers before May 1, and he might extend offers after May 1; he would proceed as he had always proceeded in selecting his law clerks. Judge Johnson offered me a clerkship in his chambers in mid-April; I accepted this offer on conveyance.

Judge Johnson did not require all applicants to come to Montgomery in person to interview. In a few cases, when it became clear to him that a candidate came from a rural, farming background, he interviewed the person by phone and made a decision based on the telephone interview, application materials, and letters of recommendation. He did this on the quite reasonable assumption that would-be clerks from family farm backgrounds did not have deep financial resources.

A law school classmate of mine, in the class one year behind mine and serving with me on the *Duke Law Journal*, had grown up in a rural community in Nebraska. Her family operated a farm, with mixed results over the years; she was the oldest child of a large family. Judge Johnson interviewed her by telephone and, shortly thereafter, offered her a clerkship in his chambers. It turns out that one of her law professors had mentioned in a letter of recommendation that she came from a large farm family and had undertaken primary responsibilities for raising several of her younger siblings—this resonated with Judge Johnson, who as the oldest of seven children in his family, had helped raise his younger siblings.

Another law clerk mentioned, in his letter of application, that he had worked on his family's blueberry farm in order to help pay for law school. The incumbent law clerks at that time told the Judge that the application looked very strong—that the applicant clearly merited an in-chambers interview. The Judge, however, had different ideas. He asked Mrs. Perry to get the fellow on the phone, interviewed him by telephone, and subsequently offered him a clerkship—no trip to Montgomery required.

After I had been working for the Judge for almost a year, and just before she arrived to start her clerkship, I asked Judge Johnson about his decision to hire my Duke Law School classmate without requiring an in-person interview. He laughed and said, "She's from a big farm family. Farm families are always struggling to make ends meet—I'm from a big farm family, and it's difficult for them financially. They don't have money to spend on plane tickets to Montgomery." It was a clear example of Judge Johnson's empathy and also of his effort to mentor people who came from relatively humble backgrounds.

Judge Johnson received a large number of applications—around eight hundred per year when in active service, and about half that number after taking senior status. He had no difficulty in finding smart, eager law graduates to work in his chambers. When he first became a federal district court judge, most of his law clerks were graduates of the University of Alabama School of Law—Judge Johnson's own alma mater. As his reputation grew over time, and his civil rights rulings received substantial attention in both the national press and in the law reviews, he began to hire law clerks from other law schools. In particular, Judge Johnson seemed to attract well-qualified candidates from Yale Law School and Cornell Law School. In the 1980s and 1990s, he usually had at least one law clerk from both places. The third clerk would come from any one of several law schools, including Alabama, Columbia, Duke, Emory, Georgetown, Harvard, New York University, North Carolina, Texas, Vanderbilt, and Virginia. In selecting law clerks, in addition to a clear soft spot for farm kids, Judge Johnson also seemed to like hiring clerks from the Deep South in general and Alabama in particular.

When interviewing clerkship candidates, Judge Johnson would ask a lot of substantive questions of clerkship applicants. In particular, he would ask candidates to discuss their views on the death penalty and would press them to justify their responses. He would also ask about the Equal Protection Clause, federal jurisdiction, and civil procedure. The Judge seemed to like applicants who had shown some interest in and aptitude for federal civil rights. At the same time, however, he seemed to shy away from applicants who had strong records of activism (of whatever stripe). I suspect that he worried about hiring a clerk who would seek to advance a particular cause from his chambers—rather than strive to get the law right.

Conclusion

Judge Frank M. Johnson Jr.'s profile in judicial courage remains highly relevant. At a time when the White House is occupied by a man who loudly and coarsely inveighs against "so-called federal judges"[66] because they have the temerity to issue rulings adverse to his spurious legal claims, we must hold fast to our core constitutional values and to our broader commitment to the rule of law itself. Now more than ever, we need judges and lawyers willing to stand up against elected officials, such as Donald Trump, who seek to place themselves above the law. Unfortunately, it would seem, George Wallace, in one form or another, will always be with us. The harder question is: will we always have a Frank Johnson to stand in his way?

Yale law professor and former assistant attorney general Burke Marshall, writing in support of Judge Johnson's nomination for an honorary doctorate in law from Yale University, observed, "I think there can be no argument but that his judicial performance . . . in the 25 years since *Brown* is the most extraordinary in the history of the federal courts—the trial Judge's equivalent of Chief Justice John Marshall on the Supreme Court."[67] Professor Owen Fiss has deployed precisely the same analogy[68] and noted, "Having desegregated the schools of Alabama, it was only natural for Judge Johnson to try to reform the mental hospitals and then the prisons of the state in the name of human rights—the right to treatment or to be free from cruel and unusual punishment—and to attempt this Herculean feat through the injunction."[69] At the same time, however, and as Fiss has observed, the work required to secure and enforce constitutional rights in places such as Alabama during the civil rights era imposed a terrible—and entirely unreasonable—burden on federal judges such as Frank Johnson.[70]

Clerking for Judge Frank Johnson was both an honor and a tremendous learning experience. My clerkship taught me many valuable lessons—lessons about the law, to be sure, and the operation of the Article III courts. But, more important, it taught me a great deal about honor, courage, character, and the ability to do one's duty (even if this requires you to put your own moral, political, or ideological beliefs to the side in the process).[71] Whatever Judge Johnson's personal beliefs and convictions—or his own internal hopes and fears—in his chambers and in his courtroom, his first and only commitment as a federal judge was fealty to the Constitution.[72]

In sum, Judge Johnson's law clerks took away better writing skills and a deeper, more nuanced understanding of the law and its operation in the federal courts. But, more important, we gained crucial insight into how to live a professional life in the service of the rule of law. I think, more than anything else, Frank Johnson inculcated in his law clerks, by his words and his deeds, the absolute necessity of maintaining the rule of law and the crucial role that lawyers play in undertaking this essential task. For me, particularly in the contemporary United States, it remains a highly salient, and cherished, lesson.

Notes

1. Tinsley E. Yarbrough, *Judge Frank Johnson and Human Rights in Alabama* (Tuscaloosa: University of Alabama Press, 1981), 87; Jack Bass, *Taming the Storm: The Life and Times of Judge Frank M. Johnson, Jr., and the South's Fight over Civil Rights* (Athens: University of Georgia Press, 2002), 194.

2. Bass, *Taming the Storm*, 3, 340, 353.

3. Jack Bass, *Unlikely Heroes: The Dramatic Story of the Southern Judges of the Fifth Circuit Who Translated the Supreme Court's Brown's Decision into a Revolution for Equality* (New York: Simon and Schuster, 1981), 79–80.

4. Steven Brill, "The Real Governor of Alabama," *New York Magazine*, April 26, 1976, 37.

5. 760 F.2d 1202 (11th Cir. 1985), *rev'd*, 478 U.S. 186 (1986). Judge Johnson's opinion in *Hardwick* held that "the Georgia sodomy statute infringes upon the fundamental constitutional rights of Michael Hardwick" (1211). This outcome was constitutionally necessary because "the activity he hopes to engage in is quintessentially private and lies at the heart of an intimate association beyond the proper reach of state regulation."

6. See *Hardwick*, 760 F.2d at 1211–13.

7. 628 F.2d 448 (5th Cr. 1980), *aff'd*, 457 U.S. 202 (1982).

8. Ibid., 457, 460–61 (invalidating Section 21.031 of the Texas Education Code, a state law that denied any state funds to local public school districts for the costs associated with educating the children of undocumented, unlawfully present agricultural workers because the policy was irrational except as a means to discriminate against children, children who "had committed no moral wrong," and explaining that under the Equal Protection Clause "Texas may not justify its discrimination by a mere desire to discriminate").

9. *Plyler v. Doe*, 457 U.S. 202 (1982). ("If the State is to deny a discrete group of innocent children the free public education that it offers to other children residing within its borders, that denial must be justified by a showing that it furthers some substantial state interest. No such showing was made here.")

10. I should note that Lane Heard, who clerked for Judge Johnson in 1978–1979, made this observation during the May 22, 1992, ceremony unveiling a bust of Judge Johnson, which had been commissioned and funded by his former law clerks, at the federal courthouse building in downtown Montgomery. Frank Lane Heard III, "Remarks at the Dedication Ceremony, Frank M. Johnson, Jr. Federal Building and

204 | RONALD J. KROTOSZYNSKI, JR.

United States Courthouse," (May 22, 1992), in *989 F.2d, LXXXIX, CXIV* (noting that Judge Johnson "was, and is, our teacher and example" and positing that "if we have the courage, when faced with a difficult decision, we ask what the Judge would do").

11. My parents lived about a three hours' drive away from Montgomery, in Moss Point, Mississippi. One Friday, when he knew I would be driving down to see them over the weekend, the Judge brought in a lovely bouquet of his prize roses with the strict instruction that I was to hand-deliver the flowers to my mother with his personal compliments. This sort of entirely unexpected kindness was typical of the Judge.

12. Hal Crowther, *Cathedrals of Kudzu: A Personal Landscape of the South* (Baton Rouge: Louisiana State University Press, 2000), 97, 101.

13. Ibid.

14. Ronald J. Krotoszynski, Jr., "A Man for All Seasons: Judge Frank M. Johnson, Jr. and the Quest to Secure the Rule of Law," *Alabama Law Review* 61 (2009): 165, 175–83.

15. Frank M. Johnson Jr., "Civil Disobedience and the Law,"*Florida Law Review* 20 (1968): 267, 271.

16. Ibid.

17. Ibid., 275.

18. The death penalty provides perhaps the best example of Judge Johnson's steadfast practice of following and enforcing settled precedent with which he disagreed—strongly disagreed in the case of the death penalty. See *McCleskey v. Kemp*, 753 F.2d 877, 908–09 (11t h Cir. 1986) (en banc) (Johnson, J., dissenting), *aff'd*, 481 U.S. 279 (1987) (arguing, in dissent, that "the Eighth Amendment prohibits the racially discriminatory application of the death penalty and McCleskey does not have to prove intent to discriminate in order to show that the death penalty is being applied arbitrarily and capriciously"); Bass, *Taming the Storm*, 448–55 (discussing Judge Johnson's strong and longstanding constitutional objections to the death penalty). As Judge Johnson explained his position to biographer Jack Bass, "'If I was making the law, I'd rule and hold—and I think there's a valid, a very valid legal basis for it—that the death penalty laws violated the Eighth Amendment" (ibid., 448).

19. *Bowers v. Hardwick*, 760 F.2d 1202 (11th Cir. 1985), *rev'd*, 478 U.S. 186 (1986).

20. *Doe v. Plyler*, 628 F.2d 448 (5th Cir. 1980), *aff'd*, 457 U.S. 202 (1982).

21. *Jager v. Douglas County School Dist*, 862 F. 2d 824 (1989). Although the Supreme Court did not review this decision, it subsequently adopted Judge Johnson's interpretation and application of the Establishment Clause. *Santa Fe Independent School Dist. v. Doe*, 530 US 290 (2000).

22. Frank M. Johnson Jr., "The Role of the Federal Courts in Institutional Litigation," *Alabama Law Review* 32 (1980–1981): 271, 274 ("Faced with defaults by government officials, however, a judge does not have the option of declaring that litigants have rights without remedies. The judge has no alternative but to take a more active role in formulating appropriate relief").

23. Frank M. Johnson Jr., "In Defense of Judicial Activism," *Emory Law Journal* 28 (1979): 901, 909 (emphasis in the original).

24. As I have observed previously, "those who assumed, based on a reading of his opinions, that Judge Johnson was a liberal maverick outside as well as inside the courtroom were routinely disappointed, for he was surprisingly traditional, indeed conservative, in his personal life, aesthetics, and sensibilities" (Ronald J. Krotoszynski, Jr., "Equal Justice under Law: The Jurisprudential Legacy of Judge Frank M. Johnson, Jr.," *Yale Law Journal* 109 [2000]: 1237, 1246).

25. Crowther, *Cathedrals of Kudzu*, 101.

26. Bass, *Taming the Storm*, 129; Bass, *Unlikely Heroes*, 80–81. ("It's hard to ostracize a fellow who does his own ostracizing. I'm the only lawyer from north Alabama that ever resigned from the Rotary Club. It was hogwash.") As Hal Crowther has observed of Judge Johnson, "Montgomery society never understood how little he cared for country club memberships or invitations to black tie balls." Crowther, *Cathedrals of Kudzu*, 100. Even so, Judge Johnson, with Mrs. Johnson, attended a black tie ball at some point in Montgomery. The Judge later described it, on the record, as the "biggest bunch of bullshit I have ever seen" (100).

27. See Bass, *Taming the Storm*, 27-29, 129-30. The social ostracism visted upon the Johnson family even extended to Sunday services at the local Baptist church. After the Freedom Riders came to Mongomery, the Johnson family was literally physically excluded from the First Baptist Church, "a large limstone structure on Perry Street that suggests a mosque" (27). Jack Bass writes that one Sunday morning, in 1961, "the deacons and other men stood outside joining hands to make sure no unwelcome visitors would come into the church" (ibid.). Johnny, the Judge's young son, was uspet at being excluded from the church in such dramatic fashion; he asked his mother why they were not welcome, observing that "I though God loved everbody" and asking "How come?" (27). Mrs. Johnson, reflecting on this incident, said that she could not provide Johnny with a satisfactory answer: "I didn't have any 'how come' answer" (ibid.). After this incident, the Johnsons stopped attending services at the church because, as Judge Johnson explained later, "during all this time that my family and I were going through this, I looked around and I did not find one supporter in that church. Not one person supported my positions" (28). Mrs. Johnson and Johnny joined the local Unitarian Church and began attending services there (without any problems or incidents).

28. Ibid., 129. As Judge Johnson put it, "it's a matter of values," and for the Judge "social matters have never been important to me" (ibid.).

29. Ian McDowell, "Incident at Looney's Tavern," Encyclopedia of Alabama, February 6, 2017, http://www.encyclopediaofalabama.org/article/h-3864 (last visited April 25, 2020) (discussing and describing "the official Alabama musical drama," as designated by the state legislature in 1993, and providing an overview of the plot, which focuses on a local school teacher's participation in the Winston County secession convention of 1861); Ala. Code § 1-2-33 (declaring *The Incident and Looney's Tavern* to be "Alabama's Official Outdoor Musical Drama"). It probably bears noting that a footnote of this sort would have annoyed, rather than charmed, Judge Johnson. The Judge would have viewed the inclusion of this additional information as, at best, constituting

206 | RONALD J. KROTOSZYNSKI, JR.

unnecessary clutter that did not materially advance or improve the quality of the main text. As a law professor, however, I live for the inclusion of esoteric footnotes. I would probably be a better, clearer writer if I followed Judge Johnson's example more often than I do when engaged in writing scholarly work. On the other hand, because scholarly work by definition involves a different audience, a nongeneralist audience, I am confident that Judge Johnson would have been more tolerant of esoteric footnotes in an academic book or law review article than in published decisions issuing from his chambers. I also suspect he was well aware of *The Incident at Looney's Tavern*'s designation as the official outdoor musical drama of the state of Alabama. There was little about Winston County that Judge Johnson did not know.

30. Robert Francis Kennedy, *Judge Frank M. Johnson, Jr.: A Biography* (New York: Putnam, 1978), 66–67 (observing that Frank Johnson's prospects for the federal judicial appointment in Montgomery "appeared dim" given strong local opposition and also because "according to custom, the judge for the Middle District seat was, and had always been, a resident of the district"); Steven Brill, "The Real Governor of Alabama," 38 ("Because he was a Republican from the northern hill country, his appointment was greeted with some suspicion and resentment by Montgomery's political insiders"). Moreover, whatever the initial attitude of the locals in Montgomery to Judge Johnson's appointment, "within a year the Johnsons were social outcasts" (39).

31. Judge Elbert P. Tuttle, "Remarks at the Dedication Ceremony, Frank M. Johnson, Jr. Federal Building and United States Courthouse," May 22, 1992, in 989 F.2d, *LXXXIX, CI-CII* (noting that after Dwight Eisenhower's election as president in 1952, "there were a good many federal positions to be filled in the State of Alabama" but that "these, of course, could be filled without the approval of the popularly elected senators from the state").

32. 142 F. Supp. 707 (M.D. Ala.), *aff'd per curiam*, 352 U.S. 903 (1956).

33. 192 F. Supp. 677 (M.D. Ala. 1961), *aff'd*, 304 F.2d 583 (5th Cir.), *aff'd*, 371 U.S. 37 (1962).

34. 208 F. Supp. 431 (M.D. Ala. 1962), *aff'd sub nom.*, *Reynolds v. Sims*, 377 U.S. 533 (1964).

35. *Williams v. Wallace*, 240 F. Supp. 100 (M.D. Ala. 1965).

36. Although Mrs. Johnson always insisted that the persistent attacks on Judge Johnson and their family did not much affect her or the Judge, their son, Johnny, told Steven Brill in an on-the-record interview that "he had been a target for constant harassment from his schoolmates" (Brill, "Real Governor of Alabama," 39). Johnny also reported that the Johnson family experienced many incidents of harassment and intimidation that they did not report "'because we did not want to give other people ideas.'" Johnny, while a law student at the University of Alabama, committed suicide on October 12, 1975. Although many factors contributed to this tragic outcome, Wallace's continual drumbeat of attacks on Judge Johnson and his family certainly could not have made life any easier for Johnny. I suspect this is why Judge Johnson rebuffed Wallace's many attempts to apologize and seek forgiveness—some of which took place during my

clerkship year. While clerking, I asked the Judge if he would ever forgive Wallace for the many years of vicious attacks on him, his court, and even his family. The Judge responded, "If Wallace wants forgiveness, then he should talk to God, not me."

37. Crowther, *Cathedrals of Kudzu*, 98.

38. See *Pugh v. Locke*, 406 F. Supp. 318 (M.D. Ala. 1976), *consolidated and aff'd in part sub nom., Newman v. Alabama* (5th Cir. 1977), *cert. denied*, 438 U.S. 915 (1978).

39. *Wyatt v. Stickney*, 325 F. Supp. 781 (M.D. Ala.), 334 F. Supp. 1341 (M.D. Ala. 1971), 344 F. Supp. 373 (M.D. Ala.), & 344 F. Supp. 387 (M.D. Ala. 1972), *aff'd in part, rev'd in part, sub nom., Wyatt v. Aderholt*, 503 F.2d 1305 (5th Cir. 1974).

40. Bass, *Taming the Storm*, 338–41; Yarbrough, *Judge Frank Johnson*, 200–202.

41. M. Roland Nachman Jr., "Remarks at the Dedication Ceremony, Frank M. Johnson, Jr. Federal Building and United States Courthouse," May 22, 1992, in *989 F.2d.*, LXXXIX, CVI-CVII (discussing Judge Johnson's judicial work during very difficult times and observing that "Judge Johnson's every judicial endeavor has embodied the concept and practice of elemental fairness, which is, after all the essence of due process of law").

42. Judge Frank M. Johnson Jr., "Remarks at the Dedication Ceremony, Frank M. Johnson, Jr. Federal Building and United States Courthouse," May 22, 1992, in 989 F.2d, LXXXIX, CX.

43. Ibid., CX–CXI.

44. For the record, the law clerks always referred to Mrs. Perry as "Mrs. Perry"— never as "Dot." Diane Stone was the Judge's other assistant during my clerkship. Mrs. Stone was a less formal person, and after I persisted for several weeks in calling her "Mrs. Stone," she admonished me: "It's 'Diane.' I want you to call me 'Diane.' When you call me 'Mrs. Stone' it makes me feel about a million years old—so don't do it, pretty please." I deferred to Diane's wishes and used her given name from that point forward. Thus: Mrs. Perry and Diane.

45. Bass, *Taming the Storm*, 38 (quoting Judge Johnson as reporting that "when I went through law school, I typed eighty words a minute on an old Underwood").

46. Ibid., 175.

47. The *Birmingham News* once described Judge Johnson's patented stare as the Judge "looking at you like he is aiming down a rifle barrel." Bass, *Taming the Storm*, 356–57. Other commentators have remarked on Judge Johnson's uncanny ability to use "the stare" to bring unruly lawyers to book: Gary May, *Bending toward Justice: The Voting Rights Act and the Transformation of American Democracy* (New York: Basic Books, 2013), 27 (describing Johnson as "a judge whose withering stare was known to cause lawyers to faint in his courtroom"); Frank Sikora, *The Judge: The Life and Opinions of Alabama's Frank M. Johnson, Jr.*, rev. ed. (Montgomery, Ala.: NewSouth Books, 2007), 194 (noting the powerful effect that Judge Johnson's "stern gaze" could have on those in his courtroom). It bears noting that until the Fifth Circuit adopted a local rule requiring all federal judges to wear a judicial robe, the Judge often did not don a judicial robe (preferring a dark suit) or use a gavel when presiding over his court (Bass, *Taming the*

Storm, 94). Judge Johnson explained that "'if a judge needs a robe and a gavel, he hasn't established control'" (Kennedy, *Judge Frank M. Johnson, Jr.*, 128).

48. Judge Pamela Pepper, e-mail message to author, July 5, 2017 (on file with author). All quotations attributed to other former law clerks to Judge Johnson, including this one, derive either from email communications with the author (on file with the author) or in-person conversations. If the source is an email, I cite it after the first quote or statement that requires a citation but do not add subsequent citations to these sources for each additional quotation.

49. Judge Pepper explains that "I wrote new lyrics to the tune of 'Rocky Top' in honor of the Judge, and we sang the song" (ibid.).

50. Former Johnson law clerk, e-mail message to author, July 5, 2017.

51. Former Johnson law clerk, e-mail message to author, July 3, 2017.

52. See, e.g., *Spencer v. Kemp*, 781 F.2d 1458, 1474 (11th Cir. 1986) (en banc) (Johnson, J., concurring in part and dissenting in part) ("In Part II of the majority opinion after many expressions and observations not involved in this case and therefore not necessary for determining the issue under consideration [see Section C. *Analysis*], this Court holds that petitioner Spencer is not procedurally barred from presenting his jury composition challenge to the federal district court. With respect to Part II, as Judge Warren Jones stated in concurring in an opinion written by Judge John R. Brown in *Wirtz v. Fowler*, 372 F. 2d 315 [1966]. 'I concur in the result and in so much of the opinion as supports the result.' *Id.* at 335 [Jones, J., concurring]"). I am indebted to former law clerk Rob Vogel (1985–1986) for calling this example to my attention.

53. Frank M. Johnson Jr., "Civilization, Integrity, and Justice: Some Observations on the Function of the Judiciary-in Honor of Judge Irving L. Goldberg," *Southwestern Law Journal* 43 (1989): 645, 652.

54. Ibid.; Stephen Breyer, *Active Liberty: Interpreting Our Democratic Constitution* (New York: Random House: 2005): 134 (arguing that the federal courts would enjoy greater public support and legitimacy if judges would "explain in terms the public can understand just what the Constitution is about").

55. Frank M. Johnson Jr., "The Role of the Judiciary with Respect to the Other Branches of Government," *Georgia Law Review* 11 (1976): 455; Johnson, "Observation: Constitution and the Federal District Judge," *Texas Law Review*; Johnson, "Civil Disobedience and the Law," *Tulane Law Review* 44 (1969); Johnson, "The Attorney and the Supremacy of Law," *Georgia Law Review* 1 (1966): 38.

56. Johnson, "Civil Disobedience and the Law," 5.

57. Johnson, "Role of the Federal Courts," 275. As the Judge put it, "It is the duty and unique responsibility of every fair-minded citizen to recognize and follow the proposition that respect for the law is the most fundamental of all social virtues, for the alternative to the rule of law is violence and anarchy" (ibid., 271).

58. Ibid., 273.

59. For the record, Judge Johnson cared far less about the specific point of copyright law, or his prior panel opinion resolving this point, than about the current panel's

failure to observe proper process for overturning a prior precedent of the circuit. Stability and predictability in the law require that future panels not simply ignore decisions of prior panels with which they happen to disagree—which is precisely what had occurred in this instance.

60. *Freeman v. Pitts*, 503 US 467 (1992). *Board of Ed. of Oklahoma City Public Schools v. Dowell*, 498 US 237 (1991).

61. Kennedy, *Judge Frank M. Johnson, Jr*, 127 (reporting that "a young Justice Department lawyer, who had caught wind of Judge Johnson's reputation for severity with those who entered his courtroom unprepared, fainted dead away with fear as he approached the judge. Johnson signaled the bailiff, and the man was carried out with no comment from the bench"); May, *Bending toward Justice*, 127 (recounting the alleged fainting incident).

62. Bass, *Taming the Storm*, 93; see also Kennedy, *Judge Frank M. Johnson, Jr.*, 125–31 (describing and discussing various anecdotes over time that demonstrate Johson's "demanding courtroom demeanor" and "uncompromising toughness and no-nonsense attittude about upholding the letter of the law").

63. Bass, *Taming the Storm*, 93.

64. Former Johnson law clerk, e-mail message to author, July 5, 2017.

65. Former Johnson law clerk, e-mail message to author, July 12, 2017.

66. Thomas Fuller, "'So-called' Judge Criticized by Trump Is Known as a Mainstream Republican," *New York Times*, February 5, 2017, A13 (describing Donald Trump's bizarre and troubling Twitter-based attack on U.S. District judge James Robart, who stayed Trump's travel ban against Muslims, and reporting on Trump's public denigration of Judge Robart "as a 'so-called judge'" and his description of Judge Robart's legal ruling "as 'ridiculous'"); Amy B. Wang, "Trump Lashes Out at 'So-called Judge' Who Temporarily Blocked Travel Ban," *Washington Post*, February 4, 2017, https://www .washingtonpost.com/news/the-fix/wp/2017/02/04/trump-lashes-out-at-federal -judge-who-temporarily-blocked-travel-ban/?utm_term=.e02ffd08ecc8 ("President Trump ripped into a federal judge's decision to temporarily block enforcement of his controversial travel ban, sending tweets throughout the day"). It bears noting that Judge Robart, whom Trump attacked repeatedly in a tweet storm, enjoys a sterling reputation as a smart, thoughtful, and even-handed jurist (Fuller, "'So-called' Judge," A13).

67. Heard, "Remarks at the Dedication Ceremony," CXIV; Brill, "Real Governor of Alabama," 38 (observing that "although [Judge Johnson] is only one of 399 federal district judges, his decisions read like a catalog of major advances in civil rights law of the last two decades").

68. Michael J. Gerhardt, "Johnson, Jr., Frank M." *Great American Judges: An Encyclopedia*, vol. 1, *A-K*, edited by John R. Vile (Santa Barbara, Calif.: ABC-CLIO, 2003), 415, 422.

69. Owen M. Fiss, *The Civil Rights Injunction* (Bloomington: Indiana University Press, 1978): 4.

70. Ibid., 90 ("It was not reasonable to expect the judges to be heroes, but the truth of the matter is that many lived up to these unreasonable expectations—they fought the popular pressures at great personal sacrifice and discomfort").

71. Frank M. Johnson Jr., "Reflections on the Judicial Career of Robert S. Vance," *Alabama Law Review* 42 (1991): 964, 966–70 (arguing that sound judgment requires three distinct virtues: reason, courage, and integrity—and explaining that that courageous judging requires "not physical bravery, but the moral courage to do what is right in the face of certain unpopularity and public criticism," and "integrity" demands "a passion for justice which propels judgment toward the just conclusion").

72. Johnson, "Role of the Judiciary," 468–69 ("Adjudication of constitutional issues requires an openness of mind and a willingness to decide issues solely on the particular facts and circumstances involved, not with any preconceived notion or philosophy regarding the outcome of the case").

BARRY SULLIVAN

John Minor Wisdom

Un Petit Hommage

"He is 'wise because his spirit was uncontaminated, because he knew no
violence, or hatred, or envy, or jealousy, or ill-will.'"
                    Henry J. Friendly, "From A Fellow Worker on the Railroad"

John Minor Wisdom was a judge of the United States Court of Appeals
for the Fifth Circuit, which is headquartered in New Orleans, for forty-
two years—from the time of his appointment by President Dwight D.
Eisenhower in 1957 until his death in 1999. That long period of judicial service
followed a long and distinguished career in the private practice of law in New
Orleans. In 1929, the Judge and Saul Stone, his close friend and Tulane Law
School classmate, had formed a partnership that would eventually become one
of the city's most respected law firms, and except for a period of military service
during World War II, the Judge practiced law with the firm continuously from
its founding until his appointment to the court.

In addition to practicing law, Judge Wisdom was a part-time professor at
Tulane Law School for many years. The Judge was also keenly interested in law
reform and was particularly proud of his early work in introducing the com-
mon law concept of trusts into the civil law of Louisiana.[1] During World War II,
Judge Wisdom served to the rank of Lieutenant Colonel in the United States
Army Air Force, working with a blue-ribbon group of lawyers, the so-called
Legal Branch, at the Pentagon.[2] After the war, the Judge was an early Louisiana supporter of General Eisenhower's 1952 presidential candidacy, and he was
principally responsible, together with his wife, the indomitable Bonnie Stewart
Mathews Wisdom, for organizing an Eisenhower slate of national convention
delegates that prevailed in a brutal credentials contest over an old-line slate
pledged to Senator Robert Taft.[3] Thereafter, the Judge and Bonnie set about

resuscitating a largely moribund Louisiana Republican Party. The Judge's appointment to the Fifth Circuit followed.

During much of the time that Judge Wisdom sat on the Fifth Circuit, the court was a particularly important one. To start with, the court's jurisdiction extended to all of the states of the Deep South—from Florida and Georgia in the east to Texas in the west—and it included the Panama Canal Zone as well. The court also was fortunate in having a core group of very able and influential judges, several of whom were appointed by President Eisenhower.[4] In addition, the court's workload was unusually robust, even in a time of burgeoning caseloads throughout the federal judicial system: the Fifth Circuit's workload was the heaviest of all the federal courts of appeals, with the average Fifth Circuit judge handling a caseload that was about 40 percent higher than the national average.[5]

The court's caseload was also diverse. The Fifth Circuit heard virtually every type of case that could be brought in federal court—from administrative law, admiralty, and antitrust to labor, oil and gas, securities, and tax. Most important, the court sat at the epicenter of the struggle for civil rights, and much of the court's work during that period involved enforcement of the antidiscrimination principle laid down by the Supreme Court's 1954 decision in *Brown v. Board of Education*[6] and subsequently reinforced by federal legislation in the 1960s and 1970s.[7] As former deputy attorney general and Yale Law School professor Burke Marshall has written:

> The Supreme Court's mandate to the inferior courts [in *Brown II*] was contained—obscurely, indirectly, and without any specific guidelines or instructions—in the final paragraph of the second Brown opinion, ordering a remand.... [E]ven though that paragraph could be taken, and might possibly have been intended to be taken, as referring only to the four cases before the Court, I have always interpreted it to reflect the Court's vision of the future. The final paragraph articulates the duty of the inferior courts to exercise their judicial discretion and to bring their experience to bear not just on segregated school systems, but also on other state-controlled institutions that perpetuated the monstrous subjugation of black people.[8]

As Professor Marshall has also pointed out, fidelity to the *Brown* mandate required Judge Wisdom and his Fifth Circuit colleagues (on both the court of appeals and the district courts) to shoulder judicial tasks that were "very special—indeed, burdensome without parallel."[9] Particularly in the early years, the judges of the Fifth Circuit faced intractable local opposition as they endeavored to enforce the antidiscrimination principle in cases involving public education, public accommodations, voting rights, and employment discrimination.[10] In many of those cases, it was Judge Wisdom who spoke for the court. He often found himself the writing judge—"the penman of the court," as one commentator has put it.[11] Those cases provided the occasion for some of the Fifth Circuit's most courageous decisions, and for some of Judge Wisdom's most significant and memorable opinions.

Judge Wisdom was born in New Orleans, had deep roots in the South, was educated almost entirely in the South, and lived virtually his whole life in the South. He was steadfast in his belief that the institutions of state-sanctioned racial subordination must give way, but he was also keenly aware of the stresses that the enforcement and extension of the antidiscrimination principle would place on the established traditions and mores of the region (to say nothing of the challenges that a new insistence on equality of opportunity would present for individual citizens as they went about their daily lives in vastly altered circumstances). For that reason, the Judge deliberately chose to frame his opinions in simple terms that could be understood and appreciated by all who would be affected by them.[12]

In *United States v. Louisiana*,[13] for example, he began his opinion by characterizing the "interpretation test"—which required would-be voters to "interpret" sometimes obscure constitutional provisions to the satisfaction of the registrar of voters and was used to prevent African Americans from voting—as "a wall . . . between registered voters and unregistered, eligible Negro voters."[14] That wall, he wrote, "is not the only wall of its kind, but since the Supreme Court's demolishment of the white primary, [it] has been the highest, best-guarded, most effective barrier to Negro voting in Louisiana."[15] He also explained that the interpretation test was not "a literacy test" and had "no rational relation to measuring the ability of an elector to read and write."[16] Thus, "We hold: this wall, built to bar Negroes from access to the franchise, must come down."[17]

The Judge's opinion in *United States v. Jefferson County*,[18] which he considered to be one of his most important, was equally elegant and straightforward. In that case, the Judge famously wrote "[The] only school desegregation plan that meets constitutional standards is one that works."[19] He also described in the plainest of terms the pattern of protracted and recalcitrant avoidance and evasion that characterized the southern school boards' response to *Brown*:

> School boards throughout this circuit first declined to take any affirmative action that might be considered a move toward integration. Later, they embraced the Pupil Placement Laws as likely to lead to no more than

a little token desegregation. Now they turn to freedom of choice plans supervised by the district courts. As the defendants construe and administer these plans, without the aid of HEW standards there is little prospect of the plans ever undoing past discrimination or of coming close to the goal of equal educational opportunities. Moreover, freedom of choice, as now administered, necessarily promotes resegregation. The only relief approaching adequacy is the conversion of the still-functioning dual system to a unitary, non-racial system—lock, stock, and barrel.[20]

The Judge added: "If this process be 'integration' according to the 1955 *Briggs* [*v. Elliott*[21]] court, so be it. In 1966 this remedy is the relief commanded by *Brown*, the Constitution, the Past, the Present, and the wavy foreimage of the Future."[22]

As eloquent and well reasoned as these opinions were, they also were the reason why Judge Wisdom was vilified in many quarters and subjected to great personal abuse: "His dogs were poisoned; rattlesnakes were thrown into his garden; he and his family were kept awake during much of the night by abusive telephone calls; and he received wholesale shipments of crude and hate-filled mail."[23] But these opinions were also the reason why, in the 1960s and 1970s, Judge Wisdom was one of the most well-known judges in America.

Like other federal appellate court judges of that era, Judge Wisdom frequently sat on three-judge district courts,[24] and some of his most famous opinions were written in that context.[25] He also served for many years as a member of the Judicial Panel on Multi-District Litigation[26] and on the Special Court for the Reorganization of the Northeastern Railroads. After the Judge took senior status in 1977, he continued to sit on the Fifth Circuit as often as the court's rules permitted, and he regularly sat as a visiting judge on other courts of appeals. Judge Wisdom was not averse to multitasking (although he would have deplored the word),[27] and his visits to the Seventh Circuit often coincided with the opening of the Lyric Opera season.

During his forty-two years on the bench, Judge Wisdom wrote well over 1,400 majority, concurring, and dissenting opinions.[28] Many of those opinions, in fields as diverse as admiralty and employment discrimination law, definitively resolved nettlesome legal questions for years to come.[29] Others, such as *Borel v. Fibreboard Paper Products Corporation*,[30] opened up whole new areas of litigation, promising the possibility of compensation for deadly but previously uncompensated harms. Many other opinions contained reasoning that was later adopted by the Supreme Court and established controlling law for the entire nation.[31] Others were included by scholars in casebooks or provided the framework for legislation or administrative rule-making.[32]

For many years, Judge Wisdom also played a major role in the work of the American Law Institute. Steeped in the Louisiana civil law tradition,[33] Judge Wisdom took a strong interest in the work of the institute, namely, the restatement and reform of the law, and he rarely missed a meeting of the council (its governing body), let alone its annual membership meeting. Among other things, the Judge served for eight years on the blue-ribbon ALI panel charged with studying the proper division of judicial work between the state and federal courts—a subject in which he had a deep professional and personal interest.[34] The work of that blue-ribbon panel was not unrelated, of course, to the practical problems he faced as a judge charged with the enforcement of federal law during a period of substantial friction between state and federal authorities, policies, and priorities.[35] Nor was it unrelated to the judicial politics involved in connection with a series of proposals to split the Fifth Circuit—a project that Judge Wisdom steadfastly opposed for almost twenty years. As the leading chroniclers of the ultimately successful efforts to split the Fifth Circuit have noted, Judge Wisdom's persistent opposition to the proposed circuit split was rooted in a deeply held conviction about the proper role of the federal courts of appeals in the federal system:

> For those who knew Wisdom, his reaction to the circuit division proposal was easy to predict. He would be strongly opposed and would most likely be relentless in his opposition regardless of the odds of success. Although he fully recognized the need for additional judges to cope with the court's caseload, he would consider splitting the circuit an unjustifiable price to pay. Wisdom, more than any other judge on the court, had a firm philosophical notion of what the courts of appeals should be. He believed that the circuit courts perform a critical role in the political system—a role he called the "federalizing function." . . . Wisdom strongly advocated that circuits be as large as practicably possible so that the courts of appeals reflect diverse interests and values. Splitting the Fifth Circuit, regardless of which geographical configuration was imposed, would create two relatively small circuits that might have a dangerous tendency toward parochialism.[36]

Judge Wisdom obviously relished the opportunity for immersion in the often challenging issues of law and policy presented by various ALI projects, and he enjoyed the debates concerning the draft restatements and other projects. But the Judge was an exceptionally gregarious person, and he also looked forward to the ALI's annual meeting as a chance to meet old friends and colleagues from around the country, including, in later years, many of his former law clerks. It was often because of the Judge's example, if not his prodding, that his former law clerks became members of the institute.[37] That was probably the case with other judges, who undoubtedly encouraged their law clerks to become members of the institute, and who also looked forward to seeing them at the annual meeting. But Judge Wisdom's was a special case. It was a mark of the special relationship that Judge Wisdom had with his clerks, and the knowledge that everyone had of that relationship, that must have caused Rod Perkins, the longtime president of the institute, to pause during the annual dinner, as he did almost every year, to acknowledge the presence of Judge Wisdom, "surrounded, as always, by his adoring law clerks."

I have always thought myself lucky to be counted amongst Judge Wisdom's "adoring law clerks," and I am certain that sentiment is shared by many others. For example, Scott Hastings, who was one of the Judge's last clerks, has written that his "year with Judge Wisdom was a life-changing experience."[38] Allen Black, an early clerk, has observed that he little realized, as he was driving to New Orleans to begin his clerkship, that "I was about to embark on an experience that would not only shape my professional career, but also in large part define who I am as a human being. The reason was the powerful intellect, the powerful personality, and the powerful humanity of John Minor Wisdom."[39] Robert Barnett expressed a similar sentiment when he wrote, simply, that Judge Wisdom was "all that a judge should be, and all that a human being can be."[40]

But what truly accounts for the "adoration" of Judge Wisdom's law clerks? It was certainly due in part to the strength of Judge Wisdom's intellect, the rigor of his thought, and his insistence on excellence, but more so, I think, to his human qualities—the steady soundness of his judgment; the pleasure he took from his work; the courage and good humor with which he met the hatred and contempt that came his way because of his judicial work; his seemingly unbounded curiosity about the world and everything in it; the depth and breadth of his knowledge, not only in diverse fields of law, but in many areas of intellectual and practical life; the penetrating powers of imagination that allowed him to see what really was at stake in a case and what the consequences of a decision might be, not simply for legal doctrine, but for the individuals and institutions that would be affected by the court's ruling; his warmth and empathy and sense of humor; his generosity and genuine interest in others; and his ability to relate to all manner of men and women, including those who could not have been more unlike him in every conceivable way, and to appreciate the meaning and significance of their situations.

Above all, perhaps, it was the sense of joy with which he did his work and lived his life. He gloried in his work and gave real meaning to Robert Frost's words in the poem "Two Tramps in Mud Time":

> Only where love and need are one,
> And the work is play for mortal stakes,
> Is the deed ever really done
> For Heaven and the future's sakes.[41]

Nothing was ever "old hat" to the Judge. He never seemed to think, as Justice Holmes did, that "there is no such thing as a hard case," or that seemingly novel questions of law were "always . . . the same old donkey . . . underneath."[42] Nor did he follow Justice Holmes in thinking that it was best for a judge to "know as little [about the facts and background of a case] as [he could] safely go on."[43] Judge Wisdom invariably wished to know as much as he possibly could about the facts and background of every case. And the joy with which he approached a legal puzzle never seemed to falter. Indeed, in the last year of his life, when he was burdened by physical frailty, he responded to my question about his health with the simple statement that he had just written "the best goddam dissent of [his] career."[44] That sense of joy pervaded his chambers, and he showed us by his example that one could be a great lawyer and judge without being crotchety or cynical or sour.

The Judge taught us much about life and work and, especially, about the meaning of a good and useful life. But, perhaps surprisingly, he also taught his clerks (particularly his male clerks) much about marriage and the relationship of men and women. In this regard, as in others, the Judge taught by example. And it was through his marriage of sixty-eight years to Bonnie Stewart Mathews Wisdom—an equal partner and every bit the Judge's match in courage, curiosity, intelligence, industry, and erudition—that he imparted these lessons to his clerks. Bonnie was formidable. She was a woman of genuine political acumen, and she had an extraordinary sense of humor. She could puncture pomposity with one well-chosen word—"le mot juste," as she would say. Bonnie was also a woman of dramatic personal style. The first time that my wife Winni and I were invited to the Wisdoms for drinks before dinner, Bonnie made a lasting impression by appearing in Chinese gold silk brocade pajamas.

Bonnie was an equal partner in the takeover and rebuilding of the Louisiana Republican Party, and she played a significant role in preventing the federal government from building Interstate 10 on a swath that it proposed to cut through the French Quarter.[45] She channeled her admiration for Shakespeare into strong support for the Folger Library, and her deep interests in history and literature led her to discover, "It was [Albion Winegar] Tourgee [the lawyer for Plessy] who supplied the dissenting justice in *Plessy* [v. *Ferguson*[46]], John Marshall Harlan, with the most powerful maxim in American law: 'Our Constitution is colorblind.'"[47] The phrase came most immediately from Tourgee's brief, but Tourgee had previously used the phrase in one of his novels, as Bonnie showed.[48]

Bonnie also had strong opinions and was not shy in expressing them. As Robert Barnett, one of the Judge's clerks, has written, the Judge's clerks got "to see how the Judge and Bonnie made marriage into a fine art. Their discussions, perhaps best described as 'intense,' ranged over everything, from politics to law to art to theatre to literature, with special emphasis on bridge. They were always each other's biggest fans."[49] Similarly, Ricki Helfer, another of the Judge's clerks, has observed, "Bonnie has enlivened every gathering with her piquant sense of humor and sharp social and cultural observations. The Judge has been heard to say, 'Sixty three years of wedded bliss and never a peaceful moment.' Bonnie has been heard to respond, 'Peace would be so boring.' Despite the warning from *Love's Labor Lost*, 'your wit's too hot, it speeds too fast, 'twill tire,' Bonnie's wit has not tired, nor dulled."[50]

Judge Wisdom was almost twenty years a judge when I had the good fortune to work for him during the 1974–1975 court term, so my perspective on the Judge is very much that of someone who clerked for him near the midpoint of his judicial career. It is also the perspective of someone who clerked for the Judge well after his judicial reputation had been established and his place in the judicial pantheon secured. That fact was made clear to me when, in a conversation with one of my high school teachers (who happened to be a graduate of Harvard Law School) about what I would be doing after law school graduation, he responded to my statement that I would be clerking for Judge Wisdom with the observation, "There's nothing like starting at the top."

I should also note that I was part of a cohort of students who studied law during the late 1960s and early 1970s, at least in part because they had been inspired by the civil rights movement and saw the practice of law as a means toward achieving a more just society. It was natural for those students to be interested in public law subjects, and that interest was reinforced in my time at the University of Chicago Law School by the presence of several exceptional public law scholars.[51] In some ways, the most influential of the group may have been Owen M. Fiss, who had worked in the Civil Rights Division of the Justice

Department during the 1960s. Professor Fiss taught first-year property (actually a course on the Fair Housing Act—which left us blissfully ignorant of such mysteries as the fee tail male) and a course on injunctions that focused on the civil rights injunction.[52] Professor Fiss's injunctions casebook showcased the work of the Fifth Circuit in general and the opinions of Judge Wisdom in particular—including the monumental opinions that emanated from James Meredith's protracted struggle to enroll at the University of Mississippi.[53] That story is, of course, well known.[54] But the opinions in the casebook provided insight, not only into the development of the law of injunctions and the contempt power, but also into the character of the Judge. In the end, Meredith succeeded in registering as a student, accompanied, as he was, by federal marshals charged with securing compliance with the court's orders.

Having entered a rule to show cause why Mississippi governor Ross Barnett should not be held in contempt of court for obstructing Meredith's matriculation,[55] a majority of the court relented, holding that Meredith's eventual matriculation had mooted the contempt proceeding. Judge Wisdom dissented.[56] Meredith may have secured admission to the university, Judge Wisdom acknowledged, but it was in spite of Governor Barnett's efforts, not because of them. He wrote: "[Governor Barnett] compounded his contempt by failing to appear before the Court, after having been summoned, and instructed his attorney to advise the Court that he had *not* purged himself of contempt. Meredith registered at the University of Mississippi October 1, 1962. To win this battle, the United States Army had more soldiers under arms at Oxford, Mississippi, or held close by in reserve, than George Washington in the Revolutionary War ever commanded at one time.[57] Judge Wisdom concluded his opinion with the observation, "There is an unedifying moral to be drawn from this case of *The Man in High Office Who Defied the Nation*: The mills of the law grind slowly—but not inexorably. If they grind slowly enough, they may even come, unaccountably, to a gradual stop, short of the trial and judgment an ordinary citizen expects when accused of criminal contempt. There is just one compensating thought: Hubris is grist for other mills, which grind exceeding small and sure."[58]

It was because of Professor Fiss's influence that many University of Chicago students became interested in Fifth Circuit clerkships. In my class, I believe that there were six of us who clerked for circuit judges on the Fifth Circuit, and at least two others clerked on the district courts. In fact, law clerks from other schools that year humorously referred to the Fifth Circuit's en banc sittings, when all the judges from across the circuit would converge on New Orleans with their clerks, as meetings of the University of Chicago Alumni Association.

By the end of my second year of law school, I had decided that I wanted to clerk for a federal judge, preferably in the Fifth Circuit, and, ideally, for Judge Wisdom. I knew that a clerkship with Judge Wisdom was a longshot, of course, because many law students aspired to clerk for the Judge, and much as he was admired at Chicago, he did not seem to be overly committed to Chicago, or to any particular school, as a source of clerks. Over the years, as I later learned, Judge Wisdom hired many clerks from Harvard and Tulane, with others coming from a variety of schools, including Chicago, Yale, Columbia, NYU, Southern California, Stanford, Loyola Los Angeles, Michigan, Minnesota, Texas, Virginia, and Washington and Lee.

While working for a Boston law firm that summer, I sent out many applications. My first positive response was an invitation to interview with Judge Bryan Simpson, a Fifth Circuit judge in Jacksonville, Florida. Judge Simpson had become well known for his courageous civil rights decisions as a district judge and was elevated to the court of appeals by President Lyndon B. Johnson.[59] With Judge Simpson's invitation in hand, I decided to call Judge Wisdom's chambers, thinking that I might be able to visit with him on my trip from Boston to the Fifth Circuit. One of Judge Wisdom's clerks told me that the Judge never interviewed clerkship applicants, but that he would check with the Judge if I wished. A short time later, the clerk called back with the good news that the Judge would indeed see me if I came to New Orleans. I arranged to meet Judge Simpson on Sunday and Judge Wisdom on Monday.

Judge Simpson, who was an unusually gracious person, arranged to meet me for breakfast at a diner near the courthouse. Toward the end of breakfast, Judge Simpson told me that he had decided to offer me a clerkship, and that he thought we would have a nicer day together if he did that then, rather than wait. We did have a very nice day together. Judge Simpson gave me a tour of the courthouse (which has since been named in his honor), showed me some of Jacksonville, and included me in his family's Sunday dinner.

At the end of the day, he drove me to the airport. Along the way, he asked where I was going next. When I told him that I was going on to New Orleans to interview with Judge Wisdom, he became quite serious. He told me that he thought that Judge Wisdom would offer me a clerkship, but that Judge Wisdom often had trouble making up his mind about hiring clerks, being predisposed to think that someone better might come along if he waited long enough. So Judge Simpson proposed that I tell Judge Wisdom that I had an offer from him, but that it would expire in a week's time. That, he thought, would help Judge Wisdom make up his mind. Judge Simpson ended by telling me that I should not feel that I had any obligation to him. I would never have another opportunity to work for someone like Judge Wisdom, Judge Simpson told me, and if I decided to clerk for him rather than for Judge Wisdom, he'd think I was a damned fool.

So off to New Orleans I went. By 1973, the Fifth Circuit had moved back to the newly renovated Court of Appeals Building (now the John Minor Wisdom Court of Appeals Building) on Camp Street from its long-time, temporary headquarters in the Louisiana Wildlife and Fisheries Building (the present home of the Louisiana Supreme Court) on Royal Street in the French Quarter. The building renovation was very well done, undoubtedly in large part because of Judge Wisdom's interest in the project, and the Judge's chambers, which clearly reflected his personal taste, were striking.

The Judge's private office was a large, high-ceilinged room in a corner of the second floor. The focal point of the room was a large brass chandelier hanging over a massive antique desk, with a high-backed wooden desk chair covered in red leather behind the desk, and a large Audubon print of a pelican (the Louisiana state bird) on the wall behind that. Next to the Judge's desk, which was piled high with books and papers, were several book carts holding the reference materials relevant to the cases on which he was working. The walls were wood-paneled but hardly noticeable because of the well-stocked, glass-fronted bookcases that covered most of the wall space. The drapes were cream-colored with a crewel pattern and covered the floor-to-ceiling windows.

There were several antique library tables stacked with papers and law books, and a number of wooden chairs with red leather seats and the letters "US" carved in their backs. As I learned later, the Judge had rescued most of the furniture in chambers from the cellar of the Customs House. One artifact that I did not notice that day, but would pass by virtually every day of my clerkship, was a small, framed certificate that was on the wall just inside his office. It was a certificate for "excellence in the study of political economy" given by Washington College in Virginia to Mortimer Wisdom, the Judge's father, and signed by the college president, Robert E. Lee.

As one might have expected, my interview with Judge Wisdom was wide-ranging. We talked about law, of course. In particular, the Judge wanted to talk about my writing sample—a course paper I had prepared for Professor Stanley N. Katz on exhaustion of remedies in civil rights cases, which the Judge encouraged me to publish.[60] We also talked about an undergraduate honors paper I had written on Jean-Jacques Rousseau's *First Discourse*. That led to a discussion of Rousseau the painter and then to a conversation about French novels and plays. Allen Black has noted that the Judge was proud of his French language skills,[61] and my recollection is that part of our interview was in French. In any event, the Judge was particularly interested in the fact that I had grown up in a small New England town where many people spoke French, and that I was taught half the day in French from kindergarten through the eighth grade. And he wanted to know more about what it had been like to grow up there, what kind of a town it was, and what was its history.

Eventually, the conversation turned back to the subject of the clerkship. Judge Wisdom said that he had enjoyed our conversation, but (as Judge Simpson had predicted) he also said that it was early in the season, and he would not be able to give me a final answer for a while. Summoning my courage, I mentioned that Judge Simpson had offered me a clerkship and had given me a week to think about it. Judge Wisdom replied that this was a wonderful opportunity: Judge Simpson was a fine man and a courageous judge, and clerking for him would be a wonderful experience. I said that I understood that, and that I greatly admired Judge Simpson, but that I would really like to clerk for him. Judge Wisdom continued his praise of Judge Simpson, suggesting that clerking for Judge Simpson would be pretty much the same as clerking for him and that I could expect to learn a great deal from Judge Simpson. I demurred. I agreed with all that Judge Wisdom said about Judge Simpson, while I still insisted that I would like to clerk for him. But it became clear that Judge Wisdom would not hear any argument that might be interpreted as expressing a preference for him over another judge. Finally, Judge Wisdom said, "What is it? Is it just that you'd rather be in New Orleans?" I saw that this was a distinction the Judge could accept and would be willing to take as an answer. So I agreed. That led to another question: "If I were to offer you a clerkship, which you understand I'm not doing, would you be inclined to accept?" At that point we had a deal.

The Judge's chambers provided a pleasant and comfortable workplace. As I have previously noted, however, the workload was heavy, and "Judge & Company," as the Judge would have put it, all worked very hard. The Judge was a serious man, and the most important thing to him, when it came to his work, was getting it right and explaining why it was right in an elegant but straightforward and convincing way. Following his undergraduate years at Washington and Lee University, Judge Wisdom had spent a year studying English literature at Harvard, and he maintained a lifelong interest in literature. One way to become a good writer, the Judge thought, was to read good writing. He enjoyed good writing all his life and urged us to do the same.

On one occasion toward the end of his life, when he and Bonnie were staying with us, the Judge happened to pick up an old copy of *A Red Badge of Courage*, which he proceeded to read in quiet moments during his visit. The Judge finished it on the way back to New Orleans, and it was returned with another book that the Judge and Bonnie thought we should read. In any event, as Stanford Goldblatt, one of the Judge's early clerks, has written, "The Judge had very clear and very firm ideas as to what constituted clear and convincing written prose. He also had a very strong sense of his own personal 'voice.'"[62] Allen Black has likewise noted that "the Judge was just as precise and careful with words as he was with grammar and punctuation. Only the right word would do."[63]

In some ways, the Judge was a very formal person. For example, he always addressed (and referred to) Dottie Dewenter, his longtime secretary, as "Mrs. Dewenter." He could also appear quite stern in court, but his sternness was only sternness; it was never rude or disrespectful, but merely a manifestation of the seriousness with which he took his work and what he believed it meant to the litigants who came before him. While the Judge clearly appreciated that some cases were more momentous than others, that seriousness extended to all of his cases, and not just to those that he deemed to be the most important. Judge Wisdom's attitude toward the court's summary disposition calendar illustrates the point.

Because of the magnitude of the Fifth Circuit's caseload, the court was required to decide many cases without oral argument or a full opinion. When the staff law clerks saw a case that seemed to present no novel or important question of law and was not therefore worthy of oral argument or a published opinion, they would recommend summary disposition to a panel of three "screening" judges, who would then review the papers in "round-robin" fashion. If one judge disagreed, the case would be restored to the oral argument calendar. The first judge to review the case would typically decide whether oral argument or a published opinion was necessary. With some judges, deciding that a case was not worthy of oral argument or a published opinion meant that it could be decided by entry of an order that simply said: "Affirmed. See Rule 18. See Rule 21," referencing the Circuit Rules that permitted the decision of cases without oral argument, in the one case, and without written opinion, in the other. In other words, no real reasons would be given.

While Judge Wisdom believed that the summary calendar was essential, if the court was to get its work done, he also recognized that judges might be tempted to use it as a way of avoiding a nettlesome problem or an opinion that might be difficult to write. In addition, the Judge thought that even the most insignificant (or seemingly straightforward) case was important to someone, and they deserved to know why they lost. Even in cases lacking genuine precedential value, the Judge thought that the better practice was to write a few sentences pointing out why the result was foreordained and undeserving of extended analysis. If the case came from other chambers with an order that simply referenced the two relevant rules, it would always receive close scrutiny and might well end up being restored to the oral argument calendar. When Judge Wisdom was the originating judge, and it was concluded that the case did not merit oral argument or a published opinion, the clerk working on the case would be expected to draft, for the Judge's review and approval, an order consisting of a few sentences to explain the result.[64]

Contrary to the practice of some courts of appeals, the same hearing panel heard arguments every day for a week in the Fifth Circuit. As I recall, the panel heard arguments in the morning and immediately conferenced on the cases they had heard. Stanford Goldblatt has noted that the Judge did not ask him to write bench memoranda in preparation for oral argument, as many judges do, but generally prepared for argument on his own.[65] The same was true when I clerked for the Judge a decade later. Occasionally, the Judge would ask one of the clerks to research a point for him, but the Judge generally prepared for argument by himself, often taking home two heavy trial bags filled with the evening's work. When the Judge was not preparing for oral argument, the same trial bags went home every night with briefs, records, and draft opinions.

During the day, the Judge would occasionally emerge from his private office, take a reporter or two from the shelves in the library, and return to his office, flipping through the pages as he walked. The Judge's practice of doing most of his argument preparation by himself freed up the clerks to spend their time on researching and writing draft opinions, but I think the practice may have appealed to the Judge for other reasons as well. By slogging through the briefs and records, the Judge was able to achieve a deep level of familiarity with each of the cases the court would hear.

During the time that I clerked for the Judge, he was usually the presiding member of a panel and would therefore be responsible for assigning the opinion if he was in the majority. A thorough understanding of the cases was obviously very useful in that regard. In addition, the Judge relied a great deal on his clerks to prepare first drafts of opinions. By having an intimate understanding of each of the cases he had drawn, the Judge was able to provide very specific guidance to his clerks as to how he wanted an opinion to be approached and structured. Moreover, as a clerk began to read the record and research the relevant points, the clerk would undoubtedly want to discuss the case in some depth with the Judge. Those discussions, which occurred before or during the preparation of a first draft, obviously would be more meaningful and efficient if the Judge already had a firm grasp of the case and the issues it presented. That was certainly true in my case. Indeed, although I might have physically prepared the first draft of an opinion, I often felt that I was merely the Judge's amanuensis, given the number of detailed discussions that the Judge and I would have had with respect to an opinion on which I was working, including even the subtlest points in the case.

Allen Black and Stanford Goldblatt have both written about the Judge's practice of keeping the most important cases for himself. Allen Black has written:

> The Judge wrote one of his most important opinions, *United States v. Jefferson County Board of Education*, during the year of my clerkship. In most cases the Judge would ask his clerks to research and prepare an initial draft of the opinion, but in *Jefferson*, as in most of his important civil rights cases, the Judge did the research and wrote the first draft himself. As other writers have properly pointed out, *Jefferson* was a masterpiece of creative legal craftsmanship. In it, the Judge devised a means for the southern federal courts efficiently and effectively to carry out their Constitutional mandate to eliminate racial discrimination from hundreds if not thousands of school districts in six states. . . . The Judge realized that the District Courts needed help, and in *Jefferson* he gave it to them.[66]

Similarly, Stanford Goldblatt has noted, "The celebrated case of *U.S. v. Louisiana*, surely the most important and noteworthy accomplishment during my tenure, was one with which I had virtually nothing to do."[67] Thus, as Goldblatt explains:

> From the time of my arrival until mid-November, the Judge disappeared into his office for most of the day leaving me to work on a series of other opinions by myself. By the time he emerged from his self-imposed exile, I was several opinions ahead of him.
>
> During this time, the Judge created what was, perhaps, his magnum opus. Occasionally, he would ask me to check a reference or look up some obscure point but, until after he was finished, he did not include me in the development of his thinking nor did he ask for anyone's help in his drafting. If you pull up 225 F. Supp. 353, you can read a forty-three page opinion in which every word was written by the Judge.[68]

Part of the clerk's job was to drive the Judge back and forth to work. This was a private time that the clerk had with the Judge and was the occasion for nonwork-related as well as work-related discussions. The clerks took turns.

Often the Judge had some errands to do, particularly when the court was not hearing arguments, and one morning I recall being asked to drive him to the home of Bonnie's nanny, an elderly woman who had passed away during the night, so that he could pay his respects to her family. I will never forget the reaction of the woman's family as they opened the door to greet Judge Wisdom, who was walking with the help of two canes at the time and had climbed some steep stairs to reach their front porch. Faces deeply marked by grief suddenly brightened as they saw who it was that had rung their doorbell.

On the way back from work, the Judge would always ask us to stop so he could buy a newspaper from a man who sold them from a shopping cart on Magazine Street. A motorist had hit the man while he was selling his papers, and the Judge frequently asked him about his lawsuit, always telling him that he had to keep after the lawyer who was handling it. The Judge would always buy two copies of the evening paper—one for himself, the other for the clerk. Sometimes he would also ask us to drive him during the day if he had some place that he needed to go. I remember once being asked to drive him to Antoine's French Restaurant, where he was meeting Justice Thurgood Marshall for lunch. As we were proceeding down a narrow street in the French Quarter, the Judge suddenly told me to stop the car in the middle of the street. I could not imagine what was wrong. It turned out that the Judge had seen a court reporter whose transcript was long overdue. The Judge rolled down the window, greeted the court reporter warmly, said something about the possibility of holding him in contempt of court, and told me to drive on. Once we were underway, the Judge told me that the problem was perennial—the court reporter was too busy to transcribe all the notes he took and too cheap to hire someone to help him.

I have noted that the Judge worked very hard and expected us to do the same. He obviously loved his work and hoped that we would as well. I have also noted that the Judge could be quite formal and exhibited a stern demeanor in the courtroom. But he was often quite playful in chambers. On one occasion that I recall, the Judge and I were in his office discussing a case when my co-clerk, Robert Walmsley, a native New Orleanian who had known the Judge from childhood, breezed into the Judge's office and asked whether one of us had "a buck." The Judge immediately took out his wallet and gave Robert a dollar. As Robert was leaving the room, however, the Judge suddenly asked him why he needed the dollar. When Robert replied that he needed to "buy some smokes," the Judge immediately got up from his chair and went over to Robert, pretending to beat him about the head and take back the dollar, all the while telling him that he did not want to support such a filthy, wicked habit. Robert and I were soon bent over in hysterics.

The Judge also demonstrated his playfulness in response to the General Services Administration's mandate that the air conditioning in chambers be turned off outside "normal business hours" whenever the Judge was not in the building—despite the fact that the windows did not open, and the clerks would still be working. That policy did not meet with the Judge's approval, since he clearly expected that his clerks would continue working when he went off to his Saturday afternoon bridge game at the Louisiana Club, as he often did. He complained to the General Services Administration without effect. Somehow, the Judge figured out that there was one side door to the courthouse that was not monitored by a security camera. With this discovery in hand, he formulated a plan. On Saturday afternoons, he would exit through the side door, while one of the clerks would go to the garage in the basement of the courthouse, get the car, pick up the Judge at the designated door, and drive him to the Louisiana Club. The plan worked perfectly until one of the marshals became suspicious that the Judge seemed to have given up his Saturday afternoon bridge game and came up to chambers to find out why.

The Judge's sense of humor did not diminish over the years. Many years later, after the courthouse had been renamed in the Judge's honor, I asked him what it was like to work in a courthouse that was now named after him. He responded with a twinkle in his eye, and in his best New Orleans accent: "Well, woik is woik. It doesn't matter where you do it." After a suitable pause, he continued: "But it does give me some pleasure when I get into a cab in the morning and say to the driver, 'Take me to *my* courthouse.'" When the Judge chose someone as his clerk, it was the beginning of a lifelong commitment. The Judge and Bonnie were always keen to hear news of the Judge's clerks, their spouses or partners, and their children. They were also anxious to meet our friends, who soon became their friends as well. They were always there to give advice when asked, and Bonnie (it is reliably reported) even guided one clerk through her courtship. The Judge performed marriage ceremonies for several of the clerks, and he proudly administered the oath of office when one of his clerks was appointed to an important post in the executive branch, the agencies, or the judiciary. He also took great pleasure in his clerks' many successes in the practice of law and in law teaching and scholarship.[69]

Every couple of years the clerks would find an excuse (the anniversary of the Judge's appointment to the bench or a significant birthday) for converging on New Orleans. We would have dinner at Antoine's on Saturday evening, with lively entertainment planned by the ever-resourceful (and devilishly funny) John Buckley. Tennessee senator Lamar Alexander often played the piano, while Judge Nora Manella and FDIC chair Ricki Tigert Helfer led the singing. Sunday brunch—always grillades and grits and the freshest possible Bloody Marys—took place at the New Orleans Women's Opera Guild.

As the years passed, many of the clerks achieved great distinction in their own careers as lawyers, judges, professors, and public servants, but the focus of these reunions was always on the Judge and Bonnie. As my wife Winni once pointed out, one never sensed the kind of edge or competition that one often feels when lawyers get together. No one seemed interested in showing how smart they were or how successful they had become. We just felt lucky to know the Judge and Bonnie and to be able to have a weekend with them.

Whenever the Judge came to Chicago to sit on the Seventh Circuit, as he often did after he took senior status, he would make a point of visiting with Winni and me. He also made a point of seeing Stan Goldblatt and his wife, Ann Dudley. He did the same with other clerks in other cities. The Washington clerks were particularly blessed in that respect, since judicial business and other professional responsibilities often took him there. Winni and I also saw the Judge and Bonnie often in New Orleans and once brought our two sons to stay with them for several days. More often, we stayed with my co-clerk Robert Walmsley and his wife, Ann, and met the Judge and Bonnie for drinks and dinner.

On one occasion, when I was in New Orleans working on a case, Robert and Ann and I took the Judge and Bonnie to dinner at Commander's Palace, which was one of their favorite restaurants. There was a small problem with the creamed spinach. It seemed that a particular kind of creamed spinach was available only on Sundays—except for Judge Wisdom. It was available for the Judge whenever he wanted it. On this occasion, Judge Wisdom ordered the "special creamed spinach," as usual, but received the ordinary variety. When the waiter cleared the plates and saw that Judge Wisdom had not eaten the creamed spinach, he asked why, whereupon the Judge explained that it was not what he had ordered. When Robert passed through the kitchen on the way to the men's room (the customary route at Commander's Palace) a few minutes later, he heard the waiter berating the chef for having made him "look like a fool in front of Judge Wisdom."

On another occasion, when the Judge was visiting Chicago, Stan Goldblatt and Ann Dudley took the Judge, Winni, and me to dinner. We sat talking quite a long time in the restaurant, and the Judge ordered several whiskeys. For some reason, the waiter did not take away the empty glasses. Finally, the Judge, noticing this, very gently said to the waiter, "Would you please take away the dead soldiers. I wouldn't want to set a bad example for my young friends."

The Judge received many honors during his life, including the Presidential Medal of Freedom and many honorary degrees, but the storeroom in chambers still contained many boxes filled with hate mail he had received earlier in his tenure, and he remained a controversial figure in certain quarters. At the time of his death, he was undoubtedly one of the best-known graduates of Washington and Lee, where I served as dean of the Law School for five years. Word of the Judge's death reached me on the morning of my final Washington and Lee Law School commencement. Ironically, the Judge had visited with us for the opening convocation at the beginning of that academic year, when it had been my duty to inform him, over breakfast, of the passing of his friend, and fellow Washington and Lee alumnus and trustee, Justice Lewis F. Powell Jr. In addition to commencement, the Law School was celebrating the conclusion of an academic year that marked both the 150th anniversary of the founding of the Law School and the 250th anniversary of the founding of the University. Chief Justice William H. Rehnquist had agreed to deliver the commencement address, and I had arranged for the invocation to be delivered by the Very Reverend Standrod Tucker Carmichael, a close family friend, Washington and Lee alumnus, and descendant of John Randolph Tucker, the legendary first dean of the Law School.[70] The ceremony would be televised by C-Span.

While the platform party was robing in Washington Hall, I mentioned to the president of the university that Judge Wisdom had passed away. The president replied that a trustee had also died during the night, and that he planned to note the trustee's passing at the beginning of the commencement ceremony, but that he did not want Judge Wisdom's death to be mentioned. The president gave no explanation for that, and I had no opportunity to pursue the subject further, as we soon fell into line to begin our ceremonial march from Washington Hall to the speakers' platform on the lawn in front of Lee House. I retired from the deanship shortly thereafter and never did learn why the president did not wish to have the news of Judge Wisdom's death acknowledged at the ceremony. I do know that the president was anxious at that time to regain the support of some potentially generous donors who had apparently become disaffected because of what they considered to be excessively progressive university initiatives concerning such matters as diversity and coeducation. Based on that, and on prior conversations, I guessed that the president thought that the university's connections with Judge Wisdom were something of a mixed blessing and ought not be given too much prominence.

Some days later, I attended a memorial service for the Judge in the Great Hall of the John Minor Wisdom Court of Appeals Building in New Orleans. Many of the Judge's other clerks were there as well. As the *New York Times* reported, "With a jazz band playing 'When the Saints Go Marching In,' hundreds of dignitaries and friends filed into a formal but joyous ceremony to pay their last respects to Judge John Minor Wisdom, a pioneer of civil rights in the Deep South."[71] Fourteen members of the Court of Appeals attended in their judicial robes. Chief Judge Carolyn Dineen King read letters from Chief Justice Rehnquist, from Justice Ruth Bader Ginsburg, and from Justice Stephen G. Breyer. As the *Times* also reported, Robert Barnett, a lawyer for President William Jefferson Clinton and one of the Judge's former clerks, read a letter from the president, who had awarded the Presidential Medal of Freedom to Judge Wisdom in 1993. "John Wisdom left his mark not only on our legal system," the letter said, "but on the generations of lawyers who served as his clerks and for whom he was a role model and mentor. He lived greatly in the law, showing the way to others through his extraordinary legal ability, his integrity and his courage."[72]

Among the others who spoke was Norman C. Francis, the longtime president of Xavier University, the historically Black Catholic university in New Orleans. The *New York Times* reported his remarks as well: "'John Minor was a major force in saving the South,' said Norman C. Francis, president of Xavier University. 'We were a divided house. . . . Yes, Americans, we owe to John Wisdom our deepest love and admiration.'"[73] Other newspapers also published stories about the memorial service, and the *New Orleans Times-Picayune* ran a picture of Bonnie Wisdom, seated at the front of the Great Hall, stylishly dressed in a black dress and a tall black hat with a veil, with the assembled judges and a large picture of Judge Wisdom in the background, clapping in time with the jazz band as the members marched past her. It was, as the *New York Times* said, a "joyous" occasion.

Fred Graham, who covered the Supreme Court for the *New York Times* and CBS News, once interviewed Judge Wisdom for a living history project. After discussing at length Judge Wisdom's courageous and steel-willed work during the time of the civil rights movement, Graham turned to a different aspect of the Judge's character, asking: "Is there a personal conflict between being a judge who is expected to be a very sober sided fellow and a person who is by inclination kind of a bon vivant?" The Judge responded very seriously, "Well I am not really a bon vivant because a bon vivant I think of as a connoisseur of wines." After a short pause, and with a twinkle in his eye, the Judge continued: "I *am* a connoisseur of Scotch whiskey."[74]

Notes

1. See John Minor Wisdom, "Progress in the Codification of Trusts," *Tulane Law Review* 14 (1940): 165; John Minor Wisdom, "A Trust Code in the Civil Law Based on the Restatement and Uniform Acts: The Louisiana Trust Estates Act," *Tulane Law Review* 13 (1938): 70. Judge Wisdom's early academic writing demonstrated the same sure sense of prose style that would later characterize his judicial opinions. See Wisdom, "Trust Code," 70 ("To the tightly logical civilian mind, regardless of the number of angels that may dance on the point of a needle, two persons cannot occupy the same point at the same time, and there cannot be two owners, legal and equitable, of the same property").

2. See Joel William Friedman, *Champion of Civil Rights: Judge John Minor Wisdom* (Baton Rouge: Louisiana State University Press, 2009): 25–29. Judge Wisdom's colleagues in the Legal Branch included two lawyers who would go on to become justices of the Massachusetts Supreme Judicial Court, as well as "a Judge of the U.S. Court of Claims, a Governor of Indiana, an Under Secretary of the Treasury, an Assistant Secretary of State, a member of the National Labor Relations Board, the dean of a law school, several law professors, a general counsel of the Internal Revenue Service, [and] an Insurance Commissioner of the State of New York" (27, quoting William L. Marbury, *In the Catbird Seat* [Baltimore: Maryland Historical Society, 1988], 155).

3. See Perry H. Howard, *Political Tendencies in Louisiana*, rev. ed. (Baton Rouge: Louisiana State University Press, 1971): 329–30; Allan P. Sindler, *Huey Long's Louisiana: State Politics, 1920–1952* (Baltimore: Johns Hopkins Press, 1956), 244–45. Judge Wisdom's role in the 1952 Republican Convention has been widely chronicled. See, e.g., Herbert Brownell and John P. Burke, *Advising Ike: The Memoirs of Attorney General Herbert Brownell* (Lawrence: University Press of Kansas, 1993), 111; Friedman, *Champion of Civil Rights*, 43–88; Anne Emanuel, *Elbert Parr Tuttle: Chief Jurist of the Civil Rights Revolution* (Athens: University of Georgia Press, 2011), 94–99; Joel Jacobsen, "Remembered Justice: The Background, Early Career and Judicial Appointments of Justice Potter Stewart," *Akron Law Review* 35 (2002): 227, 241 (discussing "brutal credential fight" involving Texas and Louisiana delegations).

4. See, e.g., Herbert Brownell, "Civil Rights in the 1950s," *Tulane Law Review* 69 (1995): 788 (discussing some of President Eisenhower's judicial appointments in the South). The exception was Judge Richard T. Rives, who was appointed by President Harry S. Truman. Jack Bass, "Richard T. Rives," *Encyclopedia of Alabama*, http://www .encyclopediaofalabama.org/article/h-3494.

5. That was the case prior to the time that Congress divided the old Fifth Circuit into two new circuits—the new Fifth Circuit and the Eleventh Circuit—in 1981. See Fifth Circuit Court of Appeals Reorganization Act of 1980, 94 Stat. 1994 (dividing

the old Fifth Circuit into two new circuits). See also Friedman, *Champion of Civil Rights*, 337. Judge Wisdom's opposition to the division was probably instrumental in delaying the split by several years. See Deborah J. Barrow and Thomas G. Walker, *A Court Divided: The Fifth Circuit Court of Appeals and the Politics of Judicial Reform* (New Haven: Yale University Press, 1980), 118–22, 179–81, 241–45. See also John Minor Wisdom, "Requiem for a Great Court," *Loyola Law Review* 26 (1980): 787 (arguing that the proper solution to the problems of judicial administration in the Fifth and Ninth Circuits was not the splitting of the circuits, but reforming the law of federal jurisdiction).

6. *Brown v. Board of Education of Topeka*, 347 US 483 (1954). The Supreme Court's decisions relating to the franchise also gave rise to much litigation in the Fifth Circuit. See *Gomillion v. Lightfoot*, 270 F.2d 594, 611 (5th Cir. 1959) (Wisdom, J., concurring), rev'd, 364 U.S. 339 (1960); *Baker v. Carr*, 369 U.S. 186 (1962); *Wesberry v. Sanders*, 376 U.S. 1 (1964); *Reynolds v. Sims*, 377 U.S. 533 (1964). In the current debate over the central meaning of *Brown*, as announcing either an antidiscrimination or an antisubordination principle, see Reva B. Siegel, "Equality Talk: Antisubordination and Anticlassification in Constitutional Struggles over *Brown*," *Harvard Law Review* 117 (2004): 1470, 1477, Judge Wisdom would have come down firmly on the side of antisubordination.

7. See, e.g., Civil Rights Act of 1964, 78 Stat. 241 (1964); Voting Rights Act of 1965, 79 Stat. 437 (1965); Fair Housing Act of 1968, 83 Stat. 73 (1968).

8. Burke Marshall, "In Remembrance of Judges Frank M. Johnson, Jr. and John Minor Wisdom," *Yale Law Journal* 109 (2000): 1207. See also *Brown v. Board of Education*, 349 US 294 (1955) (*Brown II*).

9. Marshall, "In Remembrance," 1207. See generally J. W. Peltason, *Fifty-Eight Lonely Men: Southern Federal Judges and School Desegregation*, (Urbana: University of Illinois Press, 1961).

10. See, e.g., Barry Sullivan, "John Wisdom, Watchman of the Republic, Forester of the Soul," *Mississippi Law Journal* 69 (1999): 15–16 (detailing the harassment that Judge Wisdom endured, while "undoubtedly [taking] courage from the even greater risks and sacrifices by those who invoked the protection of the federal courts"); Geoffrey Hodgson, "John Minor Wisdom: A Courageous White Judge, His Rulings Helped American Blacks," *Guardian*, May 18, 1999 ("'Everybody realized that after *Brown* there would be many important decisions,' Wisdom said in an interview in 1983. He felt, he said, that segregation 'was just plain wrong', adding that 'the more exposure you get to this problem, the more you realize that the blacks have had a raw deal for 300 years, and that we owe a debt to them. . . . These things were building up and I think they built up in me as time went along'"). Judge Wisdom often expressed the view, which was shared by others, including Burke Marshall, that the real heroes were not the judges, but the litigants in the civil rights cases that the judges decided. See Burke Marshall, "Southern Judges in the Desegregation Struggle," *Harvard Law Review* 95 (1982): 1509, 1515 ("Those whose lives, personal safety, economic security, and futures were most at stake were not lawyers or judges at all; they were the plaintiffs . . . and the participants in the civil rights movement, and they were mostly black").

11. See Frank T. Read, "The Penman of the Court: A Tribute to John Minor Wisdom," *Tulane Law Review* 60 (1985): 264 ("More often than not, John Minor Wisdom was the penman, architect, and genius who wrote the seminal decisions that integrated the public schools of the Deep South"). But Judge Wisdom would be the first to object at being singled out simply because it was often his voice that spoke for the court. He would have emphasized that he was not writing for himself alone, as some of the courageous district judges were required to do. He may have provided the words, but his colleagues courageously stood behind them. Initially, there were "the Four"— an epithet (which later became a badge of honor) used to describe Judge Richard T. Rives, Judge Elbert P. Tuttle, Judge John R. Brown, and Judge Wisdom—and they were joined in later years by other judges who were equally committed to protecting constitutional rights. See, e.g., Diane P. Wood, "Tribute to Judge Irving L. Goldberg: The Consummate Humanist," *Texas Law Review* 73 (1994): 977; Homer Ross Tomlin, *Homer Thornberry: Congressman, Judge, and Advocate for Human Rights* (Fort Worth: Texas Christian University Press, 2016); Dan R. Warren, *If It Takes All Summer: Martin Luther King, the KKK, and States' Rights in St. Augustine, 1964* (Tuscaloosa: University of Alabama Press, 2007).

12. See, e.g., Barry Sullivan, "The Honest Muse: Judge Wisdom and the Uses of History," *Tulane Law Review* 60 (1985): 314.

13. *United States v. State of Louisiana*, 225 F. Supp. 353 (1963) (three-judge court), *aff'd, Louisiana v. United States*, 380 US 145 (1965).

14. Ibid., 355.

15. Ibid.

16. Ibid., 356. The Judge obviously was mindful of the need to distinguish *Lassiter v. Northampton County Board of Elections*, 360 US 45 (1959), in which the Supreme Court upheld the constitutionality of literacy tests. In *Katzenbach v. Morgan*, 384 US 641 (1966), the Supreme Court subsequently upheld Congress's prohibition of literacy tests as an appropriate exercise of its enforcement power under Section 2 of the Fifteenth Amendment.

17. *United States v. State of Louisiana*, 356.

18. *United States v. Jefferson County Board of Education*, 372 F.2d 836 (1966) (*United States v. Jefferson County Board of Education I*), *aff'd on rehearing en banc, United States v. Jefferson County Board of Education*, 380 F.2d 385 (1967).

19. *United States v. Jefferson County Board of Education I*, 847.

20. Ibid., 878.

21. See *Briggs v. Elliott*, 132 F. Supp. 776 (1955) (three-judge court). In the foregoing passage, Judge Wisdom refers to the "*Briggs* dictum," in which a three-judge district court in the Fourth Circuit gave a narrow reading to the Supreme Court's decision in *Brown*. On remand from the Supreme Court, the three-judge district court wrote: "[The Supreme Court] has not decided that the federal courts are to take over or regulate the public schools of the states. It has not decided that the states must mix persons of different races in the schools or must require them to attend schools or must deprive

them of the right of choosing the schools they attend. What it has decided, and all that it has decided, is that a state may not deny to any person on account of race the right to attend any school that it maintains. . . . The Constitution, in other words, does not require integration. It merely forbids [segregation]" (ibid., 777).

22. *United States v. Jefferson County Board of Education I*, 878. See also Owen Fiss, *Pillars of Justice: Lawyers and the Liberal Tradition* (Cambridge, Mass.: Harvard University Press, 2017): 54–55 (discussing assistant attorney general John Doar's use of Judge Wisdom's panel opinion in his oral argument for the United States in the Fifth Circuit's en banc consideration of *United States v. Jefferson County Board of Education*).

23. See Barry Sullivan, "Dedication: For Judge Wisdom on His Eighty-Fifth Birthday," *Tulane Law Review* 64 (1990): 1345–46.

24. See, e.g., Michael E. Solimine, "The Fall and Rise of the Specialized Constitutional Court," *University of Pennsylvania Law Review* 17 (2014): 123–27 (detailing history of three-judge district court provisions).

25. See, e.g., *Dombrowski v. Pfister*, 227 F. Supp. 556, 559 (E.D. La. 1964) (Wisdom, J., dissenting), *rev'd*, 380 U.S. 479 (1965); *United States v. State of Louisiana* (Wisdom, J.), *aff'd*, *Louisiana v. United States*.

26. See Multidistrict Litigation Act, 82 Stat. 109 (1968).

27. See, e.g., Allen D. Black, "Judge Wisdom, The Great Teacher and Careful Writer," *Yale Law Journal* 109 (2000): 1267. See also John Minor Wisdom, "Wisdom's Idiosyncrasies," *Yale Law Journal* (2000): 1273, 1275 (providing stylistic advice to his clerks, including the need to avoid "Latinisms" and "ugly words," such as "which").

28. See Henry T. Greely, "Quantitative Analysis of a Judicial Career: A Case Study of Judge John Minor Wisdom," *Washington and Lee Law Review* 53 (1996): 110 (noting that Judge Wisdom, by the end of 1995, had written 1,393 published opinions, including 1,227 Fifth Circuit opinions, 117 opinions as a visiting judge on other courts of appeals, 28 while sitting as a district judge, 9 as a member of the Multidistrict Panel on Complex Litigation, and 12 as a judge of the Railroad Reorganization Court). A later source figures the Judge's total output at 1,550 opinions. See RavelLaw, https://www.ravellaw.com/reports/judge/2622/opinions.

29. See, e.g., *Offshore Company v. Robison*, 266 F.2d 769 (1959) (expanding definitions of "seaman" and "vessel" to reflect workplace reality); *Local 189, United Papermakers & Paperworkers v. United States*, 416 F.2d 980 (1969), *cert. denied, Local 189, United Papermakers & Paperworkers v. United States*, 397 US 919 (1970) (articulating "rightful place" doctrine for fashioning relief in Title VII cases). See also Alvin T. Rubin, "John Is Every Inch a Sailor," *Tulane Law Review* 60 (1985): 258 ("Th[e] formulation [in *Robison* of the elements necessary for a Jones Act case to go to the jury] deserves the classic status it has achieved. It is comprehensive and clear. It can be used by trial judges as the basis for jury instructions, for it is free of jargon and technicality").

30. *Borel v. Fibreboard Paper Products Corporation*, 493 F.2d 1076 (1973) (upholding jury verdict in products liability case involving failure to warn of asbestos dangers).

31. See, e.g., *United States v. State of Louisiana* (three-judge court), *aff'd, Louisiana v. United States; Weber v. Kaiser Aluminum & Chemical Corp,* 573 F.2d 216 (1977) (Wisdom, J. dissenting), *rev'd sub nom. United Steelworkers v. Weber,* 442 U.S. 927 (1979).

32. See, e.g., *Dallas County v. Commercial Union Assurance Co,* 286 F.2d 388 (1961); Fed R. Evid. 803 (16).

33. Allen Black, one of the Judge's clerks, has noted that "[Judge Wisdom] was an expert in Louisiana civil law, an expertise in which he took great pride, both because of its local significance and because it gave him a chance to show off his skills in the French language." Allen D. Black, "John Minor Wisdom: A Tribute and Memoir by One of His Law Clerks," *Mississippi Law Journal* 69 (1999): 44.

34. See American Law Institute, *Study of the Division of Jurisdiction between State and Federal Courts* (Philadelphia: ALI, 1969). The reporters for the project were Paul Mishkin, Charles Allen Wright, and David Shapiro. Other panel members included Henry J. Friendly, Henry M. Hart, and Herbert Wechsler. As commentators have noted, the panel membership "reads like a roster for induction into the federal courts hall of fame." William M. Richman and William L. Reynolds, *Injustice on Appeal: The United States Courts of Appeals in Crisis* (New York: Oxford University Press, 2013), 129.

35. In his concurring opinion in *United States v. Cox,* 342 F.2d 167 (1965), *cert. denied,* 381 U.S. 935 (1965)—a case involving the scope of a district judge's authority with respect to the return of a grand jury indictment in a civil rights case—Judge Wisdom characterized the dispute as "the type of case that comes up, in one way or another, whenever the customs, beliefs, or interests of a region collide with national policy as fixed by the Constitution or by Congress" (ibid., 196). Many of the Judge's cases presented variations on that theme, which he discussed in several extracurial writings. See, e.g., John Minor Wisdom, "A Federal Judge in the Deep South: Random Observations," *South Carolina Law Review* 35 (1984): 503; John Minor Wisdom, "The Frictionmaking, Exacerbating Political Role of Federal Courts," *Southwestern Law Journal* 21 (1967): 411; John Minor Wisdom, "A Southern Judge Looks at Civil Rights," *F.R.D.* 42 (1966): 437. See also Comment, "Judicial Performance in the Fifth Circuit," *Yale Law Journal.* 73 (1963): 90.

36. Barrow and Walker, *Court Divided,* 25 (quoting John Minor Wisdom, "The Frictionmaking, Exacerbating Political Role of Federal Courts," *Southwestern Law Journal* 21 [1967]: 411).

37. Some, such as Allen Black, a distinguished Philadelphia lawyer, and Judge Brock Hornby, a prominent federal district judge who previously served on the Maine Supreme Judicial Court, achieved important leadership roles in the Institute.

38. Scott Hastings to author, November 29, 2016.

39. Black, "John Minor Wisdom," 43.

40. See "Presentation of the Edward J. Devitt Distiguished Service to Justice Award to Honorable Elbert Parr Tuttle, Senior Circuit Court Judge, United States Court of Appeals for the Eleventh Circuit, and Honorable John Minor Wisdom, Senior Circuit

Judge, United States Court of Appeals for the Fifth Circuit," New Orleans, May 8, 1988, 888 F.2d (1988): civ. (letter of Robert B. Barnett, Esq.).

41. Robert Frost, "Two Tramps in Mud Time," available at https://www.poemhunter .com/poem/two-tramps-in-mud-time/.

42. Oliver Wendell Holmes to Frederick Pollock, December 11, 1909 (included in Mark DeWolfe Howe, *Holmes-Pollock Letters: The Correspondence of Mr. Justice Holmes and Sir Frederick Pollock, 1874–1932* [Cambridge, Mass.: Harvard University Press, 1941], 156.)

43. Oliver Wendell Holmes to Felix Frankfurter, December 3, 1925 (included in Alexander M. Bickel, *The Unpublished Opinions of Mr. Justice Brandeis: The Supreme Court at Work* [Cambridge, Mass.: Harvard University Press, 1957]: 230). Holmes contrasted his own approach with that of Justice Brandeis, who "always desire[d] to know all that can be known about a case." See also Barry Sullivan, "Just Listening: The Equal Hearing Principle and the Moral Life of Judges," *Loyola University Chicago Law Journal* 48 (2016): 356 (discussing expectations with respect to judicial performance).

44. Barry Sullivan, "John Wisdom: Watchman of the Republic, Forester of the Soul," *Mississippi Law Journal* 69 (1999): 13–15. Judge Wisdom's dissenting opinion ultimately prevailed when the case was reheard en banc.

45. Richard O. Baumbach Jr. and William E. Borah, *The Second Battle of New Orleans: A History of the Vieux Carre Riverfront-Expressway Controversy* (Tuscaloosa: University of Alabama Press, 1981), 90.

46. *Plessy v. Ferguson*, 163 US 537 (1896).

47. John Minor Wisdom, "*Plessy v. Ferguson*—100 Years Later," *Washington and Lee Law Review* 53 (1996): 10.

48. Ibid., 10–11. Bonnie's historical interest included an interest in family history. She was particularly proud of her great-grandfather, George Mathews, a graduate of Liberty Hall Academy (now Washington and Lee University), who was an early justice of the Louisiana Supreme Court and held in 1835 that a slave was emancipated by virtue of having been taken to France by her master. See Friedman, *Champion of Civil Rights*, 24 (discussing *Marie Louise, free woman of color v. Marot*, 9 La. 474 [1836]).

49. Robert Barnett, "John Minor Wisdom: 'O Rare,'" *Yale Law Journal* 109 (2000): 1263.

50. Ricki Tigert Helfer, "The Judge and Bonnie Wisdom: A Personal Tribute," *Tulane Law Review* 69 (1995): 1418–19.

51. The group included Gerhard Casper, a future president of Stanford University, who taught the structural part of American constitutional law as well as the "constitutional law" of the European Community; David Currie, who taught federal jurisdiction and environmental law; Kenneth Culp Davis, who taught administrative law, with a heavy emphasis on fairness of procedure; Owen Fiss, who taught courses on civil rights; Joachim Herrmann (a visiting professor from Germany), who taught comparative constitutional criminal procedure; Harry Kalven, a charismatic teacher who taught First Amendment law; Stanley N. Katz, a future president of the American Council of

Learned Societies who taught equal protection and legal history; Philip B. Kurland, who taught a seminar on separation of powers while also serving as special counsel to the Senate Judiciary Committee during the eventful spring of 1974; and James Boyd White, who taught a course on the Fourth and Fifth Amendments.

52. See Owen M. Fiss, *Injunctions* (Mineola, N.Y.: Foundation Press, 1972). See also Owen M. Fiss, *The Civil Rights Injunction* (Bloomington: Indiana University Press, 1978). Fiss also co-taught a seminar on slavery and the law with Professors Kalven and Katz.

53. See, e.g., *Meredith v. Fair*, 306 F.2d 374 (1962), *cert. denied*, 371 U.S. 828, *enf'd*, 313 F.2d 532 (1962) (en banc) (per curiam). The university put into evidence a psychiatrist's report from the time of Meredith's military service, which mentioned Meredith's "nervous stomach," presumably to demonstrate his unfitness for university study, but Judge Wisdom gave it little weight. At an earlier stage of the litigation, Judge Wisdom wrote: "It is certainly understandable that a sensitive Negro, especially one overseas, might have a nervous stomach over the racial problem. There must be a good many Negroes stateside with similar abdominal reactions. We find it significant that the psychiatrist found 'no evidence of a thinking disorder,' that he found Meredith's 'strong need to fight and defy authority' took a 'passive' form, and that no treatment was recommended. Meredith, incidentally, voluntarily went to the psychiatrist" (*Meredith v. Fair*, 305 F.2d 343, 357 [5th Cir. 1962]). Judge Wisdom thought that "Meredith's record shows just about the type of Negro who might be expected to try to crack the racial barrier at the University of Mississippi: a man with a mission and with a nervous stomach" (ibid., 358). Meredith later cited that description in his memoir. See James Meredith with William Doyle, *A Mission from God: A Memoir and Challenge for America* (New York: Atria Books, 2012), 79. See also Frank T. Read and Lucy S. McGough, *Let Them Be Judged: The Judicial Integration of the Deep South* (Lanham, Md.: Scarecrow Press, 1978), 195–253 (discussing the *Meredith* litigation).

54. See, e.g., John Doar, Nicholas Katzenbach, and Harrison Jay Goldin, "Panel Discussion: JFK and Civil Rights: Fifty Years After," panel discussion, Princeton University, Princeton, N.J., March 3, 2011, www.youtube.com/watch?v=BjeeeMi_mG4 (discussion by three Kennedy Justice Department officials concerning civil rights enforcement, including events surrounding James Meredith's matriculation at the University of Mississippi).

55. *United States v. Barnett*, 346 F.2d 99 (1965). Among the many significant questions raised by the *Meredith* case was whether Governor Barnett was constitutionally entitled to have his contempt tried to a jury. At an earlier stage of the litigation, the Fifth Circuit certified that question to the Supreme Court, which held that a jury trial was not required. See *United States v. Barnett*, 376 U.S. 681 (1964).

56. *United States v. Barnett*, 346 F.2d, 104. Judge Wisdom wrote, "To my mind, the Court's decision represents the exercise of judicial license not of judicial restraint." Moreover, he noted, the court was "not sitting in equity; the defendants are accused of criminal contempt" (ibid., 105). He continued: "The Court is less like a court than it is like St. Louis. The good French king used to sit under a spreading oak tree, not

presiding even-handedly as a judge at a trial, but dispensing justice subjectively, arbitrarily, hit-or-miss, according to his fancy of the moment as to what was best for his subjects and when it was best for him to tell them about it. Coming closer home, the law in the Court's decision is like the Law West of the Pecos" (ibid., 106).

57. Ibid., 108–9.

58. Ibid., 109.

59. See, e.g., Leon Friedman, *Southern Justice* (New York: Meridian Books, 1965), 193 ("But [there] is one federal judge who has excelled all others in his speed in enforcing the law and in his willingness to embark on new legal territory to protect Negro rights. He is Judge Bryan Simpson, chief judge of the United States District Court for the Middle District of Florida, sitting in Jacksonville").

60. See Barry Sullivan, Comment, "Exhaustion of State Administrative Remedies in Section 1983 Cases," *University of Chicago Law Review* 41 (1974): 537.

61. Black, "John Minor Wisdom," 43.

62. Stanford Goldblatt, "My Extraordinary Year," unpublished memoir, n.d., 10.

63. See Black, "John Minor Wisdom," 46. Further, "The Judge's eye for precision in writing stayed with him right up to the end. At the time of the Judge's funeral, . . . Andrew Kelly, one of his current law clerks, gave me a copy of the instructions the hospital had issued to the Judge before his last coronary operation. 'You may only take Tylenol for minor aches or headache,' the paper said. Ever the editor, the Judge had circled 'only' and moved it, so the sentence read correctly and with greater clarity: 'You may take Tylenol only for minor muscle aches or headache'"(45–46).

64. See also *Anastasoff v. United States*, 223 F.3d 898 (2000), *vacated as moot*, 235 F.3d 1054 (2000) (Richard S. Arnold, J.) (panel opinion holding that Circuit Rule stating that unpublished opinions are not precedents violates Article III of the Constitution "because it purports to confer on the federal courts a power that goes beyond the 'judicial,'" vacated by the same panel on mootness grounds).

65. Goldblatt, "My Extraordinary Year," 9–10.

66. Black, "John Minor Wisdom," 48–49. See *United States v. Jefferson County Board of Education.*

67. Goldblatt, "My Extraordinary Year," 15.

68. Ibid. See *United States v. State of Louisiana* (three-judge court), *aff'd*, *Louisiana v. United States.* See also Philip P. Frickey, "Judge Wisdom and Voting Rights: The Judicial Artist as Scholar and Pragmatist," *Tulane Law Review* 60 (1985): 276 (discussing Judge Wisdom's voting rights cases).

69. The accomplishments of the Judge's clerks are too numerous to be catalogued in this essay, but it would not be inappropriate to mention that the Judge was particularly proud of Phil Frickey, whose death from cancer prematurely ended a brilliant academic career. See, e.g., Daniel A. Farber, "Introduction: 'Practical Reason' and the Scholarship of Philip P. Frickey," *California Law Review* 98 (2010): 1111.

70. See John W. Davis, "John Randolph Tucker: The Man and His Work," *Washington and Lee Law Review* 6 (1949): 139.

71. Associated Press, "Hundreds Pay Tribute to Judge Wisdom," *New York Times,* May 28, 1999.

72. Ibid.

73. Ibid.

74. Hon. John Minor Wisdom, interview by Fred Graham (n.d.), 154. I am greatly indebted to Robert Barnett for providing me with a copy of this transcript, and to Stanford Goldblatt both for sharing his unpublished memoir and for granting me permission to quote from it. Finally, I am grateful to Jeffrey Gordon and Helaina Metcalf for excellent research assistance.

DAVID M. DORSEN

Clerking for a Giant

Henry Friendly and His Law Clerks

How much can you predict about a judge's relationship with his law clerks from his nonjudicial life? I believe quite a bit. Judges don't shed their personality and values when they put on, or for that matter take off, their robes. At least, I'm willing to bet on that proposition, based on my six-year study of Judge Henry Friendly, who served on the United States Court of Appeals for the Second Circuit. Along with Learned Hand, Henry Friendly was the greatest federal circuit judge not to have served on the Supreme Court. Not only did he write extraordinary opinions in a wide variety of fields, but he also wrote dozens of magnificent articles on a wide variety of subjects.

Friendly came from German-Jewish stock that emigrated from Bavaria in the mid-nineteenth century with the name Freundlich. His record as a student, law practitioner, and judge was unique. At Harvard College and Harvard Law School he was first in his class when he graduated in 1919 and 1922, respectively. In the latter, not only was he first in his class, but he attained the highest average since Louis Brandeis graduated (that was under a more generous grading system). Friendly's average was never exceeded and probably will not be, because Harvard has changed its grading system.

Friendly clerked for Justice Louis Brandeis, who told then-professor Felix Frankfurter, who chose Brandeis's law clerks, never to send him another clerk like Friendly. Shocked, Frankfurter asked why. "If I had another man like Friendly, I would not have to do a lick of work myself," Brandeis replied.[1]

After the Brandeis clerkship, Friendly turned down a variety of offers, including to teach at Harvard, to go into private practice with what ultimately became the law firm of Dewey Ballantine. He became a founding partner in 1945 in Cleary, Gottlieb, Friendly, Steen & Hamilton, to give it the name most remember. President Dwight Eisenhower appointed him to the Second Circuit in 1959, where he remained until 1986, when he committed suicide.

For Friendly, private practice consisted mostly of working for a new venture, Pan American Airways. It was run by a very difficult man, Juan Tripp, who had set out to monopolize the United States' international passenger market. While that effort ultimately failed, Friendly spent most of his time fighting with the likes of Howard Hughes's TWA over trans-Atlantic routes before the Federal Aviation Commission and often before the courts. Hearings that lasted months were the norm. Tripp's shenanigans, while beyond the scope of this essay, were notorious.

With rare exceptions Friendly treated associates and young partners in his firm with the same brutality that Harvard Law School professors have been portrayed as using in books and films. He had some famous remarks, such as telling an associate, "What you have done is good and original, but what is good is not original, and what is original is not good."[2] Associates and even some partners and their wives feared him.

One redeeming feature of Friendly's management style is that he did most of his work himself. For example, he would dictate briefs to a pair of secretaries, who alternated between taking dictation and typing their notes. Corrections were negligible. He demanded perfection from everyone, himself included.

Friendly's personal life is also instructive. He was socially awkward and had no serious relationship with a woman until, at age twenty-seven, he married Sophie Stern, the daughter of the chief justice of the Supreme Court of Pennsylvania and part of a wealthy and established Philadelphia family. She was outgoing and immensely popular, a free spirit whom everyone loved. Married on September 4, 1930, eleven months after the stock market began its dive, the Friendlys nevertheless had no financial problems. For one thing he sold his $7,000 stock investments in August 1929. For another, he had an excellent and secure job. The couple moved into a large apartment in a classy Park Avenue building.

The couple had three children born in the 1930s, David, Joan, and Ellen. Joan went to Radcliffe, received a Ph.D. in psychology, and eventually became a professor at the University of Pennsylvania. David, who was scientifically oriented, became a prominent child ophthalmologist. Ellen, the youngest, became a school teacher. As was usual for the period, Sophie raised the children. What was unusual, for then and for now, is that Friendly conspicuously demonstrated extraordinary favoritism toward Joan, by far the most academic of the three.

Friendly, who had no interest in and little aptitude for science and mechanics, had no interest in or rapport with David's career or David for that matter.

From all accounts, Friendly simply ignored Ellen. As Joan later explained to me, her father considered the family a wonderful presentation to him at which he was the principal member of the audience, who could bestow his favors willy-nilly on those participants he favored. Dinner conversation was about current events, not the family.

In 1959, the year Friendly became a circuit judge, David was married to Irene, a wonderful woman and a nurse. The same year Joan became engaged to Frank Goodman, a graduate of Harvard College and Law School and an editor of the *Harvard Law Review*, who later became a professor at the University of Pennsylvania Law School. Ellen, the youngest, was in college. She later married Stephen Simon, who was the nephew of Walter Annenberg, the extremely wealthy publisher, diplomat, and philanthropist. Simon would become a respected symphony orchestra conductor. At his death Friendly had nine grandchildren, who held little interest for him, although that changed for one or two who became academics.

Friendly had serious eye problems throughout his life, which led him to fear he would go blind. During his adult life, Friendly was depressed, in the popular, but probably not clinical, sense. The world was going to hell. Things were terrible. But his depression did not affect his work, sleep, or eating. Among those who might be counted as his closest friends, Judges Edward Weinfeld and Richard Posner, there was a distance. Weinfeld concealed from Friendly his eight-year bout with cancer. Posner did not know that favorite daughter Joan had a sister. Friendly was not emotionally close to his wife. Perhaps his best friend was his daughter Joan.

After Sophie died, Friendly became more despondent. While he continued to work at an extremely high level, he despaired. Almost exactly one year after her death he took his life by consuming a raft of pills, the first and last time he acted on the occasional suicidal impulse he had.

What was it like being a Friendly clerk?

Third-year law students competed intensely for a clerkship with Friendly. Aside from clerking for a Supreme Court justice (and not all of them), no other clerkship was so attractive, at least in the Northeast. Even the student with the highest average in his class at Harvard Law School could not count on being selected. Friendly hired his clerks after interviewing them.

At first, Harvard Law School professor David Cavers screened candidates and sent him a few each year, from whom one was selected. Until his eighth year on the bench, all the clerks came from Harvard, but then he started taking clerks from Yale, Columbia, Chicago, and occasionally other schools, relying largely on recommendations by professors who taught there. Friendly was interested in ability, and nothing else; for example, political leanings and politics never came up in his interviews.

When an applicant for a clerkship told Friendly that he received an A in administrative law from Professor Antonin Scalia, a scholar Friendly admired, he subjected the applicant to a withering cross-examination on the subject. Friendly not only turned him down but also wrote a letter to his sponsor, the highly regarded Professor Edward Levi of the University of Chicago Law School, to complain about the applicant's deficiencies.

For Friendly's clerks it was an unusual opportunity to work with a brilliant jurist, and almost all were positive about their experience, some exuberantly so. While the clerks recognized that Friendly rarely went out of his way to provide instruction to them, the opportunity to see him in action and to participate in the creation of excellent opinions was reward in itself. Several former clerks volunteered that Friendly was one of the best minds they had ever encountered, and many praised his sweeping intellectual curiosity.

One clerk compared the experience with "sitting next to Garry Kasparov while he explained each [chess] move."[3] Another likened Friendly to Pelé, the soccer star, though in Friendly the electrons or synapses moved faster. An academic called his clerkship "by far the single most significant year in [his] understanding and development in the law."[4] Another said that Friendly taught "entirely by example. He did his work; you did yours; then you worked together . . . in the craft of the law."[5] A third academic said that "he was a joy to work with."[6] A judge said simply, "To have been his clerk was the greatest privilege I have known."[7] While Friendly inspired a number of his clerks to become judges, he discouraged at least one. Professor Philip Bobbitt, a distinguished scholar, concluded after working for Friendly that he could not be as good a judge as Friendly, and therefore he would not become a judge.

With very rare exceptions—patent opinions and an occasional reward—Friendly wrote his own opinions. He did this in longhand, because he had only one secretary and she could not type while another secretary took dictation. Since he had a photographic memory, Friendly would pull down volumes of the *Supreme Court and Federal Reporter* as needed to complete his opinions, although occasionally he would leave a blank for the clerk to fill.

After Friendly's secretary typed his handwritten draft of an opinion triple-spaced, she would send it directly to a clerk to cite-check what the judge had written as well as supply omitted case names or citations and, when the clerk rose to the occasion, to suggest substantive changes. Friendly apparently considered this mode of input by his clerks the most efficient way to involve them in preparing his opinions. Their responsibility was summarized in a manual for clerks that David Currie, Friendly's clerk in his second year on the bench, first drafted. The 1978 manual, which had grown to forty-nine double-spaced pages, included this injunction: "The Judge welcomes criticism; challenge the draft in every reasonable way you can. Assume, at the start, that everything said, by way of fact or law, may be wrong (or incomplete) and make sure it becomes right.... This is your most important single function."[8] But the quality of Friendly's work often left little productive work for the clerk. Currie said that the clerkship was a "modest position."[9] Compared to other clerkships there was so little to do that some clerks couldn't understand why they were there.

In addition to reviewing Friendly's opinions, the clerks wrote detailed memoranda, some running dozens of pages, on intricate subjects that came up in cases, such as a history of jury trials in England before the adoption of the Bill of Rights, or the legislative history of a statute, to assist Friendly in writing an opinion. While he usually assigned the topics to clerks, some clerks read the parties' briefs and tried to predict what might help the judge. To anticipate what he might need, one pair of clerks looked on the judge's desk after he left for the day. It was not always easy trying to figure out what he wanted.

When clerks made significant contributions in the process, Friendly was delighted. "He was never happier than when a law clerk confronted him with an interesting disagreement,"[10] and when a clerk really delivered, he would light up with joy. A law clerk who exercised initiative made him beam with pleasure. He frequently gave them credit in memoranda to his fellow judges: "My law clerk's examination of the law and the facts has led me to conclude, contrary to my first impression that we should reverse." In another case: "I am indebted to my law clerk for pointing out what now seems to me the error in the way in which this matter was handled by the judge and by counsel on both sides."[11] And once after the panel had unanimously signed off on an opinion affirming the district court, clerk Mark Wolinsky wrote a fourteen-page memorandum on his own initiative that showed why the judges were wrong. Friendly circulated the memorandum to the other two judges, and the panel unanimously reversed the district judge. Decades later many former clerks mentioned as high points in their legal careers getting Friendly to change his mind, which he was willing to do when presented with cogent reasons. Some kept notes from Friendly that praised their work.

One clerk, Bruce Ackerman, now a Yale professor, described what happened when he challenged Friendly after receiving a 227-page draft, which Friendly had written in four days:

I read the opinion. Pages 137 to 193 are completely wrong. I walk in and tell him so: "Take a few days, Bruce, and write a new draft . . . ." [I] tend to wake up at 4 a.m., staring into darkness, tossing and turning, composing and recomposing.

Three weeks later my draft is done: there's still a lot of Henry Friendly there, but not a trace between pages 137 and 193. . . . We review the new draft, line by line. The Judge has made countless changes, large and small. . . . Every time I object to a new modification, he tries to answer each of my questions, and almost always revises the revision yet again—in ways neither of us had clearly anticipated.

Four hours later, we reach page 136. I wait for him to turn the page: "I think you've made a good point in the second full paragraph of 137." From then on, the draft takes an entirely new turn. My revision has convinced the Judge to drop his old fifty-five pages and to begin writing on a clean slate. The result is an opinion far stronger and deeper than either of the earlier drafts.[12]

Another clerk, Lawrence Pedowitz, described his experience:

Once the law and the facts were understood, I usually found myself in agreement with the Judge about a decision. But when disagreement remained, the real fun began, because there is nothing the Judge enjoys more than a good debate. Most often these debates provided the vehicle for the Judge to refine his initial views, and as this occurred, his arguments would become even more persuasive, which usually moved me to alter my own views. But when disagreement continued, the Judge always listened carefully and could be persuaded by a well-reasoned argument which appealed to his profound sense of justice.[13]

Friendly also called these interchanges with his clerks "fun," exceptions to his generally somber and burdened attitude. One clerk called them "open season." Friendly told clerks not to worry about his feelings, and it was absolutely fair combat. He was delighted when a clerk found he had made a mistake. He had no vested interest in his ideas or expression; if the clerk had a better idea, he'd accept it, although he could grow impatient as he quickly saw the implications of a clerk's point. One of his few requirements was that any clerk who raised a problem had to propose a solution, and he would use the clerk's version when their relative merits were close.

Nevertheless, errors, sometimes embarrassing ones, found their way into opinions, which upset Friendly. If a clerk made a mistake that crept into a published opinion, the judge would never let him or her forget it. A missed example appeared in his discussion of the sufficiency of a complaint. Friendly's published opinion reads, "For example, if a limited partner had an investment of $100,000 and was paid off with 1000 shares of stock taken at $10 per share but known to have real value of only $5, he would have been defrauded of $50,000."[14] Friendly would have been mortified at the math error.

When Friendly wanted to see a clerk, he would press a buzzer, and the clerk would enter without knocking. The number of buzzes, which were loud, would inform whether he wanted his secretary or a clerk and, when he had more than one clerk, which clerk. One problem was that when they opened his door, Friendly was already speaking. He often mumbled. Clerks generally were too intimidated to ask for clarification and would proceed on the basis of what they thought he said. Sometimes a clerk would ask the secretary to translate, trying to imitate the unintelligible mumblings and grunts. One clerk remembers Friendly greeting him with, "Why do you think the plaintiff has any right to recover on Point 2?" When he entered Friendly's domain, one of the more intrepid clerks was greeted with, "How much do they get?" Pausing, the clerk, David Deipp, asked, "What is the sentence before that one?" Friendly had not realized that the clerk had no idea which case he was talking about or who "they" were.[15]

Some clerks found the sound of the buzzer scary. In fact, one former clerk recounted that after he bought a house, he had the doorbell changed because it reminded him of Friendly's buzzer. Occasionally a clerk would stand up to Friendly, reacting to pointed criticism by telling him, "I'm going to make mistakes; I'm not you."[16] Friendly did not seem to understand what it meant to have merely a very good mind. Judge Michael Boudin said that after clerking for Friendly it was impossible to be intellectually intimidated by anyone.

Many former clerks explained that others—although rarely directly admitting it was themselves—were intimidated by Friendly. Whether or not Friendly intended it, intimidation was certainly present in varying degrees among many clerks. One clerk stated that the common denominator of all visits to Friendly's office was fear coupled with anxiety. Deadpan, Chief Justice John G. Roberts Jr. gave a specific example of this phenomenon. After explaining that he was not among those intimidated by Friendly, he shared that after Friendly once buzzed him into his office he complained that everything was darker than usual and that some of the lights must have been out. Roberts could not bring himself to tell the judge that he was still wearing his clip-on sunglasses. He told Friendly's secretary after he left his office.

When he was displeased, such as when a clerk was progressing too slowly, Friendly often showed his displeasure with sarcasm. Fast in turning out work, Friendly could be intolerant of clerks who were slower. On more than one occasion he walked over to a clerk and asked, "Have you given birth yet?" His repugnance at seeing time squandered can be illustrated by his response to Roberts getting stuck in the elevator: Friendly had someone take him briefs so he wouldn't be wasting time.

How hard clerks worked varied widely. The record for the longest hours probably went to co-clerks Gregory Palm and James Smoot, who, without telling the judge, each slept two nights a week in the chambers, showering in the judge's private bathroom before he arrived. Smoot started keeping track of his "billable" hours, but he discontinued the practice because it was masochistic and, besides, "who had time for it?"

Among Friendly's least successful clerks were those who simply accepted what he wrote as gospel. To encourage thoughtful answers, he made a practice of asking clerks for their views before he spoke. When a clerk hemmed and hawed, Friendly said through a clenched jaw, "You're not helping me any."

Friendly demanded the same level of competence and care from his clerks as he did from himself and generally had little patience for people who did not meet that standard. Thus, when a clerk misspelled the name of one of the lawyers in a case, Friendly told him, "If I cannot trust you to get the name of a lawyer right, how can I trust you to do anything else?" One clerk started a memorandum with, "At the risk of incurring your wrath once again . . ." He had little sympathy for those clerks who could not perform. Exacerbating the problem was Friendly's tendency to make early judgments about his clerks. He communicated his disappointment to them, making turnabouts difficult: "The judge was not good if something went wrong," one clerk concluded.[17]

Because of Friendly's extreme penchant for orderliness, or perhaps because of his eye problems (or both), he wanted to be sure where everything was when he took the bench to hear an appeal. Clerks drafted a map to show the placement of the parties' briefs and appendix (with all rubber bands removed), a pad of lined paper, three sharpened No. 2 pencils with their points facing to the courtroom and their erasers lined up, two pens, the Federal Rules of Appellate Procedure, and so on. It was like a map of place settings for a formal presidential dinner, and it was handed down from generation to generation. There was a routine for everything. With a few exceptions the clerks accepted their place-setting assignment with the seriousness with which it was made and were worried lest they misplace an item. But a few clerks thought it peculiar.

On one occasion Friendly found mail in his papers when he was sitting on an oral argument; he shouted at his clerk when he returned to chambers, but soon regained his equanimity. On another occasion on the bench Friendly was provided with the parties' briefs but not an appendix. He berated a lawyer in the case from the bench until she said she had filed one, and he then berated the clerk of the court for not delivering an appendix to his chambers until the clerk said he had. Learning of the problem, Friendly's law clerk, now Judge A. Raymond Randolph, found the appendix on the floor of the chambers and had to march down the aisle of the courtroom to hand it to the judge. Randolph awaited the judge's return with dread. When Friendly arrived, he stared at Randolph. "I don't know why," Randolph related, "but I started to laugh. The judge joined in. That was the end of it."[18]

Friendly's relentless adherence to routine and, to a somewhat lesser extent, to hierarchy struck all. Clerks, even some of the ones who were most satisfied with their experiences, were disappointed by his remoteness and his lack of rapport, along with his obsessive attention to detail and form. Friendly was an old-fashioned boss. Not unkindly, one clerk said that at times he felt like a private secretary to an official in the Austro-Hungarian Empire. Friendly had come from an era that was much more stratified, and his interest in history took him back even further. He tended not to see his clerks as individuals. One clerk said that Friendly tended to assume that a current clerk would know what he had told a prior year's clerk.

Friendly was not always considerate in accommodating employees' personal needs. He kept his secretary Elizabeth Flynn working the afternoon of Good Friday. That a clerk took the day off to attend his graduation from Harvard Law School—"there was no way my Polish father and Scottish mother were not going to attend my graduation"—seemed to annoy Friendly. Another clerk had to return to the office after his bachelor party and barely made it to the wedding. The wife of a clerk was due to give birth, and he did not know what to do about taking time off. He spoke to his wife, then called a couple of former clerks, "who wouldn't touch the issue." Finally, he left a note in the judge's inbox explaining the imminent birth along with the fact that he was to play an integral part in the delivery process, so that his role was almost as important as his wife's. That evening, when Friendly walked by the clerk's desk on his way home, he said, "Your role is not almost as important as your wife's." The clerk took a half day off. When another clerk called Friendly to tell him his wife had given birth that morning and he would not be in that day, Friendly's sole comment was, "See you tomorrow." The clerk thought it was funny.[19]

Friendly's chambers were a meritocracy. He had his favorite clerks, and he did not keep their names secret from his former clerks, members of law school faculties, and a number of judges and justices. In fact, if asked, he probably could have ranked his clerks from his favorite down, and the list would have correlated almost perfectly with his estimation of their ability. Topping his mental list of fifty-one clerks was Michael Boudin, with Pierre Leval a close second, both of whom served as sole clerks. Others he rated very highly included the early clerks David Currie and Bruce Ackerman, and the later clerks Raymond Randolph, Frederick Davis, William Bryson, Ruth Wedgwood, Merrick Garland, John Roberts Jr., and David Seipp. Of the eleven just mentioned, six became appellate judges, and four became professors.

Friendly also rated his clerks by how influential they were. First was Richard Daynard, who, he said at a clerks' reunion dinner, got him to change his mind more than any other clerk. He told one former clerk that the clerk who had come up with the most ideas was Bruce Ackerman, but, he asserted, "I didn't use a single one of them." He did, of course, but he may have made this remark because of Ackerman's unusually large number of ideas and his unquenchable enthusiasm for all of them.

Only one clerk had to leave early for not satisfactorily performing required duties, and even then Friendly made certain that the departing clerk received a good position. When Friendly recommended someone, whether as an applicant for a law school teaching job or for a nonacademic position, and the person performed unsatisfactorily, he blamed himself, which made the chambers an unhappy place.

In his last years Friendly had clerks go to Foley Square and track down a taxi for him and bring it to the courthouse steps, where he waited. Some clerks thought this task was inappropriate for former law students who were hired as law clerks, while others welcomed it because it gave them an opportunity to speak with the judge. Friendly dismissed their performance of tasks such as these to a fellow judge with the quip, "That's all they're good for." His sarcasm and denigrations were not characteristics that would endear him to everyone, but they may have been products of his difficulty in expressing affection. One person to whom Friendly could bring himself to speak candidly about his clerks, Judge Edward Weinfeld, assessed Friendly's views in a 1984 letter: "I assume you saw the profile in today's NY Times on William C. Bryson. With Pierre's [Leval] picture in the same paper two days ago, I suggest our Friendly, J., is swelling with pride—and justly so."[20]

Whether Friendly's remoteness was more an intellectual decision as to the proper judge-clerk relationship than the result of his inability to engage in a personal relationship is unclear, although occasional deviations from the norm suggest that it may have been the latter. For example, he took a few clerks to the theater. And when one of the later clerks told the judge in the spring that he was going to Italy and Greece with his girlfriend after the clerkship ended, Friendly prepared a ten-page handwritten program, including highlights of each hill town. Friendly may have been motivated by his passion for European culture, which he wanted others to share, but these actions were also one way he related to people. Perhaps it was also an attempt to break out of his shell.

With rare exceptions Friendly would see little of his clerks socially. Generally, a clerk had just one lunch with him, which took place on the last day and was known as "the Deficiency Lunch." It was ordinarily at Schrafft's, an upscale chain, and not at a club, where Friendly went with his equals. Along with presenting clerks with his autographed photograph, the evident purpose of the lunches was to provide evaluations. Some clerks wondered why he had not disclosed his criticisms earlier in their tenure.

Friendly and his wife had most clerks to their apartment for one dinner during the year, to which the clerk's spouse was invited—if one existed. Friendly did not see as part of his job description making the dinners particularly relaxing for the clerks. Sophie, however, tried to make them comfortable. Exceptions to the pattern included his monthly invitations to dine at his home that were extended to Peter Edelman, who was married to a federal judge's daughter; occasional dinner or theater invitations to Philip Bobbitt; a couple of dinners with Gregory Palm; and nearly monthly lunches with Todd Rakoff and Bobbitt.

Friendly was generally supportive in assisting clerks in obtaining Supreme Court clerkships and positions in the government and academia. However, he told one clerk at the start of the court term that he should not expect any assistance, and he provided damaging negative letters about people he felt were wanting. Former clerks asked Friendly to recommend them for membership in the American Law Institute, the Council on Foreign Relations, and the Harvard Club, and his files are replete with copies of his recommendations.

Once a clerk finished the year, the relationship with Friendly could become more congenial, open, and personal, a process that took many years for some and was never achieved by many. One clerk described the change as one from a distant relationship to Friendly's taking a "fatherly interest," and another clerk said that Friendly felt he had an alternative family. When they visited New York, many out-of-town former clerks would ask him to lunch, which he welcomed, although some felt awkward doing so.

After a few years on the bench Friendly began inviting his past and present clerks to an annual dinner at the Merchants Club, where former clerks, some uncomfortably, recited what they had accomplished in the preceding year. Sometimes a comment provoked Friendly, such as support for airline deregulation or a comparison of Louis Brandeis with Ralph Nader, both of which he sternly rejected. Reunion dinners continued after Friendly's death, although no longer on an annual basis. One of Friendly's clerks described the first reunion after he died: "We told each other nightmare stories, how he made you feel like crap. There was no feeling of hatred. It was like basic training—you come out the other end brutalized but the better for it."[21]

No clerk quite attained the position of Michael Boudin, who accompanied the Friendlys on a trip to Scotland and served as their driver. Boudin recalled that when he got lost, Friendly would mumble under his breath, "Mumble, mumble, cannot even figure out how to get there." Sophie would chirp in, "Now, dear, he's doing his best."

In the early 1980s the Friendlys were accompanied on a tour of the Cotswolds, near Oxford, by Boudin, Pierre Leval, Leval's wife, Susana (who totally captivated Friendly), Susana's mother, and the Levals' daughter, India, age five. Friendly got along wonderfully with India, but when the group arrived for lunch at an elegant restaurant and were told that children were not welcomed, Friendly let it be known that that was the Levals' problem. The Friendlys lunched with Boudin while the Levals went elsewhere.

Perhaps the most intriguing progression involved Philip Bobbitt, a Friendly clerk in 1975–1976. According to Bobbitt, he may have been the worst clerk Friendly ever had. "Like many great men, he was impatient. While he was a wonderful leader, I was not a good follower," Bobbitt admitted to me. His acknowledged deficits included failure to accommodate Friendly's demands for following office procedure on myriad little things. He had Friendly saying to himself, "I just don't know; I just don't know." Bobbitt was so unhappy that he asked the judge if he could leave early, something no one did. Friendly raised no objection.[22]

For reasons Bobbitt cannot fathom, he telephoned Friendly in 1979 to announce that he was working for Lloyd Cutler in the Carter White House. Friendly was delighted, in part because he regarded Cutler as perhaps the nation's best lawyer and in part because he liked his clerks to go into public service. The two saw each other often after that, mostly for lunch, and Friendly would talk to Bobbitt about politics, the legal academy, and his early professional life. Friendly told Bobbitt that although he had failed as a law clerk, he was hurt by Bobbitt's decision to leave early, a statement that shocked Bobbitt, mostly because he had trouble believing that anything he did could hurt the judge.

In his foreword to my biography of Judge Friendly, Judge Richard A. Posner cogently discussed the many facets of Friendly, the judge and the person. I end this essay with a lengthy excerpt.

> And something that may surprise some readers of the biography; brilliant people sometimes have great difficulty making productive use of other people. I am not speaking of delegation; there is too much of that among modern judges. It would have been a great waste of Friendly's time to have worked from opinion drafts of his law clerks, as most judges do nowadays, rather than writing his opinions himself, from scratch, as he did. But his clerks were very bright and energetic and could have helped more with research and even with critique of his drafts than they were allowed to do. He wasn't immodest, and he welcomed the occasional challenge from a clerk. But he didn't create an atmosphere conducive to eliciting criticisms and suggestions, or establish work protocols that would have maximized the clerks' contribution to his judicial decisions. He was so quick, so knowledgeable (having a photographic memory helped), and so experienced that he must have thought he could do everything faster and better than a law clerk could do anything—which may have been very close to the truth. The rapidity with which he wrote long opinions in nearly final form astonished the clerks; it astonishes me.[23]

Notes

A portion of this essay appears in a slightly different form in David M. Dorsen, *Henry Friendly, Greatest Judge of His Era* (Cambridge, Mass.: Harvard University Press, 2012).

1. Dorsen, *Henry Friendly*, 29.
2. Ibid., 69.
3. Ibid., 104.
4. Ibid.
5. Ibid.
6. Ibid.
7. Ibid.

8. Ibid.
9. Ibid.
10. Ibid., 105.
11. Ibid.
12. Ibid.
13. Ibid.
14. *Mayer v. Old Field Systems Corp.,* 721 F.2d 59, 66 (2d Cir. 1983).
15. Dorsen, *Henry Friendly,* 106.
16. Ibid., 107.
17. Ibid., 107–8.
18. Ibid., 108.
19. Ibid., 109.
20. Ibid., 110.
21. Ibid., 111.
22. Ibid., 112.
23. Richard A. Posner, foreword to Dorsen, *Henry Friendly,* xii.

ROBERT J. KACZOROWSKI

The Honorable A. Leon Higginbotham Jr.

T he jurist, legal scholar, writer, and historian A. Leon Higginbotham Jr., was an influential federal judge from 1964 to 1993. He was born in 1928 and raised in a poor, segregated black neighborhood outside Ewing Township, New Jersey, just a few miles from the statehouse in Trenton.[1] His mother was raised in rural Virginia, where, as a girl, she worked raising tobacco and attended a segregated school for a few months a year until the seventh grade, when her formal education ended. After immigrating to New Jersey, she worked as a maid. Leon's father was a factory worker in Trenton, as was his father's father before him. As a boy, Leon Higginbotham attended segregated public primary and secondary schools. Because his family was poor, he began working at the age of thirteen, and he worked his way through secondary school, college and law school.

The Judge continued to experience racial segregation and discrimination when he left Trenton and enrolled in Purdue University in 1944. Purdue's student body at that time consisted of six thousand white and twelve black students. The university restricted housing for the black students to the unheated attic of International House. During the winter months of his freshman year, Leon went to bed every night wearing earmuffs, and at times he also wore shoes or three or four pairs of socks and jackets to keep warm.[2] This experience prompted Leon to meet with the university president, Edward C. Elliott, and ask for permission to house the black students in one of the heated dorms, even on a segregated basis. Elliott refused. As the Judge recounted decades later, Elliot "looked me in the eye, and he said, 'Higginbotham, the law doesn't require us to let colored students in the dorm, we will never do it, and you either accept things as they are or leave the university immediately.'"[3] The harsh treatment he received from President Elliott persuaded Leon to change his career from engineering to law and to transfer to Antioch College in Yellow Springs, Ohio. The only other black student at the college was Coretta Scott, who later married Dr. Martin Luther King Jr.

While a student at Antioch, Leon Higginbotham was president of the school's chapter of the National Association for the Advancement of Colored People (NAACP). Judge Nathaniel R. Jones of the United States Court of Appeals for the Sixth Circuit played a similar role at Youngstown State University at the same time. As college students, Jones and Higginbotham met at a national NAACP conference in Warren, Ohio. Jones recalled that Higginbotham "manifested the magnificent power of articulation, the facet of his personality that ultimately became his trademark. But what impressed me the most about Leon on the occasion, and ever since," Jones reminisced, "was his passion for justice."[4] Jones explained that "Higginbotham, who was only a college sophomore at the time, seized the opportunity to urge the governor of Ohio to change his stance and support legislation that would lower the voting age to eighteen years. His argument was forceful and compelling; the governor soon took on the issue, and the legislation was passed."[5]

Leon Higginbotham graduated from Antioch College in the spring of 1949 and entered Yale Law School that fall. His admission to Yale preceded affirmative action and was clearly on merit. Indeed, he turned down a full tuition scholarship to Rutgers Law School for a partial scholarship to Yale granted by the Jessie Smith Noyes Foundation, which was created by the Wall Street "Dean of Real Estate," Charles Floyd Noyes.[6] Higginbotham was one of only three black students who entered Yale Law School in 1949, "but that was three times as many as had entered the previous year," he later recalled.[7] There were either no blacks or at most one in the entering classes of the other Ivy League law schools that year, he noted. The number of female law students in the nation's law schools was also miniscule. Moreover, "there was not one black on the faculty of any Ivy League law school, and there was not even a single black federal judge."[8]

There is some irony in the fact that Leon Higginbotham, as a member of Yale University's board of trustees, was instrumental in persuading Yale Law School to begin an affirmative action program that later benefited Clarence Thomas. Thomas became a strident opponent of affirmative action as a successor to the seat held by the first black Supreme Court Justice and civil rights activist, Thurgood Marshall; this was a seat to which Democrats and civil rights activists expected Leon Higginbotham would be appointed had Jimmy Carter won the 1980 presidential election, had Walter Mondale won the 1984 election, or had Michael Dukakis won the 1988 election.[9]

During his first year at Yale Law School, Higginbotham was assigned to Professor John P. Frank's Civil Procedure class. He quickly impressed Frank by what the professor characterized as "an extraordinary verbal talent."[10] Frank asked Higginbotham to work as his research assistant, and the two became friends.

At this time, John Frank was studying law and the history of race in the United States and assisting the NAACP in antidiscrimination cases.[11] Thurgood Marshall had asked Thomas I. Emerson and Frank to write a law professor's amicus curia brief supporting the NAACP's petition to grant certiorari in what was to become the landmark decision of *Sweatt v. Painter.* Fifty-two leading legal academics signed onto the brief.[12] Oral argument was eventually scheduled for April 3, 1950. Frank attended the oral argument, and he informed Justice Black that he wanted to bring one of his students with him. Justice Black made the arrangements for Higginbotham to attend.

This was the first time Higginbotham had traveled to Washington, D.C., and without Frank's intercession and Justice Black's arrangements, he would not have gained entry to the court that day. Not only was he admitted into the Supreme Court past the long lines of people hoping to hear the oral arguments in *Sweatt v. Painter,* but he actually sat in the courtroom with the justices' law clerks, the justices' family members and friends, and members of the Supreme Court bar!

As a federal judge, Higginbotham often shared his experiences of that day with his law clerks, recounting Thurgood Marshall's poignant argument for why the racially segregated Texas law school the state was building for black students could never be equal to the University of Texas at Austin Law School reserved exclusively for white students: "'How can it be that this law school, which does not have any alumni, can be equivalent to the University of Texas, which has so many members in the State House of Representatives, so many members in the State Senate . . .' And then he paused," Judge Higginbotham narrated. "It seemed like he stood before the podium for a full minute, and he said—'including one Justice'—looking directly at Tom Clark from the University of Texas—'who sits on this Court?'"[13]

One cannot exaggerate the powerful impact that Thurgood Marshall made on the twenty-one-year-old Leon Higginbotham that day. "As I listened to Thurgood Marshall's articulate and forceful argument," Higginbotham recalled decades later, "he seemed almost superhuman. Although counsel for other appellants were excellent craftsmen, Thurgood Marshall brought an extra emotional dimension to his presentation: he supported his argument with appropriate legal scholarship, but the tone of his voice expressed controlled outrage. He seemed to be asking why, four years after black veterans like Heman Sweatt and others helped crush Hitler and Hirohito on foreign battlefields, they still had to plead for the rudimentary justice available to other citizens without reservation."[14]

"As I left the Court that afternoon," he recounted, "I looked up again at the portals of that magnificent marble structure where 'Equal Justice Under Law' was etched. I felt confident that Thurgood Marshall and the NAACP would someday make the precept of equal justice a reality for all Americans, and I committed myself to join lawyers who would challenge this nation to eradicate governmentally enforced racism."[15]

Former Higginbotham law clerk John Q. Barrett captures the poignancy this experience held for the Judge when Higginbotham related it to John and his co-clerks in the 1980s: "It was, Higginbotham explained in emotional, impromptu remarks more than forty years later, 'an argument of such extraordinary eloquence that it gave me certain feelings of confidence which I needed and which I shall never forget.' Marshall's argument was, to Higginbotham, an eloquent assertion of the promise of equality not only for Heman Sweatt. It was, to Higginbotham, an assertion of his own equality too."[16] Barrett understood that that day at the Supreme Court was, and it remained, one of the most moving, defining moments of Leon Higginbotham's life.[17]

His student experience at Yale was also seminal for Leon Higginbotham. In his later life the Judge proclaimed that John Frank "will always be my professor ... what was really critical was that he took me seriously."[18] This relationship greatly affected a poor black kid from a racially segregated and marginalized area of Trenton, New Jersey, especially when he compared himself to more representative classmates at Yale. "We had people in our class who were grandchildren of Supreme Court Justices, who were children of Supreme Court Justices, individuals who were Rockefellers, who had power and influence—and John took me in. And I think he helped make me a far better lawyer than I otherwise would have been."[19]

Nonetheless, the Judge again experienced racial discrimination upon graduating from Yale in 1952. He graduated with honors, but major law firms refused to interview him because of his race,[20] and it must have been deeply hurtful to see these firms pursue white students with lesser credentials.[21] Dean Wesley Sturgis recommended Higginbotham to a Yale alumnus who was a partner in a major Philadelphia law firm without identifying his race. Believing Higginbotham to be a traditional Yale Law graduate, the partner wrote to Higginbotham expressing his eagerness to interview him. Impressed with his credentials, he commented that Higginbotham would have a problem deciding to accept which of the many law firm offers he would receive.[22] Dean Sturgis gave Leon money to buy a suit for his Philadelphia interview.

When he arrived at the law firm, he had difficulty persuading the secretary that he was the A. Leon Higginbotham Jr. from Yale Law School whom they were expecting. Having established his identity, he went into the Yale alumnus's office. The partner "looked me in the eye," the Judge later recalled, "and said, 'Marvelous record. Dean Sturges has written a great letter in your behalf. Of course you know there's nothing I can do for you, but I can give you the telephone number of two colored lawyers, and maybe they can help you.'"[23] Leon told the lawyer not to burden himself and described what happened next. "I went down the elevator of the Girard Trust Building, and I cried. I mean it. I cried because I thought of my mother. I thought of all the dishes she had washed, all the floors she had scrubbed, all the pain she had suffered. And after seven years [of college and law school], I couldn't get a job."[24] Major law firms refused to hire him because of his race.

Higginbotham began his legal career as a law clerk to Justice Curtis Bok of the Superior Court of Pennsylvania. Justice Bok was the father of Derek Curtis Bok, who later served as Harvard Law School's dean (1968–1971) and Harvard University's president (1971–1991). After his clerkship, Higginbotham became the youngest and first African American to be appointed an assistant district attorney for the city of Philadelphia. In 1954, he established a law firm with four colleagues. He also served in several positions for the state of Pennsylvania and as president of the Philadelphia chapter of the NAACP.

His early life experiences contributed to his becoming "a powerful, passionate and committed advocate for equal opportunity for all individuals . . . and fair treatment regardless of race or religion."[25] They also contributed to his personal commitment to Justice Hugo Black's vision of judges "'as havens of refuge for those who might otherwise suffer because they are helpless, weak, out-numbered, or . . . are non-conforming victims of prejudice and public excitement.'"[26]

President John F. Kennedy appointed Higginbotham to the Federal Trade Commission in 1962. At the age of thirty-four, he became the youngest person to be appointed to the FTC.[27] He was also the first African American appointed to a federal regulatory commission.[28] President Kennedy's brother, Attorney General Robert F. Kennedy, got to know Commissioner Higginbotham through his work on the FTC, his work on behalf of the Kennedy administration, and his visits to the Kennedy White House. The attorney general recommended to President Kennedy that he appoint Commissioner Higginbotham to the U.S. District Court for the Eastern District of Pennsylvania. The president nominated Higginbotham in 1963, but Leon was again confronted with racism when the segregationist senator from Mississippi and chairman of the Senate Judiciary Committee, James Eastland, blocked the appointment.[29]

After President Kennedy's assassination, President Lyndon Johnson appointed Higginbotham to the federal district court in Philadelphia in a recess appointment in January 1964. Ascending the bench one month before his thirty-sixth birthday, Judge Higginbotham was the youngest person ever appointed to the federal court for the Eastern District of Pennsylvania. The Senate confirmed the appointment later that year. While serving as a federal district court judge, Higginbotham became a valued adviser to President Johnson, who also appointed him to the Commission on the Causes and Prevention of Violence, following the assassinations of Rev. Martin Luther King Jr. and Senator Robert F. Kennedy. He later named Higginbotham vice chairman of the National Advisory Commission on Civil Disorders, known as the Kerner Commission, to investigate the causes of the 1967 race riots that occurred in many of the nation's cities. President Johnson later characterized Judge Higginbotham as "one of my closest advisers, sound, reliable, responsible."[30]

President Jimmy Carter elevated Judge Higginbotham to the United States Court of Appeals for the Third Circuit in 1977. He was the fourth African American to become a federal appeals court judge. The other three were William H. Hastie Jr., whom Higginbotham replaced and whose chambers overlooking Independence Hall and Mall he inherited, Thurgood Marshall, whom President Kennedy appointed to the Second Circuit Court of Appeals in 1961, and Spotswood Robinson III of the Court of Appeals for the District of Columbia. While he served as a federal judge, Leon Higginbotham wrote over 650 opinions, over fifty articles, and published two award-winning books.[31] He taught at some of the nation's leading law schools, including the University of Pennsylvania, Yale, Harvard, Stanford, University of Michigan, and New York University, and he served as an influential trustee of Yale and the University of Pennsylvania.

The Judge and His Law Clerks

In all he did, Judge Higginbotham immersed his entire being. Fulfilling his responsibilities on the bench, conducting his research and writing, and, most importantly, interacting with and developing relationships with his law clerks were of deep personal concern to him. His relationships with his law clerks transcended professional collegiality. He strove to develop personal connections with each of his law clerks. He got to know and to interact with them on a personal level, not simply on a professional level.

Not surprisingly, therefore, Judge Higginbotham was personally involved at every stage in the clerkship selection process. He reviewed each candidate's application; he personally selected each candidate to be interviewed; and he personally interviewed and selected each candidate to whom he made an offer. The Judge used the interview to get the measure of the interviewee's personality and character.

For example, when I interviewed with the Judge I was married and had two teenage sons. The Judge had three children who were older than my sons in addition to a son about the age of my two. He and I talked about the challenges and strains of fatherhood presented by demanding and time-consuming careers and how we dealt with them. I was gratified to learn that the Judge and I had similar struggles and shared similar insights and attitudes in this regard. Our revealing discussion persuaded me that he and I were kindred souls in certain important respects.

Professor Derrick Bell, who regarded Leon Higginbotham as his mentor, noted that the Judge was unlike most judges in that he did not assume that black law school graduates did not have the ability of serving as his law clerks; Higginbotham was one of the few federal judges to whom Bell could refer black students for a clerkship "with the assurance that their clerkship applications would be given serious consideration even if they were not at the top of their classes and editors of their schools' law reviews. And yet, his lengthy list of former clerks, including Eleanor Holmes Norton, Ron Noble, Kathleen Cleaver, and Ed S. G. Dennis, reads like a who's who of people of color whose careers were launched as a result of Higginbotham's great mentoring. He was not afraid of ignoring tradition in the furtherance of justice."[32]

The federal circuit courts ordinarily decide appeals in three-judge panels. Each judge is randomly assigned to a panel. When I served as a law clerk to Judge Higginbotham in the early 1980s, he was selected for seven panels, or sittings, per year. Each panel received about forty cases on appeal. The Judge distributed ten cases to each of his three law clerks. He assumed exclusive responsibility for the other ten cases.

The clerks reviewed the case files and prepared a memorandum of law for each assigned case that summarized the facts, the issues presented to the court for review, the relevant rules of law for each issue, the appropriate application of the law to the facts to resolve each issue along with an analysis explaining why the clerk believed each issue should be decided as he or she recommended.

The clerks returned the case files with their memoranda of law to the Judge when they finished their reviews of assigned cases.

Judge Higginbotham studied the cases assigned to his law clerks as carefully as he did the cases he prepared on his own. Indeed, he instructed us that thorough case preparation was the first principle of good judging. I learned at that first sitting that Judge Higginbotham knew the cases better than the lawyers who argued before him. "He had a photographic memory and was renowned for having an absolute command of the record in cases he handled," commented my co-clerk Ron Noble.[33] Judge Edward Becker emphasized this quality when he observed that Judge Higginbotham would come to oral arguments "with a knowledge of the briefs and the record that would knock counsels' socks off. I have encountered lawyers who, a decade later, remembered those searching questions, boomed at them over the half glasses in a voice that would have made Stentor green with envy. Even more memorable, is the sheer eloquence of his delivery."[34] Understandably, I felt so privileged to be associated with him.

Notwithstanding his thorough, careful preparation, the Judge was always open to discussing the views of his clerks, especially when their views differed from his. I experienced these qualities shortly after I joined Judge Higginbotham's chambers. Seven of the ten cases assigned to me that sitting, in my view, were what then–chief judge Ruggero Aldisert called "sure-pop J.O.s."

These were cases in which the district court's decision was clearly correct and should be affirmed on the lawyers' briefs and without oral argument. I recommended the other three of my assigned cases for oral argument with a view to reversing the district court's decisions. After he had reviewed my assigned cases and memoranda of law, Judge Higginbotham called me into his chambers. I felt a bit anxious over what was about to happen. The Judge, however, quickly put me at ease, and from that time I always felt his support and regard, even when I made mistakes. As it turned out, the Judge and I agreed on all but one of my cases.

Our disagreement concerned a case involving a charitable health care provider, Community Health Services (CHS) of Crawford County, in a rural, impoverished, and medically underserved county in western Pennsylvania.[35] The U.S. Department of Health, Education and Welfare (HEW) sought to recoup what it claimed were overpayments HEW made to CHS under Medicare cost-reimbursement procedures. CHS filed suit against the secretary and HEW, asking the district court to enjoin the defendants from seeking the claimed reimbursement. The district court decided the case against CHS in a summary manner, and CHS appealed.

Briefly, the facts of the case were compelling, in my view. Since 1966 CHS was under contract with the federal government to provide health care services under the Medicare provisions of the Social Security Act. In 1975 CHS entered a contract with Mercer County Consortium Services, Inc. by which it was to employ participants in a program established under the Comprehensive Employment and Training Act of 1973 (CETA). The CETA program was designed to provide job training and experience for unemployed individuals to enhance their future employability. CETA workers enabled CHS to expand the range of services it provided to meet the mushrooming demand for health services in the economically depressed area it served. Medicare regulations provided that grants or gifts its providers received must be used to pay operating expenses and must be set off against expenses submitted to Medicare for reimbursement in the provider's annual cost reports.

These regulations, however, also provided an exception to mandated offsets for "Seed Money Grants." "Seed Money" was defined in the Provider Reimbursement Manual as "grants designated for the development of new health care agencies or for expansion of services of established agencies." From 1975 to 1979, the units of service CHS provided exploded from four thousand to over a hundred thousand. CETA grants never covered more than 25 percent of CHS's costs. The central question was whether the grants CHS received under CETA should be deducted from the expenses it submitted to Medicare for reimbursement.

CHS faithfully followed administrative procedures to find an answer to this question. The administrative process precluded providers such as CHS from presenting inquiries directly to the secretary of HEW. Rather, the provider was required to ascertain an answer from the HEW's agent. In response to CHS's inquiries on five different occasions over a two and one-half year period, HEW's agent advised CHS that the CETA grants constituted seed money and were therefore exceptions to the Medicare offsets. Relying on these assurances that it would be reimbursed, CHS made expenditures in excess of $70,000. CHS also submitted its cost reports without offsetting its CETA grants from reimbursable costs, and the agent approved CHS's reports for three years. CHS used the additional money.

It turned out that the government's procedures required the department's agent to send CHS's inquiries to an HEW administrator in Washington and not to answer them itself. The agent finally did comply with required administrative procedures and referred CHS's inquiries to the proper administrator in Washington after three years. The HEW administrator decided that the CETA funds did not qualify for the seed money exception and demanded that they be offset against CHS's reimbursable costs. CHS pursued administrative remedies but was unsuccessful. It then filed this civil action for injunctive relief, but the district court entered summary judgment in favor of the government.

On appeal, CHS claimed that the secretary of HEW should be estopped from recovering the overpayments because his agent's affirmative misconduct induced CHS to include in its expense reports costs that were covered by CETA grants. The doctrine on which CHS relied is known as equitable estoppel. It prohibits a litigant from asserting a claim or a defense against another party who has detrimentally changed his position in reliance on the litigant's misrepresentation or failure to disclose some material fact. Equitable estoppel had never been applied against the federal government by the United States Supreme Court and only rarely by a lower federal court.

Judge Higginbotham made his law clerks mindful of the fact that the Third Circuit Court's decisions are subject to review and reversal by the Supreme Court. He emphasized the need to adhere to judicial precedent. You may have already surmised that Judge Higginbotham disagreed with my analysis and conclusions regarding this case. In addition to the absence of precedent supporting the application of equitable estoppel against the federal government, he noted that the amount of money involved in this case, while enough to put CHS out of business and virtually deprive the people of Crawford County of health services, on a national scale was insignificant. He also pointed out that reversing the lower court would set a precedent that could be applied not only to HEW but to every government department, including the Department of Defense, which had budgets in the billions of dollars. The court's decision in this case could set a very dangerous and costly precedent against the federal government.

Moreover, that the Supreme Court had never applied equitable estoppel against the federal government rendered our court vulnerable to reversal. "We can't decide cases on sentiment," the Judge admonished. However much one might want to reverse the district court and ensure that CHS would continue to provide the people of Crawford County with health care, Judge Higginbotham continued, "We are bound by the law." "Are you sure of the law, Bob," the Judge asked me. "Yes, Judge," I replied, but with measurably less confidence than at the beginning of our conversation. "Okay, I'll take another look and get back to you," he said.

When he did, Judge Higginbotham dictated five questions to me. "Go into the trial transcript and find the answers to these questions," he instructed. Frankly, I don't remember the Judge's questions. But I do remember realizing that the answers to these questions would either establish the government's misconduct requiring reversal of the lower court or confirm the correctness of the district court's decision. I was so impressed with the Judge's manifest genius.

I was also inspired by his dedication to the rule of law. This case dramatically demonstrated that principles and values embedded in the rule of law did not always coincide with what one might regard as the right result. The Judge demonstrated his commitment to principled judging according to the rule of law over his personal views and preferences. His example inspired my own unwavering commitment to finding the answers that led to the principled result under the law. The Judge's example has been my inspiration ever since.

My reexamination of the case file discovered the answers to the five questions Judge Higginbotham posed, and they persuaded him that the district court had erred. He asked that the case be scheduled for oral argument. I was feeling pretty good until the day of oral argument neared, and I got a call from a law clerk in Chief Judge Ruggero Aldisert's chambers. "Why did Judge Higginbotham schedule the CHS case for oral argument?" the clerk aggressively asked me. My heart sank when he added, "Judge Aldisert thinks this case is a sure-pop J.O. He doesn't understand why Higginbotham wants oral argument. Neither does Judge Meanor," a district court judge who was sitting by designation as the third member of the circuit court panel. You can understand why my anxiety shot up out of my head. I thought, my first sitting with Judge Higginbotham, the initial test of how much he can or cannot count on me, and I've screwed up.

My anxiety persisted to oral argument. The CHS case was called, CHS's lawyer presented his argument, and then it was the government's lawyer's turn. He had hardly begun when Judge Higginbotham interrupted with the first question. The government lawyer evaded answering the question. Judge Higginbotham rephrased the question and asked it again, and again the lawyer evaded answering. The Judge rephrased and asked it a third time, and when the lawyer again was evasive, Judge Aldisert leaned into the microphone, his face red with rage, and demanded that the lawyer answer Judge Higginbotham's question. Throwing himself back into his chair, Judge Aldisert uttered an expletive that echoed throughout the courtroom. The lawyer answered the question; and he answered the other four questions Judge Higginbotham put to him, and, in so doing, he lost his case. In that moment and during the arguments of the other cases scheduled that day, I felt so proud of Judge Higginbotham, who demonstrated why the legal community regarded him as one of the most learned judges of his time. I was also proud of myself and grateful for having the privilege of serving as his law clerk.

When the CHS case and the other cases were concluded, the three judges held their conference over lunch. Following the conference Judge Higginbotham returned to chambers and met with his clerks. He critiqued the lawyers in each case and used their performances to teach us techniques of good lawyering and pitfalls of bad lawyering. The Judge mentored us in this way after every oral argument. Judge Becker knew that "at heart, [Judge Higginbotham is] a teacher. It is well known that he has taught countless students at the University of Pennsylvania and at other institutions. Less well known is how much he has taught a generation of law clerks and interns."[36] His mentoring was among the most important aspects of my experience with Judge Higginbotham. I also learned more about lawyering in the sixteen months of my clerkship than I did in three years of law school.

At these postconference meetings with his law clerks, the Judge informed us of the panel's decisions. I am happy to report that Judge Aldisert was persuaded that the trial court in the estoppel case had erred, and he joined Judge Higginbotham in reversing the district court's decision. Not surprisingly, Aldisert assigned the opinion to Higginbotham, which meant that I would help the Judge write the opinion. Judge Aldisert signed onto the opinion, which concluded that "under the egregious facts of this case and in view of the affirmative misconduct of the government's agent . . . we will reverse the judgment of the district court."[37]

We were not surprised to learn that the government appealed the decision to the Supreme Court, which granted certiorari. The Supreme Court reversed the Third Circuit's decision.[38] The Court held that the government was not estopped from recovering the funds in question because CHS did not demonstrate that the elements of estoppel were present in its change in position or its reliance on the agent's advice.[39] The Court defined "estoppel" as "an equitable doctrine invoked to avoid injustice in a particular case."[40] No injustice was done, the Court explained, because CHS was never entitled to the funds it received and was required to repay the government.[41] In addition, the Court concluded that CHS's reliance on the informal, oral advice of the government's agent was not reasonable.[42] The fundamental difference between the Supreme Court and the Third Circuit was their respective interpretations of the facts.

Ronald K. Noble was the Judge's senior law clerk from August 1982 to August 1984. My clerkship with Judge Higginbotham covered most of this period. I left at the end of December 1983. Ron and I estimate that the Judge worked about eighteen hours a day, including weekends.[43] We both worked a regular business day during the business week. However, I covered the nights, and Ron covered the weekends. Because I was married and had two adolescent sons, the Judge made sure I had the weekends off.

Over the two years he clerked for Judge Higginbotham, Ron only had one day off. Ron recalled that during his two-year clerkship, the Judge never took one full day off. In describing Judge Higginbotham the man, Judge Becker acknowledges that he was "incredibly hard working. Leon Higginbotham has given that term new meaning."[44] "The hours he logged," Ron recounted, "and the work he produced would scare most rational human beings."[45] Ron formed an especially close relationship with Judge Higginbotham, whom he came to regard as his second father.

Eleanor Holmes Norton, Judge Higginbotham's first law clerk, recounted how the Judge "came to the bench with both a black man's racial identity and a judge's understanding of equality as a universal principle beyond race. His commitment to equality was a constant throughout his magnificent life."[46] She quickly discovered that "Leon was a born mentor." He never allowed

> his position to come between himself and his clerks. . . . The clerk was not only an apprentice, but also an extension of the Judge. We both wrote and we both did research because everything had to be so thoroughly researched. I edited his work and he edited mine. Though his clerk and a novice lawyer, the Judge treated me as a peer. The natural teacher was to become an actual teacher, and the Judge taught in universities for years before he left the bench. The court, where his work habits were legendary, did not begin to use up his enormous energy and talents. Nor, of course, did teaching. [47]

But the Judge "was not all work or all law. There was fun, lots of fun."

As Eleanor and Ron suggested, Judge Higginbotham was a great mentor to his law clerks. Former law clerk Audrey G. McFarlane[48] eloquently remarked on the Judge's nurturing relationship at his retirement: "For me personally, what remains most prominent in my mind about my clerkship was the wonderful way in which you taught, nurtured and inspired your law clerks. It was awe inspiring to watch you tirelessly work on court business while taking time out to share your vast knowledge with your law clerks. . . . Through it all, you maintained an impressively modest and gracious demeanor, never failing to generously give credit to those around you who may have contributed in some way."[49] Other law clerks commented on the example the Judge gave us of compassion, integrity, intellectual rigor, and tireless dedication to doing justice that characterizes the legal and judicial process at its best.[50]

The Judge's relationships with his law clerks inspired in them a fierce loyalty and devotion to him. "No judge . . . has ever had a more devoted cadre of law clerks and interns than Leon Higginbotham," Judge Becker commented. "They worked countless weekends, and some stayed on many weeks after their tour of duty was up, because of their reverence for this man." [51] Ann Whatley Chain succinctly explained why this was so:

> Law clerks to Judge Higginbotham had more than a working relationship. Once you join the family, Judge Higginbotham becomes a close friend, a surrogate father and a lifetime mentor. As a friend, he shares with us his experiences, both good and bad, and allows us to see him as a human being. Like a father, he discusses the value of money, the need to live within your means, and worries about your personal safety and happiness. As a lifetime mentor, his door is always open to those who seek his advice on important decisions or want to share with him their problems and successes. [52]

Many of his law clerks maintained their relationships with the Judge for years after their clerkships ended.

Judge Higginbotham credited Yale law professor Frank for providing him with a model for the Judge's activities as a mentor, teacher, and scholar. "The opportunity that John [Frank] gave me was very important," he declared in an impromptu speech in 1993. "I've always felt in my days of teaching that I respect the John Franks." [53] Emphasizing his role as mentor, he addressed the following words to his law clerks, particularly to those who were present for his impromptu speech: "If I transmit anything to the many law clerks I see here— all of you know I respect you and love you and admire you as students—it is partially because of the legacy I got at Yale and some extraordinarily wonderful people I met there who gave me confidence that the pursuit of justice is not an inappropriate profession for a lawyer." [54]

Judge Becker commented that he had "never met anyone who worked as prodigiously and effectively at so many things for so many years as Leon Higginbotham. His weekend work schedule is legendary." [55] Judge Higginbotham was driven by his passionate commitment to the equality of every person throughout the world. He was not just a judge, scholar, professor, and writer; he was a national and international public figure. On weekends and evenings, the Judge split his attention between his court work and his personal work.

Not so well known is the fact that the Judge hired secretaries for the evenings and the weekends and paid them out of his own pocket to avoid any possible conflicts of interest or of using government funds for his personal activities. He also had a separate telephone line dedicated to these personal activities for which he paid personally. Finally, the Judge also hired his own research assistants to help him with his scholarship. He never used his law clerks to help him with his speech writing or his academic and scholarly activities.

Assessing the Judge

Over the course of his twenty-nine years on the bench, Judge Higginbotham achieved the stature and reputation of a great judge devoted to the craft of judging, which was "reflected in his superbly crafted opinions."[56] Nevertheless, his court of appeals colleague and friend for over two decades, Judge Becker, marveled at how little the Judge changed as he achieved greatness in fact and in reputation as a federal judge. "Simply put, Leon Higginbotham, the man, is today the same nice guy he has always been—down to earth, warm, sincere, self-deprecating, possessed of a wonderful sense of humor (and a delightful giggle) and, above all, of a marvelous capacity for friendship."[57] He was in all he did and with whomever he interacted a genuine person. A man of great intellect, talents, and accomplishments, "he was, at his core, truly a modest person who preferred to focus on others rather than himself."[58]

One of Higginbotham's first law clerks later commented on the Judge's modesty and humility, noting, "from the first day on the job, I was struck with how the Judge went out of his way to accord respect to the people who were at the lower end of the courthouse bureaucracy. He knew all the elevator operators and file clerks by name and treated them with as much respect as the senior partners of the big law firms. If they had a problem, he tried to help them. . . . One would think that after having achieved so much success at such a young age, there might have been a hint of arrogance in the man; there was none, although he had tremendous self-confidence."[59]

My experience as Judge Higginbotham's clerk confirms the assessments of his excellence as a lawyer, jurist, and scholar made by Judge Becker and other jurists. Justice Thurgood Marshall said Judge Higginbotham was "a great lawyer and a very great judge. Period."[60] Judge Guido Calabresi elaborated his understanding of what makes a great judge in describing Judge Higginbotham:

> [A] judge also needs to be articulate in writing and in speech. And anyone who has read what Leon has written or who has heard him speak knows that there is no person in public life today more brilliantly articulate than

he ... yet even articulateness—as dazzling as Leon's is—pales next to his other qualities. To be truly great a judge needs wisdom, that sense of balance which allows one to weigh what cannot be measured, generosity of spirit, that compassion which causes one to know what it is like to be in trouble and in pain, and to desire instinctively to reach out and help, and above all courage, that fire which compels one to do what is right though the heavens—and one's own career—may fall. Wisdom, generosity and courage ... all these Leon Higginbotham has in the fullest of measures. Joined with his extraordinary articulateness, intelligence and learning they have made him a judge whose greatness is unchallengeable, and a person whom it is a blessing to count as a friend and teacher.[61]

Justice William Brennan characterized Judge Higginbotham as the "conscience for the legal profession."[62] Professor Derrick Bell, elaborating why he was the profession's conscience, observed, "Higginbotham saw each honor he received as an opportunity to speak the truth to those who hold positions of prestige and power."[63] Bell then recounted the Judge's speech at the one-hundredth anniversary of the *Harvard Law Review*, a black-tie event. The Judge spoke for well over one hour detailing the failings of Harvard law graduates in the area of race law even as they served on the Supreme Court, in private practice, and as scholarly contributors to the *Harvard Law Review*. Judge Higginbotham concluded by declaring:

Lawyers must be the visionaries in our society. We must be the nation's legal architects who renovate the palace of justice and redesign the landscape of opportunity in our nation. The policy choices that lawyers promote will have far more significance for our children and our grandchildren than will the credentials that we wield as we confront the intricacies of government and private enterprise. If lawyers are to play the important social and moral roles that I believe we can and should, we must begin by recognizing that our nation's basic human problems ... [of] poverty, hatred, malnutrition, inadequate health care and housing, corruption in government, and the failures of our public school system continue to haunt us today because those in power often have lacked personal morality or have failed to make real the values that they have professed to hold in the abstract. To paraphrase Justice Holmes, the life of the law must not be mere logic; it must also be values. Each lawyer—whether judge or politician, professor or entrepreneur—must make personal judgments. Those critical moral and human values cannot be acquired by even the most meticulous reading of opinions or statutes. Each lawyer must consciously and constantly assess his or her values and goals in forging rules of law for the future.[64]

Judge Higginbotham admonished the lawyers "to evaluate how successful we have been as a profession in moving towards the goal of social and legal justice for all, whether we are striving as valiantly as possible to achieve the kind of world that Dr. Martin Luther King, Jr. envisioned when he said, 'I have the audacity to believe that people everywhere can have three meals a day for their bodies, education and culture for their minds, and dignity, equality and freedom for their spirits.'"[65] He then challenged the distinguished members of the audience with the following questions:

> Where will each of you stand? Will you be aligned with those forces that expand the horizons of opportunity for the weak, the poor, the powerless, and the many who have not our options? Or will you become members of the indulgent new majority in our society who seem to feel that the quality of morality in our nation's public life is unimportant as long as they have good salaries and comfortable suburban homes or luxurious condominiums in the city? Will you as a lawyer merely become a technical expert, detached and indifferent? Will you be concerned solely with obtaining the highest fees for the least amount of effort, untroubled by the quality of life in our nation or world? Or will you care enough to make a difference?[66]

My co-clerk, Ronald Noble,[67] added context to these statements and a third distinguishing quality of the Judge: "Throughout his tenure on the federal bench, Judge Higginbotham endeavored to do justice as a jurist, striving not only to help those less fortunate than himself, but also to train those who sought to follow in his footsteps. He set a remarkable example in the way that he conducted himself—always fair, decent, and caring."[68]

Judge Nathaniel R. Jones agreed. "Throughout his long and illustrious career, Judge Higginbotham never lost his passion [for justice] nor did he, for a moment, cease teaching and inspiring others to enlist in the campaign to make our nation and our world a more just place to live."[69] His "fundamental objective was to bring about systemic change. As a lawyer, he was unrelenting in his efforts to remove the injustices that hobbled the powerless. As a jurist, he demonstrated a deep and abiding fidelity to his oath to uphold the Constitution and a powerful commitment to make its promise relevant to even the most humble citizens."[70] When he was in a position to remedy injustice, he did not hesitate to ensure that justice was done. When his judicial colleagues adhered to precedents that stood in the way of the just outcome that he believed the Constitution required, Judge Higginbotham used his pen to expose the fallacies of the majority's positions. In powerful and reasoned dissenting opinions, he set forth pathways to fair results that were consistent with the Constitution and sound public policy."[71]

But Judge Higginbotham was no ideologue who disregarded judicial precedent or statutory law. He "was respectful of the American legal system," Judge Jones proclaimed. "When the law simply did not allow for the fair outcome that he desired, the Judge dutifully enforced it."[72] But this did not stop him from advocating for change. "What really distinguished Judge Higginbotham apart from most of his judicial colleagues," Judge Jones recounted with undisguised admiration, "was his understanding that a judge's responsibility for the fair administration of justice was not restricted to the bench."[73] As a scholar, Higginbotham "developed a deep and profound understanding of the vestiges of slavery that corrupted and distorted our nation's solemn institutions and how they continued to hold sway over our lives. His personal encounters with racism and intolerance served as constant reminders of the urgent need to eradicate 'root and branch' bigotry of all kinds. . . . He audaciously ventured beyond the courtroom into other venues where he felt he could affect the way justice was administered. It was that resolve that no doubt led his friend, the late Justice William Brennan, to call Judge Higginbotham "[the] conscience for the profession."[74]

The Judge enjoyed an extraordinary reputation among his peers on the bench and at the bar.[75] He is remembered as a judicial activist. As I have already demonstrated, he was an excellent technical lawyer and was highly regarded for his principled decisions and opinions.[76] As Judge Becker noted and I can attest, "his jurisprudence was always anchored in the record."[77] Collin Seitz, fellow Third Circuit judge, commented that Higginbotham was "orthodox on most areas of the law." [78] His gift, though, was to weave progress with orthodoxy.[79] His law school professor and mentor, John P. Frank, characterized the Judge's opinions as "comprehensive, carefully analytical, and [he] never brushed aside the hard point by pretending it is not there. The observation Judge Learned Hand once made concerning Justice Benjamin Cardozo is fairly applicable here. 'He never disguised the difficulties, as lazy judges do who win the game by sweeping all the chessmen off the table: like John Stuart Mill, he would often begin by stating the other side better than his advocate has stated it himself.'"[80]

Judge Higginbotham's description of his judicial philosophy put him in the "living constitution" school of jurisprudence. He aligned his judicial philosophy with that of Justice Cardozo, a view of law that is "an evolutionary concept in terms of what is fair and just in a society."[81] He rejected strict constructionism and criticized strict constructionists as inconsistent, and I would say hypocritical, in that they "want an original intent to support and justify their conservative positions, and an evolutionary understanding of law in order to protect their conservative positions."[82]

Judge Higginbotham's jurisprudence was strongly influenced by Thurgood Marshall, whom the Judge considered his judicial mentor. Higginbotham acknowledged Justice Marshall's profound impact on him, stating:

> Because of what he did and how he did it, Thurgood Marshall made me believe that I had a place in American society. Even when I faced racial discrimination, I honestly believed that I had a "right" to good education, decent housing and access to public accommodations. I also came to understand, by the example of Justice Marshall's work, that one can overcome seemingly insurmountable obstacles with intelligent preparation, firm resolve, self-confidence and an unflagging commitment to principle. Thurgood Marshall was, for me, living proof that "nigger" was not a term that could define my existence. He, like Dr. Martin Luther King, helped me to understand that I should never bow to discrimination in pursuing my goals.[83]

And Judge Higginbotham didn't. He advocated, in his words, "what Chief Justice Warren, Justice Brennan, Justice Blackmun, and Justice Marshall and others have called the evolutionary movement of the Constitution," and he urged Clarence Thomas to follow in their footsteps on Thomas's appointment to the U.S. Supreme Court.[84]

Judge Higginbotham retired from the federal bench in 1993, but he did not retire from teaching and actively working on behalf of human rights for the weak, the poor, and the powerless, both in the United States and abroad. He relocated outside of Boston after his appointment as Public Service Professor of Jurisprudence at the Harvard University John F. Kennedy School of Government, and he also taught in the university's Department of Afro-American Studies and in the Harvard Law School. At the same time, he served as a commissioner on the United States Commission on Civil Rights and was appointed of counsel at the kind of white shoe law firm that would not even interview him when he graduated from Yale Law School in 1952. The New York firm was Paul,

Weiss, Rifkind, Wharton & Garrison, which named him one of three senior counsels in 1998. He was also the firm's elder statesman.[85] The Judge's work at Paul, Weiss was primarily pro bono on behalf of equal rights and constitutional protections of individual rights. For example, he advised the South African Children's Fund established by that country's president, Nelson Mandela. In his "retirement," the Judge continued his efforts to abolish the South African system of racial apartheid and to establish a constitution that guaranteed democratic elections and equal rights for all South Africans, regardless of race or gender. He visited South Africa six times and traveled throughout the country to witness apartheid firsthand. He worked with such organizations as the Southern African Legal Services, Legal Education Project, and the Southern Africa Project of the Lawyers Committee for Civil Rights Under Law.[86]

The Judge was one of the founders of the South Africa Free Election Fund, which raised millions of dollars to promote free elections there. Nelson Mandela selected Judge Higginbotham to be an international mediator to assure the integrity of South African elections. Mandela also selected him to assist in creating the post-apartheid South African Constitution and to create a South African constitutional court.[87] Needless to say, he was a close adviser to Nelson Mandela, who, on the Judge's death in 1998, wrote to the Higginbotham family: "[His] work and the example he set made a critical contribution to the course of the rule of law in the United States and a difference in the lives of African Americans, and indeed the lives of all Americans. But his influence also crossed borders and inspired many who fought for freedom and equality in other countries.... Judge Higginbotham played an important role in [South Africa's] first democratic elections, supported the development of public interest law work in South Africa and helped to create broader opportunities for black South African lawyers."[88] Indeed, one of the judge's law clerks for 1986–87, Sandile Ngcobo, went on to serve as chief justice of the Constitutional Court of South Africa.

In 1995 President Bill Clinton awarded Judge Higginbotham the Presidential Medal of Freedom, the nation's highest civilian honor, for working "tirelessly to advance the needs of those who have long been denied access to the American Dream."[89] As a boy whose race made him an object of legally enforced racial discrimination, combined with his impoverished economic circumstances, Leon Higginbotham started out in life as one who was denied access to the American Dream. Yet, he rose above discrimination's oppressive force and his boyhood poverty to become one of the nation's leading litigators and jurists, and an active participant in the legal struggle to dismantle the American system of racial apartheid and to broaden all Americans' access to the American dream.

Notes

1. A. Leon Higginbotham Jr., "The Dream with Its Back against the Wall—A Speech by A. Leon Higginbotham" (1989), in 46 *Yale Law Report* 34 (Spring 1990).

2. Higginbotham, "Dream."

3. Ibid. The judge also experienced discrimination as a member of Purdue's debate team. When traveling, he was unable to stay in a hotel with the other team members, who were white. A. Leon Higginbotham Jr., interview by Joe B. Frantz, October 7, 1976, Oral History Interview, LBJ Library, 1, http://www.lbjlibrary.net/collections/oral -histories/higginbotham-a.-leon-jr.html.

4. Nathaniel R. Jones, "Tribute to the Honorable A. Leon Higginbotham, Jr. for the Rutgers Law Review," *Rutgers Law Review* 53 (2000): 567–68.

5. Ibid.

6. Higginbotham, "Dream."

7. William J. Brennan Jr. et al., "A Tribute to Justice Thurgood Marshall," *Harvard Law Review* 105, no. 1 (1991): 55, 59.

8. Ibid.

9. Lincoln Caplan, "Judging Leon Higginbotham," *American Bar Association Journal* 82 (1996): 68, 69, 72; Louis H. Pollak, "A. Leon Higginbotham, Jr.: I Felt That Justice Could Overcome Anything," *University of Pennsylvania Law Review* 142 (1993): 541, 542.

10. John Q. Barrett, "Teacher, Student, Ticket: John Frank, Leon Higginbotham, and One Afternoon at the Supreme Court: Not a Trifling Thing," *Yale Law & Policy Review* 20, no. 2 (2002): 314.

11. Ibid., 312.

12. Ibid., 312–13.

13. Ibid., 319 quoting A. Leon Higginbotham, "Impromptu Remarks at the Alliance for Justice's Annual Law Day Luncheon," June 1993; Memorandum from Nan Aron to Friends of the Alliance, July 7, 1993 (copy on file with author).

14. Brennan, "Tribute to Justice Thurgood Marshall," 60.

15. Ibid., 59.

16. Barrett, "Teacher, Student, Ticket," 321.

17. Ibid.

18. Higginbotham, "Impromptu Remarks."

19. Barrett, "Teacher, Student, Ticket," 321.

20. Higginbotham, interview, October 7, 1976.

21. Brennan, "Tribute to Justice Thurgood Marshall," 55, 61.

22. Higginbotham, "Dream."

23. Ibid.

24. Ibid.

25. Ronald K. Noble, "A Tribute to a Scholar, a Wise Jurist, and a Role Model," *University of Pennsylvania Law Review* 142, no. 2 (1993): 534.

26. A. Leon Higginbotham, "An Open Letter to Justice Clarence Thomas from a Federal Judicial Colleague," *University of Pennsylvania Law Review* 140, no. 3 (1992): 1025 (quoting *Chambers V. Florida*, 309 U.S. 227 [1940]).

27. Charles J. Ogletree et al., "In Memoriam: A. Leon Higginbotham, Jr.," *Harvard Law Review* 112, no. 8 (1999): 1801–2.

28. "Higginbotham, Aloyisus Leon, Jr.," Federal Judicial Center Biography, https://www.fjc.gov/history/judges/higginbotham-aloyisus-leon-jr.

29. Higginbotham, interview, October 7, 1976.

30. Ibid.

31. A. Leon Higginbotham Jr., *In the Matter of Color: Race and the American Legal Process: The Colonial Period* (Oxford: Oxford University Press, 1980); Higginbotham, *Shades of Freedom: Racial Politics and Presumptions of the American Legal Process* (New York: Oxford University Press, 1998).

32. Bernard W. Bell, "A Tribute to Judge A. Leon Higginbotham: Higginbotham's Third Circuit Jurisprudence," *Rutgers Law Review* 53 (2000): 627, 629. For example, the judge offered a clerkship to a candidate who came from an underprivileged background and whose law school grades the candidate acknowledged did not measure up to those expected of a U.S. circuit court of appeals law clerk. Yet, he "fully justified the Judge's faith in him." L. Barry Costilo, "An Unforgettable Year Clerking for Judge Higginbotham," *Loyola of Los Angeles Law Review* 33 (1999): 1014.

33. Cliff Hocker, "A. Leon Higginbotham: 'A Legal Giant February 25, 1928—December 14, 1998,'" *National Bar Association Magazine*, 1999, 18.

34. Edward R. Becker, "Dedication: A. Leon Higginbotham, Jr.; The Man," *University of Pennsylvania Law Review* 142, no. 2 (1993): 511–12.

35. *Community Health Services, etc. v. Califano*, 698 F. 2d 615 (1983). The summary of this case is taken from the circuit court's opinion cited here.

36. Becker, "Dedication: A Leon Higginbotham, Jr."

37. *Community Health Services, etc. V. Califano*, 617.

38. *Heckler v. Community Health Services of Crawford County, Ind.*, 467 U.S. 51 (1984).

39. Ibid., 52.

40. Ibid., 59.

41. Ibid., 61–62.

42. Ibid., 64–66.

43. Hocker, "Legal Giant," 17–18.

44. Becker, "Dedication: A. Leon Higginbotham, Jr."

45. Hocker, "Legal Giant," 17–18.

46. Ogletree et al., "In Memoriam," 1829.

47. Ibid., 1829–30.

48. Audrey G. McFarlane is Dean Julius Isaacson Professor of Law, University of Baltimore School of Law.

49. Noble, "Tribute to a Scholar," 536.

50. Ibid., 536–37.

51. Becker, "Dedication: A. Leon Higginbotham, Jr.," 511–12.

52. Anne Whatley Chain, "The Honorable A. Leon Higginbotham, Jr.: Teacher, Mentor, and Friend," *University of Pennsylvania Law Review* 142, no. 2 (1993): 517.

53. Higginbotham, "Impromptu Remarks."

54. Ibid.

55. Becker, "Dedication: A. Leon Higginbotham, Jr.," 511–12.

56. Ibid., 511.

57. Ibid.

58. Barrett, "Teacher, Student, Ticket."

59. Costilo, "Unforgettable Year," 1009–10.

60. William Glaberson, "A. Leon Higginbotham Jr., Federal Judge, Is Dead at 70," *New York Times*, December 15, 1998.

61. Guido Calabresi, "What Makes a Judge Great: To A. Leon Higginmotham, Jr.," *University of Pennsylvania Law Review* 142 (1993): 513.

62. William J. Brennan Jr., "Tribute to Judge A. Leon Higginbotham, Jr.," *Law & Inequality: A Journal of Theory and Practice* 9 (1990): 383.

63. Bell, "Tribute to Judge A. Leon Higginbotham," 627, 633.

64. A. Leon Higginbotham Jr., "The Life of the Law: Values, Commitment, and Craftsmanship," *Harvard Law Review* 100, no. 4 (1987): 814–15.

65. Ibid., 815.

66. Ibid., 815–16.

67. After his clerkship, Ron served as assistant U.S. Attorney for the Eastern District of Pennsylvania, assistant attorney general and chief of staff for the criminal division of the Department of Justice, professor of law, New York University School of Law, the first non-European, the first nonwhite, the first African American, and the youngest secretary-general of Interpol.

68. Noble, "Tribute to a Scholar," 531.

69. Jones, "Tribute to the Honorable A. Leon Higginbotham, Jr.," 567–68.

70. Ibid. Judge Jones cites as examples *Jones v. Ryan*, 987 F.2d 960 (3d Cir. 1993) (reversing a denial of habeas corpus, finding a prima facie case where jurors were excluded on the basis of race in violation of the Fourteenth Amendment, and remanding for further proceedings); *Holder v. City of Allentown*, 987 F.2d 188 (3d Cir. 1993) (reversing the dismissal of a First Amendment claim of a city employee who was fired after speaking out against a city residency requirement for employees).

71. Ibid., 568–69. Judge Jones cites *Grant v. Shalala*, 989 F.2d (3d Cir. 1993), 1347 (dissenting in an opinion in which the court held that the district court did not have authority to "conduct a de novo trial" to make its own findings of fact regarding an administrative law judge's bias but instead had to rely on the DHHS secretary's findings); *Cooper v. Tard*, 855 F.2d 125, 130 (3d Cir. 1988) (dissenting in a case in which the court determined that prohibiting a group prayer without prison authority supervision did not violate equal protection rights of Muslim inmates); *Thorstenn v. Barnard*, 842

F.2d 1393, 1397 (3d Cir. 1987) (dissenting in a case in which the court held that residency requirements for applicants to the Virgin Islands bar were not invalid).

72. Ibid., 567, 69.

73. Ibid.

74. Ibid.

75. Ogletree et al., "In Memoriam," 1829, 1831.

76. Ibid.

77. Ibid.

78. Ibid.

79. Ibid.

80. John P. Frank, "Giant: A Higginbotham Memoir," *University of Pennsylvania Law Review* 142, no. 2 (1993): 379, 380, quoting Learned Hand, "Mr. Justice Cardozo," *Columbia Law Review* 39, no. 1 (1939): 379–80.

81. A. Leon Higginbotham Jr., interview, October 7, 1976.

82. Ibid.

83. Brennan, "Tribute to Justice Thurgood Marshall," 61–62.

84. Higginbotham, "Open Letter," 1005, 1011.

85. Colleen L. Adams, Rubin M. Sinins, and Linda Y. Yueh, "A Life Well Lived: Remembrances of Judge A. Leon Higginbotham, Jr.—His Days, His Jurisprudence, and His Legacy," *Loyola of Los Angeles Law Review* 33 (1999): 987–88; Caplan, "Judging Leon Higginbotham," 68, 70.

86. Charles J. Ogletree, "From Pretoria to Philadelphia: Judge Higginbotham's Racial Justice Jurisprudence on South Africa and the United States," *Yale Law & Policy Review* 20, no. 2 (2002): 386.

87. Ibid., 388–89.

88. Ibid., 387, quoting Nelson Mandela, letter to the family of A. Leon Higginbotham Jr., December 21, 1998 (on file with the Harvard Law School Library).

89. Caplan, "Judging Leon Higginbotham," 70.

ROBIN KONRAD AND KARLA McKANDERS

Creating a Family of Social Justice Advocates

Our Transformative Year as Keith Law Clerks

Robin Konrad, Law Clerk, 2004–2005

I was in my late twenties and had just started working at a big law firm in Washington, D.C., when I received a call asking me to come to Detroit for an interview with Judge Damon J. Keith, who—at that time—was a federal judge for the U.S. Court of Appeals for the Sixth Circuit. I was absolutely thrilled that I had been selected, from likely hundreds of candidates, for an interview. Judge Keith was a legend around the halls of Howard University School of Law, from which I had graduated earlier that year, and from which he had also graduated a few decades earlier. Having been mentored by civil rights leaders Thurgood Marshall and Charles Hamilton Houston (among many others), Judge Keith became a judge who protected the civil and constitutional rights of all people.

Before I went to Detroit for my interview, I reviewed the key cases that Judge Keith had decided. One of his most well-known cases—which ended up before the United States Supreme Court—involved a warrantless search of electronic information conducted by the Nixon administration before it arrested several members of the White Panther Party.[1] During the pretrial proceedings, the U.S. government argued that it did not need to turn over the information it discovered and that the warrantless searches were admissible under an exception in cases involving threats of domestic terrorism. Judge Keith, as the federal district court judge presiding over the case, disagreed and found that the Fourth Amendment's protection against warrantless searches applied with full force even under those circumstances. The Nixon administration sued Judge Keith using a legal procedure called a writ of mandamus reserved for rare circumstances when a federal judge abuses his power. The case reached the U.S. Supreme Court, and in a 1972 unanimous opinion, the Court affirmed Judge Keith's decision.

In addition to the Nixon wire-tapping case, Judge Keith issued several critical civil rights decisions in the 1970s when he sat as a U.S. federal district court
judge for the Eastern District of Michigan. He ordered the enforcement of
school desegregation in Pontiac, Michigan;[2] he struck down racial discrimination by Detroit's electric company in its hiring practices, promotion of jobs,
and compensation of black employees;[3] and he banned housing discrimination
against black people in Hamtramck, a small city surrounded by Detroit.[4] For
ten years, Judge Keith was a district court judge, appointed to the bench by
President Lyndon B. Johnson in 1967. He was eventually elevated to a federal
appellate judge in 1977 by President Jimmy Carter. He served on the federal
bench for over fifty years.

While he was an appellate court judge, Judge Keith also decided a landmark
case shortly after the attacks of September 11, 2001. In response to the terrorist
attacks, the government created a blanket rule to ban the public and the media
from attending deportation proceedings in immigration court. The lower court
applied the government's rule. On appeal, however, Judge Keith authored the
unanimous opinion striking down that rule, writing, "Democracies die behind
closed doors."[5] Using the Constitution as his guide, Judge Keith explained:
"A government operating in the shadow of secrecy stands in complete opposition to the society envisioned by the framers of our Constitution."[6]

After learning more about Judge Keith's legal legacy, I became both excited
and extremely nervous to meet this brilliant man. I went to the interview not
knowing exactly what to expect, and as I walked into his chambers, his administrative manager told me to look around while she told the Judge I was there.
I gazed upon the walls, which were filled from floor to ceiling with photographs
of Judge Keith with some of my heroes—people such as Rosa Parks, Supreme
Court justices Thurgood Marshall and William Brennan, Oprah Winfrey, Nelson
Mandela, and President John F. Kennedy. Having been out of law school for only
a few months, I was awestruck by the amount of rich history in one man's office.

Judge Keith came out, greeted me, and invited me into his office. When
I met him, I instantly felt a connection with him. We talked about our alma
mater; we talked about civil rights; we talked about my desire to use my law
degree to help the underdog. At the end of the interview, Judge Keith told me
that he could tell that I had a "fire in my belly." I walked out of chambers thinking to myself that even if I didn't receive an offer to serve as his clerk, I was still
grateful that I was able to have that one-on-one conversation with the Judge.

Fortunately, that conversation was just one of many that I would have with
Judge Keith. I received and, of course, accepted an offer to serve as his law clerk

for the 2004–2005 term. When I started my term, the Judge had just spent the summer helping save the Charles H. Wright African-American Museum from closing its doors due to lack of funding. Judge Keith had contacted his friends, urging them to get involved; within a short time, they raised over a million dollars. This was my introduction to Judge Keith. I already knew he was a prominent voice in the judiciary, but until then I had not yet come to fully appreciate the extent of his continued involvement in and commitment to his community.

Judge Keith was born and raised in Detroit, and around the city, he was a known hero. In 1987, he began hosting a Soul Food Luncheon in February, in celebration of Black History Month. In addition to bringing community members together to enjoy fried chicken, collard greens, and macaroni and cheese, the luncheon also honored a local African American who has "done exceptionally well and has made a contribution to the struggle of black people" in Detroit and Michigan.[7] Each year, Judge Keith selected and presented the Soul and Spirit Humanitarian Award to a Detroiter. Prior recipients have included people such as Aretha Franklin, Rosa Parks, Joe Dumars, or Congressman John Conyers. The Judge took great pride in this tradition, recognizing the importance of celebrating successful people in the black community. From Judge Keith, I learned that with greatness and success comes responsibility—the responsibility to give back to the community and help uplift those in need.

Judge Keith never took his position as federal judge for granted and never misused his authority and power. He prided himself on being able to say that he never held a lawyer in contempt. To Judge Keith, wearing a black robe was not a license to chastise others. Quite the opposite. When Judge Keith asked questions from the bench, he was respectful and kind. By his example, I learned that there is no reason to speak with harsh words, even to an opponent.

My clerkship with Judge Keith was for one year—a year that went by all too quickly. I was the first of three clerks to start for the term. Because of that, I was assigned the role of "senior" law clerk, which meant that I would be responsible for making sure things ran smoothly during the transition period and throughout the year. Judge Keith staggered the start date of his law clerks so that not all clerks started at the same time. I was able to work with the outgoing law clerks for a few weeks before the two incoming clerks started. This provided me the opportunity to learn both the Judge's preferences and the practical aspects of working in his chambers. In addition, I was able to learn from, and build relationships with, both my yearlong co-clerks, as well as the outgoing clerks.

During my tenure, Judge Keith was on senior status, which meant that he was not required to have the same responsibilities as an active judge. Yet despite his senior status, he still maintained a large caseload and would generally sit for oral argument in cases at least four times per year. Typically, the court would hear argument in six cases per day during a consecutive, four-day period. The Sixth Circuit is based in Cincinnati, Ohio, so we would travel from Detroit to Cincinnati whenever argument was scheduled. Judge Keith also volunteered to sit as a judge in other federal circuits that were shorthanded. While I did not have the opportunity to travel to another circuit during my clerkship, the outgoing clerks went to New York with Judge Keith to hear cases in the Second Circuit.

Preparing the Judge to hear cases was the primary duty of the law clerks. It came as no surprise to me when I learned that Judge Keith ran his chambers a bit differently than other judges in the circuit. For each case that he was going to decide, Judge Keith required his own law clerks to write a bench memorandum—a document that summarizes the legal and factual issues in the case and offers a conclusion as to how the case should be resolved. Often, an appellate judge will rely upon bench memoranda written by other judges' clerks. Judge Keith, however, asked his clerks to draft a bench memorandum for every single case. This meant that we would divide up the twenty-four cases per sitting, and we would each be assigned eight cases per argument session.

While I was clerking, I traveled on five separate occasions to Cincinnati with Judge Keith, his administrative manager, and my co-clerks. Our responsibilities in Cincinnati were different from the day-to-day work in Detroit. While in Detroit, we would typically spend our time researching and writing, fielding telephone calls, hosting visitors, and assisting the Judge with any other activities he had on his schedule, such as appearing at community events. In Cincinnati, our role was to actively prepare for the cases scheduled for the week. We met with Judge Keith every morning before oral argument to discuss the cases being heard that day. We would provide him with an oral synopsis of the case, along with our opinion on how we believed the case should be decided in light of our research. During the oral arguments, the clerks sat in the courtroom to listen to the advocates and the judges' questions. Each day, after the cases were completed, the clerks would reconvene with Judge Keith, and he would inform us how the judges voted on the cases. We never participated in the judges' deliberations but would learn only afterward who voted to affirm or reverse and who would be authoring the majority opinion. If Judge Keith was writing for the majority or a dissent, then the clerk who had written the bench memorandum for that particular case provided Judge Keith with the first draft of the opinion. This was quite a daunting task as a young attorney. But the clerks initially worked together on the draft and reviewed each other's work before we submitted anything to Judge Keith.

Once Judge Keith reviewed our draft, he would provide comments and feedback, which we then used to revise the draft. During the process, we would often speak with the Judge about any issues in the case. I recall discussing one case in particular with him where he was writing a dissent. In that case, a criminal defendant had been deprived of his constitutional right to confront a witness against him. Judge Keith voiced sincere concern for the alleged victim, while at the same time recognizing the need to uphold the constitutional rights of accused.

Judge Keith was a person who epitomized the cliché "practice what you preach." I came to learn this at an event where he shared a story about hiring me. We were at a luncheon in which Judge Keith was honored by the Wolverine Bar Association, an organization established in the 1930s to address the exclusion of African American attorneys in bar associations across the state of Michigan. As part of the ceremony, Judge Keith presented a keynote speech. At times, his law clerks would help him draft his speeches. But during this event, Judge Keith went off-script and told a story that I had never heard. He began by stressing the importance of equal justice under law—a guiding motto in his life—and of ensuring that society did not judge people based on the color of their skin. Judge Keith's entire life and career is a testament to these principles, and I had heard him tell stories underscoring the importance of these values many times in the past. But this time, he shared a personal example in which he used his own words to guide a decision he made: to hire me.

When Judge Keith saw my résumé, he said that he was sold. Not only had I graduated at the top of my class from Howard University School of Law, but I had also served as editor-in-chief of the school's law review. I had demonstrated a commitment to social justice by my work with Amnesty International, the American Civil Liberties Union, and the Human Rights Campaign. During my third year of law school, I was one of a small group of students who drafted an amicus brief to the U.S. Supreme Court in support of the University of Michigan School of Law in its desire to use race as one of many factors considered in admissions to ensure a diverse institution. After reading my background, Judge Keith assumed that because I attended a historically black university, that I, too, was black. But I am white.

During the luncheon, Judge Keith told the audience that he was taken aback by the assumptions he made regarding my identity. Judge Keith was committed to ensuring diversity among his clerks and ensuring that people who have not historically had access to federal clerkships would be given a fair opportunity to work with him. When I applied, Judge Keith had qualified applicants from different racial backgrounds, and he questioned who was best for the position. He had already filled the other two positions—one clerk was a black man; the other clerk was a white woman. As Judge Keith was telling this story, my face began to turn from pale cream to a bright red. He then told the Wolverine Bar Association that he prayed, seeking guidance on what to do. (At this point, my face had to have been brighter than the strawberries we ate for lunch!) Judge Keith explained that if he did not hire me simply because of my skin color, then he would be acting in the same way that people in power have acted for centuries. Because he wanted to practice what he preached, Judge Keith offered me the position.

I'm not going to lie. Hearing that story made me feel a little embarrassed at the time. But over the years, in thinking about the systemic oppression and discrimination that Judge Keith has faced as a black man in America, I have come to recognize, honor, and value the courage that he showed each and every day by his actions. Indeed, knowing Judge Keith and being part of his clerk family has helped me in finding the strength to live by principles of fairness and to do what is right even when it's unpopular.

As a member of the Keith clerk family, I have had the honor and privilege to be part of a circle of amazing trailblazers—including judges, educators, dignitaries, politicians, activists, and practicing attorneys—who uphold the principles instilled upon us by Judge Keith. He always treated his clerks as though we were part of his family by including us in annual events, such as the Soul Food Luncheon and his birthday celebration. Perhaps foreshadowing his future, Judge Keith was born on the Fourth of July. To celebrate both his life and his love of America, he hosted a barbeque birthday gathering at his family farm in Virginia, which was attended by his family, clerks, and other close friends.

In October 2017, at age ninety-five, Judge Keith reached his fiftieth year of service as a federal judge. In commemoration of his legacy on the bench, his clerks spearheaded a weekend-long celebration in Detroit. The main event occurred on the evening of Saturday, October 28, when over three hundred people attended a gala at the Charles H. Wright African American Museum.[8] Through music, food, and storytelling, we honored Judge Keith's life and his unwavering devotion to his country and the Constitution.

The next time I was in Detroit to once again honor Judge Keith's life was in May 2019. This time, however, Judge Keith was not there. On April 28, 2019, Judge Keith passed away in his Detroit home. That Sunday morning, I was lying in bed when I received a text message from my friend Mae (Judge Keith's former administrative manager) saying, "Call me." As soon as I read those words, I knew what they meant. I dialed Mae's number, not wanting to hear that our judge had left us. Mae said she wanted me to hear it from her before the news broke. Less than an hour later, I read the headline in the *Detroit Free Press*: "Federal Judge, Civil Rights Icon Damon Keith Dies at Age 96."[9]

Judge Keith's funeral was held on May 13 at Hartford Memorial Baptist Church. The church was overflowing with people who had come to show their love and respect for Judge Keith. Speakers at the three-hour service included the governor, the mayor, a federal appellate court judge, Wayne State University president, faith leaders, Judge Keith's former law partner, and Judge Keith's eldest daughter. Each and every person who shared their remarks continued to express the same sentiment—that Judge Keith treated everyone equally with dignity and respect regardless of their background, their faith, their job, or their so-called status in society. And that is what I, too, found so inspiring and magical about Judge Keith. He dedicated his life to serving others and led by example each and every day. I truly believe that because of Judge Keith's commitment to equal justice under law we are living in a better America.[10]

Karla McKanders, Law Clerk, 2005–2006

In 2005, I was a recent law school graduate in my late twenties when I began clerking for the Honorable Damon J. Keith. As I transitioned into my year of clerking with Judge Keith, Robin Konrad welcomed me to the office and trained me to take over her position as the senior law clerk.

I first met Judge Keith during the winter of 2003. I was working at a law firm in Detroit in the Labor and Employment Department when a junior-level associate and former Keith law clerk, Kevin Smith, invited me to come with him to Judge Keith's chambers. While I had heard numerous stories regarding the legendary Judge Keith, I did not know what to expect. My law professor from Duke University School of Law, James Coleman, was one of the first district court law clerks for Judge Keith. Professor Coleman clerked with Lani Guinier, the first African American woman to gain tenure at Harvard Law School.

Like Robin, I was amazed when I walked into Judge Keith's chambers for the first time. I was directed to the infamous wall of Judge Keith's law clerks, which displayed photographs of clerks who have continued Judge Keith's legacy of fighting for justice. Hanging on the wall were pictures of Eric Clay, a judge on United States Court of Appeals for the Sixth Circuit; Constance L. Rice, prominent civil rights activist and cofounder of the Advancement Project; and

Jennifer Granholm, Michigan's first female governor. I also saw the hundreds of photographs documenting the significant role Judge Keith played in our country's civil rights movement. On display were pictures of Judge Keith with prominent leaders such as Dr. Martin Luther King Jr., Justice Thurgood Marshall, Bill and Hillary Clinton, and civil rights icon Rosa Parks.

Judge Keith was a longtime friend of Rosa Parks. In 1957, Parks and her husband moved to Detroit, where she served on the staff of U.S. Representative John Conyers. Parks was instrumental in spearheading legislation with Conyers to create a national holiday for King. Judge Keith's connection with Parks was significant. As she aged, he helped ensure that she was taken care of—including garnering support from the Detroit community to move Parks into a secure neighborhood. Judge Keith affectionately called her "Mother Parks" in recognition of her leading role in the civil rights movement.

During my time as a law clerk, Judge Keith often told stories about Parks. Judge Keith escorted Rosa Parks to meet South African President Nelson Mandela when Mandela visited the United States. President Mandela told Judge Keith that Rosa Parks was his inspiration while he was jailed, and her example inspired South African freedom fighters. These stories transformed my clerkship into a position where I not only learned the law but also was mentored by a civil rights legend.

Shortly after I started my clerkship, Rosa Parks passed away. Judge Keith was a key organizer of Parks's home-going celebrations held in Detroit, Washington, D.C., and her home state of Alabama.[11] Regarding her passing, Judge Keith said: "Mother Parks represents everything that my legal and judicial career has stood for. It was [an] honor to celebrate her life with the rest of the world."[12]

The final home-going celebration took place in Detroit at Greater Grace Temple. Parks died fifty years and twenty-nine days from the date when she refused to give up her seat on a bus in Montgomery, Alabama. Judge Keith led national and global leaders in presiding over her funeral services. Individuals from around the world gathered to remember her symbolic act and how it changed the course of our nation's history. Among the dignitaries who gathered to pay homage to her life were then-senator Barack Obama, Minister Louis Farrakhan, Reverend Jesse Jackson, former-president William Jefferson Clinton and then-senator Hillary Clinton, Reverend Bernice King, and Reverend Al Sharpton.

As a young lawyer, I did not fully appreciate the monumental nature of the funeral services and the fact that I was being given the opportunity to participate in this historical event. President Clinton noted during the funeral that it was

Parks's "single simple act of dignity and courage that struck a legal blow to the foundations of legal bigotry."[13] Through her action, Clinton reflected, she ignited the most significant social movement in modern American history, redeeming the promise for the Thirteenth, Fourteenth, and Fifteenth Amendments.[14]

Hearing then-senator Obama speak during the funeral was also especially poignant. He reminded the audience that Parks, who was a small, quiet woman, did not hold an advanced degree from an Ivy League school or hold public office. But it is her name that will be remembered long after the names of presidents and senators have been forgotten. She "laid the foundation for a nation to live up to its creed," Obama said, by "her signature act of courage" when she "refused to be treated less than" other humans.[15] He reflected that through her simple act, and by living a life of grace and dignity, Parks showed us every single day what it means to be free.

Judge Keith's connection to Rosa Parks was extremely significant for me. When I graduated from high school in 1996, I was a recipient of a scholarship from the Rosa Parks Scholarship Foundation. In 1980, the Detroit News and Detroit Public Schools established the Rosa L. Parks Scholarship Foundation, honoring the twenty-fifth anniversary of her bus protest in Montgomery. The Rosa L. Parks Scholarship Foundation is dedicated to awarding scholarships to Michigan high school seniors attending college who hold close to Mrs. Parks's ideals while demonstrating academic skills, community involvement, and economic need.[16] During my clerkship, I served on the Rosa Parks Scholarship Board and still serve as an honorary board member.

Being present to assist Judge Keith in organizing the funeral of a monumental civil rights icon reminded me of my life commitment to pursue civil rights and social justice as a lawyer and law professor. Reflecting on my year clerking with Judge Keith, I feel humbled to state that I would not be an African American female law professor at Vanderbilt University today if it were not for both Judge Keith's and Rosa Parks's selfless acts and unwavering commitment to ensuring that the United States lives up to its promise of guaranteeing "Equal Justice Under the Law" to all persons regardless of their race, religion, ethnicity, or color of their skin.

Notes

1. *United States v. U.S. District Court*, 407 U.S. 297 (1972).
2. *Davis v. School District of City of Pontiac, Inc.*, 309 F. Supp. 734 (E.D. Mich. 1970).
3. *Stamps v. Detroit Edison Co.*, 365 F. Supp. 87 (E.D. Mich. 1973).

4. *Garrett v. City of Hamtramck*, 335 F. Supp. 16 (E.D. Mich. 1971).

5. *Detroit Free Press v. Ashcroft*, 303 F.3d 681, 683 (6th Cir. 2002).

6. Ibid.

7. Melody Baetens, "Carmen Harlan to Be Honored at Judge Keith Luncheon," *Detroit News*, February 13, 2018.

8. Sarah Rahal, "Gala Honors Damon Keith's 50th Year on the Federal Bench," *Detroit News*, October 28, 2017.

9. Cassandra Spratling and David Ashenfelter, "Federal Judge, Civil Rights Icon Damon Keith Dies at Age 96," *Detroit Free Press*, April 28, 2019.

10. See, e.g., Trevor W. Coleman and Peter J. Hammer, *Crusader for Justice: Federal Judge Damon J. Keith* (Detroit: Wayne State University Press 2013); Jesse Nesser, dir., *Walk with Me: The Trials of Damon J. Keith* (2016).

11. Cassandra Spratling, "Keith's Life and Legal Career Impact and Inspire Man," *Detroit Free Press*, June 14, 2015.

12. Nomination of the Honorable Damon J. Keith for the Sarah T. Hughes Civil Rights Award, https://fbamich.org/wp-content/uploads/2015/02/Tribute_to_Judge_Damon_J._Keith.pdf.

13. Rosa Parks Funeral Services, CSPAN, November 2, 2005.

14. Ibid.

15. Ibid.

16. The Rosa L. Parks Scholarship Foundation, http://www.rosaparksscholarship foundation.org/.

CHAD M. OLDFATHER

A Job for a Year, an Example for a Lifetime
Clerking for Judge Jane Richards Roth

The following two things seem to me to be true: The first is that the people for whom a young lawyer works early in her career are likely to have an outsized influence on that lawyer's development. It's at that point that the new lawyer is most likely to be confronted with the largest knowledge differential she will ever encounter. Her first boss is likely to have at least half a career's worth of experience, while she will have almost no experience at all. The boss's ability to understand issues, to cut through seeming complexity, and to see things the young lawyer cannot yet see will seem almost magical. If that young lawyer becomes a law clerk to a judge, that clerkship may well be the clerk's first real job, and the judge will be one of the bosses with the magical abilities.

The second is that the young lawyer, at least if he is the sort of young lawyer who obtains a federal judicial clerkship, is likely to exhibit "the combination of hubris and self-doubt that is the mark of the culture of clerks."[1] He will have done very well in law school. If he chooses to look for a job with a law firm, he will likely have found that those law firms appeared to be in competition for people like him. He might even have imagined that it was him in particular they were in competition for. People with impressive résumés will have said very nice things, and there will have been meals at fancy restaurants and choice seats at sporting events and perhaps even limousines involved. That variety of young lawyer will be eager to leave his mark. At the same time, and for many of the same reasons, he is likely to feel somewhat insecure, as though he might not have earned any of it. The fact that his new boss obviously knows so much more than he does may start to crack his A-student's faith that the kind of knowledge that succeeds in the classroom is the only kind that matters.

And here is a third thing, which I know to be true: A large part of the reason I suspect that the first two things are true is that they were true of me. By the time I started clerking for Judge Jane Roth I had been told flattering things by partners at fancy law firms, and I imagined, as the young often do, that I was much farther along the path to knowing all I needed to know than I actually was. What is more, as not only a young person but also a first-generation college graduate and product of a thoroughly rural upbringing, I lacked a strong contextual grounding based on which to know better. The difference between what Judge Roth knew and what I knew was vast, in terms of not only the law but also how to be a lawyer and a good person. I perhaps sensed this, and in any case I certainly exhibited both hubris and self-doubt. Like any embryonic professional, I needed a role model, and in that respect I could not have been more fortunate.

Judge Jane Richards Roth—An Introduction

Let's take a moment to meet Judge Jane Richards Roth. Judge Roth grew up in a family of lawyers. Her grandfather, Robert H. Richards, was one of the founders of Richards, Layton & Finger, P.A., perhaps Delaware's preeminent law firm. Among the other lawyers in the family were her great-grandfather, father, and brother, as well as an uncle and a cousin. Despite this, she did not immediately attend law school upon graduating from Smith College in 1956. Instead, she opted to act on her interest in exploring the world by joining the Foreign Service and spending six years as a clerk/typist in Tehran, Iran; Salisbury, Rhodesia (now Zimbabwe); and Brazzaville, Republic of Congo. She chose assignments in each of these locations because they were places she would not have gone to as a tourist, and proudly notes that she still recalls how to say "I like beer" in the language of the Shona tribe of Rhodesia.

Judge Roth entered Harvard Law School in 1962 as one of twenty-five women (Elizabeth Dole was another) among hundreds of men. As seems to have been his custom, Dean Erwin Griswold invited the entire group of women to a dinner at his home, where he reminded them that they had deprived twenty-five men of a future in law.[2] As was typical for women in 1962, they just sat silently with forced smiles on their faces. Judge Roth later said that she did not dare protest because she was afraid if she did she would be thrown out of school. After law school she returned to Delaware, where she was one of the first ten women members of the bar and the first female lawyer at Richards, Layton & Finger. She began her career as a family lawyer but found it was not to her liking, and she transitioned to what quickly became a successful career as a litigator.

She became Judge Roth on November 4, 1985, having been nominated by President Reagan less than a month earlier. Here, again, she blazed a trail, as the first woman to serve as a federal judge in Delaware. President George H. W. Bush appointed her to the Third Circuit in May 1991. She received her commission in July of that year and served as an active member of the court until 2006, when she took senior status. She moved from Wilmington to Washington, D.C., in 2009 to be closer to her children and grandchildren, and maintains an office in the E. Barrett Prettyman United States Courthouse. She has continued to handle a significant caseload and to serve as chair of the Third Circuit Committee on Facilities and Security.

These biographical details are impressive, and it takes little imagination to appreciate the trove of valuable and instructive experience associated with each line of her life's story. Already one can see that this was someone from whom there was much for a clerk to learn. But as is often the case, the details, or at least these sorts of details, provide an incomplete picture. Many people who have accomplished great things, and who look impressive when viewed from a distance, are less admirable when viewed up close. Talented lawyers are not always great bosses or mentors, or even especially nice people. Some federal judges, rumor has it, do not provide for a meaningful or enjoyable clerkship experience. A résumé is not a person. Fortunately for those of us who served as her clerks, Judge Roth does not merely live up to, but rather transcends her résumé.

A Judge and Her Clerks

The judge-clerk relationship is often a close one, and certainly to work in a judge's chambers is to work in a place in which the atmosphere is largely the product of one person's personality. The judge's work is the point of the whole enterprise, and the clerk's fundamental role is to advance that enterprise. The judge's primary desire, then, is to have clerks who are maximally helpful, with all that entails. And if they are enjoyable to work with, so much the better. Judge Roth wants "four enthusiastic young lawyers who are looking for the big issue in every case, but who have the sense not to find the big issue in every case."[3] Further, "the successful clerk reads carefully, writes carefully, sees the issues in an appeal without dreaming up too many constitutional issues that aren't there, and if there is a difference of opinion will persuade me to his or her way of thinking and, if he or she cannot do that, will go along with my position." In terms of personal characteristics, "most important of all" is that the clerk have a good sense of humor.

Getting this right, one imagines, can be a tricky thing, and to do so year after year is nearly miraculous. Yet Judge Roth attests that almost all of her clerks have been successful, and that she has had very little experience with clerks not meeting her expectations. Still, she identified some characteristics of a less-than-fully successful clerk. That person would not be able to commit to getting the work done as his or her primary focus, would not be available when the judge needed him or her, and would persist in a disagreement with the judge or in doing things that he or she had been asked not to do, such as to write in a style that the judge asked to be toned down. He or she would not, in other words, be helpful.

The Selection Process

Getting good clerks, and avoiding bad ones, would seem to be an art form made all the more difficult by the ever-changing nature of the clerkship market. Federal judges have only sometimes been able to adhere to a collective plan, while at other times the process has been a free-for-all. From my perspective as an applicant during a period in which there was no federal law clerk hiring plan, the market had a land-rush feel to it. Fortunately for me, I had spent the last two years of college, from which I went directly to law school, in a part-time job at the *Harvard Law Review*, so I had already been witness to an especially intense version of the process.[4]

My law school, the University of Virginia, held a meeting for those of us interested in clerking that took place midway through the first semester of our second year. At about that same time the *Virginia Law Review* circulated among its second-year members a list of the seventy-two federal judges with whom third-years had received interviews. On December 26, 1991, I mailed applications to twenty-five judges, all of whom, because I was operating on a limited budget, were located within a day's drive of Charlottesville. Then, because it was a different era in terms of communication technology, I rushed home after class each day to check the mail and the answering machine. Meanwhile, third-years who had already secured clerkships gathered and passed along information from the chambers of their judges and from members of the class ahead of theirs who were already clerking. The rumor mill turned rapidly and included the unverified claim that one of the judges on the D.C. Circuit interviewed a prospective clerk on Thanksgiving Day.

My classmates and I were largely passed over by the earliest moving judges, who tended to be fixated on the top of the class at Harvard and Yale. Judge

David Sentelle of the D.C. Circuit wrote me on January 6 to inform me that he had already concluded his hiring. Judge Stephen Williams of the same court wrote on January 3, stating that "although some interviewing and hiring has already occurred, I plan to defer a systematic review of clerkship applications for a while." But on January 21 he wrote again, thanking me for providing him with my fall semester grades while noting that "unfortunately the process has moved along not only early (a disturbing collective action problem), but swiftly, and I have already finished picking." Letters from other judges likewise bemoaned the speed with which the process moved.

My interviews began in late January, and prior to my February 14 interview with Judge Roth I had made trips to courthouses in Maryland, North Carolina, and Virginia. It was common at the time for an applicant with an interview invitation to call all the other judges chambered in the same courthouse to whom he or she had applied to let them know that he or she would be in town. This triggered a review of one's application and often generated additional interviews. (It did not always work that way, though. I once answered the phone to find a federal judge on the line to tell me, in so many words, that I was on his B-list.)

I met Judge Roth in her chambers in Wilmington on the afternoon of a day that had started at the federal courthouse in Philadelphia. I no longer remember which judge had first offered me an interview, but I had certainly used the "make some phone calls to let them know I would be in the neighborhood" trick to put together a package of interviews in the two cities. Judge Roth was my first interview in Wilmington. I had served as a research assistant for a torts professor and written my law review note on a torts topic, and these experiences formed the basis for a large part of our conversation. It seems to have gone well, because she made me an offer at the end of the interview. Knowing that I had an interview upstairs with Judge Walter Stapleton immediately after hers, and that I had just had what I thought was a good interview with one of her other Third Circuit colleagues that morning, she asked me to let her know within three days. She did so with what I now recognize as her characteristic graciousness, and knowing her as I do now I would not be surprised if she also relished the opportunity to create a mildly awkward moment for her friend Judge Stapleton.

I went up to Judge Stapleton's chambers not quite knowing how to handle the situation. A wiser twenty-something than I would have immediately described his predicament and suggested that, under the circumstances, maybe an interview would not be necessary. But I lacked any such wisdom at that point, and it took me until the end of the interview to get around to mentioning that Judge

Roth had made me an offer. Judge Stapleton did not come right out and tell me that I should accept, but he did speak very highly of Judge Roth, and I immediately marched back down to her chambers and gratefully accepted. It was among the better decisions I have ever made.[5]

Jeff Tomasevich tells a similar story:

> When the Judge called me to offer me the clerkship, my initial response was simply, "That's fantastic, thank you!" There was a pause. The Judge, in what I would later learn was her style, then queried, "Well, does that mean that you accept?" Without hesitation, I said yes, having heard horror stories about judges withdrawing their offers if a clerkship candidate asked for time to consider the offer. While it seems that many judges do that because they don't want to be bargaining chips by clerks to get other offers (Hello, I just wanted to let you know that Judge Roth has made me an offer, where do we stand?), when I mentioned this to the Judge shortly after I started clerking, she said that she wouldn't have minded at all if I had asked for more time. As she said, you had only met me for an hour or so, so it would have been natural to take some time to think it over. She was never afraid—and had the confidence—to let the chips fall where they may.

Two years after my interview I got to see the process from a different vantage point. Although we were not, as clerks, asked to provide any significant input into the selection of applicants to be interviewed,[6] I vividly remember a table outside the Judge's office on which sat a large pile of applications. And I recall us speaking with those prospective clerks who interviewed with the Judge, but also that she interviewed a relatively small number of candidates. At least one received an offer from Judge Roth at the conclusion of their interview, and I can recollect at least a couple of conversations in which she solicited our feedback on someone she just interviewed. She was also mindful of how prospective clerks treated her administrative assistants, and one later clerk mentioned an instance in which a candidate's brusque interactions with them weighed heavily in his not receiving an offer.

Judge Roth's initial response to my questions about how she selects her clerks was this: "In thinking about it, and considering that I don't interview clerk applicants unless I am pretty certain that I want to hire them—it occurred to me that I don't pick the clerks, they pick me. I look for applicants who are interested in other countries as well as our own and are interesting to talk with when I interview them." Her choices are not driven by grades alone, and she "wants some sign of a rounded personality."

Many of Judge Roth's former clerks independently passed along impressions of her approach to hiring that echo this description. They observed that she looked for clerks with whom she felt an interpersonal connection, and she often made offers on the spot. She was unfailingly gracious. Ani Satz had car trouble on her way to the interview and found herself in a ditch rather than Judge Roth's chambers at the appointed time. Judge Roth agreed to reschedule for the next day, which was a Saturday, and then found herself confronted with a soaking-wet candidate after Ani got caught in a sudden downpour. That story, fortunately, has a happy ending.

So, too, does the story of Greg Werkhesier, who attended the local law school at Widener University and secured an internship in Judge Roth's chambers during his second year. He tells of noticing the clerkship applications piling up in the judge's chambers.

A few days later, Debbie—Judge Roth's assistant at the time—said to me: "You know, you really should consider applying for a clerkship with the Judge." Initially, I scoffed at the idea. I was, I then believed, a largely unremarkable public-school educated kid from a lower middle class suburban family who had graduated from a public university and was then attending a lower tier law school. What business did I have pretending as if I had a realistic shot at Third Circuit clerkship?

Then, a few days later, Debbie again offhandedly mentioned that I should really consider submitting an application before the window closed. Within short order, one of the Judge's then current law clerks also commented that the Judge liked my work. I can occasionally be slow on the uptake, but this finally did it. Over the next few days, I updated my resume and compiled the materials necessary for my clerkship application. In short order, after submitting my materials, I was summoned into Judge Roth's inner sanctum and told that I would be one of her three law clerks for the 1996–97 term.

To this day, I am deeply grateful to Judge Roth for giving me this opportunity. Judge Roth never told me what motivated her to take a chance on a kid who, at that point in his life, had never set foot on an Ivy League campus—let alone graduated from such an institution. I can only surmise that Judge Roth—who I know has faced no small amount of adversity to get where she has in life—perceived in me some measure of legal ability and, in offering me that clerkship, was of a mind to ensure that I had the chance to make the most of my gifts.

At some point in the late 1990s Judge Roth stopped considering second-year students as clerkship candidates. "I began to have clerks out in the world who were recommending people to me, who were often new associates in the firm who had missed out in the clerkship race but were really good people," she says. Further, "I began to appreciate how much a district court clerkship really helped in terms of understanding how things actually worked, and I began to get recommendations from district court judges who had clerks who wanted to do a circuit court clerkship. I found I didn't need to look into the pile." Since then her hiring has taken place over the course of the year rather than in a concentrated period, and she finds that her clerks have been every bit as good as those chosen through the standard process.

Although I am unaware of data on which to draw confident conclusions, I share with some of my fellow Roth clerks the impression that Judge Roth's clerks may, as a group, differ from what is typical. Howard Wasserman, writing in 2013, observed that at least 20 percent of Judge Roth's clerks to that point had entered academia, and suggested that she might be an example of an "academic feeder judge."[7] The roster of her former clerks also includes, among others who have gone on to interesting and impressive careers within and outside the law, United States senator Chris Coons, Delaware Chancery Court vice chancellor J. Travis Laster, and former assistant to the president for Homeland Security and Counterterrorism Lisa Monaco. Whether we found Judge Roth or she found us, her clerks seem to share her curiosity about the world and to exhibit her desired enthusiasm about the law, which is a combination that no doubt leads to the sort of clerk who will tend to find academia and other nontraditional careers alluring.

Use of Clerks

Judges' use of their clerks varies from one to the next, depending on individual preference and the nature of the court. Some judges delegate less, others more. Some conduct their chambers like a seminar, with lots of discussion between and among the judge and the clerks, while others prefer a set of individual working relationships, and still others interpose a senior clerk between the judge and the remaining clerks. The work itself will differ depending on whether the judge sits on a trial court, intermediate appellate court, or court of last resort.

During the era in which I was a law clerk, the Third Circuit followed a somewhat extraordinary practice pursuant to which most appeals were resolved via the issuance of a one-sentence "judgment order" noting that the decision of the trial court was affirmed.[8] Few, if any, of these cases received oral argument. Because Judge Roth herself performed the initial review of the briefs in all of the cases in a sitting and made her requests for oral argument based on that review, we as clerks had substantial involvement in only a portion of all the cases in a given sitting. She assigned the cases selected for oral argument evenly among the three of us to prepare bench memos, and the default was that the clerk who had drafted the bench memo would prepare the initial draft of any opinions assigned to Judge Roth. (Any adjustments would be to account for an uneven workload resulting from the opinion assignments not falling evenly among the clerks.) We regularly circulated drafts of opinions among one another for comment, but not because Judge Roth required it.

Over the intervening two-plus decades Judge Roth has changed the way she uses her clerks, in part because they are based in Philadelphia while she is based in D.C., but largely because she has concluded that there are benefits for both her and her clerks to doing things differently. Rather than assigning cases herself, she now asks her clerks to figure out for themselves how they will divide things up, and she is less actively involved in monitoring their respective workloads. And now she asks the clerks to review all of the cases for a sitting and to make recommendations concerning which cases should be argued, with Judge Roth focusing at that stage of the process primarily on those cases in which one of her clerks has recommended argument but for which neither of the other judges on the panel has voted. Finally, she actively encourages clerks to review one another's work and view it as a group product, and at times she receives memos discussing the existence of disagreement among the clerks.

My recent conversation with Judge Roth revealed that she has a better recollection of some of the cases I worked on as a clerk than I do. It shook loose memories of all the interesting cases and issues I got to work on during that year, which brought home to me in vivid detail just how wonderful the experience was. Sometimes it is the facts that loom largest in my memory, such as in the litigation arising out of the "Chilean grape crisis" of 1989, where anonymous calls to the U.S. Embassy in Chile led to the testing of fruit imported from Chile, which in turn led to the banning of Chilean fruit after potentially (spurious) testing by the Philadelphia FDA laboratory appeared to reveal cyanide had been injected into grapes.[9] Other memorable cases included one concerning whether the Americans with Disabilities Act required the city of Philadelphia to install curb cuts at pedestrian crossings every time it repaved a street,[10] and the one involving a man who was wrongfully arrested and incarcerated due at least in part to what appeared to be significant prosecutorial misconduct.[11] The court's resolution of an appeal concerning who was responsible for the cost of detaining stowaways on ships and airplanes when those stowaways seek political asylum was covered by both the *National Law Journal*[12] and the *New York Times*.[13]

And while many of the specific legal issues have faded from my memory, some remain. One of the highlights in that regard involves a case in which Judge Roth was not even assigned the opinion. *Schoonejongen v. Curtiss-Wright Corp.*[14] presented some relatively technical ERISA questions, including whether a plan's provision reserving to "the Company" the right to amend the plan amounted to "a procedure for amending" the plan and one "for identifying the persons who have authority" to do so. I vividly recall working with Judge Roth on the text of what became footnote 3 to Judge Stapleton's opinion for the court, which notes that Judge Roth "does not agree with our reasoning" on a particular point and provides an alternative perspective on the issue.

The Supreme Court took the case in the following term and substantially (and unanimously) based the reasoning in its opinion on the logic of that footnote.[15] I was in practice by then, and Judge Roth called me shortly after the Supreme Court issued its opinion. I was not in the office at the time she called, which led to the creation of a nice memento. I still have the message my secretary took: "Scoony-Rungan [*sic*] case reversed 3rd circuit decision based on footnote you two wrote."

To focus on specific cases or issues, though, is to fail to do justice to the entire experience. The imprint that clerking left on my legal skills was no less real for being irreducible to nuggets of doctrine. Some of the briefs were, quite simply, bad, and I learned that I could fill in the gaps. And while I might not have been consciously aware of it at the time, I was, to deploy a phrase I often use with my own students today, learning much more "how" than "what." Digesting and assessing the arguments in briefs across a wide variety of subject areas helped refine my feel for how the various ingredients of informed legal judgment relate to one another. What is more, clerking, at least for me, was the sort of "intellectual feast" that Judge Robert Bork infelicitously referred to during his ill-fated Supreme Court confirmation hearings. At that stage of my career, all of the cases were interesting, all of the issues were new, and all of the paths to solving them seemed to involve, indeed require, acts of imagination. Not too far along into the year it occurred to me to wonder whether I would ever have a job that good again, and I continued to have that same thought for many years after.

To some viewing the process of judging from the outside it appears to involve little more than applied politics. That's not what I imagined myself to be engaged in as a clerk, nor did I perceive the judges to be doing so. My bench memos recommended the disposition that I felt the law required, although I cannot say that I always found the law's requirements to be clear, and I can attest that Judge Roth did not always see things my way. In one case I reached the conclusion, after the oral argument and during the process of drafting an opinion, that the judges had gotten it wrong. I wrote a memo to Judge Roth—most likely after asking her whether writing a memo about it would be worthwhile—in which I laid out my reasoning. She found it at least persuasive enough to circulate it to the other judges on the panel for their consideration, but my arguments did not carry the day. I then did what a good clerk does, which was to draft the best opinion I could in support of the result I disagreed with.

Jeff Tomasevich, who clerked for Judge Roth while she was on the district court, tells a story from his clerkship that captures a great deal of what her clerks learned from her:

> Shortly after arriving, I was reviewing summary judgment briefs submit-ted by a prominent Wilmington firm and the Delaware Attorney Gen-eral's office. Both sides had missed recent, on-point, and controlling precedent from the Third Circuit. As a newly-minted lawyer, I was aghast at what I perceived to be flagrant malpractice. I read and re-read the case. I approached the Judge late in the day, and told her that I thought we had a problem—both sides had missed controlling precedent. Her response: "Can you give me a copy of the case and the briefs, and I'll look at it tonight." The next morning, I was sure she was going to be as incredu-lous as I was. Had they purposefully meant to mislead the court? How could they—partners in a prestigious Wilmington firm and experienced government attorneys—both have missed this case, which an attorney with a whopping four months under his belt was able to find? The Judge's response was, again, classic Judge Roth. She said, "You're right. They missed it. Let's put it in the opinion. The case makes my decision easy." When I asked whether she wanted to sanction the lawyers on both sides for misleading the Court, she paused, smiled, and said, "No, there's no need to sanction anyone. You found the case. You did your job. Remem-ber, they are balancing many cases, trying to do the best they can for all of their clients. Once you're in private practice, you'll see what I mean. And not all of them clerked for a federal judge."

The Life Lessons

In 2013, in connection with the dedication of her official portrait, at least one of Judge Roth's clerks from each of her years on the bench contributed to a collection of memories of their time with the Judge. The themes are consistent. Her fairness and equanimity. Her lack of ideological motivations. Her curiosity about the world. Her terrific sense of humor. The respect with which she treated everyone with whom she interacted. One of her earliest clerks perfectly captured her essence, and the lessons that many (one hopes all) of her former clerks took from the experience: "I learned that you don't have to be humorless or hierarchical to be respected. And you don't have to be impractical to be principled. You can be impartial and still be opinionated. And I learned that some people can wear a robe with St. Bernard fur on it with dignity."

St. Bernards, as Delawareans of that era knew, were a signature of the Roth family. Judge Roth's husband, United States Senator William V. Roth Jr., whose most visible legacy is the Roth IRA, would take one of the dogs with him on the campaign trail.[16] We would occasionally get to see him in action on the streets of downtown Wilmington, and on those days the dogs would make an appearance in chambers as well. For many of us, getting to see the interaction between Judge Roth and Senator Roth was one of the most memorable features of our clerkship. It is no exaggeration to suggest that they were a bona fide power couple. But it was abundantly clear to any of us who got to see them up close that they had not let it go to their heads, and their primary form of engagement was to turn their sharp senses of humor on one another. One of my co-clerks, Jeff Steger, had worked for Senator Roth prior to his clerkship, which led to the following incident:

> One Friday evening, after a sitting in Philadelphia, the Judge and I were driving back to Wilmington. We had a discussion of other careers the Judge had considered, including politics, and we discussed her job as a court of appeals judge compared to the Senator's job. I said something to the effect that I thought the Judge's job was harder because of the amount of reading she had to do. I did not think about the conversation over the weekend, but on Monday, I was working in my office, which was right next to the Judge's office, and the Senator came to meet the judge for lunch. The Senator started to playfully jab me about how at a dinner party that weekend, the Judge was telling everyone that I told her that she was "smarter" than he was. Before I could defend myself, the Judge came

shooting out of her office and spiritedly said to the Senator: "See, you can't even get that right!"

Judge Roth would regularly have lunch with her clerks, which led to this recollection from Greg Werkheiser:

> One of my fondest memories of my clerkship year—perhaps because it reinforced with me that Judge and Senator Roth were fundamentally decent and genuine people—were those clerkship lunches when the Senator would join us. I can no longer recall what the conversation was about. What sticks with me is that they genuinely enjoyed one another's company. Without fail, as part of her lunch, the Judge would order one serving of french fries. The Senator, as I recall, would not order his own fries. Instead, he would proceed to steal fries from the Judge's plate. While she would make a show at being annoyed, at the next lunch, the same pattern would repeat.

That is how it was. We were delighted by it at the time, but of course lacked the perspective to be able to appreciate just how remarkable it was. No matter, because it, too, left a deep and lasting mark. For me, it was an early spur to the realization that while the rules of this professional life I was entering would in many ways be different from those with which I had grown up, the basic standards of goodness and decency were the same.

Conclusion

Karl Llewellyn once praised the institution of the judicial clerkship based on his belief that "the recurring and unceasing impact of a *young* junior in the task is the best medicine yet discovered by man against the hardening of a senior's mind and imagination."[17] The constant flow of newly minted lawyers into a judge's chambers, he reasoned, would provide "a reasonable sampling of information and opinion derived from the labors, over the three past years, of an intelligent group of men specializing in the current growth and problems of our law: the faculty which has reared the new apprentice."[18]

Llewellyn at least partially missed the mark in touting what he called the "new model every year" benefits of clerks. The academy and the judiciary have grown apart. Faculty at the elite schools that produce the most law clerks—and perhaps especially those faculty who are likely to be among the group that the top students who get clerkships tend to emulate—are unlikely to be producing scholarship that bears much of a direct relationship to the day-to-day work of judges. One might instead imagine that the mechanism has become a source of hazard, as clerks are likely to bring with them half-formed versions of the Big New Ideas to which they were exposed in law school, and without the benefit of the experience necessary to put them in perspective.

But Judge Roth suggests that he was right in one sense. "I feel a lot younger than many of my contemporaries, and I think it's because I talk to my clerks like a person for whom age doesn't matter," she told me. And so it seemed to me. For my money, Llewellyn was right about another benefit of clerkships, too. He observed that law clerks tend to emerge from the experience with the knowledge "from the inside that the appellate courts move with continuity, and move with responsibility, that they answer to their duty to the 'law,' that they move not as individuals or persons, but as officers."[19] That, too, rings true. I may have the occasional doubt when it comes to elected judges, but nothing I saw of the federal appellate courts left me with any sense but that the task is in capable hands acting in good faith.

I flew to Washington, D.C., to interview Judge Roth for this essay. Because she had an appointment in the morning I met her at her home. We talked there for a bit before she drove us to the courthouse to meet my co-clerk Jeff Steger for lunch. Of all the memories I will carry from that day, it will be the drive that stands out most. There I was, riding shotgun with someone who has been one of the greatest influences on my life, who fifty-five years earlier had started to navigate a world in which women were discouraged from becoming lawyers, and who had made her way successfully through that world. She drove me through D.C. traffic while fully engaged in a conversation about the Second Amendment and the Third Circuit's approach to it. And she did all of this while making liberal use of the horn and offering salty commentary on the deficiencies of other drivers. My admiration for her grew even greater in the moment.

Right around the time I interviewed Judge Roth I came across this quote from C. S. Lewis: "The process of living seems to consist in coming to realize truths so ancient and simple that, if stated, they sound like barren platitudes. They cannot sound otherwise to those who have not had the relevant experience."[20] I've had enough experience to appreciate Lewis's wisdom, and to see that a similar principle applies to the examples by which one chooses to guide one's own life. Maturation is a water-on-stone-like process of slow change. There are things that the young, no matter how book smart they may be, simply cannot know. I appreciated Judge Roth's value as a role model as her twenty-something law clerk, but nowhere near as fully as I do now. As a person—as a boss, as a partner in a marriage, as a human being—her example was impecca-ble. As a jurist, she was not an originalist, or a textualist, or a subscriber to any other sort of ism. She had been a lawyer, and then she became a judge, in the fullest and best sense of the word. These perhaps sound like barren platitudes, but they are not.

Two arguably conflicting strands of thought struck me as she and I con-versed in her office, she behind her desk and me in a chair, just has we had been seated one afternoon in February of 1992. One was that more than a quarter century had passed since we first met, and that in that time I had made a career and perhaps even cultivated some wisdom and perspective of my own, and that her insistence that I call her "Jane" signified a shift in our relationship. The other was that it was as if almost no time had passed at all.

Notes

1. Anthony T. Kronman, *The Lost Lawyer* (Cambridge, Mass.: Harvard University Press, 1993), 347.

2. Griswold had done the same thing a few years earlier, with a class of entering female students that included Ruth Bader Ginsburg. "Dean Griswold asked them, as a matter of ritual, the same question: What was each doing in law school, occupying a seat that could be held by a man? Ginsburg would always remember her diffident answers: that her husband was a year ahead and she hoped study would help her under-stand his work. And she would always esteem the wonderful classmate who had the nerve to answer the dean with her own question: with five hundred Harvard men and only nine women, "'what better place to catch a man?'" Fred Strebeigh, *Equal: Women Reshape American Law* (New York: W. W. Norton, 2009), 36.

3. Judge Jane Richards Roth, interview, June 14, 2017. Any quoted remarks attributed to her are taken from that interview.

4. This was the era before cellphones, so at least some of the editors were taking calls from judges at the law review offices. Because taking calls involved a very public pag-ing process, the editors were undoubtedly aware of which of them were especially in demand. It was there, too, that I first heard stories of judges withdrawing offers because they weren't accepted on the spot, or because a prospective clerk simply hadn't been quick enough at returning a phone call. I learned as well that some judges were better bosses than others, and that some were best avoided entirely. The group of friends I made there was very helpful as I navigated the process myself a couple years later, and one of them was connected enough that he left me a message congratulating me on my clerkship with Judge Roth before I had even arrived home from the interview.

5. A final note on my experience as a clerkship applicant. Although I have no record of it, I am sure that I let all of the judges who had not yet rejected me know that I had

accepted an offer from Judge Roth. Out of however many of them there were, only Judge Royce Lamberth of the D.C. District Court responded, sending me a handwritten note congratulating me and wishing me well. It's a gesture that I remembered and have at least occasionally sought to emulate. As luck would have it, a couple decades later he and I were assigned to be co-presenters at an event put on by the Federal Judicial Center.

6. One of Judge Roth's later clerks does recall having a role in winnowing down the pool of applicants.

7. Howard Wasserman, "Honoring Judge Jane Roth," blog, PrawfsBlawg, May 13, 2013, http://prawfsblawg.blogs.com/prawfsblawg/2013/05/adam-levitin-georgetown -miriam-baer-brooklyn-chad-oldfather-marquette-seth-tillman-teaching-overseas -tomiko-brown.html.

8. "From 1989 to 1996, the Third Circuit not only used the JO in approximately 60 percent of its cases, but it also may have used the JO in some of its hardest cases. By contrast, the majority of other circuits, while using other short-form dispositions, almost never used the JO form of case disposition." Mitu Gulati and C. M. A. McAuliff, "On Not Making Law," *Law & Contemporary Problems,* Summer 1998, 162.

9. *Fisher Bros. Sales, Inc. v. United States,* 46 F.3d 279 (1993) (en banc). Judge Roth's majority opinion for the panel was vacated when the court voted to hear the case en banc. She then wrote the dissenting opinion.

10. *Kinney v. Yerusalim,* 9 F.3d 1067 (1993).

11. This opinion was unpublished and is not available on Westlaw, but the gentleman who was wrongly arrested had a memorable name, and I was able to discover that he later wrote a book about the experience, and also that he was shot to death under mysterious circumstances a couple decades later. The prosecutor's later history includes having his law license suspended.

12. Harvey Berkman, "Court Rebuffs INS on Lodging of Stowaways," *National Law Journal,* July 18, 1994.

13. Clifford J. Levy, "Court Upsets Law on Costs of Stowaways," *New York Times,* June 30, 1994.

14. *Schoonejongen v. Curtiss-Wright Corp.,* 18 F.3d 1034 (3d Cir. 1994).

15. *Curtiss-Wright Corp. v. Schoonejongen,* 514 U.S. 73, 80 (1995).

16. His campaigning with a St. Bernard was enough of a signature that it was the subject of three paragraphs in his obituary in the *New York Times.* Matthew L. Wald, "William V. Roth, Jr., Veteran of U.S. Senate, Dies at 82," *New York Times,* December 15, 2003.

17. James L. Magrish, "The Common Law Tradition: Deciding Appeals, by Karl N. Llewellyn." *Indiana Law Journal* 36, no. 4 (1961): 9.

18. Ibid.

19. Ibid.

20. C. S. Lewis, *The Collected Letters of C. L. Lewis,* vol. 2, *Books, Broadcasts, and the War, 1931–1949,* edited by Walter Hooper (San Francisco: HarperCollins, 2004), 258.

CONTRIBUTORS

ALFRED C. AMAN clerked for two years for the Honorable Elbert P. Tuttle of the United States Court of Appeals for the Eleventh Circuit after graduating from the University of Chicago Law School. Aman spent several years in private practice before joining the faculty at Cornell Law School. Deanships at the Indiana Maurer School of Law and Suffolk University Law School followed. Aman is presently the Roscoe C. O'Byrne Professor of Law at Indiana Law School. He is also the author of three books on administrative law.

LYNN E. BLAIS clerked for the Honorable William Wayne Justice of the United States District Court for the Eastern District of Texas and the Honorable Harry A. Blackmun of the United States Supreme Court after graduating from Harvard Law School. She currently serves as the Leroy G. Denman, Jr. Regents Professor of Real Property Law at the University of Texas School of Law. For the last decade, Blais has also served as the co-director of the Texas Law School's Supreme Court Clinic.

ROLAND E. BRANDEL is currently senior counsel in the San Francisco office of Morrison & Foerster. Brandel graduated from the University of Chicago Law School and clerked for the Honorable Roger J. Traynor of the Supreme Court of California. Brandel has authored several books in the field of financial services as well as multiple articles on a wide range of legal topics.

RONALD K. L. COLLINS clerked (1980-81) for the Honorable Hans A. Linde of the Oregon Supreme Court and was thereafter a Supreme Court Fellow under Chief Justice Warren Burger. After working with the Legal Aid Foundation of Los Angeles and the Legal Aid Society of Orange County, Collins taught at the George Washington University Law School and Temple Law School. Before he retired, he was the Harold S. Shefelman Scholar at the University of Washington School of Law. Collins is the author, coauthor, or editor of twelve books, including *The Fundamental Holmes: A Free Speech Chronicle & Reader* (2010), and coauthor of *The Judge: 26 Machiavellian Lessons* (2017). His next book is on Justice Holmes and the Civil War.

MARGARET CONNORS earned a master's degree (history) from Villanova University and a J.D. from Villanova University School of Law. She then clerked for three different state court judges, including the Honorable Juanita Kidd Stout of the Supreme Court of Pennsylvania. She is presently of counsel with the firm of Mayerson Law in Pottstown, Pennsylvania.

POLLY WIRTZMAN CRAIGHILL, a former law clerk for the Honorable Burnita Shelton Matthews, earned her B.A. from Sweet Briar College, her J.D. from George Washington University School of Law, and her LL.M. from the Georgetown University Law Center. For over two decades, Craighill served in the Office of the Legislative Counsel of the United States Senate. She has also held the position of lecturer in law at the George Washington University Law School.

DAVID M. DORSEN is the author of the award-winning biography *Henry Friendly, Greatest Judge of His Era* (2012). He spent the first part of his legal career serving as an assistant United States attorney under Robert M. Morgenthau and then as a chief counsel of the Senate Watergate Committee. A long-time lawyer in Washington, D.C., Dorsen is also the author of *The Unexpected Scalia: A Conservative Justice's Liberal Opinions* (2017).

CARMEL "KIM" PRASHKER EBB clerked for the Honorable Jerome Frank of the United States Court of Appeals for the Second Circuit after graduating first in her class from Columbia Law School. Ebb subsequently worked in both private practice and for the federal government.

ANNE S. EMANUEL is the author of *Elbert Parr Tuttle: Chief Jurist of the Civil Rights Revolution* (2011) and is a former Tuttle law clerk. After a second clerkship with the Honorable Harold N. Hill of the Georgia Supreme Court, Emanuel joined the law faculty at George State University. She is the winner of the Lifetime Achievement Award from the Southern Center for Human Rights.

RUTH BADER GINSBURG, a graduate of Columbia Law School and a former law clerk to the Honorable Edmund L. Palmieri of the United States District Court for the Southern District of New York, was an associate justice on the United States Supreme Court.

HENRY M. GREENBERG, presently a shareholder at the firm of Greenberg Traurig, LLP, graduated from Syracuse University College of Law and then clerked for the Honorable Irving Ben Cooper of the United States District Court of the Southern District of New York and the Honorable Judith S. Kaye of the New York Court of Appeals. Greenberg has also served as former counsel to the New York state attorney as well as president of the New York State Bar Association.

ANNA R. HAYES, a graduate of the University of North Carolina School of Law, where she served on the editorial board of the *North Carolina Law Review,* is a former partner in the law firm of Manning, Fulton in Raleigh. She is the author of the award-winning *Without Precedent: The Life of Susie Marshall Sharp* (2008).

RONALD J. JOHNSON, a graduate of Southwest Texas State University and St. Mary's School of Law, clerked for both the Honorable John W. Wood Jr. and Adrian A. Spears. He is presently a solo practitioner.

ROBERT J. KACZOROWSKI, a longtime faculty member at the Fordham University School of Law, holds a Ph.D. from the University of Minnesota and a J.D. from New York University Law School. After graduating from law school, he clerked for one and one-half years for the Honorable A. Leon Higginbotham Jr. of the United States Court of Appeals for the Third Circuit. Kaczorowski is also the author of books on constitutional law, judicial interpretation, and the history of Fordham Law School.

ROBIN KONRAD, a graduate of Boston University and Howard University School of Law, clerked for the Honorable Damon J. Keith of the United States Court of Appeals for the Sixth Circuit before spending over a decade as an assistant federal public defender. As a public defender, she represented death row inmates in four states as well as on the federal death row. Konrad's work led her to the United States Supreme Court, where she argued the lethal injection case of *Glossip v. Gross*. After working as the Death Penalty Information Center's Director of Research and Special Projects, Konrad joined the law faculty at the Howard University School of Law.

JAMES E. KRIER, a graduate of the University of Wisconsin School of Law, subsequently clerked for the Honorable Roger J. Traynor of the Supreme Court of California before beginning a distinguished teaching career. Krier is currently the Earl Warren DeLano Professor Emeritus of Law at the University of Michigan Law School. His scholarship includes case books, book chapters, and over twenty-five law review and legal journal articles.

RONALD J. KROTOSZYNSKI, JR., is presently the John S. Stone Chairholder of Law at the University of Alabama School of Law. Krotoszynski graduated from Emory University and Duke University School of Law before clerking for the Honorable Frank M. Johnson Jr. of the United States Court of Appeals for the Eleventh Circuit.

KIRSTEN LEVINGSTON, the director of the Racial Justice Program at Wellspring Advisors, previously held the position of program officer at the Ford Foundation and the criminal justice program director at the Brennan Center for Justice. Levingston holds a law degree from Harvard Law School and a master's in fine arts from the New School.

MITCHELL A. LOWENTHAL, a graduate of Cornell University and Cornell Law School, spent one year clerking for the Honorable Edward Weinfeld. He subsequently joined the law firm of Cleary Gottlieb, where he worked for over thirty years. He is now senior counsel with the firm. Lowenthal has published on the topics of securities litigation and complex civil procedure in a host of different law reviews and legal journals.

JEREMY MALTBY attended Harvard College and Columbia Law School before clerking for the Honorable Eugene Nickerson of the United States District Court for the Eastern District of New York, the Honorable Pierre Leval of the United States Court of Appeals for the Second Circuit, and the Honorable David Souter of the United States Supreme Court. A former member of the White House Counsel's Office, Maltby is currently a partner at the law firm of O'Melveny and Myers in Washington, D.C.

KARLA MCKANDERS is the current head of the Immigration Law Clinic at Vanderbilt Law School and is a graduate of Spellman College and Duke University Law School. After clerking for the Honorable Damon J. Keith of the United States Court of Appeals for the Sixth Circuit, Kanders held teaching positions at Villanova University School of Law, the University of Tennessee College of Law, and Howard University School of Law.

CHAD M. OLDFATHER, a graduate of Harvard College and the University of Virginia School of Law, clerked for the Honorable Jane Richards Roth of the United States Court of Appeals for the Third Circuit. Oldfather subsequently worked for the Minnesota State Public Defender's Office and in the Minneapolis office of Faegre and Benson, LLP before beginning his teaching career. A prolific scholar, Oldfather is currently a professor of law at the Marquette University Law School.

TODD C. PEPPERS holds the Henry H. & Trudye H. Fowler Chair of Public Affairs at Roanoke College, and he is also a Visiting Professor of Law at the Washington and Lee University School of Law. He is the author of *Courtiers of the Marble Palace: The Rise and Influence of the Supreme Court Law Clerk* (2005) and the coeditor of *In Chambers: Stories of Supreme Court Law Clerks and Their Justices* (with Artemus Ward; 2012) and *Of Courtiers and Kings: More Stories of Supreme Court Law Clerks and Their Justices* (with Clare Cushman; 2015).

BARRY SULLIVAN is currently the Cooney & Conway Chair in Advocacy and the George Anastaplo Professor of Constitutional Law and History at the Loyola University Chicago School of Law. Sullivan graduated from Middlebury College and the University of Chicago Law School before clerking for the Honorable John Minor Wisdom of the United States Court of Appeals for the Fifth Circuit. Sullivan's subsequent professional career has included service as dean of the Washington and Lee School of Law.

J. HARVIE WILKINSON III, a graduate of Yale University and the University of Virginia School of Law, clerked for Supreme Court Justice Lewis Powell. He is currently a judge on the United States Court of Appeals for the Fourth Circuit as well as a prolific scholar and author.

Note: The justices for whom the law clerks worked are indicated in parentheses after each clerk's name—for example, Brandel, Roland E. (Traynor). Photographs in the unfolioed illustration gallery are indexed according to sequence (e.g., *gallery page 1*)